INTERNATIONAL HUMAN RIGHTS AND THEIR ENFORCEMENT IN AFRICA

INTERNATIONAL HUMAN RIGHTS AND THEIR ENFORCEMENT IN AFRICA

Morris Kiwinda Mbondenyi

lawAfrica

Published by

LawAfrica Publishing (K) Ltd
Co-op Trust Plaza, 1st Floor
Lower Hill Road
P.O. Box 4260 - 00100 GPO
Nairobi, Kenya
Phone: +254 20 2722579/80
Fax: +254 20 2722592

LawAfrica Publishing (U) Ltd
Office Suite, No. 2
Plot 10A, Jinja Road (Opposite NEMA House)
P.O. Box 6198
Kampala, Uganda
Phone: +256 41 255808
Fax: +256 41 347743

LawAfrica Publishing (T) Ltd
Co-Architect Building, 7th Floor
India Makunganya Street
P.O. Box 38564
Dar-es-Salaam, Tanzania
Phone: +255 22 2120804/5
Fax: +255 22 2120811

Email: sales@lawafrica.com

Website: www.lawafrica.com

© Morris Mbondenyi 2011; LawAfrica

ISBN 9966-1532-4-1

lawAfrica

TABLE OF CONTENTS

Chapter 3: Historical Dimensions of the African System on Human and Peoples' Rights

Part II: The Normative Instruments of the African System on Human and Peoples' Rights

Chapter 4: The Constitutive Act of the African Union

Chapter 5: The African Charter on Human and Peoples' Rights

Chapter 6: The African Charter on the Rights and Welfare of the Child

Chapter 7: The Protocol to the African Charter on Human and Peoples' Rights on the Rights of Women in Africa

Chapter 10: The African Court on Human and Peoples' Rights

Chapter 11: African Committee of Experts on the Rights and Welfare of the Child

Part IV: Challenges and Reforms to the African System on Human and Peoples' Rights

Chapter 12: Normative Challenges and Reforms to Africa's Regional Human Rights System

Chapter 13: Institutional Challenges and Reforms under the African Human Rights System

Chapter 14: Mainstreaming and Rationalising the African Human Rights System

DEDICATION

In loving memory of my dear late father,
Lewis George Mbondenyi

ACKNOWLEDGEMENTS

This work is to me both a reminder and commemoration of the inputs of many people and institutions. It has taken years of hard work, sacrifice and relentlessness for this book to be compiled. Without the strength and hand of the Almighty God over my life, this work would definitely not have seen the light of the day. I am therefore grateful to my gracious LORD for His mercy, love, strength and care; for protecting me, saving me and guiding me through every stage of this work.

Some of the chapters in this book were developed from my Doctor of Laws (LLD) research hosted by the University of South Africa (UNISA) College of Law, under the supervision of Professor André Mbata Betukumesu Mangu. Indeed, Professor Mangu's invaluable comments and inputs at every stage of my doctoral work are highly appreciated and acknowledged. However, while I am grateful for his contribution, shortcomings, errors and omissions in this book are entirely mine.

Many other institutions have also been a stepping-stone towards the compilation of this book. These include the United Nations International Criminal Tribunal for Rwanda (UN-ICTR), whose small but resourceful library I was able to consult when working at the institution as a legal researcher. Others are: the University of Witwatersrand (Wits) library in Johannesburg, South Africa; University of Pretoria Library; University of Swaziland (UNISWA) library; and the South African Human Rights Commission (SAHRC) library in Johannesburg.

Of equal importance to this achievement are members of my family to whom I attribute a great deal of my success. They did not spare anything to support, nurture and educate me. I am particularly indebted to my mother, Mrs. Lenah Nakijwa Mbondenyi and my late father, Lewis George Mbondenyi, for their parental guidance, assistance and care. Moreover, through the collaborative efforts of my many friends, relatives, teachers and colleagues, this dream has finally become a reality. Because of their optimism and constant encouragement, they will forever be remembered as long as the development and completion of this book is concerned. Special thanks also go to my spiritual guardians, mentors and pastors for their guidance, advice and ceaseless prayers. They taught me to build on the solid foundation, which is the word of God.

Lastly, I am indebted to those writers, scholars, leaders and activists whose works have been quoted extensively in this book. This study would not have attained its present status and form without the academic resources produced by them. Their efforts and contribution to the human rights agenda of the continent is acknowledged.

Morris Kiwinda Mbondenyi
Nairobi, Kenya, 2011

PREFACE

Before the late 1980s, international protection of human rights in Africa was more of a myth than a reality. The mere mention of human rights attracted great resistance from the political elite who viewed the doctrine with a lot of suspicion. The now defunct Organisation of African Unity (OAU) maintained overt passiveness in condemning human rights violations in the continent, rather choosing to over-glorify the principle of non-interference in the internal affairs of member states. Accordingly, the multiple gross violations of human rights that were perpetuated by despotic regimes escaped the rather blind eye of the OAU.

As a result of the need to contain the egregious violation of human rights and the attendant culture of impunity, numerous human rights treaties were concluded at the global level, courtesy of the United Nations Organisation (UN). The global movement towards the protection of human rights received support from European and American states, eventfully leading to the emergence and evolution of regional human rights systems. Soon afterwards, Africa was forced to conform to these global trends in human rights protection. A number of important events influenced the emergence and evolution of a regional human rights system in Africa. These include, encouragement at the UN level for regional human rights mechanisms, NGO lobbying and the unprecedented acknowledgement by some African leaders that human rights violations in other states were also their concern.

Whilst the establishment of the African human rights system was a good gesture that signalled the recognition of the value and essence of international human rights in the continent, a continuous study of the system has become necessary. This is particularly in light of the fact that the continent is in desperate need of well established and effective regional human rights enforcement mechanisms. At the moment, the regional human rights system is stuck between prospects and pitfalls because of the gap that exists between the promise of human rights and their actual realisation. By all means, this trend needs to be reversed.

The main objective and purpose of this book therefore is to underscore the challenges besetting the effective enforcement of international human rights law in Africa and the prospects and promises of an effective regional human rights system. The book, a revised and updated version of my earlier book entitled The African System on Human and Peoples' Rights: Its Promises, Prospects and Pitfalls, captures succinctly the recent developments of the system, since the publication of its predecessor. This is done with the understanding that the African human rights system is gradually progressing, despite the fact that it is not only the least developed but also the least effective as compared with its American and European counterparts.

LIST OF ACRONYMS

ACHPR	African Charter on Human and Peoples' Rights
ACHR	American Convention on Human Rights
ACJ	African Court of Justice
ACRWC	African Charter on the Rights and Welfare of the Child
AEC	African Economic Community
AHRLJ	African Human Rights Law Journal
AHSG	Assembly of Head of States and Government
AIDS	Acquired Immune Deficiency Syndrome
AJIL	African Journal of International Law
AM. J	American Journal
APRM	African Peer Review Mechanism
ART	Article
AU	African Union
CAAU	Constitutive Act of the African Union
CAT	Convention against Torture
CE	Council of Europe
CEDAW	Convention on the Elimination of All Forms of Discrimination against Women
CEN-SAD	Community of Sahel-Saharan States
CERD	Convention on the Elimination of All Forms of Racial Discrimination
CILSA	Comparative and International Law Journal of Southern Africa
CIP	Country Issue Paper
CODESTRIA	Council for the Development of Economic and Social Research in Africa
COMESA	Common Market for Eastern and Southern Africa
COMP.L	Comparative Law
CRM	Country Review Mission
CSAR	Country Self-Assessment Report
CSM	Country Support Mission

CSSDCA	Conference on Security, Stability, Development and Cooperation in Africa
DANIDA	Danish International Development Agency
DEVAW	Declaration on the Elimination of Violence Against Women
DRC	Democratic Republic of Congo
EC	Executive Council (of the African Union)
ECCAS	Economic Community of Central African States
ECHR	European Convention on Human Rights and Fundamental Freedoms
ECOSOC	Economic and Social Council
ECOWAS	Economic Community of West African States
ED(S)	Editor(s)
ESC	European Social Charter
EU	European Union
FGM	Female Genital Mutilation
GA	General Assembly
GA. Res.	General Assembly Resolution
GDP	Gross Domestic Product
HPs	Harmful Practices
HRC	UN Human Rights Committee
HSGIC	Heads of State and Government Implementation Committee
HUM.RTS	Human Rights
IACHR	Inter-American Convention on Human Rights
ICC	International Criminal Court
ICCPR	International Covenant on Civil and Political Rights
ICERD	International Covenant on the Elimination of all forms of Racial Discrimination
ICESCR	International Covenant on Economic, Social and Cultural Rights
ICJ	International Court of Justice
ICTR	International Criminal Tribunal for Rwanda

ICTY	International Criminal Tribunal for the Former Yugoslavia
IGAD	Intergovernmental Authority for Development
IHRR	International Human Rights Report
ILM	International Legal Material
ILO	International Labour Organisation
IMF	International Monetary Fund
INTL	International Law
LJ	Law Journal
LLB	Bachelor of Laws
LLD	Doctor of Laws
LLM	Master of Laws
MAP	Millennium Africa Recovery Plan
MDC	Movement for Democratic Change
MDG	Millennium Development Goals
MOU	Memorandum of Understanding
NAI	New African Initiative
NEPAD	New Partnership for Africa's Development
NGC	National Governing Council
NGO	Non-Governmental Organisation
OAS	Organisation of American States
OAU	Organisation of African Unity
ODM	Orange Democratic Movement
OSCE	Organisation for Security & Co-operation in Europe
OSIWA	Open Society Initiative for West African
P.	Page
PARA	Paragraph
PCIJ	Permanent Court of International Justice
PNU	Party of National Unity
POA	Programme of Action
PP	Pages
PRS	Permanent Representative Committee

RECs	Regional Economic Communities
RSA	Republic of South Africa
SA	South Africa
SADC	Southern African Development Community
SAJHR	South African Journal of Human Rights
SALJ	South African Law Journal
SAP	Structural Adjustment Programme
SAPL	South African Public Law
SAYIL	South African Year Book of International Law
SCSL	Special Court for Sierra Leone
STCs	Specialised Technical Committees
UDHR	Universal Declaration on Human Rights
UK	United Kingdom
UMA	*Union du Maghreb Arabe*
UN	United Nations
UNCRC	United Nations Convention on the Rights of the Child
UNDP	United Nations Development Programme
UNESCO	United Nations Educational, Scientific, and Cultural Organisation
UNGA	United Nations General Assembly
UNHCR	United Nations High Commission for Refugees
UNICEF	United Nations Children's Fund
UNISA	University of South Africa
UNISWA	University of Swaziland
UNP.	Unpublished
UNTS	United Nations Treaty Series
US/USA	United States/United States of America
USSR	Union of Soviet Socialist Republic
V.	Versus
VOL	Volume
WILDAF	Women in Law and Development in Africa
ZANU-PF	Zimbabwe African National Union-Patriotic Front

TABLE OF CASES

Communications 140/94, 141/94, 145/95, *Constitutional Rights Project, Civil Liberties Organisation and Media Rights Agenda v. Nigeria,* Thirteenth Annual Activity Report of the African Commission on Human and Peoples' Rights (Annex V)

Communications 143/95, 150/96, *Constitutional Rights Project and Civil Liberties Organisation v. Nigeria,* Thirteenth Annual Activity Report of the African Commission on Human and Peoples' Rights (Annex V)

Communication 144/95, *William Curson (acting on behalf of Severo Moto) v. Equatorial Guinea,* Eleventh Annual Activity Report of the African Commission on Human and Peoples' Rights (Annex II)

Communications 147/95, 149/96, *Sir Dawda K Jawara v. The Gambia,* Thirteenth Annual Activity Report of the African Commission on Human and Peoples' Rights (Annex V)

Communication 148/96, *Constitutional Rights Project v. Nigeria,* Thirteenth Annual Activity Report of the African Commission on Human and Peoples' Rights (Annex V)

Communication 151/96, *Civil Liberties Organisation v. Nigeria,* Thirteenth Annual Activity Report of the African Commission on Human and Peoples' Rights (Annex V)

Communication 153/96, *Constitutional Rights Project v. Nigeria,* Thirteenth Annual Activity Report of the African Commission on Human and Peoples' Rights (Annex V).

Communication 155/96, *The Social and Economic Rights Action Centre and the Centre for Economic and Social Rights v. Nigeria,* Fifteenth Annual Activity Report of the African Commission on Human and Peoples' Rights (Annex V).

Communication 159/96, *UIDH, FIDH, RADDHO, ONDH, ANDH v. Angola,* Eleventh Annual Activity Report of the African Commission on Human and Peoples' Rights (Annex II).

Communication 18/88, *El Hadji Boubacare v. Benin,* Law Reports of the African Commission Series A, Volume 1, ACHPR/LR/A1 (1997).

Communication 197/1997, *Bah Ould Rabah v. Mauritania,* Seventeenth Annual Activity Report of the African Commission on Human and Peoples' Rights (Annex VII).

and Peoples' Rights (Annex V).

Communication 225/98, *Huri-Laws v. Nigeria,* Fourteenth Annual Activity Report of the African Commission on Human and Peoples' Rights (Annex V).

Communication 228/99, *The Law Offices of Ghazi Suleiman v. Sudan,* Sixteenth Annual Activity Report of the African Commission on Human and Peoples' Rights (Annex VII).

Communication 231/99, *Avocats Sans Frontières (on behalf of Gaëtan Bwampamye) v. Burundi,* Fourteenth Annual Activity Report of the African Commission on Human and Peoples' Rights (Annex V).

Communication 232/99, *John D. Ouko v. Kenya,* Fourteenth Annual Activity Report of the African Commission on Human and Peoples' Rights (Annex V).

Communication 233/99, *Interights (on behalf of the Pan African Movement and Citizens for Peace in Eritrea) v. Ethiopia,* Sixteenth Annual Activity Report of the African Commission on Human and Peoples' Rights (Annex VII).

Communication 234/99, *Interights (on behalf of the Pan African Movement and Inter-Africa Group) v. Eritrea,* Sixteenth Annual Activity Report of the African Commission on Human and Peoples' Rights (Annex VII).

Communication 236/2000, *Curtis Francis Doebbler v. Sudan,* Sixteenth Annual Activity Report of the African Commission on Human and Peoples' Rights (Annex VII).

Communication 240/2001, *Interights et al (on behalf of Mariette Sonjaleen Bosch) v. Botswana,* Seventeenth Annual Activity Report of the African Commission on Human and Peoples' Rights (Annex VII).

Communication 241/2001, *Purohit and Moore v. The Gambia,* Sixteenth Annual Activity Report of the African Commission on Human and Peoples' Rights (Annex VII).

Communication 242/2001, *Interights, Institute for Human Rights and Development in Africa; Association Mauritanienne des Droits de l'Homme v. Mauritania,* Seventeenth Annual Activity Report of the African Commission on Human and Peoples' Rights (Annex VII).

Communication 254/2002, *Mouvement des Réfugiés Mauritanien au*

Communication 71/92, *Rencontre Africaine pour la Defence des Droits de l'Homme v. Zambia,* Tenth Annual Activity Report of the African Commission on Human and Peoples' Rights (Annex X).

Communication 73/92, *Mohammed Lamine Diakité v. Gabon,* Thirteenth Annual Activity Report of the African Commission on Human and Peoples' Rights (Annex V).

Communication 74/92, *Commission Nationale des Droits de l'Homme et des Liberties v. Chad,* (1997) 4 IHRR.

Communication 74/92, *Commission Nationale des Droits de l'Homme et des Libertés v. Chad,* Ninth Annual Activity Report of the African Commission on Human and Peoples' Rights (Annex VIII).

Communication 91/93, *Commission Internationale de Juristes v. Togo.*

Communication 97/93, *John K. Modise v. Botswana,* Tenth Annual Activity Report of the African Commission on Human and Peoples' Rights (Annex X).

Communications 25/89, 47/90, 56/91 & 100/93, *Free Legal Assistance Group, Lawyers' Committee for Human Rights, Union Interafricaine des Droits de l'Homme, Les Temoins de Jehoveh v. Zaire,* Ninth Annual Activity Report of the African Commission on Human and Peoples' Rights (Annex VIII).

Communications 27/89, 46/91, 49/91, 99/93, *Organisation Mondiale Contre La Torture and Association Internationale des juristes Democrates) Commission Internationale des Juristes (C.I.J) Union Interafricaine des Droits de l'Homme v. Rwanda,* Tenth Annual Activity Report of the African Commission on Human and Peoples' Rights (Annex X).

Communications 53/90 and 53/91, *Alberto T. Capitao v. Tanzania,* Seventh Annual Activity Report of the African Commission on Human and Peoples' Rights (Annex IX); Eighth Annual Activity Report of the African Commission on Human and Peoples' Rights (Annex VI).

Communications 64/92, 68/92 and 78/92, *Krishna Achuthan (on behalf of Aleke Banda), Amnesty International (on behalf of Orton and Vera Chirwa v. Malawi,* Seventh Annual Activity Report of the African Commission on Human and Peoples' Rights (Annex IX); Eighth Annual Activity Report of the African Commission on Human and Peoples' Rights (Annex VI).

TABLE OF STATUTES

INTRODUCTION

International human rights law is recognised as a distinct branch of law with its own institutions, jurisprudence and norms.[1] Currently, it registers a tremendous positive impact on the legal systems throughout the world[2], although this was hardly the situation years ago.[3] Umozurike correctly observed that this branch of law appeared to enjoy low esteem during the 1970s, particularly in Africa.[4] His observations were predicated on the overt passiveness the former Organisation of African Unity (OAU)[5] maintained in condemning human rights violations in a number of independent African states by 'unduly emphasising the principle of non-interference in the internal affairs of member states.'[6] Accordingly, the massacre of thousands of Hutus in Burundi, as well as the despotic regimes of dictators Idi Amin of Uganda, Macias Nguema of Equatorial Guinea and Jean-Bedel

---

1   See O Eze *Human Rights in Africa: Some selected problems* (1984) 1. Eze observed that after the Helsinki Accord of 1975 on European security, human rights issues were injected into and apparently form part of the equation of international relations.

2   See generally the arguments advanced in D Titus *The applicability of the international human rights norms to the South African legal system* (1993) 2-3. Titus acknowledged that it is not until as recently as 1946 when the impact and importance of international human rights law began to be felt, particularly in Africa, but more so, in South Africa.

3   See M Kirby 'The role of the judge in advancing human rights by reference to international human rights norms' (1988) 62 *Australian Law Journal* 530.

4   U O Umozurike 'The African Charter on Human and People's Rights' (1983) 77 *American Journal of International Law* 902.

5   Established in 1963, through the OAU Charter, adopted 25 May 1963. For a discussion on OAU, see generally, A Chanda 'The Organisation of African Unity: An appraisal' (1989) *Zambia Law Journal* 1-29; C Amate *Inside Organisation of African Unity and its Charter* (1968); D Mazzeo (ed.) *African regional organisations* (1984).

6   Umozurike (n 4 above) 902. Umozurike expressed his disapproval of the OAU's inability to end the culture of impunity on the continent by quoting President Sékou Touré's assertion that the Unity was not 'a tribunal which could sit in judgement on any member state's internal affairs.' He sees this attitude as a self-imposed inhibition by the OAU members, 'not so much to protect their legitimate states', as to fend off international concern for gross abuses of Human rights in some African states.'

Bokassa of the Central African Republic seem to have escaped the rather blind eye of the OAU.[7]

In all fairness though, it is important to note that the passiveness to international protection of human rights was more of a 'global syndrome' than an African creation. Indeed, even events in the international circles at that time were less conducive to the thriving of a robust human rights culture.[8] For example, international law emphasised the doctrine of sovereignty of states which in a way created focus on the consolidation of political power rather than the protection and promotion of human rights.

Thus, in pursuit of sovereignty, independent states were constantly in conflict amongst themselves while the non-independent ones strove for their independence.[9] There was therefore an upsurge of violence and by extension, violation of human rights. As a result of the need to contain this state of chaos and stem the egregious violation of human rights and the attendant culture of impunity, numerous treaties were concluded at both the global and regional levels.

At the global level, the United Nations (UN) created, for example, reporting mechanisms in the Convention on the Elimination of all Forms of Racial Discrimination (CERD)[10], the First Optional Protocol to the International Covenant on Civil and Political Rights (ICCPR), the Convention Against Torture (CAT)[11], and more recently, the Optional Protocol to the Convention on the Elimination of All Forms of Discrimination Against Women.[12] At

---

7   As above.

8   See M Mbondenyi & N Sifuna 'A review of procedural and jurisdictional challenges in enforcing international human rights law under the African Charter regime' (2006) *Berkeley Legal Press Working paper No. 1869* at http://law.bepress.com/expresso/esps/1869 (accessed on 13 April 2010).

9   As above.

10   CERD art 14; Adopted and opened for signature and ratification by General Assembly Resolution 2106 (XX) of 21 December 1965; entry into force 4 January 1969, in accordance with Article 19.

11   CAT art 22. The procedures stipulated under this Convention are similar in a number of ways to those provided for under the CERD.

12   The United Nations General Assembly adopted the Optional Protocol in October 1999 (A//res/54/4). The Optional Protocol entered into force on 22 December 2000, after ten states had become parties thereto.

regional levels, such mechanisms were initiated through the adoption of the European Convention on Human Rights and Fundamental Freedoms[13], the American Convention on Human Rights[14] and the African Charter on Human and Peoples' Rights.[15] Some mixed-model approaches have also been sought, partly inspired by the desire to overcome the weaknesses of both the international and national mechanisms.[16]

Arguably, whereas the universal system of human rights established under the UN played a vital role in the enforcement of international human rights law immediately after the Second World War, its wide geographic jurisdiction undermined its efficacy.[17] Other factors such as the lack of adequate resources to accommodate the increasing numbers of human rights violations, the adverse effects of the cold war which pitted one nation against another and the issue of veto powers, made it even harder for human rights to be effectively enforced at that level.[18]

Additionally, some states, particularly those in Africa, were not comfortable with the human rights standards established by the UN because their participation 'in the early years of the human rights revolution was meagre.'[19] It has been argued that in the early years

---

13   Arts 25-34, Convention for the Protection of Human Rights and Fundamental Freedoms, 213 U.N.T.S. 222; *entered into force* 3 September 1953, *as amended by* Protocols nos. 3, 5, 8, and 11 *which entered into force* on 21 September 1970, 20 December 1971, 1 January 1990, and 1 November 1998, *respectively*.

14   See, art 44 of American Convention on Human Rights, O.A.S. Treaty Series no. 36, 1144 U.N.T.S. 123; entered into force 18 July 1978.

15   Adopted 27 June 1981; entered into force 21 October 1986. Arts 56 to 59 of the Charter provide further directions on how the Commission is to deal with the Communications presented to it.

16   Following a civil war in Sierra Leone, the UN Security Council adopted Resolution 1315 on 14 August 2000 requesting the UN Secretary-General to start negotiations to create a Special Court to prosecute 'those most responsible for committing human rights violations' in the country during that period. On 16 January 2002, an agreement establishing the court was signed between the government of Sierra Leone and the UN. This court has adopted a statute that prosecutes both international and national crimes.

17   During this period, the UN was the key (if not the only) enforcer of human rights globally, making it practically impossible for it to effectively address all concerns on human rights violations.

18   G Mugwanya *Human rights in Africa: Enhancing human rights through the African regional human rights system* (2003) 24-29.

19   As above, 26.

of the UN, Africa was still largely colonised; only four of its states, which were independent at that time, were founding members of the UN.[20] The remaining states were 'represented' by their colonial masters.[21]

Thus, it is further contended, Africans were not consulted during the drafting and adoption of the Universal Declaration on Human Rights (UDHR)[22] in 1948.[23] All the above factors, which were a source of disquiet with the universal system, might have motivated the establishment of the existing regional human rights systems, namely, the European[24], Inter-American[25] and African systems.[26]

---

20   As above. These were Ethiopia, Egypt, the Union of South Africa and Liberia. Egypt was admitted to the UN membership on 24 October 1945, while the Union of South Africa, Liberia and Ethiopia were admitted on 7, 12 & 13 November respectively.

21   As above.

22   See the Universal Declaration on Human Rights G.A Res. 217 (III); adopted on 10 December 1948.

23   See M Mutua 'The ideology of human rights' (1996) 36 *Virginia Journal of International Law* 605.

24   For detailed discussions on the European system of human rights, see generally, R Higgins 'The European Convention of Human Rights' in T Meron (ed), *Human rights in international law: Legacy and policy issues* (1984) 495; E Jacobs 'The European Convention on Human Rights' in R Benhardt & J Jolowicz (eds) *The international enforcement of human rights* (1987) 31; F Castberg *The European Convention on Human Rights* (1974); C Morrison *The developing European law of human rights* (1967); J Wright *The European Convention on Human Rights: An analysis and appraisal* (1978); J Fawcett *The application of the European Convention on Human Rights* (1987); R Beddard *Human rights and Europe: A study of the machinery of human rights protection of the Council of Europe* (1980); P Mahoney 'Speculating on the future of the reformed European Court of Human Rights' (1999) 20 *Human Rights Law Journal* 1.

25   See generally, D Harris & S Livingstone (eds) *The Inter-American system of human rights* (1998); S David *The Inter-American human rights system* (1997); H Vander Wilt 'The OAS system for the protection of human rights' in R Hanski & M Suksi (eds) *An introduction to the international protection of human rights: A textbook* (1997); T Buergenthal *Human rights in a nutshell* (1995); T Buergenthal 'The advisory practice of the Inter-American Human Rights Court' (1985) 79 *American Journal of International Law* 1; D Shelton 'The jurisprudence of the Inter-American Court of Human Rights' (1994) 10 *American University Journal of International Law and Policy* 333.

26   See generally E Ankumah 'Universality of human rights and the African Charter on Human and Peoples' Rights' (1992) *Universaliteit van Mensenrechten* 25-38; W Benedek 'The African Charter and Commission on Human and Peoples' Rights: How to make it more effective' (1993) 1 *Netherlands Quarterly of Human Rights* 24-40; K Busia 'The status of human rights in pre-colonial Africa: Implications for contemporary practices' in E McCarthy *et al* (eds) *Africa, human rights, and the global system* (1994); R Carver 'How African governments investigate human rights violations' (1988) *Third World Legal Studies* 161-83; C Flinterman & E Ankumah 'The African Charter on Human and Peoples' Rights' in H Hannum (ed) *Guide to international human rights practice* (1992) 159-69; R Kiwanuka 'The meaning of "People" in the African

In Africa, a number of important events influenced the emergence and evolution of a regional human rights system. These include, encouragement at the UN level for regional human rights mechanisms, NGO lobbying and the unprecedented acknowledgement by some African leaders that human rights violations in other states were also their concern.[27] These events culminated to the adoption of the African Charter on Human and Peoples' Rights (hereafter 'ACHPR', 'the African Charter' or 'the Charter') by the OAU Assembly of Heads of States and Government (AHSG).[28]

With the subsequent entry into force of the Charter in October 1986, the essence of regional promotion and protection of human rights in Africa was somehow officially acknowledged by the OAU.[29] Apart from guaranteeing a catalogue of rights, the Charter also provides for the establishment of their enforcement mechanism, namely, the African Commission on Human and Peoples' Rights (hereafter 'the African Commission' or 'the Commission').[30]

Whilst the adoption of the African Charter was a good gesture that signalled the recognition that human rights violations in one state were a concern to other states, the African human rights system generally, and the African Commission in particular, have been found wanting in a number of areas.[31] The system is not only the least

---

Charter on Human and Peoples' Rights' (1988) 82 *American Journal of International Law* 80-101; M Mutua 'The Banjul Charter and the African Cultural Fingerprint: An evaluation of the language of duties' (1995) 35 *Virginia Journal of International Law* 339-80; M Mutua 'The African human rights system in a comparative perspective: The need for urgent reformulation' (1993) 5 *Legal Affairs* 31; S Neff 'Human rights in Africa: Thoughts on the African Charter on Human and Peoples' Rights in the light of case law from Botswana, Lesotho and Swaziland' (1984) 33 *International & Comparative Law Quarterly* 331-47; J Swanson 'The emergence of new rights in the African Charter' (1991) 12 *New York Law School Journal of International & Comparative Law* 307-33; C Welch 'The African Commission on Human and Peoples' Rights: A five-year report and assessment' (1992) 14 *Human Rights Quarterly* 43-61.

27   R Murray *Human rights in Africa: From the OAU to the AU* (2004) 22.

28   Adopted 27 June 1981.

29   Murray (n 27 above).

30   The African Commission on Human and Peoples' Rights was established in 1987 'to promote human and peoples' rights and ensure their protection.' See art 30 of the African Charter.

31   J Mubangizi 'Some reflections on recent and current trends in the promotion and protection of human rights in Africa: The pains and the gains' (2006) 6 *African Human Rights Law Journal* 147.

developed but also the least effective as compared with its American and European counterparts.[32] This is rather strange especially because the African Charter, which was intended to anchor the system, is the most widely ratified regional human rights instrument in the world.

Perhaps, this explains why, in spite of the Charter's ratification by all the OAU/AU member states, human rights have continued to be relentlessly violated on the continent.[33] This lends credence to Baimu's observation that 'the fact that conflicts, and the associated massive human rights violations, have continued to engulf the continent when most of the African states are bound by the provisions of the Charter indicates that the African Charter is still not taken seriously by many African states.'[34]

To compensate for the Commission's inadequacies and to strengthen the regional human rights system, the African Court on Human and Peoples' Rights (hereafter 'the African Court' or 'the Court') was subsequently established.[35] While some scholars have high hopes for the Court, believing it will make African leaders more conscious of their human rights obligations,[36] others doubt that it will do much to improve the already pathetic human rights

---

32   As above, 148.

33   K Hopkins 'A new human rights era dawns on Africa?' (2003) 18 *SAPR/PL* 360.

34   E Baimu 'Commission and the Court', *Conflict Trends* (2001) 3 19.

35   See generally, A Van der Mei 'The new court on human and peoples' rights: Towards an effective human rights protection mechanism for Africa?' *Leiden Journal of International law* (2005) 18/1 113-29; C Heyns 'A human rights court for Africa' *Netherlands Quarterly of human rights* (2004) 22/3 325-7; F Viljoen 'A human rights court for Africa and Africans' (2004) 1/30 *Brooklyn Journal of International law* 1-66.

36   See for example, A O'Shea 'A critical reflection on the proposed African Court on Human and Peoples' Rights' (2001) 1 *African Human Rights law Journal* 285; N Udombana 'Toward the African Court on Human and Peoples' Rights: Better late than never' (2000) 3 *Yale Human Rights and Development Law Journal* 45; J Mubangizi & A O'Shea 'An African Court on Human and Peoples' Rights' (1999) 22 *South African Yearbook of International Law* 256; M Mutua 'The African Human Rights Court: A two-legged stool? (1999) 21 *Human Rights Quarterly* 342; G Naldi & K Magliveras 'Reinforcing the African system of human rights: The Protocol on the establishment of a regional court of human and peoples' rights' (1998) 16 *Netherlands Quarterly of Human Rights* 431; A Stemmet 'A future African court for human and peoples' rights and domestic human rights norms' (1998) 21 *South African Yearbook of International Law* 233; and G Naldi & K Magliveras 'The proposed African Court on Human and Peoples' Rights: Evaluation and comparison' (1996) 9 *African Journal of International and Comparative Law* 944.

situation on the continent.[37] Some have argued that the Court, given its normative and institutional frameworks, is a typical reflection of the fear of the OAU/AU member states to create a powerful regional human rights mechanism that would from time to time call them to account for violations in their domestic jurisdictions.[38] Whether or not the Court has the potential and capacity to adequately reinforce Africa's regional human rights system is analysed in detail elsewhere in this book. However, it is important to note at this juncture that the Court is a timely innovation, whose establishment cannot be underrated.

Noteworthy, apart from the need to complement the African Commission, the establishment of the regional human rights court was partly a response to the gross impunity that escalated from the early 1990s. The degenerating human rights situation was indeed an issue of great concern that necessitated the innovation of appropriate measures to salvage the continent which was at the brink of the precipice. At the end of the second millennium, therefore, Africa began to re-position and set itself on a firm path to development, peace and respect for human rights.[39]

Hence, other than the establishment of the regional human rights court, this period witnessed the emergence of other pan-continental institutions and programmes with human rights responsibility, such as the New Partnership for Africa's Development (NEPAD) and the African Peer Review Mechanism (APRM). The period also witnessed the restructuring of old institutions such as the OAU, which later became the African Union (AU), perhaps, to make them more compliant with the human rights tide that was sweeping the globe more intensely than before. These initiatives somehow marked

---

37   See generally, A Dieng 'Introduction to the African Court on Human and Peoples' Rights' (2005) 15 *INTERIGHTS Bulletin* 3; G Bekker 'The African Court on Human and Peoples' Rights: Safeguarding the interests of African states' (2007) 51/1 *Journal of African Law* 153.

38   See these arguments in O Nmehielle 'Towards an African court of human rights: Structuring and the court' (2000) 6/1 *Annual Survey of international and Comparative Law* 96-109; A Loyds & R Murray 'Institutions with responsibility for human rights protection under the African Union' (2004) 48/2 *Journal of African Law* 165-86.

39   See K Kithure 'The normative and institutional framework of the African Union relating to the protection of human rights and the maintenance of international peace and security: A critical appraisal (2003) 3 *African Human Rights Law Journal* 99.

the beginning of the end of the passiveness to impunity that had all along been displayed by the majority of African states.

Besides the emergence of new institutions and restructuring of old ones, the continent, during this period, experienced a flood of activities in the form of conferences, seminars and workshops, convened to look for ways to articulate human rights in its agenda. These include: the Grand Bay (Mauritius), Kigali (Rwanda), Cairo (Egypt) and Algiers (Algeria) conferences. These initiatives notwithstanding, regional enforcement of human rights in Africa is still beset with a multiplicity of challenges.

This book, which is a comprehensive study of the African system on human and peoples' rights, therefore provides an insight into international human rights law and their enforcement in Africa. In other words, it analyses Africa's regional human rights system in terms of its historical and philosophical backgrounds, its normative and institutional frameworks and unveils the nature and scope of the challenges besetting it. Additionally, it proposes possible normative and institutional reforms to the regional human rights system in order to foster the effective enforcement of human rights on the continent.

THE BOOK

This book is a revised and updated version of my earlier book entitled *The African System on Human and Peoples' Rights: Its Promises, Prospects and Pitfalls*. Its main objective and purpose is to underscore the challenges besetting the effective enforcement of international human rights law in Africa. Towards this end, the book aims at illuminating a number of issues concerning the African system on human and peoples' rights. First, it aims at analysing the philosophical and historical foundations of human rights in Africa. This is essential because, as shall be seen later, human rights have been said to be foreign and irrelevant in Africa and to Africans. Appreciating that human rights are relevant to Africa, and indeed not foreign to Africans as purported in certain quarters, will therefore go a long way to emphasise the need to strengthen their enforcement on the continent, particularly at the regional level.

Secondly, the book aims to unveil the theoretical and historical origins and developments of the African human rights system. As shall be shown elsewhere below, the system is a product of prolonged negotiations and activities that took place over a long period. It is therefore imperative to underscore the journey taken to bring the system to its present status. This will also give room to the assessment as to whether or not the system is progressing, stagnant or retrogressing.

Thirdly, the book aims to review the normative and institutional mechanisms of the regional human rights system. Noteworthy, at the centre of the debates on the system lies the alleged inadequacy of its normative and institutional mechanisms. Further, the book shall provide an insight into the challenges of enforcing international human rights law in Africa at the regional level. This will not only help to uncover the pitfalls but would also emphasise the future prospects of enforcing human rights in the region. Finally, the book aims to recommend possible ways on how to deal with some of the challenges to effective enforcement of human rights under the African system.

In summary, this book was motivated by the desire to conduct a comprehensive study on the African human rights system, not only with regard to its institutional mechanisms, but also the challenges encountered in the course of enforcing its substantive human rights norms. This, however, is not to say that no study has been conducted on the African human rights system. Indeed, a lot has already been said, and this book is an added voice to the ongoing research on the system. A continuous study of the system is necessary particularly in light of the fact that the continent is in desperate need of well established and effective regional human rights enforcement mechanisms. At the moment, the regional human rights system is stuck between prospects and pitfalls because of the gap that exists between the promise of human rights and their actual realisation. By all means, this trend needs to be reversed.

STRUCTURE OF THE BOOK

This book consists of fourteen chapters divided into four parts. Part I discusses the philosophical and historical backgrounds to human rights in Africa. The part is divided into three chapters. Chapter One reviews the concept and philosophy of human rights. Chapter Two discusses human rights in Africa by tracing their existence from pre-colonial Africa to the modern day state. Chapter Three discusses the historical dimensions of the African system on human and peoples' rights.

Part II of the book, which consists of Chapters Four to Seven, reviews some of the key normative instruments of the African system on human and peoples' rights. The instruments reviewed are: the Constitutive Act of the African Union (CAAU); the African Charter on Human and Peoples' Rights; the African Charter on the Rights and Welfare of the Child; and the Protocol to the African Charter on Human and Peoples' Rights on the Rights of Women in Africa, respectively.

Part III revisits the institutional mechanisms of the system. The part comprises of four chapters. Chapter Eight, the African Union and its organs; Chapter Nine, the African Commission on Human and Peoples' Rights; Chapter Ten, the African Court on Human and Peoples' Rights; and Chapter Eleven, the African Committee of Experts on the Rights and Welfare of the Child.

Part IV, which mainly deals with the challenges facing the African human rights system, also examines the possible reforms to the system. Specifically, Chapters Twelve and Thirteen illuminate the normative and institutional deficiencies of the system, respectively. Chapter Fourteen proposes two important institutional reforms to the system, namely, mainstreaming and rationalisation.

PART I

PHILOSOPHICAL AND HISTORICAL BACKGROUNDS OF HUMAN RIGHTS IN AFRICA

CHAPTER 1

A REVIEW OF THE CONCEPT AND PHILOSOPHY OF HUMAN RIGHTS

International human rights law is a product of both international law and human rights law. Alston correctly acknowledged that, while the antecedents of this branch of law lie in domestic legal, social and political developments, the process through which it emerged has been very much a top-down rather than a bottom-up one.[1] This is because 'it was the inclusion in the United Nations Charter of a commitment to human rights and the subsequent elaboration of more precisely defined obligations in international law that marked the transition of human rights from a field of philosophical inquiry and moral invocation to its present universal status.'[2]

Whereas international human rights law has registered a remarkable degree of acceptance within the relatively short period of its existence, its conceptual and philosophical foundations have remained a subject of great controversy.[3] Since time immemorial, the concept of human rights has attracted intense philosophical challenges, especially in Africa. This is certainly true in relation to the raging debate on relativism versus universalism. This debate shall be revisited in the next chapter of this book. Meanwhile, this chapter shall review the philosophical basis of human rights and the evolution of the concept of international human rights law.

Noteworthy, before human rights became an international concern, they were promoted, protected as well as violated at the domestic level; as much as they are today. Hence, we cannot blindly focus on human rights as an international concept and ignore their domestic background, otherwise our study on the African human rights system would be partial. In other words, it is imperative to

---

1   P Alston (ed) *Human rights law* (1996) Xii.

2   As above.

3   The disputed philosophical foundations largely centre on whether the concept of human rights is universal or contextual and on its existence in pre-colonial African societies.

re-examine the definition, scope and philosophy of human rights, before embarking on their internationalisation. This would go a long way to enhance our understanding of the philosophical and conceptual basis of the African human rights system.

Suffice it to state that Africa's regional human rights system is a product of various philosophical perceptions. This is indeed permissible, owing to the socio-political and cultural diversities that define the continent. Historical factors, such as colonialism, have also contributed to the divergence of perceptions on the concept. While this is the case, this chapter will re-visit the traditional theories or philosophies of human rights that have most likely influenced the emergence, evolution and content of Africa's regional human rights system. The chapter, to a large extent, appreciates that the African system did not originate from a 'philosophical vacuum', but was rather built on philosophies and theories of law and human rights that subsisted prior to its inception.

1.1   DEFINITION, CLASSIFICATION AND SCOPE OF HUMAN RIGHTS

1.1.1   DEFINITION OF HUMAN RIGHTS

The apparent difficulty to identify human rights has reduced their definition to a subject of great controversy among scholars.[4] For instance, scholars such as Shestack associated human rights with attributes such as 'important', 'moral' and 'universal'.[5] Such an approach is, however, too generalised because not all entitlements with such attributes qualify as human rights. Arguably, the terms 'important' and 'moral' may not necessarily have universally accepted interpretations in the sense that what is 'important' or 'moral' to one community or person may not be the same to another.

On his part, Cassese defines human rights on the basis of 'an expansive desire to unify the world by drawing up a list of guidelines for all governments ... an attempt by the contemporary world to

---

4   A Brendalyn *Democratisation and the protection of human rights in Africa* (1995) 29.

5   J Shestack 'The Philosophic foundations of human rights' in R McCorquodale *Human rights* (2003) 4.

introduce a measure of reason into its history.'[6] If this observation is anything to go by, it would mean that human rights are not inherent in all human beings but are rather conferred through the so-called 'list of guidelines.' In other words, based on this observation, governments have the discretion to decide whether or not human rights are relevant to their people. This is because there is nothing absolute about 'guidelines'. Rather, they can be varied, depending on the prevailing circumstances, to suit the whims of those implementing them.

The perception of human rights as 'guidelines' is therefore myopic because it is antithetical to the understanding that human rights are inherent entitlements which cannot be granted to anyone nor be deprived without a great affront to justice.[7] Hence, Cassese's assertion cannot be embraced uncritically because the promotion and protection of human rights goes beyond the desire to unify the world. Any suggestion in this regard should therefore not be entertained.

It has further been suggested that human rights are those entitlements individuals possess by virtue of being human.[8] This implies that all human beings are equal and have rights in equal measures regardless of age, sex, race, social class, talent, or religion.[9] In tandem with this position, Henkin concluded that human rights are universal rights accruing on all human beings that are fundamental to human existence and can neither be transferred, forfeited, nor waived.[10] One would agree with this definition simply because, unless it is appreciated that human rights are inherent in all persons, it will not be possible to enforce them, especially in Africa. It cannot be gainsaid that the concept of human rights has, at some point, been dismissed as a Western idea or creation which has no bearing

---

6   A Cassese *Human rights in a changing world* (1990) 3.

7   M Cranston 'Human rights: Real or supposed' in D Raphael (ed) *Political theory and the rights of man* (1967) 52.

8   Brendalyn (n 4 above).

9   As above.

10   L Henkin *The Age of rights* (1990) 2.

or relevance to Africans.[11] The discussion on whether or not Africa has a history of human rights shall be revisited in the next chapter.

Legal positivism regards human rights as those entitlements which have become part of a positive legal system and derive either from the will of the state or the command of the sovereign.[12] This proposition is not very appropriate to Africa because, if states are allowed to become the ultimate source of rights, it is not unlikely that such status would be used to violate human rights with impunity.[13] Legal positivism fails to appreciate the fact that the so-called 'will of the state' or 'command of the sovereign' can only give effect to rights that are inherent but not create them through legislation. This is to say, if human rights are legislated by a state, it simply means that the state has the power to confer them only to the extent it acknowledges their importance to its people. In this regard, a state may choose to guarantee or violate human rights at whims without necessarily being called to question.

Amidst all these contradicting legal positions, one would agree with Azinge's observation that, to postulate a precise definition of human rights is a highly elusive task.[14] Justice Oputa of Nigeria alluded to this definitional problem when he posited:

> If therefore we attempt to probe human rights in the political and legal culture of Nigeria without a clear idea of rights, a clear theory of rights in general, and of human rights, in particular, we shall not be right about human rights.[15]

---

11   See generally the arguments advanced in this regard in K Appiagyei-Atua 'A rights-centred critique of African philosophy in the context of development' (2005) 5 *African Human Rights Law Journal* 335-357; K Quashigah 'The philosophic basis of human rights and its relations to Africa: A critique' (1992) *Journal of Human Rights Law and Practice* 22-38; K Wiredu 'Democracy and consensus in African traditional politics: A plea for a non-party polity' in O Eze *Postcolonial African philosophy: A critical reader* (1997) 303; P Hountondji 'The master's voice: The problem of human rights in Africa' in P Ricoeur (ed) *Philosophical foundations of human rights* (1986) 319; E Anthony 'Beyond the paper Tiger: The challenges of a human rights court in Africa' (1997) 32 *Texas International Law Journal* 519-521.

12   Brendalyn (n 4 above) 29. See also D Lloyds *Introduction to jurisprudence* 291-292.

13   As above.

14   E Azinge 'Milestone decisions on human rights' in A Kalu & Y Osinbajo (eds) *Perspectives on human rights* (1992) 196.

15   'Human rights in the political and legal culture of Nigeria', Second Justice Idigbe Memorial Lecture, University of Benin, (1986) cited in Azinge (n 14 above) 196.

Oputa seems to suggest that, for human rights to be properly defined, the starting point of the enquiry should be to define the term 'right'. Accordingly, the term 'right' could either be defined in the abstract or concrete sense. In the abstract, it refers to 'justice', 'ethical correctness', or 'consonance with the rule of law or the principles of morals'.[16] In the concrete sense, it means 'power', 'privilege', 'faculty' or 'demand', inherent in one person and incidental upon another.[17] Accordingly, some legal positivists defined 'legal right' as a legally protected interest,[18] while natural law thinkers, viewing the term in correlation with nature, concluded it is something inherent in humanity.[19]

It has therefore been contended that those claims which are based on, or are in accord with, some objective standards, be it a code of moral values or laws, can rightly be termed as 'rights'.[20] In tandem with this perception, Eze defined human rights as 'demands or claims which individuals or groups make on society, some of which have become part of *ex lata* while others remain aspirations to be attained in future.'[21] In Eze's understanding, only that which is recognised and protected by the legal system can be considered as a right. This perception is somewhat limited.

Arguably, while some rights are recognised and protected by law for various reasons, others are not, yet they are important as they are inherent in man. The law or legal system should not be seen as a 'grantor' but a 'protector' of rights. It is true that in most legal systems, especially those founded on the Common Law tradition, one cannot assert a claim unless it is recognised by the legal system. In the case of human rights, however, this fact should not be taken to mean that all rights are conferred by the legal system. Rather, it should be an emphasis of the fact that the legal system enforces and protects what already inherently exists in man.

---

16   Azinge (n 14 above) 197.

17   As above.

18   See P Fitzgerald *Salmond on jurisprudence* (1966) 217.

19   See generally J Finnis *Natural law and natural rights* (1980).

20   Azinge (n 14 above) 197. See also the arguments advanced in F Dowrick (ed) *Human rights, problems, perspectives and texts* (1979) 8.

21   O Eze *Human rights in Africa* (1984) 5.

It is in tandem with this argument that Cranston maintains, and rightly so, that 'a human right is something of which no one may be deprived without a great affront to justice.'[22] According to him, 'there are certain deeds which should never be done, certain freedoms which should never be invaded, some things which are supremely sacred.'[23] When this position is extrapolated further, one would arrive to the conclusion that if the deprivation of human rights would result to 'a great affront to justice', no institution or individual qualifies as a grantor of human rights. At the same time, it could be argued that all institutions and individuals are expected to be protectors of human rights.

Despite numerous attempts to find a composite definition of human rights, it is now accepted that the province of this concept cannot easily be determined. This means that human rights are continually evolving, lending credence to Laski's observations that 'a legal system is surrounded by the penumbra of an attainable ideal which it must reach as the price of its preservation.'[24] In the context of this book therefore, human rights are defined as the demands or claims individuals or groups make that are essential for individual well being, dignity, and fulfilment,[25] the deprivation of which may lead to a great affront to justice. Accordingly, they are demands or claims:

> which stand above the ordinary laws of the land and which in fact [are] antecedent to the political society itself. It is a primary condition to a civilised existence and ... could be immutable to the extent of the non-immutability of the constitution itself.[26]

Any definition of human rights cannot ignore the fact that they are inherent, indivisible, interrelated, universal and belong to every society regardless of geographical, historical, cultural, ideological, political or economic orientation. It is easy to contest the authenticity of such a definition with respect to the rights of vulnerable persons such as women, children, the old and disabled.

---

22   Cranston (n 7 above) 52.

23   As above.

24   H Laski *A grammar of politics* (1967) 91-92.

25   As above.

26   *Ransome Kuti v. Attorney-General of Nigeria* cited in Azinge (n 14 above).

Thus, as if motivated by the need to cater for these categories of persons, Humana defined human rights as laws and practices that have evolved over the centuries to protect ordinary people, minorities, groups, and races from oppressive rulers and governments.[27] This, however, is a narrow definition which fails to cater for those outside the purview of these categories. Although 'oppressive rulers' may not be 'ordinary people', they too have rights by reason of being human. In other words, the essence of human rights would be lost if they are meant for only the 'good' or 'vulnerable' people in society.

Therefore, if Humana's definition is anything to go by, then human rights shall be confined, not to claims asserted and recognised 'as of right', but to claims based on charity or benevolence.[28] This has never been the essence of human rights. Instead, human rights have always been 'those liberties, immunities and benefits which by accepted contemporary values, all human beings [are] able to claim 'as of right' of the society in which they live.'[29] They are not privileges granted by the state or society but are the ideals and distinguishing marks of a civilised society.[30]

Noteworthy, although the term 'human rights' as it is commonly used today is a twentieth century concept for what was referred to as 'natural rights' or 'the rights of man'[31], its philosophical and historical foundations can be traced back to the existence of mankind. We shall revert to this debate at a later part of this chapter.

1.1.2   CLASSIFICATION OF HUMAN RIGHTS

Human rights may be divided into different categories. These are: civil, political, social, economic and cultural.[32] These rights could be enjoyed individually (individual's rights) or collectively (group or collective rights). Civil and political rights include, but are not limited

---

27   C Humana *World human rights guide* (1983) 7.

28   Azinge (n 14 above) 197.

29   L Henkin 'Human rights' in R Bernhardt (ed) *Encyclopaedia of international law* (1985) 8 268.

30   A Nsirimovu *Human rights education techniques in schools* (1994) 24.

31   M Cranston *What are human rights* (1973) 1.

32   See this classification in, for example C Aka 'Military, globalisation and human rights in Africa' (2002) *New York Law School Journal of Human Rights* 371.

to, the right to self-determination; the right to life; freedom from torture and inhuman treatment; freedom from slavery and forced labour; the right to liberty and security of the person; freedom of movement and choice of residence; right to fair trial; right to privacy; freedom of thought, conscience and religion; freedom of opinion and expression; the right to assembly; freedom of association; the right to marry and found a family; the right to participate in one's government either directly or through freely elected representatives; the right to nationality and equality before the law.[33]

Economic, social and cultural rights envisage, *inter alia,* the right to work; the right to just conditions of work; the right to fair remuneration; the right to an adequate standard of living; the right to organise, form and join trade unions; the right to collective bargaining; the right to equal pay for equal work; the right to social security; the right to property; the right to education; the right to participate in cultural life and to enjoy the benefits of scientific progress.[34]

Noteworthy, while civil and political rights impose restraints on the exercise of state power and are therefore negative rights, socio-economic rights tend to extend the scope of state activities, translating them into positive rights.[35] It is equally important to note that human rights are not static; their codification is an ongoing and never ending process both nationally and internationally. Sometimes they are codified in response to a specific threat or act of repression. An example frequently cited in this regard is freedom of religion, which was codified in reaction to the powerful Catholic church in Europe and the religious wars and government coercions that the church provoked.[36]

---

33   As above. See also generally the African Charter on Human and Peoples' Rights arts 2-14; Universal Declaration on Human Rights (UDHR); European Charter on Human Rights and Fundamental Freedoms and the American Convention on Human Rights.

34   As above. See also the International Covenant on Economic, Social and Cultural Rights (ICESCR).

35   W Eno 'The African Commission on Human and Peoples' Rights as an instrument for the protection of human rights in Africa' (1998) *LLM Thesis University of South Africa* 7.

36   As above.

The classification of rights into the various categories listed above should not be construed as rigid because, as stated earlier, human rights are interrelated and interdependent.[37] Moreover, the enjoyment of these rights is not absolute and may be limited or derogated from on the basis of, for example, state security, national survival or any other necessary circumstances.[38] That is why some modern Constitutions entrench limitation and derogation clauses that would enable them to limit the enjoyment of certain rights and derogate from others in cases of emergencies that threaten the life or security of a nation.[39]

1.1.3   Scope of Human Rights

Human rights are of broad application; they are recognised in the Constitutions of many states whose political principles are otherwise quite divergent.[40] Accordingly, they are applicable both nationally and internationally. Initially, human rights were purely a matter of national concern. However, the adoption of the UN Charter, after the Second World War, ushered in a process leading to their gradual universalisation. The Charter after reaffirming, in the preamble, faith in fundamental human rights, in the dignity and worth of the human person, in the equal rights of men and women, pronounces in Article 1(3) that one of its purposes is to promote and encourage respect for human rights and fundamental freedoms. Thus, the UN has been able to consolidate the principle that human rights are a matter of international concern and that the international community is required to promote and protect them.[41]

The protection and promotion of human rights cannot be effectively discussed without recognition of the efforts to enforce them at the regional level. Conspicuous regional achievements in this regard are the adoption of the European Convention on Human Rights and Fundamental Freedoms; the African Charter

---

37   See art 5 of the Vienna Declaration and Programme of Action.

38   M Nowak *Introduction to the international human rights regime* (2003) 2.

39   See, for example, The Constitution of the Republic of South Africa 1996, arts. 36 & 37.

40   Azinge (n 14 above) 199.

41   As above, 200.

on Human and People's Rights; and the American Convention on Human Rights. Consequently, people from different regions of the world now have established institutionalised processes through which they can ultimately find recourse to the violation of their rights. Human rights can now be regarded as the benchmark below which no national law may fall.[42] They can be enforced at the international level when they become a matter of treaty obligation or to the extent that their respect has become a customary rule of international law.[43]

In the *Barcelona Traction Case*[44], the International Court of Justice (ICJ) found that the principles and rules concerning basic human rights were binding on all states. Principally, the protection and promotion of human rights is a prerequisite for all governments. Hence, they are expected to incorporate human rights standards into their domestic legal systems. Arguably, the level of a state's development is determined or even affected by the extent to which its citizens enjoy human rights in all their ramifications. It follows therefore, that peace, progress and stability are predicated on the respect for human rights.

Consequently, as Umozurike correctly observed, human rights have become 'a potent instrument of diplomacy to which has been added democracy.'[45] For instance, how a state treats nationals of another state residing in its territory would determine whether the two states will have a good diplomatic relationship. The yardstick used to determine or define such a relationship is usually predicated on the respect for human rights of the concerned individuals. Unfortunately, the paradox in human rights is that their would-be most effective protectors— governments— are most often their

---

42   U Umozurike *The African Charter on Human and Peoples' Rights* (1997) 6.

43   See *Nationality Decrees of Tunis and Morocco* PCIJ Ser. B no. 4 1923. In this case, the Permanent Court of International Justice answered the question whether the extension of French nationality decrees in Tunis and Morocco to British citizens was a matter within domestic jurisdiction. Giving a negative answer, the court found that the status of a matter depended on the development of international relations. Accordingly, a matter was removed from the domain of domestic jurisdiction once it became the subject of treaty obligation.

44   International Court of Justice Report (1970) 32 para 34.

45   As above.

worst violators.[46] The challenge has therefore not been to lay down standards for states but also to ensure, through effective enforcement mechanisms, that states carry out their human rights obligations.

1.2   PHILOSOPHICAL FOUNDATIONS OF HUMAN RIGHTS

Having attempted a definition of human rights, it is equally important to review their philosophical foundations. Other than the role philosophy plays in unveiling truth, there are a myriad of reasons for exploring the philosophical origins of human rights. In the main, unless the philosophies that shape human rights are underscored, the understanding of the concept is likely to remain obscure.[47] Further, understanding the philosophical foundations of the concept will 'help to devise a translation formula that will permit men and women to speak to each other across the gulf of creed and dogma, a necessary exercise for universal recognition of human rights principles.'[48] This is because, there has been a general confusion as to what human rights really are and whether they are relevant to people of certain cultural inclinations. Such issues could be resolved through the systematic discussion of the philosophical underpinnings of the concept.

For the above reasons, we shall discuss some philosophical theories of human rights. However, our discussion shall be confined to three main theories–naturalism, positivism and Marxism. The reason for such a restrictive discussion stems from the fact that the three are largely regarded as the 'traditional theories' that purport to explain the philosophical foundations of law and human rights. While this may be true, it should be noted that social sciences have also attempted to postulate a number of disparate theories based on people's cultures, conflicts, and interests. Such theories, including the sociological and utilitarian theories, tend to emphasise the all important point that human rights are largely a product of social forces and human interactions.

---

46   O Okongwu 'The OAU Charter and the principle of domestic jurisdiction in Inter-African affairs' (1973) 13 *Indiana Journal of International Law* 589.

47   Shestack (n 5 above) 202.

48   As above.

Although the 'traditional theories' are more pronounced in the demystification of the philosophical foundations of human rights, it is nonetheless not correct for any society to claim monopoly over the evolution of the concept. Likewise, no society can claim to be a paradise for human rights. It should be emphasised, even though a particular concept is more pronounced in a certain society, that should not be taken to mean that the concept is foreign to other societies.[49] In this regard, we contend that traditional (pre-colonial) African societies had a culture of human rights, whose philosophical foundations may be akin to those discussed herein below. Hence, the fact that the philosophical foundations of human rights in this chapter are analysed in the light of the Natural, Positivist and Marxist theories should not be construed as lending credence to the argument that human rights owe their origin in Europe or America. We maintain that Africa too has a human rights tradition, whose parameters shall be highlighted in the next chapter.

1.2.1   NATURAL LAW (RIGHTS) THEORY

According to this theory, human rights were perceived as the natural right of every individual. The postulation of this theory is credited to Sophocles and Aristotle, although it was later elaborated by the stoics of the Greek Hellenistic period and by those of the Roman period.[50] Thomas Aquinas, one of the early proponents of this theory, perceived natural law as part of the law of God that confers certain immutable rights upon individuals.[51] The particular rights and freedoms that were thus thought to be natural concomitants of being human were identified by contemplating the condition of an individual in a stateless society.[52]

---

49   K Busia 'The status of human rights in pre-colonial Africa: Implications for contemporary practices' in E McCarthy *et al* (eds) *Africa, human rights, and the global system* (1994) 46.

50   Some of the chief early proponents of this theory include Callicles, Plato, Aristotle, Sophocles, St. Augustine, St. Thomas Aquinas, Stoic, Wiliam Ockham, Thomas Hobbes and John Locke. See W Roux 'Natural law theories' in D Moellendorf & C Roederer *Jurisprudence* (2006) 25-61.

51   Eno (n 35 above) 6, citing, St. Thoman Aquinas, *Summa Theologica,* Lib. II, pt. II (1475).

52   Centre for Human Rights Pretoria, *From human rights to human wrongs* (1995) 50.

However, as feudalism declined, modern secular theories of natural law arose, particularly as enunciated by Grotius and Pufendorf. Their philosophy detached natural law from religion, laying the groundwork for the secular, rationalistic modern version of the theory. According to Grotius, a natural characteristic of human beings is the social impulse to live peacefully and in harmony with others. Therefore, whatever conformed to the nature of men and women as rational social beings was right and just; whatever opposed it by disturbing the social harmony was wrong and unjust. Thus, Grotius defined natural law as a 'dictate of right reason'.[53]

Natural law theory led to natural rights theory the theory most closely associated with modern human rights.[54] The chief proponent of this theory was John Locke, who premised his philosophy on the imagination of the existence of human beings in a state of nature.[55] In that state, men and women were free, able to determine their actions, and were also equal in the sense that no one was subjected to the will or authority of another. The state of nature, however, suffered from certain limitations due to the absence of a superior power that would regulate the conflicting interests of individuals.[56]

To instil order and harmonious co-existence, individuals entered into a 'social contract' by which they mutually agreed to form a civil society (*pactum unionis*) and set up a political authority to protect their respective rights. That way, they retained the rights to life, liberty, and property.[57] At the same time, government was obliged to protect the rights of its subjects, failure to which, it forfeited its validity and force. According to this theory, the government derived justification for its existence and continuous exercise of political power from the contractual duty to protect the rights of its subjects.[58]

Locke's theory was the basis for the principle that law should protect the basic human rights of the individual against the abuses

---

53   H Grotius *De jure belli et Pacis* (Book 1, 1689) cited in Eno (n 35 above).

54   J Cobbah 'African values and the human rights debate: An African perspective' (1987) *Human Rights Quarterly* 314.

55   As above.

56   Roux (n 50 above) 41.

57   Eno (n 35 above) 7.

58   As above.

of governments. This can at least be traced back to his *Two treatises of government,* published in 1690.[59] In his celebrated work, Locke believed that human beings, not governments, came first in the general order of things. He therefore argued that:

> If man in the state of nature be so free, as has been said; if he be absolute Lord of his own person and possession, equal to the greatest and subject to nobody, why will he part with his freedom? Why will he give up his empire, and subject himself to the dominion and control of another power? To which tis obvious to answer, that though in the state of nature he hath such a right, yet the enjoyment of it is very uncertain, and constantly exposed to the invasion of others. For all being kings as much as he is, every man his equal, and the greater part no strict observer of equity and justice, the enjoyment of the property he has in this state is very unsafe, very unsecured. This makes him willing to quit a condition, which however free, is full of fears and continual dangers: And tis not without reason, that he seeks out, and is willing to join in society with others who are already united, or have a mind to unite for the mutual preservation of their lives, liberties and estates.[60]

Thus, under this theory, human rights were regarded as people's inherent possession, having nothing to do with the intervention or support of society.[61] This simply means, they were created with those rights and in turn, they created society to protect the rights by enacting suitable laws.

Natural rights theory is believed to have been the philosophical impetus for the wave of revolts against absolutism during the late eighteenth century.[62] The theory is visible in the French Declaration of the Rights of Man,[63] in the US Declaration of Independence,[64] in the Constitutions of numerous states created upon liberation from colonialism, and in the principal UN human rights documents.

---

59   J Locke *Two treatises of government* (Latest rev ed. 1963) 395. See also Roux (n 50 above) 43-45.

60   Cited in Roux (n 50 above) 43-45.

61   Eno (n 35 above).

62   Z Motola 'Human rights in Africa: A cultural, ideological and legal examination' (1989) *Hastings International & Comparative law review* 374.

63   Declaration of the Rights of Man and of Citizens (France 1789).

64   Motola (n 62 above) 374.

Hence, through various philosophical writings found in the works of Locke, Montesquieu and Jefferson, among others, the ideas of individual rights and popular sovereignty gained acceptance in Europe and America in the eighteenth century.[65] For example, in 1776 in Virginia, a bill of rights was adopted at a convention of delegates representing the thirteen original states of the United States of America (US)[66], which stated that all men are equally free and independent by nature and in possession of certain inherent rights of which they cannot be divested, namely the right to life, liberty and property.[67]

The natural rights theory, however, was seen as a barrier between the individual and the government, when individual rights were invoked as a legal tool against the latter.[68] To ensure this barrier is not penetrated, advocates of natural rights devised mechanisms to limit the government's powers.[69] Most notable of these mechanisms was the doctrine of separation of powers and the notion of the rule of law.[70] Consequently, this led to the creation of institutions that would ensure the essential natural rights were not infringed upon by the government.[71]

Generally, the natural rights theory makes an important contribution to the human rights discourse. It identifies with and provides for the respect for human dignity, freedom and equality, from which other human rights flow. The theory, however, has some overt limitations. For example, it fails to elucidate how one could determine the norms that are to be considered as part of the law of nature and therefore inalienable.[72] Under Locke's view of human beings in the state of nature, all that was needed was the opportunity to be self-dependent; life, liberty, and property were the inherent

---

65   As above 375.

66   E Kenyon 'Constitutionalism in revolutionary America' in J Pennock & J Chapman (eds) *Constitutionalism* (1979) 93.

67   The Virginia Declaration of Rights, adopted in Virginia on 12 June 1776.

68   J Swanson 'The emergence of new rights in the African Charter' (1991) 12 *New York Law School Journal of International & Comparative law* 325.

69   As above.

70   A Pollis & P Schwab (eds) *Human rights cultural and ideological perspectives* (1979) 20.

71   Swanson (n 68 above).

72   Eno (n 35 above) 8.

rights that met this demand.[73] However, it is doubtful that the theory is flexible enough to accommodate the demands of the modern-day society, given their complexity.

As Shestack observed, the lack of flexibility has formed the basis for the chief criticism of natural rights theory.[74] In short, the principal problem with natural law is that the rights considered natural can differ from one theorist to another, depending on their conceptions of nature.[75] Because of this and other difficulties, natural rights theory became unpopular with philosophers like Bentham, who termed the theory as a fallacy.[76] However, natural rights philosophy had a renaissance after World War II. Cobbah noted that over the years, after World War II, it has been recognised that human rights are not just pious declarations, but are declarations that must be practicably enforceable.[77]

The recognition of the practicality and enforceability of human rights has meant that governments have to put in place limits both on the exercise of these rights by the individuals, as well as on the powers of their agents.[78] Hence, human rights have to be enjoyed with due regard to the rights and freedoms of others. Limitations on the enjoyment of individual human rights have today found expression in a number of human rights instruments.[79]

1.2.2   Positivist Theory

Legal positivism is a theory that is typically founded on empiricism and the rejection of metaphysics.[80] The positive method in social sciences was first set out by August Comte in his *Cours de philosophie positive*.[81] Comte rejected metaphysical speculation and argued that

---

73   Swanson (n 68 above).

74   Shestack (n 5 above) 208.

75   As above.

76   As above.

77   Cobbah (n 54 above) 309.

78   Shestack (n 5 above) 210.

79   See, for example, art. 36 of the Constitution of the Republic of South Africa, which provides for the limitation of rights under certain circumstances.

80   I Kroeze 'Legal positivism' in Roederer & Moellendorf (n 50 above) 63.

81   See generally A Comte *Cours de philosophie positive* (1975) cited in I Kroeze (n 80 above).

science ought to concern itself with empirical facts. Once these facts are established, general rules or laws of nature can be abstracted by means of induction. In this way, the theory was premised on the need for man to control and rule over nature and not the other way round.[82] Hence, some early legal positivists opposed the natural law postulation due to its unscientific nature and its tendency to insist on the *status quo* rather than reforms.[83] They contended that natural law in its essence and form was against legal reforms.[84]

It should be clear from the onset that legal positivism is neither a simple nor a single doctrine. This is essentially because it has undergone numerous changes in the course of time as a result of the numerous differences among its postulants.[85] What has remained constant in the theory is the insistence on a view of law as a product of human action.[86]

Classical positivists ascribed all authority to the state and its officials. They rejected any attempt to define and articulate law as a phenomenon that transcended from a source other than the existing legal systems. Accordingly, the source of human rights could only be in the enactments of a system of law with sanctions attached to it. Views on what the law 'ought to be' had no place in classical positive law and were therefore worthless.[87] Regarded in this sense, the theory hinged on the need to distinguish 'law as it is' from 'law as it ought to be.'

In the words of Austin, 'the science of jurisprudence … is concerned with positive laws, or with laws strictly so called, as considered without regard to their goodness or badness.'[88] On this premise, therefore, natural law and natural rights could not be used to deduce what law actually is because at best they provided a standard or ideal for what the law ought to be. Put differently, it

---

82   As above.

83   See this argument in D Johnson, S Pete & M Du Plessis *Jurisprudence: A South African perspective* (2001) 64-65.

84   As above.

85   Kroeze (n 80 above) 73.

86   As above.

87   Shestack (n 5 above) 208.

88   J Austin *The province of jurisprudence determined* (1894).

would not be a waste of time to consult natural law when trying to establish the definition and content of law.

Some positivist scholars insisted on the separation of law and morals.[89] Kroeze argued that the influence of Bacon, Burke and Kant could have generated this kind of thinking among this category of scholars.[90] According to Kant, one of the scholars who insisted on this premise, terms like 'rights' and 'duties' meant different things in legal and moral contexts respectively.[91] In the legal context, these terms could only have a meaning determined by positive law. Similarly, Bentham dismissed 'deontological morality' or natural law as nonsense on stilts.[92] To him, whatever could not be established or verified empirically failed to exist. Whereas this is the case, it has been argued that legal positivists never denied that morality influences the law.[93] Accordingly:

> What they deny is the use of morality to determine whether a rule is a valid rule or not. The validity of a particular rule is one question, the morality of that rule is an entirely different question. The insistence on the separation of law and morality therefore deals with questions of validity and not with evaluation …. Hart's view of the separation of law and morality is a much more nuanced one than of his predecessors. He accepts that natural law has a role to play. For a group of people to constitute a society, a number of basic rules must apply. This he calls the 'minimum content of natural law.'… These minimum rules occur in both law and morality and, as such, there is an overlap between the two. But they are not the same. However, Hart does not believe that the validity of law is dependent on morality, because law does not derive its validity from such a higher source.[94]

As a result of its insistence on the separation of law and morals, legal positivism has been accused of negating the moral philosophical basis of human rights.[95] It is contended that, by divorcing a legal

---

89   See this view in A Alerk *Jurisprudence: An introduction* (1998) 27.

90   Kroeze (n 80 above) 65.

91   J Raz *The authority of law: Essays on law and morality* (1979) 37-38.

92   J Bentham 'Anarchical fallacies' in J Waldron *Nonsense upon stilts: Bentham, Burke & Marx on the rights of man* (1987) 53.

93   Kroeze (n 80 above) 67.

94   As above.

95   Shestack (n 5 above) 209.

system from the ethical and moral foundations of society, positive law encourages the belief that the law must be obeyed, no matter how immoral it may be, whether or not it disregards the individual.[96] For instance, the anti-Semitic edicts of the Nazis although abhorrent to morality, were obeyed as positive law. The same could be said of the immoral apartheid practices that prevailed in South Africa for many years.[97]

Further, positivism has been criticised for its tendency to undermine an international basis for human rights because of its emphasis on the supremacy of national sovereignty.[98] Positivism regards rules of international law as not being law but merely rules of positive morality set or imposed by opinion.[99] This assumption has been one of the major impediments to effective human rights protection in Africa. The doctrine of state sovereignty, which is a culmination of legal positivism, has hampered human rights promotion and protection in Africa, particularly at the regional level.

1.2.3   MARXIST THEORY

Marxism, like the natural law theory, is also concerned with the nature of human beings in society. However, the theory's approach is rooted in the causal role of things such as the forces of production, relations of production, and political and legal arrangements.[100] The proponent of this theory, Karl Marx, regarded the 'law of nature approach' to human rights as idealistic and ahistorical.[101] He saw nothing natural or inalienable about human rights. In a society in which capitalists monopolised the means of production, Marx regarded the notion of individual rights as a bourgeois illusion.[102]

According to the Marxist theory, concepts such as law, justice, morality, democracy, freedom, and others, were considered

---

96   Eno (n 35 above) 10.

97   As Above.

98   Shestack (n 5 above) 209.

99   As above.

100   See D Moellendorf 'Marxism and the law' in Roederer & Moellendorf (n 50 above) 138.

101   Shestack (n 5 above) 210.

102   As above.

historical categories, whose content was determined by the material conditions and the social circumstances of a people. Accordingly, as the conditions of life change, so would the content of notions and ideas.[103] Noteworthy, Marxism sees a person's essence as the potential to use one's abilities to the fullest and to satisfy one's needs. Actualisation of potential, according to the theory, is contingent on the expression of men and women as social beings, which can only occur in a communist society devoid of class conflicts.[104] The only rights, so goes the argument, are those granted by the state, and their exercise is contingent on the fulfilment of obligations to society and the state.[105]

The Marxist theory has been said to be inconsistent with international human rights because it does not recognise international norms.[106] This was evident in the days of Communism in that, while Communist states conceded to the promulgation of international norms, they held the application of those norms to be a matter of exclusive domestic jurisdiction. In international fora, they repeatedly asserted that their alleged abuse of human rights was not just a matter of protecting sovereignty, but was an expression of the communist theory of the unlimited role of the state to decide what is good for the people.[107] The theory was therefore associated with more evil than good and with the gross human rights violations that occurred across the globe after World War II, particularly in the former Union of Soviet Socialist Republic (USSR).[108]

In wrapping up our discussion on the philosophical foundations of human rights, it may be argued, some of the ideals in the above theories can be traced in the practice of human rights in pre-colonial Africa. For example, the natural rights ideal that all people possess human rights simply by being humans also transpired in pre-colonial African societies. Similarly, the African 'communitarian ideal', which

---

103   As above.

104   See A Cassese *International law in a divided world* (1986) 69.

105   Shestack (n 5 above) 211.

106   As above.

107   See, for example, V Chalidze *To defend these rights: Human rights and the Soviet Union* (1974) 15.

108   See Moellendorf (n 100 above) 150-153.

emphasised group over individual rights, can closely be linked to the postulations in Marxism.

The bottom line is, regardless of the divergence in the theoretical and philosophical ramifications of the concept, human rights were known to all human societies since time immemorial. However, the effects of colonialism and related vices led to the insubordination of some cultures to such an extent that the concept was perceived as a Western invention rather than a preserve for all human beings. This skewed perception was somehow clarified when human rights eventually became an international concern.

1.3　INTERNATIONALISATION OF HUMAN RIGHTS

As stated earlier, the concept of human rights as a universal legal obligation of states is of recent origin and its historical antecedents can be traced to the events during and after the Second World War.[109] Mugwanya argued that the consequent awareness of the nexus between respect for human rights and dignity and peace motivated the Allies to set in motion a revolution that culminated in the universalisation of human rights. This was epitomised by the inclusion of certain provisions in the UN Charter that made a qualitative leap towards the promotion and protection of human rights for all.[110] Soon after the universalisation of human rights through the UN and its organs, international protection of human rights devolved to the continental level in what later came to be known as 'regional human rights systems'.

Traditionally, international law granted states national sovereignty whereby every state had complete freedom to deal with its own nationals (personal sovereignty) within its own territory (territorial sovereignty).[111] This principle dictated that in all matters falling within the domestic jurisdiction of any state, international law could not permit interference or intervention by another state. In other words, such matters did not fall within the concern of international

---

109　G Mugwanya *Human rights in Africa: Enhancing human rights through the African regional human rights system* (2003) 16.

110　As above.

111　Eno (n 35 above) 9.

law.[112] Accordingly, as long as personal sovereignty continued to be regarded as exclusively within the domestic jurisdiction of sovereign states, 'what a government did to its own citizens was its own affair and beyond the reach of international law or legal interference by other states.'[113]

However, the position was different when it came to the treatment of aliens. As part of its national sovereignty, a state was always entitled to demand respect for its own nationals abroad, otherwise their maltreatment could constitute a violation of the personal sovereignty of the state to which they belonged.[114] Unfortunately, only states were allowed to claim compensation under international law.[115] If a state fell short of protecting another state's nationals, for example, by expropriating their property, the compensation was due to the state whose personal sovereignty had been violated and not the individual whose property had been expropriated. Whether that state chose to pass the compensation to the injured individual was entirely its own affair.

Thus, for centuries, one proposition remained unchallenged: by reason of the doctrine of national sovereignty, international law could not recognise any rights vested in any individual against any sovereign state, whether his own or another.[116] In other words, individuals featured only in so far as they were subjects of states. Thus, an injury to an individual by the nationals of another state could be interpreted as injury of one state by another.[117] The emphasis on sovereignty of states and the attendant insubordination of the

---

112   As above.

113   J Humphrey *The international law of human rights* (1973) 12. This principle was emphasised in the Covenant of the League of Nations, whose section 15 was categorical that nothing contained in the Covenant would authorise the League to intervene in matters that are 'exclusively within the domestic jurisdiction of states'. The same principle was subsequently reiterated in art 2 (7) of the UN Charter of 1945.

114   See the *Mavromatis Palestinian Concession Case* PCIJ Series A no. 2, in which the court pointed out that 'by taking up the case of one of its subjects, and by resorting to diplomatic action or international judicial proceedings on his behalf, a state is in reality asserting its own right to ensure in the person of its subject, respect for international law...'

115   M Shaw *International law* (1986) 421.

116   P Seighart *The international law of human rights* (1982) 12.

117   R Piotrowicz & S Kaye *Human rights in international and Australian law* (2000) 7.

individual have therefore been the hallmark of international law. A number of examples could be cited in this regard, the best one being the jurisdiction of the International Court of Justice (ICJ).

Even though described as the principal judicial organ of the UN (popularly referred to as the 'World Court'), the ICJ is expressly prohibited from having individuals commence actions or appear before it.[118] It is exclusively for the use of states and an extremely limited class of international organisations. The interests of an individual can only be brought to the notice of the court in the event that a state chooses to act on the individual's behalf.[119] Even when the state takes up the matter, the individual has no right of appearance, nor any ability to influence the case.[120]

Further, international law traditionally emphasised the notion of sovereign equality of states.[121] Since each state is equal, at least on the basis of this doctrine, no state is allowed to impose its will on another.[122] Hence, international rules can only be adopted by consent and each state within its own territory is sovereign, with its freedom of action, 'only fettered by some obligations as it, itself, chooses to assume.'[123] Accordingly, this concept permitted a state to 'impose draconian measures on its own populace ... provided it does not impact upon the sovereignty of any other state, or breach an obligation which it has voluntarily undertaken ...'[124]

By the nineteenth century, however, international law developed a doctrine of 'humanitarian intervention' in cases where a state committed atrocities against its own nationals which 'shocked the conscience of mankind'.[125] At that time, there was a growing realisation of the inseparable link between individual liberty and international peace and security. It was therefore imperative for world leaders to discuss how to ensure the protection of liberties,

---

118   See art 34 of the Statute of the International Court of Justice.

119   Piotrowicz & Kaye (n 117 above) 8.

120   As above.

121   Eno (n 35 above) 9.

122   As above.

123   Piotrowicz & Kaye (n 117 above) 8.

124   As above.

125   Seighart (n 116 above) 13.

not only within their own territories but also internationally.[126] This humanitarian intervention doctrine was invoked largely against the Ottoman Empire in 1827 on behalf of the Greek people; by French in Syria in 1860-1861; and again in 1876 when a large number of Christians were massacred by irregular Ottoman troops in what is today Bulgaria.[127]

It cannot be gainsaid, therefore, prior to the outbreak of the First World War in 1914, international law had a very different view of the manner in which force could be deployed against individuals, both within a state and against the nationals of another state. War was seen as a legitimate method of diplomacy; being referred as merely the extension of diplomacy by other means.[128] Territory could be acquired by conquest without regard to the inhabitants, whose property could be forfeited and who could be denied any role in the government of their land.

Thus, by 1914, most of the earth's land territory was part of the various colonial empires, and other states such as China, Turkey and those of Central and South America were effectively dominated by the 'Great Powers'.[129] In that state of affairs concern over the rights of individuals within the colonial power did not apply to the same extent, if at all, in the colonised territory. Similarly, the core of rights that constituted international humanitarian law were in an extremely primitive state, with little regard being paid to the care of the wounded in the battle-field, and the methods by which force could be employed.[130]

Efforts to protect individuals under international law intensified after the First World War, during which period treaties were concluded to protect the rights of linguistic and ethnic minorities.[131] The protection of minorities took three main forms. First, there were five special treaties on minorities with the Allied or newly created

---

126   As above.
127   As above.
128   Piotrowicz & Kaye (n 117 above) 16.
129   As above.
130   As above.
131   Eno (n 35 above) 11.

states: with Poland (Versailles, 1919), with Czechoslovakia and Yugoslavia (St. Germain-en-Laye, 1919), with Romania (Trianon, 1920), and with Greece (Sevres, 1920). Secondly, chapters on the rights of the minorities within borders were included in the peace treaties with the ex-enemy states such as with Austria (St Germain-en-Laye, 1919), Bulgaria (Neuilly, 1919), Hungary (Trianon, 1920) and later with Turkey (Lausanne, 1923).[132] Thirdly, certain states made declarations before the Council of the League of Nations as a condition of their admission to the League.[133]

Generally, the various initiatives for the protection of the rights of minorities provided for equality before the law with regard to civil and political rights, freedom of religion, the right of members of the minorities to use their own language, and the right to maintain their own religious and educational establishments.[134] Moreover, it was recognised that these various provisions protecting the rights of minorities constituted 'obligations of international concern', which were placed under the guarantee of the League of Nations and could not be modified without the consent of the Council of the League.[135]

Members of minority communities could petition the League with complaints as to their treatment, which would in turn pass on the complaint to the state concerned.[136] Further, a minorities' section was set up within the Secretariat of the League in 1920. The ICJ was on the other hand asked by the League to give advisory opinions on various practices and laws in states with regard to minorities, to determine the scope of the protection contained in the treaties.[137]

---

132   As above.

133   These states included: Finland (1921, as regards the Aland Islands), Albania (1921), Lithuania (1922), Latvia (1923), Estonia (1923), and later Iraq (1932).

134   H Robertson & J Merrils (eds) *Human rights in the world* (1993) 21.

135   As above.

136   The usual procedure was that, if the Secretary-General considered the case admissible, the Council would appoint an *ad hoc* minorities committee to investigate the matter and try to reach a friendly settlement. If it failed, the complaint was referred to the full Council. The Council in turn could refer the matter to the Permanent Court of International Justice. See in this regard, Robertson & Merrils (n 134 above) 20.

137   As above.

The period after the First World War also witnessed the intensification of international collaboration in the abolition of both the national and international slave trade.[138] Noteworthy, many efforts had been made prior to this period, with a number of agreements between states entered in this regard.[139] The General Act of the Brussels Conference was the most comprehensive instrument on this subject until the outbreak of the First World War.[140] Thereafter, the mandate system established by Article 22 of the League Covenant declared that the well-being and development of the peoples in the mandated territories should form a 'sacred trust of civilisation' and that the mandate powers should administer the territories under conditions 'which will guarantee freedom of conscience and religion … and the prohibition of abuses such as slave trade.'[141] As a result of these efforts, the International Convention on the Abolition of Slavery and the Slave Trade was concluded under the auspices of the League of Nations in 1926.[142]

Meanwhile, the doctrine of sovereignty of states still dominated the international law agenda and the relationship between states. As recently as the late 1930s and early 1940s, international law was still silent on how sovereign states should treat their citizens or subjects. The turning point and the subsequent downfall of the doctrine of sovereignty of states, at least as far as it relates to human rights, came when unprecedented atrocities were perpetrated by Italy, Russia, Germany and other dictatorial regimes in Europe and Asia, against

---

138   Eno (n 35 above) 11.

139   By the treaty of Paris of 1814, the British and French governments agreed to cooperate in the suppression of the traffic in slaves. This undertaking was generalised and accompanied by a solemn condemnation of the practice by the major European states at the Congress of Vienna in 1815. Similarly, more than fifty bilateral treaties on the subject were concluded between 1815 and 1880, and the Conference of Berlin on Central Africa of 1885 was able to state in its General Act that 'trading in slaves is forbidden in conformity with the principles of international law as recognised by the signatory powers.' This led to the signing and ratification of the Anti-Slavery Act by eighteen states, which not only condemned slavery and the slave trade, but also drew up a list of agreed measures for their suppression both in Africa and on high seas. See Robertson & Merrils (n 134 above) 17.

140   As above.

141   As above.

142   As above. This Convention proclaimed, in part, the objective of the nations to completely suppress slavery in all its forms and of the slave trade by land and sea.

millions of their own citizens.[143] A frequently cited example in this context is the Turkish genocide in Armenia in 1915.[144]

The fallacy of international law was also made clear during the Second World War when many people were brutally and innocently assassinated and international humanitarian law was atrociously violated.[145] This partly explains why at the end of the Second World War, shocked by the barbaric atrocities committed and sufferings caused by some states against their nationals, the victorious Allied Powers were determined to introduce into international law new concepts designed to outlaw such events in the future, or to make their recurrence at least less likely.[146] The means adopted was the establishment of new inter-governmental organisations, such as the UN, and the development of a new branch of international law, specifically concerned with relations between governments and their own subjects.[147] This branch of international law eventually came to be known as international human rights law.

The Allied Powers realised that it was the infringement of individual liberty within member states that had led to the Second World War.[148] They then pledged to ensure that protection of individual rights internationally would have to become their major priority if there was to be international peace and security. To make sure that their pledges became a reality, they adopted legally binding treaties that exposed the treatment of individuals by their governments to international scrutiny.[149] Thus, in the aegis of the UN, the Allied Powers embarked on a serious mission of universalising

---

143   Eno (n 35 above) 11.

144   M Nowak *Introduction to the international human rights regime* (2003) 21.

145   As above.

146   As Above, 12.

147   For a detailed discussion on the role of the UN in the promotion and protection of human rights, see generally, United Nations *The United Nations and human rights 1945-1995* (1996); A Lewis 'Treaty-based procedures for making human rights complaints within the UN system' in H Hannum (ed) *Guide to international human rights practice* (1999); E Krause & M Rosas (eds) *Economic, social and cultural rights* (1985) 41-62.

148   See generally J Symonides *Human rights: International protection, monitoring and enforcement* (2003) 15.

149   As above.

human rights.[150] This was especially through the adoption of, for example, the UDHR in 1948, as well as the International Covenant on Civil and Political Rights (ICCPR) together with its Optional Protocols; the International Covenant on Economic, Social and Cultural Rights (ICESCR)[151] and other human rights instruments.

In order to implement human rights norms and call states to account for their violations, the international community of states also established various institutional mechanisms. For example, through the UN Economic and Social Council's (ECOSOC) Resolution 1235 of 1967, followed by ECOSOC Resolution 1503 of 1970, foundation was laid for UN Charter-based mechanisms for the protection of human rights.[152] From 1976, ECOSOC adopted a series of resolutions, which culminated in the establishment of the Committee on Economic, Social and Cultural Rights, a permanent body with the mandate to promote the implementation of ICESR.[153]

Treaty-based institutions and mechanisms have also been evolved to reinforce the UN Charter-based mechanisms. These treaty-based institutions and mechanisms are, for example, the UN Human Rights Committee (now known as the Human Rights Council), which is the enforcement mechanism for the ICCPR.[154] The Committee on the Elimination of Racial Discrimination came into being with the entry into force of the International Convention on the Elimination of All Forms of Racial Discrimination.[155] Various other treaty-based institutions such as the Committee on the Elimination of Discrimination Against Women and the Committee

---

150   See in this regard T Burgenthal (ed) *International human rights in a nutshell* (1995); L Sohn & T Burgenthal *International protection of human rights* (1973).

151   Adopted 16 December 1966; entered into force 23 March 1976.

152   Mugwanya (n 109 above) 17.

153   M Scheinin 'Economic and social rights as legal rights' in Krause & Rosas (n 147 above) 41.

154   As above.

155   Convention on the Elimination of all forms of Racial Discrimination (CERD) adopted and opened for signature and ratification by General Assembly Resolution 2106 (XX) of 21 December 1965; entry into force 4 January 1969, in accordance with art 19.

on the Rights of the Child are also in place.[156] Further, Specialised Agencies of the UN, such as UNESCO and ILO, have over the years adopted special mechanisms to deal with human rights violations falling within their scope of competence.[157]

Despite all attempts to give it international credence, the concept of human rights faced great resistance during the Cold War period, a time when the question of human rights protection was deeply politicised.[158] There was tension between the Western capitalist and the Eastern socialist nations. Western industrialised states criticised the socialist states and the South for their gross and systematic human rights violations based on their own (Western) standards. Hence, from the 1970s, the Conference for Security and Cooperation in Europe (CSE), along with the UN, began to serve as platforms for the human rights clash between the East and West.[159]

As of the late 1970s, the US, the European Union (EU), as well as several European donor states formulated development policies with the intention to extract human rights concessions.[160] To counter this move, the East responded by pointing to violations of economic, social and cultural rights in capitalist states. However, their defence was a mere attempt to conceal the massive violations and the deteriorating human rights situation in the East.[161] The East, which professed and was inclined to the socialist human rights philosophy, rejected to be monitored by any international mechanism. Instead, it opted to take cover under the doctrine of state sovereignty.[162]

To complicate the situation further, the South too began to resist the doctrine of international human rights, especially in the

---

156 See M Mbondenyi & N Sifuna 'A review of procedural and jurisdictional challenges in enforcing international human rights law under the African Charter regime'(2006) *Berkeley Legal Press Working paper No. 1869* http://law.bepress.com/expresso/esps/1869 (accessed on 13 April 2010) 3.

157 See UNESCO 104 EX/Decision (1978). See also P Alston 'UNESCO's procedure for dealing with human rights violations' (1980) 20 *Santa Clara Law Review* 665.

158 Nowak (n 144 above) 25.

159 As above.

160 Dowrick (n 20 above) 135.

161 As above.

162 As above.

period between 1980s and 1990s.[163] The block generally felt that the concept of 'universal human rights' was being imposed without due regard to cultural and ideological differences.[164] The universalism concept drew lots of suspicion from non–Western states, which saw it as a move by the Western states to impose its culture on others. In the late 1980s, the socialist regimes in Central and Eastern Europe began to collapse, signalling victory for human rights.[165] The end of the Cold War was therefore an opportune time for the advancement of the international human rights agenda.[166]

It was the 1993 Vienna World Conference on Human Rights that eventually set out the parameters for this advancement agenda.[167] The conference reaffirmed 'the solemn commitment of all states to fulfil their obligations to promote universal respect for, and observance and protection of, all human rights and fundamental freedoms for all in accordance with the Charter of the United Nations, other instruments relating to human rights, and international law.'[168] Hence, apart from some isolated controversies over the concept of human rights,[169] generally, there is a degree of consensus that human rights are universal, inalienable, and inherent to every human being in every

---

163   Nowak (n 144 above) 25.

164   For an exposition on the doctrine of universality of human rights, see generally L Lindholt *Questioning the universality of human rights: The African Charter on Human and Peoples Rights in Botswana, Malawi and Mozambique* (1997); R Howard *Human rights in Commonwealth Africa* (1986); J Nickel *Making sense of human rights* (1987); J Donnelley *Universal human rights in theory and practice* (1989); J Tang (ed) *Human rights and international relations in the Asia-Pacific region* (1995); R Howard *Human rights and the search for community* (1995); R Howard 'Cultural absolutism and the nostalgia for community' (1993) 15 *Human Rights Quarterly* 315; J Oloka-Onyango 'The concept of human rights in the international order' in Kalu & Osinbajo (n 14 above) 1-9.

165   Nowak (n 144 above) 26.

166   As above.

167   As above. Nowak observed that 'had it not been for the more than 1,500 NGOs both from the North and the South, which parallel to the conference were trying to push through the idea of 'all human rights for all', the World Conference would perhaps have foundered because of the issue of universalism of human rights which was then being spearheaded by the Western world. On the very last day, following tough negotiations, the 171 states were able to agree on the wording of the Vienna Declaration, which states that 'all human rights are universal, indivisible and interrelated.'

168   See the Vienna Declaration and Programme of Action of 25 June 1993, s I, para 1.

169   On some of the controversies, see generally Cranston (n 7 above) 43; Dowrick (n 20 above); T Campbell T *et. al* (eds) *From rhetoric to reality* (1986).

society.[170] Further, all rights are interdependent notwithstanding the fact that different measures may be required to implement them.[171]

It cannot therefore be gainsaid that the protection and promotion of human rights at the international level has been one of the most outstanding developments since the end of the Second World War.[172] This is especially because, notwithstanding national and regional differences in historical, cultural and religious backgrounds, the Vienna Declaration recognised that it is the responsibility of all states to protect human rights and fundamental freedoms. The Declaration seems to have settled, at least for the time being, the heated debate on the philosophical and ideological differences in perception of the human rights concept.

It is imperative to note, however, despite the international acknowledgement of the concept, widespread violations of human rights show that the attempts to provide international protection are not as effective as they ought to be and that a great deal remains to be done to augment the ongoing international efforts.[173] To bring such efforts to fruition, it must be conceded that the effective enforcement of human rights will, to a large extent, depend on how well the various conceptions held by the different peoples of the world are harmonised. People from different parts of the globe recognise the need to protect human rights but adopt methods that suit their particular needs and circumstances.[174]

As a result of the divergent conceptions and perceptions, international enforcement of human rights has turned to be more effective through regional human rights mechanisms. Ironically, before they gained momentum, it was initially believed that these mechanisms would detract from the perceived universality of human rights. As the European and Inter-American systems evolved, however, this view later changed.[175] Initially, the UN intended to

---

170   On this consensus see the Vienna Declaration paras 1 & 5.

171   As above.

172   Robertson & Merrils (n 134 above) 1.

173   As above.

174   As above. This position is reiterated in The Final Act of the International Conference on Human Rights, Tehran, 1968, as published in UN document A/Conf 32/41.

175   Mugwanya (n 109 above) 32.

create regional human rights regimes of its own but later resolved to delegate the task to the member states.[176] It therefore appealed to states not belonging to regional human rights regimes to 'consider agreements with a view to the establishment within their respective regions of suitable regional machinery for the promotion and protection of human rights.'[177]

It should be pointed out that the inadequacy of the universal system was one of the reasons that prompted the establishment of regional human rights systems. For instance, from its inception in 1945, it took nearly two decades for the UN to come up with the ICCPR and ICESR.[178] Due to such long-stalled efforts, it became clear that more expedient mechanisms were required to enhance the speedy enforcement of international human rights norms.[179] Whereas this may be the case, the universal and regional human rights systems should be seen as complementary, aimed at giving effect to the rights first comprehensively guaranteed in the UDHR as 'a common standard of achievement for all people and all nations.'[180] These systems should therefore work together to ensure that human rights are enjoyed by all people, regardless of their geographical, cultural, social, economic or political differences.

---

176   As above.

177   See GA. Res. 32/127, 32 UN. GAOR (105th plen. Mtg.), UN Doc. A/32/458 (1977) reprinted in 31 Y.B UN. 740 (1977). Two subsequent resolutions reiterated the plea of the General Assembly. G.A Res. 33/167, 33 UN. GAOR (90th Plen. Mtg.), UN. Doc. A/33/509 (1978), reprinted in 32 Y.B. U.N. 734 (1978), and G.A Res. 34/171, 34 U.N GAOR (106th plen. Mtg.), U.N. Doc A/734/829 (1979), reprinted in 33 Y.B. U.N. 871 (1979).

178   Mugwanya (n 109 above) 34.

179   As above.

180   See the Universal Declaration on Human Rights, preamble.

CHAPTER 2

HUMAN RIGHTS IN AFRICA

The existence of human rights in traditional African societies has been a controversial issue for many decades. According to some Western scholars, human rights did not exist in pre-colonial Africa.[1] To them, pre-colonial societies were lawless and savage and could not in any way have regard for human rights. In fact, some positioned the continent outside history and civilisation.[2] This positioning, however, is not correct because there is historical evidence that depicts Africa as the cradle of mankind and civilisation.[3] Although Africa's pre-colonial societies differed in a number of ways, there is ample proof that there not only existed legal systems but also some measure of protection of human rights during that period.[4] Numerous anthropological, sociological, economic and historical works have unravelled the mysteries surrounding Africa's past and have greatly contributed in providing useful information in this regard.[5]

---

1   See R Howard 'Group versus individual identity in the African debate on human rights' in A An- na 'im & F Deng (eds) *Human rights in Africa: Cross-cultural perspectives* (1990) 159; R Howard 'Evaluating human rights in Africa: Some problems of implicit comparisons' (1984) 6 *Human Rights Quarterly* 160; J Donnelly 'Human rights and Western liberalism' A in An-na 'im & F Deng (eds), *Human rights in Africa: Cross-cultural perspectives, op cit*; J Donnelly *Universal human rights in theory and practice* (1989).

2   See 'Alternative histories and non-written sources: New perspectives from the South' (Proposal for an International Seminar organised by the South-South Exchange Programme for Research on History of Development (SEPHIS), Amsterdam, at La Paz, 12-15 May 1999), cited in O Nmehielle *The African human rights system: Its laws, practice and institutions* (2001) 7.

3   See in this regard A Diop *The African origin of civilisation: Myth or reality?* (1974).

4   O Eze *Human rights in Africa: Some selected problems* (1984) 9.

5   See, for example, W Rodney *How Europe underdeveloped Africa* (1972); B Davidson *Old Africa rediscovered* (1970); S Amin *The class struggle in Africa* (1985); C Meek *A Sudanese Kingdom* (1937); K Dike *Trade and politics in the Niger Delta 1830-85* (1956); M Gluckman *The judicial process among the Barotse of Northern Rhodesia* (1967); Y Ghai & B McAuslan *Public law and political change in Kenya: A study of the legal framework of government from colonial times to the present* (1970); T Elias *The nature of African customary law* (1962); T Elias *British colonial law* (1962); J Salacuse 'An introduction to law in French-speaking Africa' (1969) 1 *Africa South of the Sahara*; M Hooker *Legal pluralism: An introduction to colonial and neo-colonial Laws* (1975).

The existence of such proof notwithstanding, Africa has generally been depicted as a place of doom and despair in as far as human rights are concerned. Consequently, the analysis of its level of compliance with human rights focuses more on its failure to adopted Western standards. In other words, the continent's success or failure to promote and protect human rights is construed against the background of Western 'models'. In this case, Africa is not primarily studied in terms of its own dynamics, but is rather 'an appendix or a periphery to the centre (the West) and considered valuable only by its submission to the West and its conformity to Western standards.'[6]

Evaluation of human rights standards in Africa against those of the Western countries has, therefore, to say the least, painted a poor image of the continent's commitment to human rights values. This, however, is not to say that Africa's human rights record is excellent and needs not to be criticised in the light of other jurisdictions. The point being made is that, whereas one would concur with the view that human rights are not highly esteemed in Africa, the same could also be said of other continents. European and Asian countries, as well as America, the self-styled 'mother of democracy and human rights', also have their share of human rights violations. We cannot close our eyes to the fact that some of these continents have at one time in their history experienced massive violations of human rights, even to the magnitude of genocide, war crimes and crimes against humanity.

For instance, diverse forms of discrimination, particularly on racial grounds, have been and continue to be, perpetrated in some Western countries. Like the 'Mosaic law', respect for human rights is fundamentally premised on the proposition that 'if you break one, you break all.' Thus, when the West points the accusing finger on the violations committed in Africa, it should do likewise to those committed within its borders. A violation is a violation, by whatever name called, notwithstanding its magnitude or the colour of its perpetrator.

---

6   A Mangu 'The road to constitutionalism and democracy in post-colonial Africa: The case of the Democratic Republic of Congo' (2002) *LLD Thesis University of South Africa* 36.

It is therefore not correct to argue that the reason why many contemporary African societies still violate human rights with impunity is because the concept was non-existent in pre-colonial Africa. Such an argument is presumptuous and should not be entertained because it is not based on accurate historical facts. To explain the existence, or otherwise, of human rights in the political, social and economic lives of a people, it is necessary to have recourse to their history.[7] This chapter therefore examines the historical antecedents of human rights in Africa. Thus, three periods that mark the history of Africa shall be considered. These periods are: pre-colonial, colonial and post-colonial. The study of the status of human rights in Africa during these three periods is very essential since their effective enforcement in the region will, to a large extent, depend on how their historical and philosophical foundations are perceived.

2.1   HUMAN RIGHTS IN PRE-COLONIAL AFRICA

To reiterate what was stated at the beginning of this chapter, there has been a protracted disagreement among scholars on the existence of human rights in pre-colonial Africa. Mutua believed that much of the discussion on whether African pre-colonial societies knew of and enforced human rights has taken place in the absence of considered studies of, and reference to, judicial processes and socio-political formations in those societies.[8] As a result, scholars

---

7   U Umozurike *The African Charter on Human and Peoples' Rights* (1997) 1.

8   M Mutua 'The Banjul Charter and the African Cultural fingerprint: An evaluation of the language of duties' (1995) 35 *Virginia Journal of International Law* 350.

have engaged in an unending academic battle on this issue.[9] This observation may not be entirely true because substantial research on pre-colonial African societies had already been conducted prior to Mutua's assertion. Arguably, what was lacking in previous research on these societies was an in-depth search to establish whether or not they had a human rights tradition. In other words, much has already been said on the judicial processes and systems and socio-political formations in pre-colonial Africa but without a clear focus on the status of human rights during this period. This position is also gradually changing as more scholars are taking interest in studying the status of human rights promotion and protection in pre-colonial Africa.

---

9   See, for example, Mangu (n 6 above) 235-257; M Mamdani 'Social movements and constitutionalism in the African context' in I Shivji *State and constitutionalism: An African debate on democracy* (1991) 237; J Wiseman *Democracy in black Africa* (1990) ix-xi; G Nzongola-Ntalaja *The state and democracy in Africa* (1997) 10; K Busia 'The status of human rights in pre-colonial Africa: Implications for contemporary practices', in E McCarthy-Arnolds *et al*, *Africa, human rights, and the global system: The political economy of human rights in a changing world* (1994) 49; K Appiagyei-Atua 'A rights-centred critique of African philosophy in the context of development' (2005) 5 *African Human Rights Law Journal* 335-357; K Quashigah 'The philosophic basis of human rights and its relations to Africa: A critique' (1992) *Journal of Human Rights Law and Practice* 22-38; K Wiredu 'Democracy and consensus in African traditional politics: A plea for a non-party polity' in O Eze *Postcolonial African philosophy: A critical reader* (1997) 303; P Hountondji 'The master's voice: The problem of human rights in Africa' in P Ricoeur (ed) *Philosophical foundations of human rights* (1986) 319; E Anthony 'Beyond the paper Tiger: The challenges of a human rights court in Africa (1997) 32 *Texas International Law Journal* 519-521; O Diganke '*Protection of human rights in Africa*' *(2000)* 10 *Transnational law & Contemporary Problems* 374-378; I Shivji *The concept of human rights in Africa II* (1989); J Cobbah 'African values and the human rights debate: An African perspective' (1987) 9 *Human Rights Quarterly* 309-331; J Swanson 'The emergence of new rights in the African Charter' (1991) 12 *New York Law School Journal of International & Comparative law* 324-329; Z Motola 'Human rights in Africa: A cultural, ideological and legal examination' (1989) 12 *Hastings International & Comparative Law Review* 408-409; R Gittleman 'The African Charter on Human and Peoples' Rights: A legal analysis' (1982) 22 *Virginia Journal of International law* 671; J Okere 'Human rights and the African Charter' (1984) 6 *Human rights quarterly* 153-156; A Pollis & P Schwab (eds) *Human rights cultural and ideological perspectives* (1979); H Berger 'Are human rights universal?' (1977) *Commentary* 62; C Welch 'Human rights as a problem in contemporary Africa' in C Welch & R Meltzer (eds) *Human rights and development in Africa* (1984) 16; A El-Obaid & K Appiagyei-Atua 'Human rights in Africa: A new perspective of linking the past to the present' (1996) 41 *McGill Law Journal* 829-836; J Donnelly *The concept of human rights* (1985) 8; C Mojekwu 'International human rights: The African perspective' in J Nelso & V Green (eds) *International human rights: Contemporary issues* (1980); L Marasinghe 'Traditional conceptions of human rights in Africa' in Welch & Meltzer, *op cit*, 37; A Legesse 'Human rights in African political culture' in K Thompson (ed) *The moral imperatives of human rights: A world survey* (1980) 125.

To speak of human rights in pre-colonial Africa therefore necessitates a comprehensive inquiry into some critical questions, such as: What was the nature of Africa's pre-colonial societies? Were human rights a concern in those societies? What arguments have been advanced to refute claims that human rights were an entity in pre-colonial Africa? Are these arguments authentic, if not, why? Some of these questions are explored below.

2.1.1 THE NATURE OF AFRICA'S PRE-COLONIAL SOCIETIES

As a point of departure, it is important to note that Africa's pre-colonial period witnessed the prevalence of traditional communities living under various socio-political arrangements.[10] Our analysis will therefore assume a more generalised position because it would be misleading to pretend that a universal socio-political arrangement subsisted during this period. However, although Africa's pre-colonial societies differed in a number of ways, there is ample information to prove that they not only had legal systems but also some measure of respect for and protection of human rights.[11] There is evidence that human rights, which are entitlements that accrue to all people by virtue of being human, were known on the continent even prior to foreign intervention.[12] They were observed and even violated in pre-colonial Africa just like in the subsequent historical periods.

According to Mutua, pre-colonial Africa consisted of two categories of societies. The first comprised those societies with centralised authority, administrative machinery, and standing judicial institutions, such as the Zulu and the Ashanti, while the second are those with more communal and less intrusive governmental paraphernalia, such as the Akamba and Kikuyu of Kenya.[13] However, almost all pre-colonial African societies characteristically displayed ethnic, cultural, and linguistic homogeneity, a common trait that

---

10   El-Obaid & Appiagyei-Atua (n 9 above) 821.

11   Eze (n 4 above) 9.

12   See generally the arguments advanced in M Mbondenyi 'The potential of Taita customary law in the promotion and protection of human rights in Kenya: A critical survey' (2003) *LLB Dissertation: Moi University* 13-15.

13   Mutua (n 8 above) 349.

gave them fundamental cohesion.[14] This latter observation was confirmed by Umozurike when he asserted that most pre-colonial African societies were at one time socialistic and communalistic.[15] Cohen also took note of this aspect by observing that:

> Many African cultures value the group-one should never die alone, live alone, remain outside societal networks unless one is a pariah, insane, or the carrier of a feared contagious disease. Corporate kinship in which individuals are responsible for the behaviour of their group members is a widespread tradition. ....[16]

In tandem with this position, Okere observed that the 'African conception of man is not that of an isolated and abstract individual, but an integral member of a group animated by a spirit of solidarity.'[17] Mbiti illustriously summed up this philosophy by stating, 'I am because we are, and because we are, therefore I am.'[18]

By reason of most of pre-colonial societies being 'socialistic' or 'communalistic', rights and privileges of their members were respected and regarded as rights and privileges of the community itself.[19] Those rights and privileges were thus not isolated or held against the community 'but formed a great admixture with community rights so that members had an interest in the well being of other members.'[20] Consequently, rights and privileges were restricted to the members of the community and were not regarded as universal.[21]

The communality of most African societies notwithstanding, the individual and his or her dignity and autonomy were equally

---

14   As above.

15   U Umozurike 'The significance of the African Charter on Human and Peoples' Rights' (1997) 44.

16   R Cohen 'Endless teardrops: Prolegomena to the study of human rights in Africa' (1990) *Human rights and governance* 44.

17   B Okere 'The protection of human rights in Africa and the African Charter on Human and Peoples' Rights: A comparative analysis with the European and American systems' (1984) 6 *Human Rights Quarterly* 141.

18   J Mbiti *The African religions and philosophy* (1970) 141.

19   Mutua (n 8 above) 349.

20   Cohen (n 16 above) 44.

21   As above.

protected, as were individual rights.[22] Nyerere and Wai attested to this when they argued, separately, that pre-colonial societies supported individual welfare and dignity and did not allow gross inequalities between members.[23] This position was confirmed by studies conducted by a number of scholars, including Busia, Wilks and Rattray.[24] Busia, for example, noted that an individual could exercise his right to depose of a king, if he could show that the king had breached an oath of office or any other obligation.[25]

In his study of pre-colonial West Africa, Loucou also insisted that various ethnic societies, namely the Abbey, Abidij, Abourè Adjoulkrou, Ahizi, Alladian, Akyè, Avikam, Ebriè, Ega, Ehotilè, Essouma, Krobou and Mbatto, practised 'democracy of age classes.'[26] The Akan, Mandè and Baoulè societies were democratic monarchies with even slaves exercising senior administrative and political responsibilities, especially in the Mandè kingdom.[27] In sub-Saharan African kingdoms, unwritten laws existed that limited the power of the monarch. This was illustrated by some examples from the Anyi kingdoms in Ivory Coast and Ghana.[28] The king could be impeached or removed from office. A college of electors, political and military chiefs of villages, called *Asafohene,* chose several candidates or postulants, based on their individual qualities and not their genealogical positions.[29]

To add to this generalised perception of pre-colonial African societies, Eze observed that all human societies have had to go through certain stages in the process of their development.[30] At

---

22   As above.

23   See generally D Wai 'Human rights in Sub-Saharan Africa' in An-na 'im & Deng (n 1 above) 115; J Nyerere *Essays on Socialism* (1968) 102.

24   See K Busia *Africa in search of democracy* (1967) 22-26; K Busia *The position of the Chief in modern political system of Ashanti* (1951) chapter 3; I Wilks *Ashanti in the nineteenth century: The structure and evolution of political order* (1975) R Rattray *Ashanti law and Constitution* (1969).

25   Busia (n 9 above) 54.

26   J Loucou 'Le multipartisme en Cote d'Ivoire' *Afrika Zamani* (1996) 111-126.

27   Mangu (n 6 above) 244.

28   As above.

29   As above.

30   Eze (n 4 above) 13.

one stage, because of the primitivism of the means of production, collective ownership, collective labour and equal distribution of the fruits of labour were necessary for subsistence.[31] There was no room for private acquisition and accumulation of wealth. Since the society had no classes, there was neither the need for a state nor law. Such machinery would only be necessary where exploitation of man by man occurred.[32] Whatever rules of conduct existed could at best be described as non-legal, even if they were 'binding' usages and rules of custom. The adage that *ubi societas ubi jus'*— where there is a human society there is law-was not applicable at this stage.[33]

With the passage of time, pre-colonial African societies evolved to such a level that primitive communalism, slave owning and feudalism became the predominant socio-economic structures immediately prior to colonial incursion.[34] The slave-owning societies and feudalism structures were characterised by the existence of laws which were promulgated to govern social relations.[35] Nmehielle attributed the origin of law in pre-colonial Africa to these two forms of socio-economic structures.[36] Accordingly, this explains the argument from certain quarters to the effect that societies in pre-colonial Africa had achieved a reasonable degree of political, social and economic, organisation akin to the modern state.[37] Not only so, there is sufficient historical evidence that kingdoms flourished in Africa as far back as the fourth century.[38]

In West Africa, for example, there were the Ghana, Songhai, Mali and Walata empires. In the South-East, there was the Zulu empire, in Central Africa the kingdom of Monomotapa, and in East

---

31   As above.

32   See K Marx & L Engels *Selected works* (1982) 461-556; P Wilmot *Sociology: A new introduction* (1985) chapter 4; O Eze 'Theoretical Perspectives and problematics' in O Eze *Society and the rule of law* (1987) chapter 1.

33   Eze (n 4 above) 13.

34   As above.

35   As above.

36   Nmehielle (n 2 above) 8.

37   As above. According to Elias, 'in African law although theories about social contract have not been formulated in this way, yet the indigenous ideas of government are not essentially dissimilar, at least in its presuppositions, to that of Grotius as well.' See T Elias *Africa and development of international law* (1988) 13.

38   Nmehielle (n 2 above) 8.

Africa the ancient Bunyoro Empire and the Buganda Kingdoms.[39] Basing his argument on the confirmation of the first Europeans to reach East and West Africa by sea, Rodney concluded that the levels of development between Europe and Africa were comparable, although the former had an edge.[40] The impressive nature of legal and political developments in pre-colonial Africa was further enunciated by Elias, according to whom:

> African societies with strong centralised political systems tended to have a more advanced body of legal principles and judicial techniques than had those with more or less rudimentary political organisation. In the former, there were usually hierarchically graded courts ranging from the smallest chiefs' to kings' courts, with well-defined machinery for the due enforcement of judicial decisions. In the latter, rules rather than rulers, functions rather than institutions, characterised the judicial organisation of these societies.[41]

Further, Gluckman's study found the Lozi to be a society with a fairly advanced legal system.[42] He found that in Lozi, as in Western countries, the sources of law consisted of customs, judicial precedents, legislation and laws of natural morality.[43] The bottom line of his argument is that the judicial process in Loziland corresponded to, rather than differed from, the judicial process known in Western societies.[44]

Notwithstanding the above observations, the existence of law generally and human rights in particular, in pre-colonial Africa has been doubted. It has been contended that law did not exist in traditional African societies.[45] This has partly been attributed to the fact that those societies were largely governed by customs which were extremely rigid and whose obedience could only be ensured

---

39   As above.

40   Rodney (n 5 above) 82.

41   Elias (n 5 above) 30.

42   Gluckman (n 5 above) 231.

43   As above.

44   As above.

45   See 'Alternative Histories and Non-Written Sources: New Perspectives from the South' 4 (Proposal for an International Seminar organised by the /South-South Exchange Programme for Research on History of Development (SEPHIS), Amsterdam, at La Paz, 12-15 May 1999) cited in Nmehielle (n 2 above) 7.

by the overwhelming power of group sentiment.[46] Under such circumstances, it was impossible to make any distinction between legal, moral or religious rules, all of which were 'interwoven into the single texture of customary behaviour.'[47]

Eze rightly queried the above observation. He contended, the argument that traditional African societies did not possess legal systems was based either on inadequate information or the lack of appreciation of the true nature of pre-colonial African societies on the one hand; and on the other, Western scholars' concept of law as emanating from the state.[48] Nmehielle was similarly right to conclude that defining law as an offshoot of the state ignores the possibility that it could also emanate from other sources, as it did in traditional African societies and as it does from the international circles such as the United Nations.[49] One would also agree with the reasoning that this argument has the implication that African societies operated in total legal vacuum before foreign intervention.[50]

It cannot be disputed that indeed, there were certain barbaric practices in some pre-colonial African societies which could lead one to presume the absence of law or even human rights. Umozurike succinctly captured this phenomenon as follows:

> One of the most heinous acts committed in some societies was the practice of human sacrifice. This practice was conducted for atonement or cleansing for serious crimes or to avert major catastrophes. Primitive belief in the spirit world also necessitated that on their death, dignitaries should be buried along with slaves and servants that would serve them. Similarly, the practice of killing of twins was very radical as well as controversial. Whereas twins were admired, for example, among the Yoruba of Western Nigeria, they were loathed among the Igbo, Efik and Ibibio of Eastern Nigeria. To the latter, they symbolised the wrath and displeasure of the gods and had no right to live. Twins were thus put to death and their mothers excommunicated, banished or sent back to their parental homes. In the contrary, their fathers were

---

46   As above.

47   See D Lloyd *Introduction to jurisprudence* (1972) 566.

48   As above.

49   Nmehielle (n 2 above) 7.

50   Eze (n 4 above) 10.

not condemned, something that clearly depicted gender disparity and discrimination.[51]

Another general characteristic of pre-colonial African societies was their emphasis on morality. Morality was of the greatest importance in both private and public relations.[52] As a moral dictate, anyone who claimed a right or privilege was also required to carry out the obligations that accompanied it.[53] Societies had stabilising factors which included the sense of obligation to one's kith and kin, the fear of the deity that was omnipotent and omniscient, and accountability to him for all human actions on earth.[54] This had a restraining effect on human activities, since the good expected to be appropriately rewarded and the wicked or their successors to be condemned.[55]

The foregoing discussion on the nature of Africa's pre-colonial societies sets the basis for our evaluation of the arguments on the existence, or otherwise, of human rights in these societies. This solicits answers to a number of questions, such as: is the notion of human rights a Western invention, Western import in Africa and is the West the model thereof? Were human rights experienced in pre-colonial Africa or are they foreign to African societies? There is an ongoing debate on these issues. Our aim is to assess both sides of the argument and also add our voices to the already existing scholarly contribution on this debate.

2.1.2 ARGUMENTS ON THE EXISTENCE OF HUMAN RIGHTS IN PRE-COLONIAL AFRICA

Some scholars argued that non-Western cultural and political traditions lacked not only the practice of human rights but also the

---

51   Umozurike (n 7 above) 16.

52   L Marasighe 'Traditional conceptions of human rights in Africa' in C Welch & P Alston (eds) *Human rights and development in Africa* (1984) 32-45; L Adegbite *African attitudes to the international protection of human rights* (1968) 69.

53   Mutua (n 8 above) 358.

54   Umozurike (n 7 above) 17.

55   As above.

very concept.[56] Donnelly, for example, asserted that recognition of human rights simply was not the way of traditional Africa.[57] He further observed that 'even in many cases where Africans had personal rights vis-à-vis their governments, these rights were community, status or [assumed] some other ascriptive characteristic.'[58] Howard stretched this view further when she contended that African proponents of the concept confuse human dignity with human rights. Accordingly:

> The African concept of human rights is actually a concept of human dignity, or what defines the inner (moral) nature and worth of the human person and his or her proper (political) relations with society. Despite the twinning of human rights and human dignity in the preamble of the Universal Declaration of Human Rights and elsewhere, dignity can be protected in a society not based on rights. The notion of African communalism, which stresses the dignity of membership in, and fulfilment of one's prescribed social role in a group (family, kinship group, tribe), still represents how accurately, how many Africans appear to view their personal relationship to society.[59]

As Busia noted, it appears, at least from the foregoing, that Donnelly and Howard, like most of their colleagues in this argument, had a problem with the fact that African ideals could accommodate the concept of human rights.[60]

The arguments on human rights being foreign to Africa are not confined to the sentiments of Donnelly and Howard. In fact, some scholars went further to contend that even democracy and constitutionalism, which are fundamental to the promotion and protection of human rights, are also foreign to Africa.[61] These concepts have been said to have no future on the continent because

---

56   R Howard & J Donnelly 'Human dignity, human rights and political regimes' (1986) 80 *American Political Science Review* 891-919. See also R Howard 'Group versus individual identity in the African debate on human rights' in An-Na'im & Deng (n 1 above) 159; R Howard 'Evaluating human rights in Africa: Some problems of implicit comparisons' (1984) 6 *Human Rights Quarterly* 160.

57   J Donnelly 'Human rights and Western liberalism' in An-Na'im & Deng (n 1 above) 243.

58   J Donnelly *Repression and development* (1990) 304.

59   Howard (n 56 above) 165-166.

60   Busia (n 9 above) 226.

61   For a detailed discussion on the existence, or otherwise, of constitutionalism and democracy in pre-colonial Africa, see generally, Mangu (n 6 above) 233-257.

they are unsuitable, especially in 'black Africa'. Thus, the West has been perceived as the model of human rights, constitutionalism and democracy.[62] Allegedly, pre-colonial African traditions either ignored or had no idea of these concepts.

Constitutionalism, democracy and human rights, it was further alleged, were either 'at variance with African traditions' or 'out of tune with the needs of [Africans] at this stage in their history.'[63] Sadly, this perception was not only championed by European and American scholars but also some African scholars.[64] Simiyu, for example, insisted that democracy had no roots in Africa no matter how organised the traditional political systems were. Accordingly, he insisted that:

> In black Africa, whether the political system was that of the highly centralised states or of the amorphous non-centralised communities, it did not belong to a democratic tradition. There were rudiments of democratic principles and practices, especially in the non-centralised communities, but it would be dangerous to equate those practices with advanced forms of democracy.[65]

This position was also echoed by Akindes who considered the ancient Dahomey as typical of the authoritarianism of pre-colonial Africa,[66] and Kedourie, who argued that 'African and Asian societies are victimised by their own despotic traditions.'[67] Conversely, a number of African scholars have risen in defence of the existence of human rights in pre-colonial Africa, thereby sharply refuting the views held by Donnelly, Howard and their cronies.[68] For example, Nzongola-Ntalaja correctly argued that a very disturbing phenomenon is:

> The tendency of Northern countries on both sides of the Atlantic to think that Africans do not deserve the same rights as peoples elsewhere,

---

62   As above, 236.

63   R Hiden 'Africa and democracy' (1963) 8 *Encounter Pamphlet* 2-3.

64   See the criticism in Nzongola-Ntalaja (n 9 above) 10.

65   C Simiyu 'The democratic myth in African traditional societies' quoted in Mangu (n 6 above) 237.

66   Akindes quoted in Mangu (n 6 above) 237.

67   Kedourie quoted in Mangu (n 6 above) p. 237.

68   See generally K Wiredu 'An Akan perspective of human rights' in An-Na 'im & Deng (n 1 above) 243; Mutua (n 8 above) 339.

and that strong men are what is needed to keep a restless and volatile continent at peace. Thus, what is absolutely intolerable elsewhere can be justified as understandable, 'by African standards'.[69]

Indeed, it is not proper for the West to pretend to be the inventor or the model of human rights. Human rights, constitutionalism and democracy are not un-African; nor were they unknown in pre-colonial Africa. They also belong to Africa. Ake deplored the attitude of the West and its conventional approach to the study of Africa by stating that:

> Through decades of involvement in Africa, the North's attitude has been that democracy is not for Africa. That attitude was an important component of the ideology of colonisation, which held that Africans were unfit to govern themselves, that they needed the civilisation of colonial tutelage as their one hope of eventually achieving self-determination and development.[70]

Nzongola-Ntalaja refuted the Eurocentric attitude of perceiving Africans as being incapable of determining their own affairs and by extension having no history of democracy and human rights. He correctly emphasised that:

> Such an approach not only glosses over the impact of the Atlantic slave trade on political institutions and practices in West and Central Africa but also minimises the role of colonial despotism as a school of post-colonial rulers.[71]

Further, Mamdani ruled out the Western 'paternity' of the concept of human rights by stating that:

> It is difficult to accept, even in the case of Europe, that human rights was a concept created by 17th century Enlightenment philosophy. True, one can quote Aristotle and his ideological justification of slavery as evidence that the idea of human rights was indeed foreign to the conscience of the ruling classes in ancient Greece ... What was unique about Enlightenment philosophy, and about the writings of the French and American Revolutions, was not a conception of human rights,

---

69   G Nzongola-Ntalaja *From Zaire to the Democratic Republic of Congo* (1998) 14.

70   C Ake *Democracy and development in Africa* (1996) 130.

71   Nzongola-Ntalaja (n 69 above) 11-12.

but a discussion of these in the context of a formally articulated philosophical system.[72]

No country has the monopoly of human rights respect or abuses; nor can any society claim to be a paradise for human rights. Dismissing the Western 'paternity' of democracy and constitutionalism, Mangu rightly noted that Athens and Rome that allegedly 'invented' democracy ended up in authoritarianism and dictatorship, while Greece, the supposed 'mother of Western democracy', was still a dictatorship in the 1970s.[73]

Unfortunately, it is too easy for Western scholars to give lessons and present themselves as the 'model' for human rights. Busia was therefore right to discredit the Westernised analyses of the concept of human rights as 'facile generalisations not reflecting the entire reality of human rights in pre-colonial social formations of Africa.'[74] Hence, 'an inquiry into the origin of human rights is not only a false search but a precarious adventure which can only resurrect the cultural relativist's argument which is now running out of steam.'[75]

The failure of Eurocentric Western scholars to locate human rights in pre-colonial Africa could be attributed to the lack of understanding of the cultures of the people. Pre-colonial African societies had intricate cultural formations and values which could not be understood by simply juxtaposing them with Western cultures. Hence, a number of African scholars have laboured to vindicate that African cultures were after all not devoid of human rights as supposed by their Western colleagues. For instance, Quashigah maintained that:

> ... each and every human society, whatever its stage of development, from absolute primitivity to modern statehood, logically recognises some rights which could be rightly termed human rights. The concept of human rights is, therefore, not alien to African societies; if anything at all, it is absent only in any articulated philosophical form.[76]

---

72   M Mamdani *et al* (eds) *Social movements, social transformation and the struggle for democracy in Africa* (1988) 236-237.

73   Mangu (n 6 above) 249.

74   Busia (n 9 above) 49.

75   As above, 65.

76   Quashigah (n 9 above) 30.

At a more practical level, Wiredu attempted to locate human rights in the Akan cultures by tabulating the rights and responsibilities borne by the community in the pre-colonial era. These included rights to political participation, land and religion, as well as the duty to defend the nation.[77] Moreover, Wai confirmed that some traditional African rulers were bound by checks and balances to limit their power and guarantee a 'modicum of social justice and values concerned with individual and collective rights.'[78] It has also been reported that the Akamba of Kenya believed that all members of the society were born equal and were therefore treated as such regardless of their sex or age.[79] The same was said of pre-colonial Taita society.[80]

One notable cultural difference between African and Western societies, which could have led to the conclusion that the former lacked a human rights tradition, is the emphasis of the collective (group) more than the individual. In Africa, communal rights were more esteemed and pronounced than individual rights.[81] Confirming this position, Cobbah asserted:

> Africans do not espouse a philosophy of human dignity that is derived from natural rights and individualistic framework. African societies function within communal structure whereby a person's dignity and honour flow from his or her transcendental role as a cultural being ... We should pose the problem in this light, rather than assuming an inevitable progression on non-Westerners toward Western lifestyle.[82]

On the same note, Eze correctly concluded, human rights were recognised and protected in pre-colonial Africa, but this fact must be looked at in the context of societies that were communal and at the same time unified by mythological beliefs.[83] Because African societies were humanistic and socialistic, they could not have failed to pay attention to human beings and all that appertained to them,

---

77   See Wiredu (n 9 above) 303.

78   See Wai (n 23 above) 352.

79   As above, 349.

80   See Mbondenyi (n 12 above) 15.

81   Shivji (n 9 above) 56.

82   Cobbah (n 9 above) 331.

83   Eze (n 4 above) 15.

particularly their rights.[84] Hence, to understand the concept of human rights as articulated in pre-colonial Africa, the starting point 'is not the individual but the whole group including both the living and the dead.'[85]

The above sentiments notwithstanding, there are other African scholars who perceived the enjoyment of human rights in pre-colonial Africa not solely from communalistic, but also individualistic perspective. Asante, for example, argued that 'human rights, quite simply, are concerned with asserting and protecting human dignity, and they are ultimately based on a regard for the intrinsic worth of the individual.'[86] Indeed, since human rights are concerned with the preservation of human dignity and the recognition of the intrinsic worth of the individual, there is no conceivable reason why they should not be a preserve for all societies.

This essentially means, notwithstanding their differences, both Western and African cultures embodied both respect for and abuse of human rights. As elsewhere, there was democracy and human rights in Africa, in addition to tyranny and other forms of human rights abuses.[87] If the concept of human rights was a Western discovery, as argued by the host of Eurocentric scholars, the same should also be said of concepts such as genocide, slavery, absolute monarchy, inquisition, authoritarianism and so on.[88]

The above argument, however, should not be taken to mean that there are no cultural differences which inform the various philosophical perceptions of the human rights concept. Rather, it emphasises the obvious fact that, since the values of human dignity are applicable and therefore relevant to all societies, so does the human rights concept. To this effect, Kannyo pointed out that:

> ... the factors which gave rise to the need for constitutional guarantees and led to the evolution of the philosophy of human rights in the

---

84   As above.

85   Cobbah (n 9 above) 321.

86   Asante (n 9 above) 102.

87   Mamdani (n 9 above) 249.

88   For a similar argument with regard to democracy and constitutionalism, see Mangu (n 6 above) 252.

West have become equally relevant in other parts of the world. ...
Traditionally, most of the cultures have given the greatest importance
to the preservation of life and the promotion of human welfare.[89]

This observation is sensible especially because, as shown above, a close
nexus exists between the modern human rights corpus and some
pre-colonial African practices. The arguments that human rights
could only exist in a post-feudal state and that the concept was alien
to specific pre-capitalist traditions should therefore be seen as an
attempt, by certain quarters, to claim cultural superiority.[90] However,
the socio-cultural realities of ancient Africa are too complex to be
simplified through the lenses of Afro-centric romantics, or those of
Afro-pessimists.[91]

Indeed, human beings occupied pre-colonial Africa. By virtue
of this fact, it is impossible to adopt the position that pre-colonial
African societies knew not of human rights. This would definitely
turn out to be a misplaced argument for the very reason that human
rights are inherent in all humans. As already pointed out, this should
not be taken to mean that human rights were not violated in pre-
colonial Africa. It should be noted, however, such violations were
not peculiar to Africa. Factually, all cultures suffer from this 'duality
of the good and the bad.'[92]

The point that has been emphasised all along in this discussion
is that the whole debate on the existence of human rights in pre-
colonial Africa is quite controversial. This is because, the nature and
character of a particular society has always determined the categories
of rights to be protected, their scope and ultimately who is to enjoy
them.[93] This argument is premised on the observation that human
rights protection evolved gradually on a stage-by-stage sequence as
societies developed.

The nature of the rights protected differed depending on
whether the society was based on the slave mode, feudal mode or

---

89   Kannyo (n 9 above) 4.

90   Mutua (n 8 above) 351.

91   Nzongola-Ntalaja (n 9 above) 10.

92   Mutua (n 8 above) 355.

93   Eze (n 4 above) 15.

nascent capitalism.[94] Hence, those scholars who deny the existence of human rights in pre-colonial African societies appear to be perpetuating Euro-centric views, which at best conjure memories of colonialism. On the other hand, their opponents, who not only defend the existence but also go further to assert the 'African uniqueness' of the concept, have been dismissed as overzealous Africanists.[95]

In fact, the latter category of scholars tends to complicate the debate on human rights in Africa by proposing an autochthonous construction of the concept. In this regard, we need to ask ourselves a number of questions such as: should the concept of human rights, as known in the West, be 'imported' as it is in Africa or should it be clothed with autochthonous or domestic forms, or should Africans totally ignore Western ideas and stick to their understanding of the concept?

Again, is it proper to posit a 'unique' African concept of human rights, distinct from that of the West? Such a debate will definitely induce an in-depth analysis of two concepts-universalism and relativism. It is therefore expedient to discuss these concepts in the light of the ongoing debate on the African concept of human rights.

2.1.3   THE AFRICAN CONCEPT OF HUMAN RIGHTS

The seemingly un-ending debate on the relevance and place of human rights in both pre-colonial and post-colonial African societies has been exacerbated by the agitation to evolve a 'unique' African concept of human rights. In this respect, there are African scholars who insist that human rights should be contextualised to take root on the continent.[96] Such scholars are inclined to cultural relativism that views human rights from a relativist perspective. Other scholars, however, opine that human rights are universal and

---

94   As above.

95   As above.

96   For general perceptions on African notions of human rights, see, for example, Mutua (n 8 above) 351-357; Eze (n 4 above) 8-31; Motola (n 9 above) 373-410; Marashinge (n 9 above) 37.

should be construed without cultural overtones.[97] Two theories are therefore fundamental in any discussion on the African human rights concept-cultural relativism and universalism.

Cultural relativism is a concept based on the proposition that human rights should not be construed as absolute because there is infinite cultural variability in every society.[98] The concept has several different possible meanings. Teson defined it as the position according to which local cultural traditions properly determine the existence and scope of human rights enjoyed by individuals in a given society.[99] According to this view, no trans-boundary legal or moral standards exist against which human rights practices may be judged acceptable or unacceptable.[100]

Thus, as a point of departure, substantive human rights standards vary among different cultures and necessarily reflect national idiosyncrasies. In the superficial sense, this essentially means that what may be regarded as a human rights violation in one society may probably be considered lawful in another.[101] Additionally, this proposition holds that even if, as a matter of customary or conventional international law, a body of substantive human rights norms exists, its meaning varies substantially from culture to culture.[102]

Universalism, on the other hand, contradicts cultural relativism. The terms 'universal' or 'universality' can be defined as 'of, belonging to, done by, all; affecting all', and a universal rule as one with no exception.[103] According to this definition, in order for a rule or concept of human rights law to be defined as universal, it would have to have been established by a consensus of all states and must apply

---

97   For this position see the arguments in Howard (n 1 above) 160-179; Howard (n 1 above) 159-183; L Lindholt *Questioning the universality of human rights: The African Charter on Human and Peoples' Rights in Botswana, Malawi and Mozambique* (1997) 7.

98   Lindholt (n 97 above) 33.

99   F Teson 'International human rights and cultural relativism' in P Alston (ed) *Human rights law* (1996) 11.

100   As above.

101   Lindholt (n 97 above) 33.

102   See A Pollis 'Liberal, socialist and Third World perspectives on human rights' in A Pollis & P Schwab (eds) *Towards a human rights framework* (1982) 23.

103   Oxford advanced learners dictionary of current English (1989).

to all individuals within each of these states.[104] Panikkar correctly commented that:

> ... In order for a concept to become universally valid it should fulfil at least two conditions. It should, on the one hand, eliminate all the other contradictory concepts. ... On the other hand, it should be the universal point of reference for any problems regarding human dignity. In other words, it should displace all other homeomorphic equivalents and be the pivotal centre of a just social order. To put it another way, the culture which has given birth to the concept of human rights should also be called upon to become a universal culture.[105]

Supporters of universalism base their arguments on the significance of the 1948 Universal Declaration on Human Rights (UDHR). Some argue that its inception marked the transition of human rights from a contextual (national) to a universal (international) concept.[106] The UDHR is not only the first global instrument to clearly define a general catalogue of human rights and freedoms, but is also recognised as the 'human rights pioneer' in the preambles of most of the subsequent global and regional instruments, besides the Constitutions of most independent states of the world.[107] Its relevance in the promotion of the culture of human rights on the globe was reiterated in the First World Conference on Human Rights, held in Teheran, where it was termed as 'an obligation for the members of the international community.'[108]

Similarly, the Second World Conference on Human Rights, held in Vienna in 1993, reaffirmed the universality of human rights.[109] In its Declaration and Programme of Action, the conference emphasised that the 'universal nature of these rights and freedoms is beyond question.'[110] At paragraph 3, the Vienna Declaration and Programme of Action stated that:

---

104   Lindholt (n 97 above) 33.

105   R Panikkar 'Is the notion of human rights a Western concept?' in Alston (n 99 above) 170.

106   J Shestack 'The Philosophic foundations of human rights' in R McCorquodale *Human rights* (2003) 228.

107   As above.

108   Umozurike (n 7 above) 6.

109   See Vienna Declaration and Programme of Action, para 1.

110   As above.

All human rights are universal, indivisible and inter-dependent and inter-related. The international community must treat human rights globally in a fair and equal manner, on the same footing and with the same emphasis. While the significance of national and regional particularities and various historical, cultural and religious backgrounds must be borne in mind, it is the duty of states, regardless of their political, economic and cultural systems, to promote and protect all human rights and fundamental freedoms.

This is a strong and definitive ideological statement, which would somehow urge one to ascribe to universalism. However, it has been difficult for the theory to gain acceptance in Africa, especially due to the insistence on the need to evolve a 'pure' or 'unique' African concept of human rights. This insistence is partly premised on the argument that Africans have a human rights culture and philosophy that is different to that of Western countries.

Moreover, it is believed that at the time the UDHR and the two International Covenants on human rights were drafted, most of the member states of the UN were states 'with white populations and largely Christian traditions.'[111] Consequently, 'the individualistic conception of human rights that is reflected in the UDHR indicates the domination of the Western world.'[112] From this point of view, 'the rights contained in the UN documents are not necessarily valid for all peoples at any time.'[113] This perception did not only inspire the search for a 'uniquely African' regional human rights instrument,[114] but also sparked the ongoing search for a 'unique' African concept of human rights.[115]

The African concept of human rights, according to Mojekwa, 'was fundamentally based on ascribed status ...'[116] Unlike the Western concept of human rights which emphasises individual rights, the African concept shares significant similarities with the Islamic concept in that both emphasise rights based on community.

---

111   Gittleman (n 9 above) 671.

112   Motola (n 9 above) 377.

113   Swanson (n 9 above) 326.

114   This document ended up to be the 'African Charter on Human and Peoples' Rights'.

115   Swanson (n 9 above) 326.

116   Mojekwa (n 9 above) 91.

It is important to note, the concept is not static but dynamic and has been subject to various forces both internal and external, which have influenced and continue to a certain degree, to shape its essence and content.[117] Eze is of the view that, in order to fully appreciate the African concept of human rights, it is necessary to, among other things:

> locate it in the context of Africa's history spanning from pre-colonial pre-capitalist-formations to the present day; examine the dynamics of its internal evolution before and, after contact with external forces, bearing in mind the pervasive influence of African and imported religions with their tendency towards fostering mythical and naturalist conceptions of human rights; take due account of the process of universalisation of the principles of human rights ...; determine whether in view of the overwhelming impact of external variables on Africa's socio-economic and political formations and the resultant acculturation, it can seriously be maintained that there is much left of the 'traditional' African conception of human rights, and; ascertain, given the heterogeneity of African societies whether there existed and still exists a sufficient degree of homogeneity, to justify the assertion of the existence of an African notion of human rights ...[118]

Undoubtedly, Africa presents a paradoxical picture in the study of human rights. This is because the realities of post-colonial Africa differ greatly from those of the pre-colonial and colonial periods, thus contributing significantly to the divergence in the conceptual understanding of human rights. As argued elsewhere above, human rights certainly existed in pre-colonial Africa, only that the philosophical explanations of the concept differed in key respects from those propounded by the European colonisers. It is these differences in conceptualisation that are at the core of the ongoing debate on the African concept of human rights. Three examples need to be cited to vindicate this argument.

First, unlike in the Western set-up, human rights in traditional African societies were not sanctioned by a normative system, constitutional framework or 'Grundnorm'. Rather, they were premised on social values fortified by beliefs and transmitted to

---

117   As above.

118   Eze (n 4 above) 8.

posterity through oral history and manifested through positive practices.[119] Thus, human rights were underpinned by social forces peculiar to each society and were not the creation of the subsisting legal systems. The absence of a constitutional order, therefore, did not have any effect on the traditional approaches to human rights in Africa.

Secondly, while in modern societies human rights enforcement relies on courts and other judicial or quasi-judicial agencies, most traditional African societies mainly, although not wholly, relied on reconciliation, consensus, communal solidarity and the moral upbringing of its people.[120] According to Mutua, it was believed that if individuals were properly brought up to respect one another and live in solidarity with one another, there would be no room for human rights violations.[121] Keba M'Baye noted that:

> According to African conception of the law, disputes are settled not by contentious procedures, but through reconciliation. Reconciliation generally takes place through discussions which end in a consensus leaving neither winners nor losers. ... People go to court to dispute rather than to resolve a legal difficulty.[122]

M'Baye seemed to suggest that there exists a discernible tradition in Africa favouring reconciliation over litigation. The assertion can be said to be a simplistic over-generalisation of African societies. Even a cursory glance at the practices of some pre-colonial African societies does not seem to support M'Baye's proposition. The Amhara of Ethiopia, for example, historically thrived on litigation and the vigorous examination and cross-examination of witnesses.[123] The Taita of Kenya also had a judicial mechanism, comprised of the council of elders, similar in many respects to the modern-day court systems.[124] Hence, to suggest that courts are created for disputes

---

119   W Eno 'The African Commission on Human and Peoples' Rights as an instrument for the protection of human rights in Africa' (1998) *LLM Thesis University of South Africa* 18.

120   See generally Welch (n 9 above) 31-45.

121   Mutua (n 8 above) 342.

122   International Commission of Jurists 'Human and peoples rights in Africa and the African Charter: Report of a conference' (1985) 27.

123   Anthony (n 9 above) 520.

124   Mbondenyi (n 12 above) 24.

rather than for legal resolution is to flagrantly misrepresent the function and purpose of judicial institutions.[125]

Thirdly, in the Western traditions, human rights were considered universal and individualistic in nature and applied on the same footing to every human being irrespective of their geographical location.[126] Conversely, under the African set-up, human rights existed within the context of a particular group or community.[127] Generally, 'African law' was a law of the group, not only because it applied to micro-societies (lineage, tribe, ethnic group, clan or family), but also because the role of the individual was largely insignificant.[128] It was within the group, for example, that the individual could probably find the pleasure to enjoy his or her rights.

It follows therefore, the African concept of human rights is influenced by, among other things, the African 'communitarian ideal'. This ideal could be seen in, for instance, the fact that decisions in traditional African societies were made by consensus rather than by competition.[129] Thus, as Shivji succinctly put it, 'African traditional society is based on collectivity (community) rather than on an individual and therefore, the notion of individual is foreign to African ethno-philosophy.'[130]

Some scholars, however, have been quick to dismiss the so-called 'communitarian ideal.'[131] Silk, for example, contended that the emphasis on groups is arbitrary since groups by their very nature do not exist without the individual in them.[132] It has also been argued, and rightly so, that the apparent absence of the 'individual ideal' in traditional African societies should not be taken to mean the absence of individual rights.[133] Individual rights and interests were

---

125   Anthony (n 9 above) 520.

126   Welch (n 9 above) 11.

127   Marashinge (n 9 above) 33.

128   As above.

129   R Howard 'Is there an African concept of human rights?' in R Vincent (ed) *Foreign Policies and Human Rights: Issues and Responses* (1986) 13.

130   Cited in Eno (n 119 above) 18.

131   See, for example, Silk (n 9 above) 293-294; Asante (n 9 above) 102.

132   Silk (n 9 above) 293-294.

133   Eze (n 4 above) 8.

defined in groups or communities through which the individual found expression.

Be that as it may, the African concept of human rights has been said to envisage at least two important elements: the pre-eminence of the group over the individual and the preference of consensus over competition.[134] In addition, the concept thrives on the preservation of human dignity and morality. The inherence of human rights in every person in the community, according to this concept, stems from the fact that every human being has inherent dignity which must be respected by all.[135] By extension, every bearer of rights has the attendant duty to protect the rights of others. Thus, the African concept of human rights advocates for rights which are intertwined with duties. This aspect of the concept found its way into some of the treaties of the African human rights system, such as the African Charter.[136]

In spite of its being romanticised by certain African scholars, the African concept of human rights has sharply been criticised by others for various reasons. In the main, there has been a protracted debate among scholars on whether in the first place Africa has a tradition of human rights.[137] The arguments in this regard have been discussed in detail elsewhere above and it is needless to repeat them here. With this debate still going on, and notwithstanding the various aspects of it discussed above, what is needful is the enquiry whether it is proper to talk of a 'pure', or even 'unique', African concept of human rights. If we sum up the various positions societies find themselves at the various stages of development, it is clear that it is not possible to have a pure or unique African concept of human rights.[138] However, while maintaining that Africa is not one society and that diversity exists, it is possible to make certain generalisations on the 'African-ness' of the concept.[139]

---

134   Howard (n 1 above) 50.

135   As above.

136   See generally arts 27-29 of the African Charter on Human and Peoples' Rights; adopted 27 June 1981, entered into force 21 October 1986.

137   See, for example, Howard (n 1 above) 159-183.

138   Lindholt (n 97 above) 17.

139   As above.

In tandem with Lindholt's suggestion, to arrive at such generalisations, the important distinction between form and essence must first be drawn.[140] Hence, looking for an African human rights concept in the same form as it is known from a European perspective may not be fruitful.[141] There is obviously nothing sacrosanct about the forms evolved in the West because they differ from one Western country to another. Thus, every nation should be allowed to express itself according to its own wishes and traditions.

The enforcement of human rights must be premised on local conditions because the simplistic adoption of models designed elsewhere is likely to be unsuccessful.[142] Although African countries slavishly imitated their former colonial masters' institutions, these institutions have to a large extent failed to yield tangible results as they cannot function in the same way in a culturally, historically and socially different context.

However, while it is proper to predicate human rights enforcement on local conditions, insisting on an 'autochthonous' or a 'unique' African concept of human rights would be contradictory to the view that human rights also belong to Africa and that pre-colonial Africans were familiar with them. This is because the debate on autochthony insists that human rights are 'Western' inventions or notions foreign to Africa that should be domesticated in order to develop or consolidate.[143]

Further, the issue of a unique African concept of human rights is highly problematic and controversial since it is hard to define what constitutes 'African' and what may actually constitute an 'African version' of the concept that would be uniformly applicable on the entire continent.[144] Simply put, Africa has diverse cultures and its societies have always differed in many respects, making it difficult for one to talk of an 'African version' of human rights.

---

140   As above.

141   See generally the argument in J Okere 'Human rights and the African Charter' (1984) 6 *Human rights quarterly* 153-156.

142   Wiseman (n 9 above) 10.

143   Mangu (n 6 above) 262.

144   As above.

This viewpoint was emphasised in the first meeting of the group of experts preparing a Draft African Charter in Dakar in November 1979 as follows:'You have to be careful that your Charter may not be a Charter of the 'African man'. Mankind is one and indivisible and the basic needs are similar everywhere.'[145] This means that Africa can have a model where human rights are universal in their essence, but allow for cultural diversity in their form and in their interpretation and practical application.[146]

Adherence to universalism does not imply that African peoples have no contribution to make to the development of the concept. Indeed the continent has contributed invaluably, in more than one ways, to the concept and its development.[147] In fact, all societies, be they modern or traditional, have contributed to the development of the human rights concept by upholding certain essential values.[148] However, the way these values are conceptualised differ.[149] Put differently, although the conceptualisation of human rights differs from one society to another, all societies manifest the notion.

Principally, universalism, it is argued herein, does not in itself preclude the expression of regional or national preferences and peculiarities. Thus, what may be deemed to be 'universally valid' are the standards or values that define and perpetuate the inherent dignity of all human beings. These standards or values are what define the core of human rights, *viz* inalienability, indivisibility, interdependence, interrelation and inherence.[150] It is upon these standards or values that all human rights hinge, thus giving them a universal appeal.

By extension, this means that universalism of human rights is only applicable to the extent that it is appreciated that all persons are

---

145   W Benedek & K Ginther 'New perspectives and conceptions of international law:An Afro- European dialogue' *Australian Journal of Public and International law* (1983) 148.

146   Lindholt (n 97 above) 17.

147   See generally F Viljoen 'Africa's contribution to the development of international human rights and humanitarian law' (2001) 1 *African Human Rights Law Journal* 18-39.

148   Berger (n 9 above) 62.

149   Motola (n 9 above) 279.

150   See para 3 of the Vienna Declaration.

vested with inalienable, interdependent, interrelated and indivisible rights by virtue of being custodians of inherent human dignity. Anything short of this recognition waters down the relevance of the universalism concept. These standards may be uniformly (universally) enforced and realised notwithstanding the divergent interpretations (contextual application) of human rights across socio-economic or political divides or geographical locations. It is argued that the fact that human rights are interpreted and applied contextually does not mean they are not universal.

Essentially, no single document, or even society, can represent a blueprint of the 'full content' of human rights.[151] This is because, as stated earlier, the substance of human rights depends on the cultural setting of a particular society. As Quashigah observed, 'since societal development has never been universally in *pari materia*, human rights contents which are specific ideas rooted in certain social facts of the particular societies cannot be expected to be universal.'[152] He, however, acknowledged that certain human rights are 'indisputably universally ascribable to persons of every historical, geographical and cultural background.'[153] This view seems to bridge the gap between the hypothetical absolute universalism and the purely relativistic view. It emphasises an approach which on the one hand recognises that universalism exists to some extent but that some space must also be given to relativism.

Indisputably, most African governments have accepted the UN Charter and UDHR, which have significantly attempted to universalise human rights.[154] However, to conclude that the mere acceptance of these instruments by states has succeeded to universalise human rights standards is to be ignorant of the political, economic, cultural and social factors that underpinned the promulgation of these instruments.[155] Besides, some governments adopt international instruments as a mere formality or as a public relations exercise.

---

151   Motola (n 9 above) 373.

152   Quashigah (n 9 above) 22.

153   As above.

154   Motola (n 9 above) 378.

155   See Pollis & Schwab (n 9 above) 7.

Again, in many regards, the UDHR is universal in essence but not in form. This is because, although it contains certain provisions which are respected in all societies and cultures, for example, the right to life and the right against torture, the interpretation and application of these rights tends to differ from one society to the other. For example, while the right to marry in most parts of the world involves members of the opposite sex, in some states, particularly in the West, it is increasingly being extended to homosexuals, despite strong objections from certain quarters.[156] Similarly, in states where the death sentence has been abolished, the right to life appears to be absolute, while in those states where this sentence is recognised, the right is qualified or limited. Again, whereas freedom of worship includes the right to change one's religion, Muslim states, by virtue of Islamic tenets, may regard such a change as apostasy.

It follows that 'radical universalism' is subject to remarkable specificities and peculiarities, a phenomenon that puts its relevance to question. Hence, it might take some time for universalism to be acknowledged in practice and be legally recognised by all states.[157] On a more positive note, however, it is inevitable to note that the African human rights system, which was previously more inclined to cultural relativism, is gradually shifting to a less radical approach.

This approach, at least to some degree, recognises the universality of human rights, though not in the strict sense of the word. For instance, the African Charter is based on a compromise between a wide-ranging diversity of national legal and cultural backgrounds.[158] At the same time, the African human rights system looks upon the UN and other regional human rights systems when developing its normative and jurisprudential frameworks.

From the foregoing discussion it may be concluded that there is no validity in the argument that human rights represent 'Western imperialism', because the African human rights system, a system Africans specifically crafted, is inspired by, and reinforces 'universal'

---

156   The only country in Africa that has recently decided to extend this right to homosexuals is South Africa. Other African countries do not recognise it for various reasons which could either be religious or cultural.

157   Mutua (n 8 above) 348.

158   As above.

human rights norms. Thus, the African human rights concept can only be valid if it does not 'trample' on the universal standards that acknowledge and reinforce man's inherent dignity. Ultimately, in pursuit of a 'unique' African human rights concept, caution needs to be exercised to avert the possibility of giving the impression that human rights are foreign to Africa and Africans. Suffice it to state, we maintain that at the moment we cannot truly talk of a 'unique' African human rights concept, given the reasons advanced above. At the same time, 'universality' of human rights is more hypothetical than a practical concept.

2.2 THE STATUS OF HUMAN RIGHTS IN AFRICA DURING THE SLAVE TRADE PERIOD

Whereas it is true that human rights were violated in pre-colonial Africa, the nature, scope and dynamics of the violations took a dramatic turn for the worst since her contact with the Islamic jihadists, Arab merchants and later Euro-American slavers and imperialists.[159] Since the seventh century, the continent experienced successive waves of military assault, massive destructions and killings. For instance, as soon as the Arab traders arrived in Northern Africa, they began to organise military expeditions and slave raids into the Southern regions of Morocco and as far south as the boundaries of Ancient Ghana. It is reported that in several occasions, they unleashed persecution, summary execution, illegal expulsion and arbitrary arrests on the inhabitants of those areas.[160]

The worst violations of human rights in Africa's history have been attributed to the slave trade.[161] The trade was epitomised by wars, ironically waged just to capture slaves. Its victims were mainly men, women or children who were thought to have brought dishonour to the family, the village or the clan. They were often sold into slavery to prevent further disrepute.[162] From the time they were captured to when they were sold, slaves were subjected to inhumane,

---

159 E Alemika 'Protection and realisation of human rights in Africa' in A Kalu & Y Osinbajo *Perspectives on human rights* (1992) 153.

160 As above.

161 See Eze (n 4 above) 16.

162 As above.

agonising and torturous experiences. By reason of being regarded as commodities or animals, rather than human, they were tied to each other with chains around their necks and their hands tied behind their backs. Some had their lips perforated and locked with a view to preventing them from eating when desired. Such acts were not only barbaric but also undermined human dignity.

In the ship, the slaves, still in shackles, were packed like sardines.[163] The conditions therein were so pathetic that many of them died before they reached their desired destination. Worse still, stubborn or sick ones were thrown overboard. William Wilberforce is quoted to have said: 'Never can so much misery be found condensed into so small a space as in a slave ship.'[164] According to statistics, it was not unusual to have an 80% casualty-rate in a slave ship. It was also estimated that for every 300 slaves that reached their destination in the Americas, 700 had died 500 during the raids and the march to the coast, 125 in slave ships and 75 after landing.[165] Slaves who survived the long journey across the Atlantic sea finally reached their destinations where they were subjected to hours of daily toil, further torture, the denial of adequate food and satisfaction of innate human desires.[166]

The trade in slaves culminated to gross depopulation in Africa. It is estimated that about twenty million people were transported out of the continent during this period.[167] Besides having negative implications on human rights, the trade was totally extractive of human resources, negated political, economic, social and cultural development and stultified the growth of civilisation.[168] It destroyed kingdoms and prevented the development of legitimate trade. Additionally, personal insecurity was highest during this period with consequent degradation of the quality of life.[169]

---

163   As above, 17.

164   Quoted in T Wallbank *Contemporary Africa: Continent in Transition* (1964).

165   Eze (n 4 above) 17.

166   Umozurike (n 7 above) 17.

167   Eze (n 4 above) 17.

168   Eno (n 119 above) 33.

169   As above.

Shocking as it now appears, the institution of slavery was generally legal under the national laws of many European countries and America by the end of the eighteenth century.[170] It was legal in the United States until 1863, in Brazil until 1880, and in some countries into the twentieth century. According to the *Somerset's case*, the trade was already illegal in England by 1772. At the turn of the ninteenth century, a humanitarian movement, inspired by William Wilberforce, sought to prohibit it internationally.

In 1807, slave trade was prohibited in British colonies. It was also abolished in France, and by the treaty of Paris of 1814 the British and French governments agreed to cooperate in the suppression of the traffic in slaves. This undertaking was generalised and accompanied by a solemn condemnation of the practice by the major European states at the Congress of Vienna in 1815.[171] More than fifty bilateral treaties on the subject were concluded between 1815 and 1880, and at the Berlin Conference of 1885 the practice was forbidden in conformity with the principles of international law.[172]

All the efforts and successes to end the trade in slaves notwithstanding, a permanent imprint has been left on the face of the continent on how brutal human beings can be against one another. Thus, the subsequent attempts, centuries later, by Western states to reprove African states for their poor human rights records have gone largely unheeded and have often been dismissed as pretentious.[173]

Unfortunately, slave trade was just the beginning of the nightmarish ordeal Africans would experience for a couple of centuries thereafter.[174] With the demise of the trade in slaves came the urgent need among the European powers already in Africa to translate their presence into other commercial activities.[175] Following series of events, which initially began as a pursuit of genuine commercial interests by Europeans, Africa was colonised.

---

170   H Robertson & J Merrills *Human rights in the world* (1997) 15.

171   The congress of Vienna of 1815 considered that the slave trade was 'repugnant to the principles of humanity and of universal morality.'

172   Robertson & Merrills (n 170 above) 15.

173   Umozurike (n 7 above) 17.

174   Nmehielle (n 2 above) 17.

175   As above.

The colonisation of Africa had certain implications on human rights promotion and protection then, as it still has today.

2.3   HUMAN RIGHTS IN COLONIAL AFRICA

Throughout the second half of the nineteenth century, some European states brutishly jostled one another for influence and control over trade of certain valued commodities in Africa.[176] So intense was the competition that in 1884 Chancellor Bismarck of Germany convened a conference of European nations 'to establish rules for recognising spheres of commercial suzerainty.'[177] Eventually, Africa found itself under the control of European colonialists. The major colonial powers at that time were France, Britain and Belgium. Portugal, Germany, Italy and Spain exerted some measure of colonial authority as well, though they had no great impact as the other three.[178]

It is important to reiterate that before the coming of foreigners to Africa, local societies were mainly governed by customary law and traditions.[179] Foreign intrusion later led to the decline and subsequent demise of the then subsisting African kingdoms, chiefdoms and empires. But in spite of this, there remained a substantial part of the cultural, political systems and customs inherited from the past.[180] In other words, some aspects of African customary law survived the onslaught of foreign invasion, even after vehement attempts to subjugate it. Foreign invasion did, however, have a direct and decisive impact on it.

In the first place, with the coming of Arab slave traders and later the European colonialists, African customary law no longer evolved according to African needs. African societies became subject to political, economic and social domination, and local cultures were either ignored or supplanted with foreign ones.[181] Besides tampering

---

176   G Ayittey *Africa betrayed* (1992) 81.

177   Nmehielle (n 2 above) 17.

178   As above.

179   As above.

180   Eze (n 4 above) 14.

181   As above.

with the socio-economic and political formation of the then existing societies, foreign intervention was characterised by gross violation of human rights.[182] In many instances, Africans were regarded as beasts rather than human.

It is against this background that we examine the status of human rights in Africa in the wake of colonialism. The term 'colonial period' is deliberately used to depict that period when Africa was subjugated by the cruel hand of its European foreign 'masters', who initially poised as its trading partners only to reveal their true intentions later on. Hence, 'colonial period' essentially envisages the entire epoch from the coming of the European imperialists to when they relinquished their dominion over the continent.

It should be noted that European foreigners employed different techniques to bring the African inhabitants to submission as well as plunder their resources. As a result, the techniques and systems of administration preferred, for example, by the British, French, and Belgian colonialist to govern their subjects varied significantly. These systems could loosely be dabbed: indirect, direct/paternalism and the assimilation systems. Differences in the systems were based on the philosophical and historical experiences of the colonisers. It is therefore imperative to consider them separately in order to determine the status of human rights under each of them.

2.3.1　The Status of Human Rights under the Indirect-rule System

The indirect-rule system of colonial administration was coined and perpetuated by the British in their colonies. The system was 'indirect' because it encouraged the use of existing institutions and the traditional political leaders.[183] In other words, the African traditional chief became a tool in the hands of the British colonisers for the main purpose of maximising exploitation. According to this system, each colony was demarcated into provinces, districts and regions governed by Provincial Commissioners, District Commissioners

---

182　Nmehielle (n 2 above) 18.

183　Eze (n 4 above) 19.

and Chiefs, respectively.[184] The system recognised and provided for the application of African customary law.

Although the system utilised the services of local chiefs and rulers, indirect-rule had two major disadvantages that are worth mentioning. First, it introduced authoritarianism by bestowing on the rulers powers which would not have been condoned in the traditional African set-up.[185] Secondly, it inhibited the un-interrupted evolution of African indigenous institutions that would have increasingly developed and become more democratic with the passage of time.[186] Further the indirect-rule system was discriminative because even the applicable English common law did not recognise the full and equal enjoyment of rights between indigenous Africans and Britons. Instead, it encouraged the exercise of powers of political detention or deportation and use of laws of sedition and censorship framed more widely than those of England.[187]

With regard to administration of justice, the system established and maintained policies and procedures that were authoritarian and discriminative, to say the least.[188] Unlike the French and Belgian systems, it did not create adequate appeal mechanisms, nor did it place fundamental and justiceable limitations of power on either the legislature or executive. The legislature had a wide measure of freedom in the areas in which it could legislate and the emergency powers granted to it could only have exacerbated the denial of fundamental rights and freedoms.[189]

The point remains that the indirect-rule system was disrespectful of African traditions and values. It relegated Africans to subservience in all fields. It arrested and destroyed the internal dynamics of the evolution of African societies.[190] Undoubtedly, by abolishing certain objectionable traditional practices that were prevalent in pre-

---

184   Ayittey (n 176 above) 86.

185   Nmehielle (n 2 above) 25.

186   As above.

187   As above.

188   See Y Ghai & J McAuslan *Public law and political change in Kenya* (1970) 407- 408.

189   Nmehielle (n 2 above) 27.

190   As above.

colonial Africa, such as human sacrifice, slavery, killing of twins, among others, the colonialists did contribute, to a certain extent, to the development of human rights.[191] However, the negative effects of colonialism generally, and the indirect-rule system particularly, on colonial and independent Africa cannot be taken lightly.

2.3.2   THE STATUS OF HUMAN RIGHTS UNDER THE DIRECT-RULE/PATERNALISM SYSTEM

Direct-rule or paternalism system was employed by, among other colonial powers, Belgium, to govern its colonies in Africa. Belgian colonies were concentrated in the Congo basin and embraced also the Rwanda-Burundi regions. This system was motivated by the assumption that Africans were incapable of ruling themselves and were therefore to be controlled by the colonialists in every aspect of their lives.[192] Consequently, Belgian colonies were governed directly from Brussels from where all decrees emanated. The Congolese were not consulted in the administration of their own affairs.

Prior to the introduction of this system, the influence of king Leopold II of Belgium prevailed in the Congo region. The king not only reaped benefits from the region but also regarded the territory as his private property. He called the region 'Congo Free State', meaning that anyone interested could exploit the region without any hindrance but subject to his directions and instructions.

The treatment of the Africans was so harsh that the other colonial powers pleaded with the king to exercise some form of restraint. His brutality and exploitation also attracted widespread protests from the inhabitants of the region. This forced the Belgian Parliament to bring the 'Congo Free State' under Belgian state rule, after the adoption of the Colonial Charter of 1908. It then became 'Belgian Congo' and the colonial policy was one of direct-rule, also known as paternalism or tutelage.

Colonial rule in the Congo was a tripartite arrangement: rule by corporation, which consisted of the crown, the Catholic church and large companies in which the crown held substantial stock.

---

191   Umozurike (n 7 above) 17.

192   Nmehielle (n 2 above) 22.

The administration was brutal and imposed stringent conditions on the subjects.[193] It presided over massive transfers of wealth from the territory to Belgium. It limited Africans in a number of ways and regarded them as inferior to the Belgians. For example, Africans received only limited education, which would allow them to read the Bible, take orders efficiently from the missionaries, and function, at best, as clerks in the colonial bureaucracy. Additionally, they were not allowed to travel in the Congo without a permit, possess arms or indulge in certain social activities.[194]

Despite the absolute control that Belgium had over its colonies, the subjects were never granted the right to citizenship.[195] Unlike the British and the French, the Belgians diligently kept their subjects out of Belgium. Africans in other European colonies could attend universities in Europe, but not the Congolese.[196] Simply put, the policies under the Belgian administration were not for the betterment of Africans. They were racist and degraded Africans in many respects, to say the least. Human rights were therefore more of a myth than a reality under this system of colonial administration.

2.3.3   THE STATUS OF HUMAN RIGHTS UNDER THE ASSIMILATION SYSTEM

The assimilation system was the handmaiden of the French colonial administration. Under this system, the colonised people were expected to adopt the French culture. The rationale for assimilation was based on the belief that French culture was superior.[197] The system made it impossible to have a uniform application of policies. Policies in many cases had to be modified to accommodate the various categories of persons present in society.[198] Most often, this meant that the rights of Africans to participate in their own government had to be suspended. This system posed the gravest

---

193   As above.

194   See Ayittey (n 176 above) 86.

195   See generally, C Young 'Colonial rule through direct rule: The Belgian model' in W Cartey & M Kilson (eds) *The African reader: Colonial Africa* 87-88.

196   As above.

197   Nmehielle (n 2 above) 20.

198   As above.

danger to indigenous African institutions, especially the great paramount chieftaincies, which were deliberately destroyed.[199]

The system made a distinction between various categories of Africans, on the one hand, and the French, on the other.[200] For example, customary law was applicable to persons who were considered as having customary status (*statut coutumier*), while persons to whom the French law applied acquired the French civil status (*statut civil Francais*). Assimilation was limited to very few Africans and the French were forced to employ indirect-rule when they failed to do otherwise.[201] Notwithstanding the applicable system, chiefs who were at the apex of traditional African societies were reduced to agents of French colonial administrators.

The system disregarded the rights of the African masses. For example, freedom of movement was restricted so as to ensure the provision of cheap labour both for the administration and the colonial corporations and for this adequate pay was not given.[202] Forced labour was also practiced. The *indigenat*, which consisted of regulations that allowed colonial administrators to inflict punishment on African subjects without obtaining a court judgement or approval from the metropolis, was largely applied under this system.[203] It allowed the colonial officers to jail any African for up to two years without trial, to impose heavy taxes and punitive fines, or to burn the villages of those who refused to pay.[204]

In summary, therefore, there is no doubt that no one system of colonial administration was better than the other. A closer look at these systems will reveal that they had the same objectives and produced more or less similar consequences.[205] By whatever name called, or philosophies under which they were formulated, all the systems were fashioned to exploit the colonies in the maximum way

---

199   Ayittey (n 176 above) 86.

200   Eze (n 4 above) 15.

201   As above.

202   Above.

203   Nmehielle (n 2 above) 20.

204   As above.

205   As above.

possible. Colonial policies and legislation were generally racist, and degraded Africans in many respects.

Even where native law and customs were applicable, they could not be observed or enforced if they were repugnant to natural justice, equality and good conscience, or incompatible with any Ordinance in force in the territories.[206] Ironically, the standards of natural justice, equality and good conscience by which they were to be judged were of colonial origin.[207] Additionally, all colonisers practised forced labour; were disrespectful of African traditions and values and intentionally destroyed the internal dynamics of the evolution of African societies.[208]

Colonialism denied the people the right to determine their political, economic, and social future. No wonder, in many cases, the history and legacy of violations of the rights of African peoples that began during the colonial period easily became the basis on which post-colonial despots undermined international efforts against human rights abuses on the continent. Thus, former President of Zaire (now 'the Democratic Republic of Congo'), the late Mobutu Sese Seko, one of the leading despots in Africa, was able to claim without remorse:

> We are often accused of violating human rights. Today it is Amnesty International and tomorrow it is a human rights league and so forth. During the entire colonial period, the universal conscience never thought it necessary to have a human rights organisation when indignities, humiliations and inhuman treatment inflicted in those days against the people of the colonies should have been condemned. It is rather odd. Everybody waited until we became independent suddenly to wake up and start moralising all day long our young states.[209]

While Mobutu's sentiments cannot be upheld as a justification for the continued violation of human rights in Africa, it must be conceded that indeed the exploitation and human rights abuses witnessed during the colonial era were done with impunity, in utter

---

206   Eze (n 4 above) 17.

207   As above.

208   Nmehielle (n 2 above) 29.

209   Quoted in F Reyntjens 'Authoritarianism in Francophone Africa from colonial to the post-colonial state' *Third World Legal Studies* (1988) 73.

violation of international law. Ironically, international bodies such as the League of Nations, which was later replaced by the United Nations (UN), turned a blind eye to those abuses. In fact, member states misused international law against Africa while the League remained passive.[210]

For instance, the 1935 Italian invasion and colonisation of Ethiopia, an independent member state of the League, did not provoke any reaction from the international community.[211] Umozurike argued, certain states failed to regard Ethiopia as a sovereign state, 'because it was African.'[212] One would therefore conclude that the overt failure by the UN to respond promptly and adequately to the ongoing gross violations of human rights in Africa is just a continuation of the legacy of marginalisation and oppression of Africa by the international community.

2.4   HUMAN RIGHTS IN POST-COLONIAL AFRICA

The status of human rights protection and promotion in Africa took a slightly different turn from the late 1950s when the then colonised states began to emerge from colonial bondage.[213] By then, colonialism had greatly damaged the socio-economic and political structures of the traditional African societies by putting in place new systems, which were totally in contrast with the values and norms of the local populace.[214] Thus, the emerging states had to face the challenge of embracing new values, systems and institutions, on the one hand, and the universal agitation for human rights promotion and protection, on the other.[215]

Amidst these challenges states that were independent resolved to consolidate their efforts and forge a common front to bloat out colonialism in its entirety from the face of the continent. This move saw the emergence of pan-continental organisations such as the

210   U Umozurike *International law and colonialism in Africa* (1979) 66.

211   See A Zumach 'Parallels between the League of Nations and the UN: The Specter of Abyssinia' in Amnesty International *Global Rights: UN 50 years after take off* (1995) 27.

212   Umozurike (n 210 above) 66.

213   Eze (n 4 above) 23.

214   Nmehielle (n 2 above) 27.

215   As above.

Organisation of African Unity (OAU), whose historical parameters shall be examined in detail in the next chapter. Further, albeit reluctantly, independent African states also saw the need for regional mechanisms for the protection of human rights on the continent. This came along with the unending concern for an African concept of human rights, whose parameters were demystified elsewhere above.

It is equally important to point out that with the emergence of independent African states, there were high hopes for the effective protection and promotion of human rights and the restoration of human dignity on the continent.[216] Arguably, this would have been tenable, given the transition of political governance to indigenous leaders who were better placed to understand and appreciate the problems of their people. Independence should also have presented the opportunity to revive the traditional institutions that were undermined by colonialists, of course with some reforms that would accommodate the incumbent socio-economic and political diversity.[217]

This, however, turned out not to be the case. Instead, many of the emerging states adopted Constitutions and legal systems similar to those of the colonial powers, notwithstanding the fact that they were not in tandem with the socio-economic and political set-up of the traditional societies.[218] With these legal and constitutional systems came a package of guarantees, such as, multiparty system of government, independence of the judiciary, respect for the rule of law, and the promotion and protection of human rights, among others.

Sadly, the end of the 1960s was characterised by the negation of the pledged democracy as well as gross violation of human rights with impunity across the continent. The pledged multiparty democracy became a by-word as opposition parties were regarded as 'clogs in the wheels of progress.'[219] Ruling parties which had become more intolerant of the opposition politics denied government resources and facilities to their opponents and some even veered

---

216   Umozurike (n 7 above) 22.

217   As above.

218   As above.

219   As above, 23.

to the single party system.[220] Consequently, a wave of coups swept across the continent, where the military overthrew governments, purportedly to clean the socio-economic and political messes.[221] Whereas military regimes were usually enthusiastically received, little did people know what was in store for them. With time, they fell into the same errors as the civilian administration.[222]

The pathetic human rights situation on the continent was worsened by the vengeful deportation of foreigners from a number of African states, which in most cases led to the deprivation of their property. For example, Nigerians were deported from Cameroon soon after independence, Ghanaians from Ivory Coast, Rwandans from Burundi and vice versa. Ghana deported foreigners in 1969 and 1970 in order to check unemployment.[223] Liberians were deported from Ivory Coast and Nigerians from Zaire. Kenyans, Tanzanians and Asian Ugandans were expelled from Uganda. Aliens were ejected from the Congo Republic and Nigerian labourers in Equatorial Guinea were deprived of their property, many of them were killed and the women were raped.[224]

Clearly, although African leaders were expected to promote and protect human rights at independence, they violated the same with impunity. As Babu sarcastically noted, liberation was duly climaxed by the following tendencies:

> Arbitrary arrest of citizens; disrespect for the right of habeas corpus; imprisonment without trial; denial of freedom of movement; ... organised and systematic police brutality; domination of government by secret police; mass arrests and detentions; concentration camps; physical and mental torture of prisoners; public executions; and the whole apparatus of violent repression.[225]

---

220   For example, in 1982 Kenya became a *de Jure* one party state following the enactment os s.2A in its Constitution.

221   Umozurike (n 7 above) 22. Umozurike explains that there were mutinies in Burundi and Rwanda in the 1970s and 1990s and in Nigeria, as early as 1966. In the same period, Ghana witnessed ten-minute trials and executions of former heads of government, following a successful military coup.

222   As above.

223   As above.

224   As above.

225   A Babu *African socialism or socialist Africa?* (1981) 171.

This has been an ongoing situation in Africa. In fact, human rights violations have taken new forms and status, such as genocide, war crimes and crimes against humanity. As recently as 1994, for example, the continent experienced one of the gravest genocides in its history where approximately 800,000 people were brutally massacred in Rwanda.[226]

The situation did not get any better even after the Rwandan genocide from which many African states were expected to draw viable lessons. Instead, in the first decade of the twenty-first century, many African states were engulfed in human rights and related crises. Countries like Sierra Leone, for example, experienced a civil war that saw many people dead and others wounded, besides encountering other forms of gross human rights violations. This prompted the UN and the government of Sierra Leone under the leadership of President Ahmed Tijan Kaba to set up the Special Court for Sierra Leone in 2002.[227]

Additionally, Burundi, the Democratic Republic of Congo (DRC), The Gambia, Togo, Nigeria and Liberia have also had a share of trouble in the form of civil wars, political assassinations and other forms of gross human rights violations. The situation in Northern Uganda is also perturbing because there is an incessant warfare between the government and rebel forces which has, over the years, led to kidnapping of children and recruiting them as soldiers, contrary to international norms.[228]

Similarly, Sudan is in a crisis as a result of the ongoing war in its Darfur region. Although talks have been initiated in a bid to end the war, human rights have continued to be violated with impunity.[229]

---

226   For more information on the Rwandan genocide and the ongoing trials of its perpetrators, visit www.ictr.org.

227   The UN Security Council adopted Resolution 1315 on 14 August 2000 requesting the UN Secretary-General to start negotiations to create a Special Court to prosecute 'those most responsible for committing human rights violations' in the country during that period. On 16 January 2002, an agreement establishing the court was signed between the government of Sierra Leone and the UN. This court has adopted a statute that prosecutes both international and national crimes.

228   See 'Conflicts in Africa' available at http://www.globalissues.org/Geopolitics/Africa.asp (accessed on 1 March 2010).

229   See generally, Human Rights Watch *World Report 2007* (2007).

Somalia, which has just emerged from a war that lasted for more than a decade, is still staggering to have a stable government in place. Clan feuds instigated by the government and rebel forces are the order of the day in that country.[230]

Some countries in Southern Africa have also had their share of atrocities and violations of human rights. For example, before April 1994, when the first multi-racial democratic elections were held in the Republic of South Africa, the country was shackled in the bondage of apartheid and racial discrimination. The end of the apartheid regime was indeed good news to many who had directed their efforts and resources to end it.

Even so, the new democratic dispensation is still fighting to gain ground on the residues of this brutish legacy.[231] The government is still battling to overcome racial discrimination, xenophobia and related intolerance. Some government policies in South Africa have also been criticised as perpetrating discrimination of certain sections of the society. More particularly, its policies and legislation concerning 'unfair discrimination' have been received with a lot of suspicion.[232]

Zimbabwe is also between the rock and a hard place under the autocratic rule of its 'founding father', president Robert Mugabe. The President, who has been in power since the country attained her independence in 1980, has joined the ranks of the world's worst ten dictators.[233] Although elections are held regularly, they are never free and fair and the ruling ZANU/PF party, except in March 2008, has invariably retained parliamentary majority.[234] Its human rights

---

230   As above.

231   See South African Human Rights Commission 'Shadow Report on South Africa's compliance with the provisions of the International Convention against all Forms of Racial Discrimination (ICERD)' (August 2006) (*Presented to the International Committee on the Elimination of All Forms of Racial Discrimination, Geneva, Switzerland*).

232   As above.

233   D Wallechinsky 'The world's ten worst dictators' available at http://archive.parade.com/2005/0213/0213_dictator.html (accessed 11 April 2010). Those listed alongside Mugabe are: Omar Al-Bashir of Sudan, Kim Jong-il of North Korea, Than Shwe of Burma, Islam Karimov of Uzbekistan, Hu Jintao of China, King Abdullah of Saudi Arabia, Saparmurat Niyazov of Turkmenistan, Seyed Ali Khamane'I of Iran and Teodoro Obiang Nguema of Equatorial Guinea.

234   See 'Zimbabwe: Is a fair vote possible?' available at http://news.bbc.co.uk/2/hi/talking_point/debates/african_ debates/798820.stm (accessed 1 March 2010).

record is an embarrassment to the AU and the continent at large. Additionally, having adopted land policies that have largely attracted criticism from all and sundry, the country is under economic sanctions that have contributed to its high inflation rates and currency devaluation.

Today, in Zimbabwe, there isn't much difference between a pauper and a millionaire because both cannot engage in any meaningful commercial transaction for the lack of commodities to buy. Moreover, the opposition in the country has been gagged and frustrated, the press censored and the judiciary reduced to a tool of oppression in the hands of the executive, just to mention a few incidents. As a result of the deteriorating situation, many Zimbabweans have been reduced to 'economic refugees' in other countries, such as South Africa. The situation in the country has gradually been going from bad to worse.

Other countries in southern Africa, such as Swaziland, Lesotho, Namibia, Angola and Mozambique are either recovering from long spells of civil wars or are in the labyrinth of diverse forms of human rights violations. Poverty, which originates not only from the vestiges of colonialism but also from economic plunder by the post-colonial leaders, has been the hallmark of the lives of the citizens of these countries. There are countless instances of gross human rights abuses throughout the continent, Generally, the continent is still wallowing in a miasma of confusion, while trying to remain afloat in the sea of turmoil.

The complexity of the situation in Africa produces consequences which when carefully considered run counter to the interests of regional enforcement of human rights. One would therefore agree with Alemika's assessment that:

> The chronic and worsening conditions of human rights in Africa have produced serious political, social and economic consequences. … The violations of political and civil rights by rulers often either include or result in the denial of the citizens of full participation in the formulation and implementation of vital policies affecting them and their society. Human rights violations, therefore, produce a vicious

circle of repression, economic stagnation and regression, and political instability …[235]

Indeed, even the democratic wave that swept across Africa from the mid-1990s and witnessed the demise of many authoritarian regimes only minimised the practice of human rights violations; it did not abate it. There are still reports of opposition activists being jailed without trial for daring to seek level playing fields in politics; journalists being detained or sometimes forced into exile for exposing corruption in high places; academics being threatened with arrests for writing about poor governance; workers being dismissed for attempting to unionise or to ask for better remuneration in the face of currency devaluations and inflation.[236]

The prevailing human rights situation in Africa has made it exceptionally difficult for the regional human rights system to be as effective as it ought to be. Generally, states have totally failed to take human rights seriously within their domestic domain. Subsequently, this has translated to their neglect and violation at the regional and international levels. It is needless to emphasise that human rights have in the past been viewed with a lot of suspicion by African leaders; as a tool for neo-colonialism and not as inherent entitlements of mankind.

This explains why the attempt to craft a vibrant African system on human and peoples' rights was stiffly resisted. However, with the emergence of a new crop of political leaders, there seems to be a general consensus on the need for an effective regional human rights system that would contain the rising tide of impunity and redress the failures of domestic legal systems. Arguably, human rights are better understood today than they were before, especially by the African political elite.

---

235   Alemika (n 159 above) 160.

236   J Akokpari 'Policing and preventing human rights abuses in Africa: The OAU, the AU & the NEPAD Peer Review' (2004) 32/2 *International Journal of Legal Information* 461.

CHAPTER 3

HISTORICAL DIMENSIONS OF THE AFRICAN SYSTEM ON HUMAN AND PEOPLES' RIGHTS

The expression 'African system on human and peoples' rights' refers to the regional system of norms and institutions for enforcement of human and peoples' rights in Africa. There has been an academic controversy over the scope and definition of this system. Gutto, for example, argued that a distinction should be made between the broader 'African human rights system' and the narrower 'African Charter system'.[1] Accordingly, whereas the African Charter system centres around two enforcement institutions, namely, the African Commission and the African Court on Human and Peoples' Rights, the African human rights system goes beyond to include the political institutions and other organs created under the African Union (AU), formerly known as the Organisation of African Unity (OAU).[2]

Gutto's observations could be faulted because the African Charter, which is at the core of his so-called 'African Charter system', is a very important instrument of the 'African human rights system'. Hence, the 'African human rights system' cannot be construed separately from the 'African Charter system.' Secondly, it is not proper to view the 'African Charter system' distinctly from the pan-continental political institutions principally because the latter seem to anchor the former. This is confirmed by the fact that the African Charter effectively puts the African Commission under the control of the Assembly of the Heads of States and Government (AHSG).[3]

Further, just before the inception of the AU, the former OAU Council of Ministers called for the incorporation into the union, 'organs, institutions/bodies which have not been specifically

---

1 S Gutto 'The reform and renewal of the African regional human and peoples' rights system' (2001) 2 *African Human Rights Law Journal* 176.

2 As above, 184.

3 See art 58 of the African Charter on Human and Peoples' Rights (hereafter the 'African Charter' or 'Charter').

mentioned in the Constitutive Act.'[4] The AU Assembly, at its first ordinary session, decided that, 'the African Commission on Human and Peoples' Rights and the African Committee of Experts on Rights and Welfare of the Child shall henceforth operate within the framework of the African Union.'[5] These are a few illustrations of the links and synergies between the 'political institutions' and the 'African Charter system' which makes it difficult for one to conclude that their existence is distinct.

As a variant of Gutto's proposition, we consider the African human rights system as one that embodies two inter-related components, namely the 'political' (AU-based) and the 'legal' (African Charter-based) components.[6] While the former is more concerned with regional politics than with human rights, the latter is wholly involved in human rights affairs. The meeting point of the two components, however, is their involvement in regional promotion and protection of human rights. In other words, both have a hand and are necessary in the human rights agenda of the region.

Odinkalu contended for a much broader definition of the expression 'African human rights system.'[7] According to him, the system encapsulates not only the subsisting regional human rights mechanisms but also supra-national, pan-continental systems and mechanisms and the domestic legal systems in Africa.[8] This depiction, however, is overbroad and therefore misleading. It ignores the all important fact that, whereas supra-national and domestic systems in Africa may enforce regional human rights norms, the latter are not mandated to enforce, or even interpret, supra-national

---

4   N Udombana 'The institutional structure of the African Union' (2002) 33 *California Western International Law Journal* 84.

5   As above.

6   With regard to this arrangement, see the observations in E Baimu 'Human rights mechanisms and structures under NEPAD and the African Union: Emerging trends towards proliferation and duplication' (2002) *Occasional No. 15*, Centre for Human Rights.

7   C Odinkalu 'The role of case and complaints procedures in the reform of African regional human rights system' (2001) 2 *African Human Rights Law Journal* 227.

8   As above.

or domestic laws. They may only interpret and enforce those norms created under, or that are relevant to, the system.[9]

Under the African human rights system, the rule of exhaustion of domestic remedies serves as the link between domestic and regional human rights mechanisms.[10] However, contrary to Odinkalu's argument, this rule does not make the domestic mechanisms part of the regional human rights system.[11] Rather, the rule was evolved to uphold sovereignty of states by granting them the first opportunity in domestic dispute resolution.[12] The African Commission confirmed this position when it stated that the exhaustion of domestic remedies rule prevents it from acting as a court of first instance as long as domestic remedies are available, effective and sufficient.[13] Through this assertion, the Commission wanted to distinguish the roles between domestic and regional human rights systems.[14]

Odinkalu's position should therefore not be entertained because one could be misled to understand that the African human rights system includes the human rights norms and institutions created in the aegis of the United Nations (UN), as long as African states are parties to UN treaties. As stated above, we adopt the position that the 'African human rights system' refers to the regional system of norms and institutions for enforcement of human and peoples' rights on the continent. This system consists of the pan-continental 'political' mechanisms on human rights, such as the AU and some of its norms and organs, and the 'legal' mechanisms, such as the African Charter, its Protocols and enforcement institutions.

---

9   See for example art 3(1) of the Protocol to the African Charter on Human and Peoples' Rights Establishing the Africa Court on Human and Peoples' Rights. The article provides that 'the jurisdiction of the Court shall extend to all cases and disputes submitted to it concerning the interpretation and application of the Charter, this Protocol and *any other relevant human rights instrument ratified by the States concerned.*' (emphasis mine)

10   See art 56(6) African Charter.

11   Odinkalu (n 7 above) 227.

12   See F Viljoen 'Admissibility under the African Charter' in R Murray & M Evans *The African Charter on Human and Peoples' Rights: The system in practice 1986-2000* (2002) 62.

13   Communications 147/95, 149/95, *Sir Dawda K Jawara v The Gambia*, Thirteenth Annual Activity Report.

14   Viljoen (n 12 above) 62.

In conformity with this definition, it may be argued that the system, created under the auspices of the OAU/AU, comprises a number of normative instruments. These include: the Constitutive Act of the African Union (CAAU)[15]; the African Charter on Human and Peoples' Rights[16]; the Convention Governing the Specific Aspects of Refugee Problems in Africa[17]; the Convention on the Elimination of Mercenaries in Africa[18]; the African Charter on the Rights and Welfare of the Child[19]; the Cultural Charter for Africa[20]; the Convention on the Prevention and Combating of Terrorism[21]; the Protocol to the African Charter on Human and Peoples' Rights on the Rights of Women in Africa[22]; and the Protocol to the African Charter on Human and Peoples' Rights on the Establishment of an African Court on Human and Peoples' Rights.[23]

There are also two African treaties dealing with the environment, although not from a human rights perspective, which have been included by some scholars in the list of norms informing the African human rights system.[24] These are the African Convention on the

---

15   See the Constitutive Act of the African Union adopted by the 36th ordinary session of the Assembly of Heads of State and Government, 11 July 2000, Lomé, Togo. Art 3(h) of the CAAU stipulates that the Union aims, among other things, at 'promoting and protecting human and peoples' rights in accordance with the African Charter on Human and Peoples' Rights and other relevant human rights instruments.'

16   Adopted on 27 June 1981, OAU DOC CAB/LEG/67/3, rev 5.

17   Adopted on 10 September 1969, entered into force on 20 June 1974, OAU Doc CAB/LEG 24.3.

18   Adopted June 1977, entered into force 1985, OAU Doc CM/433/Rev L Annex I (1972). For a discussion on the political, human rights, legal and security aspects of the problems of mercenaries in Africa, see J Fayemi & A Musah (eds) *Mercenaries: An African security dilemma* (2000).

19   Adopted in July 1990, entered into force on 29 November 1999, OAU Doc CAB/LEG 153/REV 2. The Children's Charter is reprinted in C Heyns (ed) *Human rights law in Africa 1997* (1999) 38.

20   Cultural Charter for Africa of 1976 (1990) reprinted in Heyns (n 19 above) 55.

21   Adopted by the 35th ordinary session of the Assembly of Heads of State and Government, Algiers, Algeria, 14 July 1999.

22   Adopted by the Second Ordinary Session of the Assembly of the Union in Maputo, July 11 2003.

23   Protocol to the African Charter on Human and Peoples' Rights on the Establishment of an African Court on Human and Peoples' Rights, OAU Doc OAU/LEG/EXP/AFCHPR/PROT (III), available at http://www.achpr.org (accessed 28 November 2007).

24   See Gutto (n 1 above) 176.

Conservation of Nature and Natural Resources and the Bamako Convention on the Ban of the Import into Africa and the Control of Trans-boundary Movement and Management of Hazardous Wastes within Africa.[25]

In addition to the normative instruments, a number of institutions are involved, either directly or indirectly, in the enforcement of the norms of the system. These are: the African Union (AU) and its organs[26]; the African Commission on Human and Peoples' Rights (the Commission), established under the African Charter on Human and Peoples' Rights; the African Court on Human and Peoples' Rights created by the Protocol to the African Charter on Human and Peoples' Rights on the Establishment of an African Court on Human and Peoples' Rights; and the African Committee of Experts on the Rights and Welfare of the Child, established under the African Charter on the Rights and Welfare of the Child.[27] Despite the proliferation of norms and institutions, the African Charter remains the main human rights instrument of the African system.[28] Similarly, the African Commission has, since the inception of the Charter, been the sole institution that ensures state compliance with the Charter's norms. The African Court on Human and Peoples' Rights was recently established to complement the Commission.

The African human rights system is the youngest and least developed of the three regional human rights systems. Generally speaking, to attain its present status, the system evolved under difficult circumstances. Its inception was resisted by the then OAU leadership because of the fear that elevating human rights to the regional status

---

25   Adopted at Bamako, Mali, 29 June 1991, reprinted in (1993) 1 *African Yearbook of International Law* 269.

26   The CAAU makes reference to the African Charter in its objectives (art 3(h) Constitutive Act). Additionally, various institutions and organs have since been established within the AU framework, most of which will be directly or indirectly responsible for human rights protection and promotion.

27   The Committee was inaugurated in 2002. See C Heyns 'The African regional human rights system: In need of reform?' (2001) 2 *African Human Rights Law Journal* 155-156.

28   G Wachira 'A critical examination of the African Charter on Human and Peoples' Rights: Towards strengthening the African human rights system to enable it effectively meet the needs of the African population' in F Viljoen (ed) *The African human rights system: Towards the co-existence of the African Commission on Human and Peoples' Rights and the African Court on Human and Peoples' Rights* (2006) 16.

would most likely compromise state sovereignty, which to them was more important at that time. Against this background, this chapter reviews the historical origin and evolution of the institutional and normative mechanisms of the system.

It should be noted that it is not the intention of this chapter to review all the mechanisms under the system. Rather, our focus shall be on the main human rights treaty in the region, the African Charter on Human and Peoples' Rights and its enforcement institutions, the African Commission and Court on Human and Peoples' Rights. The OAU/AU which is the 'political arm' of the system shall also be examined in light of its role in regional human rights promotion and protection. Other important OAU/AU programmes, such as the New Partnership for Africa's Development (NEPAD) and the African Peer Review Mechanism (APRM) will also be explored within the same context.

3.1   THE EMERGENCE AND ROLE OF THE OAU IN HUMAN RIGHTS PROTECTION IN AFRICA

The birth of the OAU can be attributed to series of events in various parts of the continent, aimed at ending colonial domination. In 1959, for example, a conference of nine independent African states was convened in Monrovia to discuss the situation in Algeria following the establishment of the country's provisional government.[29] Building on the successes of this conference, more conferences were subsequently held in early 1960s to encourage and organise non-violent revolutions aimed at liberating colonised African states.[30] These conferences spearheaded widespread condemnation of human rights abuses, among others, the deprivation of property, racial discrimination and disenfranchisement of the right to universal adult suffrage. At least, this initial move was a good indication of the potential of independent African states in promoting and protecting human rights.

---

29   Ethiopia, Ghana, Guinea, Liberia, Libya, Morocco, Sudan, Tunisia and United Arab Republic.

30   R Murray *Human rights in Africa: From the OAU to the Africa Union* (2004) 2.

These states later sought to consolidate their efforts through the creation of a regional organisation that would help them speak in one voice. They did not, however, agree on the nature of the organisation, with some falling into the 'Monrovia' bloc,[31] favouring a 'more classical, 'confederal' approach where, 'far from aiming at the integration of African states, sovereignty would be preserved in the framework of a much looser arrangement.'[32] In contrast, other states under the leadership of Ghana's President Nkurumah, in what became known as the 'Casablanca' bloc[33], had signed the more federalist Casablanca Charter for economic cooperation, stressing elements of self-defence and the need to eliminate colonialism.[34]

In May 1961 a pan-African conference was held in Monrovia, attended by representatives of twenty-two of the twenty-seven independent African states, excluding those affiliated to the 'Casablanca' bloc.[35] The conference recommended, *inter alia,* that a Charter, establishing an organisation of African and Malagasy states, should be adopted.[36] In January 1962, the newly formed Assembly of Heads of States and Government (AHSG) convened in Lagos, to consider drafting the Charter.[37] It was proposed that the intended regional organisation should comprise three principal organs, namely, an Assembly of Heads of States, a Council of Ministers and a Secretariat, with a Secretary-General. It was eventually adopted as 'the Charter of the Organisation of African and Malagasy states' (or the 'Lagos Charter') by seventeen states in December 1962.[38]

---

31   Cameroon, Central African Republic, Chad, Congo, Dahomey, Ethiopia, Gabon, Liberia, Libya, Malagasy, Mauritania, Niger, Nigeria, Senegal, Sierra Leone, Somalia, Togo, Tunisia and Upper Volta.

32   P Sands & P Klein *Bowett's law of international institutions,* (2001) 244.

33   United Arab Republic, Ghana, Guinea, Mali and Morocco.

34   Sands & Klein (n 32 above) 244.

35   Murray (n 30 above) 3.

36   See T Elias 'The Charter of the Organisation of African Unity' (1965) 59 *American Journal of International Law* 243-244.

37   As above.

38   The Casablanca bloc was still not present at any of these meetings.

Subsequent events led to the merger of the two blocs and the adoption of the Charter of the OAU in 1963,[39] bringing to an end years of division. Principally, the OAU was established to ensure independence of all African countries and promote their unity. Emerson correctly observed, the history of colonisation to which nearly all of Africa had been subject, the resulting groupings among newly independent African states and the idea of a sense of African unity, were behind the creation of the OAU.[40]

It was within the remits of the OAU that the independence of African states should be safeguarded and that all forms of colonialism and racism, especially as manifested in southern Africa, be ended.[41] According to Kannyo, 'the strong and unanimous desire to complete the process of decolonisation and dismantle the system of apartheid in South Africa',[42] reinforced the organisation.

The OAU Charter, however, did not intimate the protection and promotion of human rights as one of its principal goals. Instead, its objectives simply mentioned the eradication of 'all forms of colonialism' from Africa, while its preamble glossed over the desire of its members to observe human rights, in the following words:

> Conscious of our responsibility to harness the natural and human resources of our continent ... persuaded that the Charter of the United Nations and the Universal Declaration of Human Rights, to the principles of which we reaffirm our adherence, provide a solid foundation for peaceful and positive cooperation among states ...

Dlamini observed that besides the issues of apartheid and decolonisation, the only sense in which the OAU could be considered as an organisation for the promotion of human rights was in relation to its general goal of 'total advancement of our peoples in spheres

---

39   See Charter of the Organisation of African Unity, adopted 25 May 1963, 47 UNTS 39; 2 ILM (1963) 766.

40   R Emerson 'Pan-Africanism' (1962) 16/2 *International Organisation* 282.

41   Art 21(1) of the Charter of the OAU.

42   E Kannyo *Human rights in Africa: Problems and prospects* (1980) 15; D Venter 'Black Africa and the Apartheid issue: A South African response?' (1981) *Journal of Contemporary African studies* 84.

of human endeavours.'[43] Kannyo attributed the absence of human rights provisions in the Charter of the OAU to the purpose for which the organisation was established, that is, the termination of foreign dominion.[44]

Perhaps one of OAU's major failures was its lack of emphasis on human rights protection and promotion; which could have been the reason why some of its member states lacked comprehensive Bill of rights in their independence Constitutions. Apparently, its member states were expected to ascribe to the human rights fundamentals entrenched in the Universal Declaration of Human Rights (UDHR).[45]

Despite its obvious failure to entrench human rights through the provisions of its Charter, the OAU's role in agitating for the right to self-determination in Africa cannot be overemphasised. For instance, it relentlessly played a crucial role in strengthening and invigorating the UN's efforts against colonialism and apartheid by setting up a Liberation Committee through which it channelled support to the liberation movements fighting in Mozambique, Angola, Namibia, Guinea (Bissau) and South Africa.[46] The organisation gave its official approval to the Lusaka Manifesto of 1969 adopted by the Heads of States of East and Central Africa and secured its adoption by the UN General Assembly.[47] The manifesto renewed faith in 'the belief that all men are equal and have equal rights to human dignity and respect, regardless of colour, religion or sex ...'[48]

Additionally, the OAU addressed the plight of refugees in the region by adopting the 1969 Convention on the Specific Aspects of Refugee Problems in Africa.[49] It also co-operated with international

---

43   Preamble of the Charter; C Dlamini 'The OAU and the protection of human rights in Africa' (1991) *Obiter* 69.

44   Kannyo (n 42 above) 17.

45   See H Othman 'Africa and the protection of rights' (1995) 6/1 *African Law Review* 51-55.

46   O Nmehielle *The African human rights system: Its laws, practice and institutions* (2001) 70.

47   C Hamalengwa, M Flinterman & V Dankwa (eds) *The international law of human rights in Africa* (1988) 104-110.

48   As above, 104.

49   R Murray & A Lloyd 'Institutions with responsibility for human rights protection under the African Union' (2004) 48/2 *Journal of African Law* 167.

agencies and helped the host states financially to support refugees who had fled their countries in Africa.[50] The OAU's role was also emphasised by the myriad conferences[51] and summits held to discuss the issue of conflicts and human rights affecting the continent, from which an array of treaties, protocols, declarations and communiqués emanated.[52] Other Commissions established under the organisation's Charter also had the mandate to consider human rights matters. These included the Labour and Social Affairs Commission, the Population Commission and the Women's Committee on Peace and Development.[53] All these initiatives evidenced a willingness by African states to see human rights as a matter within the OAU's remit.[54]

In spite of the above stated achievements, the OAU suffered a serious legitimacy crisis in as far as it remained passive while its members grossly violated human rights. The organisation was strongly accused for unduly emphasising the principle of non-interference in the internal affairs of its member states.[55] Similarly, during its tenure, many armed conflicts on the continent escaped its rather blind eye and deaf ear. Among its many failures, the OAU was generally criticised for its inability to halt the genocide in Rwanda, stop the civil war in Liberia, mitigate the crisis in Burundi and put an end to the conflict in the Democratic Republic of Congo (DRC).[56]

---

50   As above.

51   See, for example, the *Resolution on the Ministerial Conference on Human Rights in Africa*, CM/Res.1673 (LXIV); *Grand Bay Mauritius Declaration and Plan of Action, adopted by the Ministerial Conference on Human Rights* in April 1999, CONF/HRA/DECL (I).

52   For a discussion on all the legal instruments adopted by the OAU since its establishment, see generally, T Maluwa 'International law making in the Organisation of African Unity: An overview' (2000) 12 *African Journal of International and Comparative Law* 201.

53   This body was a joint initiative of the OAU and UN Economic Commission for Africa, to increase the participation of women in decision making on conflict at the international level. It is composed of government representatives, NGOs and individual experts and has a task of advising on conflict and gender-related issues.

54   Murray (n 30 above) 6.

55   U Umozurike 'The significance of the African Charter on Human and Peoples' Rights' (1997) 45.

56   See A Abass & M Baderin 'Towards effective collective security and human rights protection in Africa: An assessment of the Constitutive Act of the new African Union' (2002) 49 *Netherlands International Law Review* 12.

At the end of the Second Millennium, there was the need to consolidate development, peace and the respect for human rights on the continent.[57] This therefore provoked the transformation of the OAU to the AU whose Constitutive Act entails more human rights provisions than the OAU Charter. The evolution and normative parameters of the AU are discussed in detail elsewhere below. Meanwhile, it is important to note that it was during the subsistence of the OAU that the continent witnessed the evolution of its regional human rights mechanisms. However, as different scholars have argued, the creation of this system was not of the OAU's liking.[58] In fact, the OAU was utterly opposed to its formation for various reasons.

3.2   THE EMERGENCE OF AFRICA'S REGIONAL HUMAN RIGHTS MECHANISMS

The African human rights system is a product of prolonged negotiations from both within and outside the continent. Its emergence centres on a series of events that also instigated the rise and fall of the OAU.[59] The OAU leadership, for political expediency, resisted agitation by non-state actors for a proactive regional human rights system.[60] The incumbent OAU leaders were reluctant to embrace a human rights regime that would strictly define benchmarks for their compliance.[61] Given the alarming levels of violations and the attendant impunity, there was so much agitation that resistance by the OAU could no longer hold back reforms.

Notably the agitation for change had by then got the eye of the international community which precipitated international response

---

57   See K Kithure 'The normative and institutional framework of the African Union relating to the protection of human rights and the maintenance of international peace and security: A critical appraisal (2003) 3 *African Human Rights Law Journal* 99.

58   W Reisman 'Through or despite governments: Differentiated responsibilities in human rights programs' (1987) 72 *Iowa Law Review* 392; Dlamini (n 43 above) 68.

59   M Mbondenyi & N Sifuna 'A review of procedural and jurisdictional challenges in enforcing international human rights law under the African Charter regime' (2006) *Berkeley Legal Press Working paper No. 1869* at http://law.bepress.com/expresso/esps/1869 (accessed on 13 April 2010) 28.

60   Dlamini (n 43 above) 68.

61   W Reisman 'Through or despite governments: Differentiated responsibilities in human rights programs' (1987) 72 *Iowa Law Review* 392.

by powerful nations such as the US calling for a proactive human rights dispensation on the continent.[62] As Umozurike succinctly put it:

> Chief among these was the emphasis that President Carter placed on human rights in the international relations of the United States. The Helsinki Final Act of 1975, signed by the United States, Canada, and 33 European countries, emphasised respect for human rights. Watch committees were subsequently set up to monitor observance and this kept the issue alive in international politics. ... Though unsuccessful, an attempt was made to include human rights in the renewed EEC-A-C-P pact, the Lome II Convention. The stage was thus set both internally and externally for the debut of the African Charter on Human and Peoples' Rights.[63]

President Carter of the US promoted human rights in his African policy to the point of cutting off aid to Uganda and placing an embargo on the importation of coffee as a sanction against Idi Amin's violations of human rights.[64] In addition, the activities of the UN on human rights and the pressure of non-governmental organisations, especially Amnesty International, popularised and strengthened the demand for the respect and promotion of human rights on the continent.[65]

The search for a new human rights dispensation in Africa goes back to as early as 1961 when African jurists met in Lagos, Nigeria, under the auspices of the International Commission of Jurists (ICJ) and proposed the promulgation of a human rights Charter for Africa. The African Conference on the Rule of Law, as it was called, took steps to carry out the intentions of the ICJ to ensure global adherence to the rule of law principle.[66] Here, the Conference proclaimed the 'Law of Lagos', which stated, among other things:

---

62   As above.

63   Umozurike (n 55 above) 904; See also A Young-Anawaty 'Human rights and the ACP-EEC Lome: II Convention' (1980) 13 *New York University Journal of International Law & Policy* 63.

64   O Ojo & A Sesay 'The OAU and human rights: Prospects for the 1980s and beyond' (1986) 1/9 *Human Rights Quarterly* 92.

65   Young-Anawaty (n 63 above) 63.

66   Kannyo (n 42 above) 17.

That in order to give full effect to the Universal Declaration of Human Rights of 1948, this Conference invites the African governments to study the possibility of adopting an African Convention of Human Rights.[67]

Interestingly, the Conference also proposed the establishment of an African court of human rights, which proposal was temporarily abandoned during the drafting of the African Charter in favour of a more promotional-oriented Commission.[68] During the 1960s and 1970s the process towards the creation of a legal framework for human rights protection and promotion in Africa, began in Lagos, intensified, expressed through a series of conferences and seminars.[69] Some of the most important milestones of this process were the UN Human Rights Commission seminar in Cairo in 1967 pressing for the establishment of an African human rights commission,[70] and the 1971 seminar in Addis Ababa which adopted this proposal.[71] It was common cause that regional human rights commissions would be meaningful if set up by the members of the regions themselves and not imposed from outside.[72]

The UN Human Rights Commission then advised the UN Secretary-General to organise seminars in those regions where no human rights commissions existed with a view to discussing their need.[73] In 1969, another UN seminar was held in Cairo, Egypt, at the close of which the participants, including 19 African states, requested the UN Secretary-General to, *inter alia*, communicate the report and its recommendations to the OAU Secretary-General and members. One of the recommendations was the setting up of a

---

67   Quoted in L Lindholt *Questioning the universality of human rights: The African Charter on Human and Peoples Rights in Botswana, Malawi and Mozambique* (1997) 73.

68   As above.

69   Nmehielle (n 46 above) 70.

70   Later in 1967, jurists from Francophone African states meeting in Dakar, Senegal, reiterated this call. See W Seriti 'The African Charter on Human Rights' (1995) 6/1 *African Law Review* 13.

71   As above.

72   As above.

73   Umozurike (n 55 above) 904.

regional commission in Africa that would be fully supported by the OAU member states.[74]

The Cairo seminar opened the floodgate for other seminars, meetings and conferences in various parts of Africa. These were held in Lusaka, Zambia in 1970;[75] Addis Ababa, Ethiopia in 1971;[76] Yaoundé, Cameroon in 1971;[77] Libreville, Gabon in 1971;[78] and Dar-es-Salaam, Tanzania in 1973.[79] Most of these meetings echoed the urgent need for an African human rights commission or some other regional human rights protection mechanism.[80]

Another significant event worth mentioning here was the ICJ seminar on 'Human Rights in a One-Party State' co-hosted with the government of Tanzania in 1976. The seminar drew up the important conclusions that human rights included both 'individual and collective rights', and stated that the establishment of civil and political rights must go hand in hand with the promotion of economic, social and cultural rights. These statements were to represent some of the most characteristic aspects of the African Charter.[81]

Later, seminars took place in 1978 in Butare, Rwanda and in Dakar, Senegal, both under the heading 'Human Rights and Economic Development in Francophone Africa'.[82] The seminar

---

74   As above.

75   'Seminar on the Realisation of Economic and Social Rights with particular reference to the Developing countries', Lusaka, Zambia, 23 June-4 July 1970.

76   'Conference of African jurists on (the) African legal process and the individual', Addis Ababa, Ethiopia, 19-23 April 1971.

77   'Seminar on measures to be taken on National Level for the implementation of the United Nations Instrument Aimed at Combating and Eliminating Racial Discrimination and for the Promotion of Harmonious Race Relations', Yaoundé, Cameroon, 16-29 June 1971.

78   'Seminar on the Participation of Women in Economic Life', Libreville, Gabon, 27-29 August 1971.

79   'Seminar on the study of New Ways and Means for Promoting Human Rights with special Attention to the Problems and Needs of Africa, Dar-es-Salaam', Tanzania, 23 October-5 November 1973.

80   C Dlamini 'Towards a regional protection of human rights in Africa: The African Charter on Human and Peoples' Rights' (1991) *XXIV CILSA* 189.

81   E Bello 'Human rights: African developments' *Encyclopaedia of Public International Law* (1985) 287.

82   As above.

in Dakar was particularly important since it succeeded in drafting concrete proposals for a human rights document. Here, President Sengor of Senegal agreed to sponsor a draft resolution which would provide for an African human rights commission. Furthermore, he delegated Keba M'baye, President of the Supreme Court of Senegal and a judge of the ICJ, to draft a text on human rights, which was later to form the basis of the African Charter.[83]

In more than one respect the road had then been paved for the initiation of the process that would result in the elaboration and adoption of the African Charter. The founding principles had already been laid down and even more significant was perhaps the OAU's constructive change of policy towards more direct interference against the massive human rights violations in some African states.[84] Significant in this respect was the establishment of the Bokassa inquiry in May 1979, where an independent OAU Commission of five judges from the Ivory Coast, Liberia, Rwanda, Senegal and Togo publicised its findings of substantive violations of human rights.[85] Unable to bear the intense pressure and agitation for a regional human rights mechanism, the OAU caved in to the demands.

At a summit held in Monrovia in July 1979, the OAU resolved to facilitate the process of establishing a pan-continental commission on human rights.[86] Later in the same year the UN convened another seminar to discuss the possibility of establishing an African human rights Commission. The outcome of these meetings was the establishment of a working group to draft concrete proposals for the creation of an African Commission on Human Rights.[87] The actual drafting process of the Charter began with the first meeting of experts in Dakar, in November and December 1979, which

---

83   G Naldi *The Organisation of African Unity* (1989) 110.

84   Bello (n 81 above) 290.

85   As above.

86   This conference was preceded by a symposium organised by the OAU Secretariat in Monrovia, Liberia, from 12-16 February 1979, to discuss the theme 'What kind of Africa by the year 2000?' Experts in various fields attended the symposium.

87   'UN seminar on the Establishment of Regional Commissions on Human Rights with Special Reference to Africa', Monrovia, 10-21 September 1979, UN Doc. ST/HR/SER.A/4 (1979); See also Kannyo (n 42 above) 28.

produced a draft 'specifically suited to cater for the special problems relating to human rights in Africa.'[88]

The next step was for the Ministers of Justice of the OAU member states to review the draft. The first meeting in this regard, held in March 1980 in Addis Ababa, failed to materialise, mainly due to political reasons. Subsequently, however, the Council of Ministers managed to meet twice in Banjul, Gambia, although the first of these sessions in June 1980 was unsuccessful, resulting in the review of only 11 articles at the end of the session.[89] The basis for these difficulties was mainly the lack of consensus and a general atmosphere of suspicion among some delegates, and a prevailing tendency to maintain a cautious attitude on certain subjects.[90]

Fortunately, the tension diffused remarkably at the second meeting of ministers in January 1981, also in Banjul, and in only two weeks the delegates succeeded in fully revisiting and adopting the text of the Charter.[91] In January 1981, the preliminary draft of the African Charter on Human and Peoples' Rights was finally adopted by the OAU Council of Ministers with some modifications. The 18th Assembly of Heads of State and Government later adopted the Charter in its session held in Nairobi, Kenya.[92] In accordance with its Article 63(3), the Charter was to come into force 3 months after a simple majority of the member states of the OAU had ratified or acceded to it. The number of member states of the OAU was at that time 50, and a simple majority therefore meant that 26 states would have to ratify the Charter in accordance with the provisions of article 63(1) and (2) in order for it to come into force.[93]

The process of ratification of the Charter was initially slow, with only one state ratifying it in 1981, five in 1982 and in 1983, and four

---

88   Bello (n 81 above) 30.

89   Lindholt (n 67 above) 80.

90   As above.

91   Bello (n 81 above) 30.

92   This was on the 26 of June 1981.

93   Lindholt (n 67 above) 80.

in 1984.[94] No state ratified the Charter in 1985, giving way to grave speculations and widespread scepticism about its future. In 1986, however, as many as 13 states ratified it, leading to its entry into force on 21 October.[95] Lindholt argued that the period of five years from the adoption of the Charter to its coming into force was not unduly long, considering the fact that the UN Covenants took eleven years to accomplish the same.[96]

The adoption of the Charter heralded the establishment of the African Commission on Human and Peoples' Rights. This Commission was formally initiated on November 2, 1987 and its Banjul Headquarters were established in mid-1989. The time span between the initiation of the Commission and the establishment of its headquarters in Banjul speaks volumes about the 'cold reception' it got from its political principal, the OAU. Bello tried to explain this phenomenon by observing that:

> Apart from concern held by governments, who were clearly unwilling to give up too fast their chosen policy of violating human and peoples' rights for fear of losing comfortable privileges and positions, a substantial number of African leaders since the days of independence in the mid-sixties regarded almost all jurisdictional bodies, particularly of an international nature, with suspicion, and therefore were hesitant, at best, to accept supra-national provisions regarding human and peoples' rights.[97]

---

94   Egypt ratified the African Charter on 20 March 1984 and reserved as follows: 'Article 8 (freedom of conscience, religion and the professions) and Article 18(3) (elimination of discrimination against women and the protection of women and children) are subject to Islamic laws, while Article 9 (right to receive and impart information) is subject to Egyptian law.' Zambia ratified on 10 January 1984 subject to the following reservations: Article 13(3) should read: 'Every individual shall have the right of access to any place, services or public property intended for use by the general public.' Zambia also wanted an article additional to article 62 so that states that have neither ratified nor acceded should render periodic reports on their human rights situations and the difficulties that prevent ratification or adherence. See U Umozurike *The African Charter on Human and Peoples' Rights* (1997) 27. Lindholt (n 67 above) 80.

95   For a detailed exposition of the Charter see, for example, R D'Sa 'Human and Peoples' Rights: Distinctive features of the African Charter' (1985) *Journal of African Law* 73.

96   Lindholt (n 67 above) 80.

97   Bello (n 81 above) 135.

The fact that the Charter has today been ratified by all the AU member states, however, indicates the growing commitment and willingness, at least on paper, of African states to improve the state of human and peoples' rights on the continent.

Although it has been said to be a 'faulty document', the African Charter is on record as the first major attempt by African leaders to establish regional mechanisms for the implementation of the human rights of Africans.[98] It reaffirms the support of African leaders for the protection of human rights and freedoms, as declared in the UDHR.[99] Having thus given consent to the internationalisation of human rights, African leaders can no longer plead that human rights are matters reserved exclusively for the domestic jurisdiction. Consequently, the concept of 'state sovereignty' will no longer provide a cover up for grave breaches of human rights.[100]

Like its counterparts, the European Convention on Human Rights and Fundamental Freedoms and the Inter-American Convention on Human Rights, the African Charter entails a catalogue of rights. These rights shall be discussed in detail elsewhere below. However, it is important to note that despite the international acclaim that heralded the adoption of the Charter, and its subsequent entry into force, the demand for its reform began barely within five years of its existence.[101] One reason for this demand is its failure to provide for adequate or effective enforcement institutions. For example, it has been argued that, while the African Commission has an elaborate promotional mandate, it does not possess sufficient protective powers.[102]

---

98   As above.

99   See the African Charter's preamble.

100   See this argument in G Mugwanya *Human rights in Africa: Enhancing human rights through the African regional human rights system* (2003) 31-32.

101   For a comprehensive discussion on the inadequacies of the African Charter and its possible reforms, see generally, Heyns (n 27 above); M Mbondenyi 'Improving the substance and content of civil and political rights under the African human rights system' (2007) 17/2 *Lesotho Law Journal* 39-105; Nmehielle (n 46 above); E Ankumah *The African Commission on Human and Peoples' Rights* (1997) 111-176.

102   See this argument in, among others, Nmehielle (n 46 above) 236; E Ankumah *The African Commission on Human and Peoples' Rights* (1996) 74-75.

There was therefore the need to supplement the Commission's mandate by creating other institutional mechanisms, such as a regional human rights court. At another level, it was necessary to transform moribund institutions, such as the OAU. Such transformation eventually witnessed the creation of new institutional mechanisms and programmes such as the New Partnership for Africa's Development (NEPAD) and the African Peer Review Mechanism (APRM).

Consequently, the beginning of an important chapter in the history of regional promotion and protection of human rights on the continent was opened. What follows therefore is a discussion on the evolution of the African human rights system from its initial status, under the OAU and the African Commission's regimes, to the present status, under the AU and the African Court on Human and Peoples' Rights.

3.3   THE EVOLUTION OF THE AFRICAN HUMAN RIGHTS SYSTEM TO ITS PRESENT STATUS

From the 1990s, there has been a rapid transformation in the international human rights discourse which by extension has affected regional promotion and protection of human rights in Africa. This period witnessed what has been described as the 'New World Order', whose dictates have led to both positive and negative consequences in the protection and promotion of human rights. The New World Order actually began with the collapse of the Berlin wall in 1989, which in turn marked the beginning of the end of the ideological division between the East and the West.[103]

As this process continued, African states struggled to integrate themselves continentally through increased sub-regional and regional coalitions and associations. By losing the benefits of East-West ideological divisions, they not only lost the political and ideological protection they had enjoyed since independence and throughout the Cold War era, but also became vulnerable as their Western allies turned their backs on those regimes whose outrageous human rights records had previously been 'overlooked' in the interests of retaining

---

103   Mugwanya (n 100 above) 20.

'African friends' for strategic, economic, political, military and other reasons.[104]

With the end of the Cold War, the West applied new conditions and pressures on those African governments that were perceived to be perpetuating human rights abuses.[105] Pressure was exerted in different ways, including political isolation, economic embargos and the use of political force.[106] This forced African states to embark on a series of initiatives, meetings and conferences aimed at purging the continent's poor human rights record. These initiatives were a marked departure from the passiveness to human rights issues previously displayed by a majority of the states.

Most importantly, the Second World Conference on Human Rights held in Vienna, Austria, in 1993, perhaps inspired the positive attitude of African governments to human rights. The greatest demonstration of Africa's determination to improve its human rights situation occurred when the African Ministers of Justice and Attorneys-General met in Tunis in November 1992 to prepare an 'African Position Paper' that was presented during that conference.[107] At the end of this meeting, they had adopted an 'African Declaration of the Regional Meeting for Africa of the World Conference on Human Rights'. In this Declaration, stress was laid on 'the need to promote and protect human rights everywhere in Africa by all concerned institutions, groups and individuals, as well as by governments, national institutions, non-governmental organisations and other bodies.'[108]

The main objective of the 1993 conference was to set out the parameters of international human rights law. In its Declaration and Programme of Action, it was categorically stated:

> The promotion and protection of all human rights and fundamental freedoms must be considered as a priority objective of the United

---

104   W Eno 'The African Commission on Human and Peoples' Rights as an instrument for the protection of human rights in Africa' (1998) *LLM Thesis University of South Africa* 38.

105   As above.

106   As above.

107   M Nowak *Introduction to the international human rights regime* (2003) 26.

108   As above.

Nations in accordance with its purposes and principles, in particular the purpose of international cooperation. In the framework of these purposes and principles, the promotion and protection of all human rights is a legitimate concern of the international community.[109]

In spite of the outcome of the conference, violations of human rights increased during the 1990s due to the prevailing political situations in various parts of Africa, most notably Burundi, the DRC (formerly Zaire), Liberia, Nigeria, Sierra Leone, Rwanda, South Africa and the Sudan. At the same time, demands and pressure on African governments to enhance the promotion of human rights both locally and internationally were also intensified.[110] This forced African governments to individually and collectively embark on efforts to resolve internal and regional conflicts in order to protect human rights.

A number of meetings and conferences were therefore convened to look for ways to articulate human rights in the continent's agenda. These conferences include the Grand Bay (Mauritius), Kigali (Rwanda), Cairo (Egypt) and Algiers (Algeria) conferences. Some of the conferences and summits led to the establishment of the AU, NEPAD, APRM and the African Court on Human and Peoples' Rights.

3.3.1   THE TRANSFORMATION OF THE OAU TO AU

On 8 and 9 September 1999, forty-four African leaders met in Sirte, Libya at an Extraordinary Summit of the OAU called by Muammar Gaddafi, to discuss the formation of a 'United States of Africa.'[111] The theme of this Summit was 'Strengthening OAU's capacity to enable it to meet the challenges of the new millennium.' At this meeting, the Sirte Declaration[112] was adopted, calling for, among other things, the establishment of the AU.[113] The legal parameters of the Union were to be defined by the legal experts who were

---

109   See the Vienna Declaration and Programme of Action, art 4.

110   Nowak (n 107 above) 26.

111   (1999) 36 *Africa Research Bulletin* 13677.

112   OAU Doc EAHG/Dec1 (IV) Rev 1, reprinted in (1999) 7 *African Yearbook of International Law* 411.

113   Para 8(ii) Sirte Declaration.

instructed to model it like the European Union (EU), taking into account the Charter of the OAU and the Treaty establishing the African Economic Community (AEC).[114]

The OAU legal unit then drafted the Constitutive Act of the African Union (herein 'CAAU' or 'the Act'). The draft Act was debated in a meeting of legal experts and parliamentarians and later at a Ministerial Conference held in Tripoli from 31 May to 2 June 2000.[115] The involvement of the African parliamentarians was intended to ensure that the Union becomes more closely connected with the people. The Act was adopted by the OAU AHSG in Lomé in July 2000.[116]

All members of the OAU had signed the Act by March 2001,[117] and therefore the OAU Assembly, at its 5th extraordinary summit held in Sirte, Libya from 1 to 2 March 2001 declared the establishment of the AU.[118] However, for the Union to be operationalised, the CAAU had to be ratified by two-thirds of the member states of the OAU.[119] This was achieved on 26 April 2001 when Nigeria became the thirty-sixth OAU member state to deposit its instrument of ratification.[120] The AU became a reality a month later, when the Act entered into force.

The CAAU is more responsive to human rights than its predecessor, the OAU Charter. This is clear in its preamble, objectives and guiding principles. For instance, one of its objectives is to promote and protect human and peoples' rights in accordance with

---

114   (1999) 36 *Africa Research Bulletin* 13678.

115   Para 247, OAU Secretary-General report <http://www.oau-oua.org/LOMÉ2000/ENGLISH%20INTRO%Note%20SG.htm> (accessed 3 May 2010).

116   36th ordinary session of the Assembly held in Lomé, Togo 10-11 July 2000.

117   OAU 'Decision on the Africa Union' 5th OAU extraordinary session of the Assembly of the Heads of State and Government 1-2 March 2001 Sirte, Libya EAHG/Dec 1-4 (V).

118   As above.

119   The CAAU entered into force 30 days after the deposit of the instruments of ratification by two- thirds of the members of the OAU. See art 28 of CAAU.

120   OAU 'The Constitutive Act of the African Union attains the legal requirement for entering into force. Press release No 52/2001 at <http://www.oau- oua.org/oau_info/pressrelease/PRESS%20RELEASE%20NO%2052-%202001.htm>(accessed 3 May 2010).

the African Charter and other relevant human rights instruments.[121] This provision, which concretises the relationship between the regional human rights system and its political affiliate, the AU, is an indication of the latter's resolve to take human rights issues seriously.[122] The human rights provisions of the CAAU are been discussed at length in a separate chapter below.

The CAAU also provides for the creation of organs within the AU framework, some of which could be used to enhance the promotion and protection of human rights on the continent.[123] These organs include the Assembly of the Union, the Executive Council, the Pan-African Parliament, the Court of Justice, the Commission, the Permanent Representative Committee (PRC), the Specialised Technical Committees (STCs), the Economic, Social and Cultural Council, and the Financial Institutions.

It is inevitable to note that the transformation of the OAU to AU ushered in a new dimension to regional enforcement of human rights in Africa. While the full impact of the Union is yet to be seen or felt, its inception is a bold step intended to further the realisation of human rights in the region. Its Constitutive Act is also an instrument that somehow strengthens the African human rights system. Noteworthy, the creation of the AU culminated in a series of other activities of relevance to the human rights discourse in the region. For example, the Union held its 'First AU Ministerial Conference on Human Rights in Africa' in May 2003, which culminated in the adoption of the Kigali Declaration.[124]

This Declaration forms the basis of the revised agenda of the AU on human rights in Africa.[125] It reaffirmed the AU member states' commitment to the objectives and principles contained in the CAAU, the African Charter on Human and Peoples' Rights, the solemn Declaration of the Conference on Security, Stability,

---

121   CAAU, art 3(h).

122   CAAU, art 3(g). See also E Baimu 'The African Union: Hope for a better protection of human rights in Africa? (2001) 2 *African Human Rights Law Journal* 311.

123   CAAU, art 5(1) & (2).

124   Kigali Declaration, MIN/CONF/HRA/Decl. 1(I), adopted at the First AU Ministerial Conference on Human Rights in Africa, 8 May 2003.

125   See Murray & Lloyd (n 49 above) 172.

Development and Cooperation in Africa (CSSDCA), the NEPAD, the Declaration on the Code of Conduct on relations between states, all relevant AU declarations and decisions as well as the UN Charter and the UDHR and the Vienna Declaration of 1993.

The Kigali Declaration should therefore be seen as an added impetus to the human rights revolution that has been sweeping across the continent particularly at the dawn of the new Millennium. It is expected that many more developments will be made in this regard. In fact, many other conferences, of relevance to human rights promotion and protection in the region, took place before and after the Kigali Conference.[126] It is unfortunate that most of these conferences ended with declarations which are anything but binding on states. Some of the conferences, however, have been productive in the sense that they ushered in new developments in the human rights agenda of the continent. For example, it was in such conferences where the NEPAD and APRM were conceived and born.

3.3.2   THE NEW PARTNERSHIP FOR AFRICA'S DEVELOPMENT (NEPAD) AND THE AFRICAN PEER REVIEW MECHANISM (APRM)

The emergence of the NEPAD and the APRM is an indication that regional enforcement of human rights in Africa is rapidly evolving. NEPAD is a programme that started off as the Millennium Africa Recovery Plan (MAP) conceived by Presidents Mbeki of South Africa, Obasanjo of Nigeria and Bouteflika of Algeria in the year 2000.[127] MAP merged with the 'OMEGA plan', developed by President Wade of Senegal, to form the New African Initiative (NAI) in July 2001. The title NAI was later changed to NEPAD in October 2001.[128]

---

126   For example, the Grand Bay Conference, Algiers Conference, Cairo Conference and Sirte Summit, among others.

127   See J Ohiorhenuan 'NEPAD and dialectics of African underdevelopment' (2002) 7 *New Agenda* 10.

128   Para 5(b) of the Communiqué issued at the end of the first meeting of the HSIC, Abuja, Nigeria, 23 October 2001.

The MAP document had its immediate origins in the OAU summit held in Togo in July 2000. This summit mandated former Presidents Mbeki of South Africa, Obasanjo of Nigeria and Bouteflika of Algeria to engage Western countries with a view to developing a partnership for the renaissance of the continent.[129] Around the same time, the newly elected president of Senegal, Wade, conceived a plan titled OMEGA.[130] The MAP and OMEGA plans were presented, respectively, by Presidents Obasanjo and Wade during the fifth Extraordinary Summit of the OAU held in Sirte, Libya from 1 to 2 March 2001.[131]

Recognising the synergies and complementarities between the two plans on continent-wide development, the Sirte Summit recommended their integration.[132] The decision to have a single, coordinated African plan was premised on the need to avoid confusing Africa's partners, diffusing the focus, eroding capacity, splitting resources and undermining the credibility of the plans.[133] The result of this merger, which was finalised on 3 July 2001, was NAI. The NAI was approved by the 37th OAU Assembly of Heads of State and Government held in Lusaka in July 2001.[134] The NAI had to be reorganised to clear repetition and inconsistencies emanating from the hasty merger of the MAP and OMEGA plans. The finalisation of the NAI document was achieved on 23 October 2001, when its name was also changed to NEPAD.[135]

Later, the AU inaugural summit held in July 2002 in Durban, South Africa, adopted a Declaration on the implementation of

---

129   Para 321 of the OAU Secretary-General Report (2001). Pursuant to this mandate, the three leaders relentlessly engaged the industrialised countries in the north and multi-lateral organisations on the partnership at various fora. For example, the three leaders made a presentation on the MAP at the World Economic Forum in Davos in January 2001.

130   Para 323 of the OAU Secretary-General Report (2001).

131   As above, para 318.

132   E Baimu 'Human rights in NEPAD and its implications for the African human rights system' (2002) 2 *African Human Rights Law Journal* 303.

133   As above.

134   See OAU Declaration on the New African Initiative [MAP and OMEGA] 37th ordinary session of the Assembly of the Heads of State and Government of the OAU, July 2001 Lusaka, Zambia, OAU Doc AHG/Decl 1 (XXXVII) para 9.

135   See Baimu (n 132 above) 303.

NEPAD, endorsing the NEPAD Progress Report and Initial Action Plan[136] and encouraging AU member states to adopt the NEPAD Declaration on Democracy, Political, Economic and Corporate Governance (DDPECG)[137] and to accede to APRM.[138] The APRM was officially launched during the 9th summit of the Heads of State and Government Implementation Committee (HSGIC), held in Kigali, Rwanda in February 2004.

Generally, NEPAD should be seen as a strategic framework for Africa's renewal, practically designed to support the vision, objectives and principles of the AU.[139] Although it is an economic development programme, it emphasises that human rights, peace and development are interdependent matters.[140] The initiative has a number of implementation mechanisms, the main ones being: the HSGIC, its Secretariat and the APRM.[141]

The APRM is 'an instrument voluntarily acceded to by member states of the African Union as an African self-monitoring mechanism.'[142] Participation in the APRM is open to all AU member states on a voluntary basis. The mechanism entails a series of reviews[143] which include visits to the country under review by a Panel of Eminent Experts.[144] A detailed discussion on the NEPAD and APRM and their relevance to human rights promotion in Africa is conducted in the chapter dealing with the African Union, its organs and initiatives.

---

136   Doc AHG/235 (XXXVIII).

137   As above, Annex I.

138   As above, Annex II (APRM Base Document).

139   See 'NEPAD in brief', available at http://www.nepad.org/2005/files/inbrief.php (accessed 1 March 2010).

140   See W Nagan 'Implementing the African Renaissance: Making human rights comprehensive for the new millennium', available at http://www.cha.uga.edu/CHA-CITS/Nagan_paper.pdf (accessed 1 March 2010).

141   C Heyns 'The African regional human rights system: The African Charter' (2004) 108/3 *Penn State Law Review* 684.

142   See NEPAD Document, Doc AHG/235 (XXXVIII), para 28.

143   African Peer Review Mechanism, Annex II, para 13.

144   As above, paras 5 & 6.

3.3.3   THE ESTABLISHMENT OF THE AFRICAN COURT ON HUMAN AND PEOPLES' RIGHTS

Following the creation of the African Commission and the consequent dissatisfaction with its output, efforts were directed at the establishment of a pan-continental human rights court. The idea of a regional court, however, generated another debate of almost a similar magnitude to the one that preceded the creation of the African Commission. For instance, at the Third Afro-Americo-European Conference held in Strasbourg in June 1992, some of the participants were of the view that the creation of an African court should be postponed to a later stage.[145] They argued that, given the financial difficulties facing the Commission, it would have been unwise to establish another pan-continental human rights institution at that time.[146] Without underestimating the importance of a court, it was therefore deemed wise to strengthen the Commission and revert to the issue of the court at the appropriate future time.

After prolonged discussions in subsequent meetings, it was resolved that a Protocol creating a regional human rights court for Africa should be drafted. The process of drafting the Protocol was initiated at a Summit of Heads of State and Government of the OAU in Tunis in June 1994.[147] A resolution adopted at this Summit requested the Secretary-General of the OAU to convene a meeting of government experts to examine ways of enhancing efficiency of the African Commission and to consider in particular the question of the establishment of an African Court on Human and Peoples' Rights. A Draft Protocol, prepared by the OAU Secretariat, was submitted to a meeting of government experts in Cape Town, South Africa, in September 1995.[148]

The Cape Town meeting was followed by a number of intermediary meetings, until the meeting of Ministers of Justice in

---

145   W Benedek & W Heinz (eds) *Regional systems of human rights protection in Africa, America and Europe: Third Afro-Americo-European Conference, Strasbourg, June 1992* (1992).

146   As above.

147   Nmehielle (n 46 above) 255.

148   Resolution no. AHG 230 (XXX), doc. OAU/LEG/EXP/AFC/HPR, September 1995.

December 1997 at which the draft Protocol was adopted, before being ratified by the Summit of Heads of State and Government in Ouagadougou, Burkina Faso on 9 June 1998. The Protocol came into force on the 25th of January 2004, after the fifteenth instruments of ratification was deposited by Comoros.[149]

Meanwhile, the Protocol to the AU Court of Justice, whose creation is mandated by the CAAU, was also being drafted. This therefore meant that two regional courts would operate under the AU. Fortunately, in July 2004, the Assembly of Heads of State and Government (AHSG) resolved to merge the Court of Justice and the regional human rights court.[150] The motivation for such a merger was financial expediency.[151] However, due to the prolongation of the negotiations on the intended merger, it was deemed proper to go ahead with the operationalisation of the human rights court. Hence, on 2 July 2006, the first eleven Judges of the court were sworn in.[152]

The establishment of the court was applauded as a milestone towards the strengthening of the African human rights system.[153] Given the continent's history of serious human rights violations, the court is a significant development in the protection of human rights at the regional level. The adoption of the Protocol thus demonstrated a resolve by African governments to realise the spirit of the African Charter and ensure the protection of human rights in Africa.[154] It is expected that through the court, victims of human rights violations or their representatives would have recourse to judicial redress.

It is equally expected that the Court will provide the right forum to articulate international law principles. At the same

---

149   See Explanatory Notes to the Protocol to the African Charter On the Establishment of an African Court on Human and Peoples' Rights 1 (6-12 September 1995), Cape Town South Africa.

150   See paras 4 & 5 of Assembly/AU/Dec 45(III). See also F Viljoen & E Baimu 'Courts for Africa: Considering the co-existence of the African Court on Human and Peoples' Rights and the African Court of justice' (2004) 22/2 *Netherlands Quarterly of Human Rights* 241-267.

151   As above.

152   See Viljoen (n 28 above) iii.

153   See Amnesty International, *Credibility in question: Proposals for improving the efficiency and effectiveness of the African Commission on Human and Peoples' Rights*, AI Index: IOR 63/02/1998.

154   As above.

time, it is supposed that domestic courts in Africa will look to it for direction and precedents in their application of human rights instruments at the domestic level.[155] Ultimately, the Court could be an important institution in the realisation of human and peoples' rights in the region. When the African Charter was adopted and the Commission established, Africa was the continent with the worst human rights record in the world.[156] Although this position might not have changed significantly, it is hoped that the establishment of the Court will transform the regional human rights landscape.[157]

---

155   As above.

156   J Joiner 'Beyond commitments, towards practical action' in E Sall & L Wohlgemuth (eds) *Human rights, regionalism and the dilemmas of democracy in Africa* (2006) 19.

157   See generally the argument in A Mangu 'The Changing human rights landscape in Africa: Organisation of African Unity, African Union, New Partnership for Africa's Development and the African Court' (2005) 23/3 *Netherlands Quarterly of Human Rights* 380.

PART II

THE NORMATIVE INSTRUMENTS OF THE AFRICAN SYSTEM ON HUMAN AND PEOPLES' RIGHTS

CHAPTER 4

THE CONSTITUTIVE ACT OF THE AFRICAN UNION

The Constitutive Act of the African Union (hereafter 'CAAU' or 'the Act') is the treaty that establishes the African Union (AU), the political institution within whose framework the African human rights system operates. Its adoption by the Organisation of African Unity (OAU) Assembly of Heads of State and Government (AHSG) in 2000[1] can be said to have been an attempt to transform Africa's human rights landscape. The Act places the promotion and protection of human rights in the agenda of the AU, something which was not visible in the OAU Charter.[2]

The inferior status of human rights in the OAU Charter affected their promotion and protection on the continent. Under the Charter, the rights of OAU member states superseded those of individuals, thus giving credence to authoritarianism, single-party or military rule, armed conflicts and the whole host of human rights violations experienced during the subsistence of the organisation.[3] Specifically, Article III of the Charter was a safe haven for states that perpetrated gross human rights violations. Pursuant thereto, OAU member states solemnly affirmed and declared their adherence to principles such as: the sovereign equality of all member states; non-interference in the internal affairs of states; and respect for the sovereignty and territorial integrity of each state and for its inalienable right to independent existence.[4]

---

1   36th ordinary session of the Assembly held in Lomé, Togo 10-11 July 2000.

2   According to the preamble of the Act, member states pledge their determination to promote and protect human and peoples' rights, consolidate democratic institutions and culture and to ensure good governance and the rule of law.

3   See this observation in A Mangu 'The changing human rights landscape in Africa: Organisation of African Unity, African Union, New Partnership for Africa's Development and the Human Rights Court' (2005) 23/3 *Netherlands Quarterly of Human Rights* 383.

4   See Charter of the Organisation of African Unity, art III.

These principles effectively locked out any attempt by the international community to intervene in a state that violated its citizens' rights. The principles also perpetuated double standards in the sense that, whereas violations of the rights of African peoples by colonial powers could not be countenanced[5], it was permissible for African leaders to do the same on their people without being reproved by the rest of the world. It is not surprising that this rather extreme assertion of sovereignty evolved by the OAU leadership kept human rights outside the political and diplomatic priorities of the continent until the very end of the 20th century.[6]

Due to such double standards, coupled with the rising impunity on the continent, there was mounting pressure on African leaders to change their approach to human rights. This led to the adoption and ratification of a number of pan-continental human rights instruments. It also led to the disbandment of the defunct OAU and the establishment of the AU, whose Constitutive Act has been hailed by many scholars for entrenching the culture of human rights on the continent. For example, whereas Mangu considered the adoption of the Act as a major contribution to changing the human rights landscape in Africa[7], Murray saw it as evidence of an approach towards incorporating human rights in the activities of the OAU/AU.[8]

Although the Act is not a source of substantive rights, its emphasis on human rights protection and promotion in the region and its establishment of the 'political institutions' of the African human rights system needs to be underscored. The importance of this instrument cannot be ignored owing to the fact that the regional human rights system was not only founded by the OAU/AU but also, to a large extent, if not entirely, depends on this pan-continental political body for its survival. Due to its strategic position, the OAU/AU has contributed generously to the promises, prospects and pitfalls of the African human rights system.

---

5   As above, arts I(c)-(d) & III(6).

6   C Odinkalu 'Back to the future: The imperative of prioritising for the protection of human rights in Africa' (2003) *Journal of African Law* 2.

7   Mangu (n 3 above) 388.

8   R Murray *Human rights in Africa: From the OAU to the African Union* (2004) 267.

4.1 STRUCTURE AND FEATURES OF THE CONSTITUTIVE ACT OF THE AU

The Act consists of 33 Articles. Although it retained a number of the purposes and principles of the OAU, it goes further to include new objectives and principles aimed at promoting and protecting human rights on the continent. In principal, it reiterates the determination of the African Heads of States and Government to 'promote and protect human and peoples' rights, consolidate democratic institutions and culture, and to ensure good governance and the rule of law.'[9] This explains why a number of the principles and objectives of the AU entrenched in the Act relate to human rights promotion and protection. These objectives and principles shall be discussed elsewhere below.

One remarkable feature of the Act is the imposition of sanctions on members that fail to comply with the decisions and policies of the AU.[10] Notably, there was no such provision in the OAU Charter. Although it may be debatable how far this provision has been put in practice, the decision to suspend the Central African Republic from participating in the AU policy organs as a result of the *coup d'etat* in March 2003 at least offered a ray of hope for its implementation.[11] It is also encouraging to note that the provision was implemented against Madagascar, which was barred from the AU inauguration Summit in 2002, because of doubts over the legitimacy of its president.[12] The state was however re-admitted in 2003, at the second AU Summit.[13]

The Act also provides for the creation of organs within the AU framework, some of which could be useful in the promotion

---

9   See the preamble to the CAAU.

10   Art 23 provides as follows: '2 ... any member state that fails to comply with the decisions and policies of the Union may be subjected to other sanctions, such as the denial of transport and communications links with other member states, and other measures of a political and economic nature to be determined by the Assembly.'

11   Ninetieth Ordinary Session of the Central Organ of the Mechanism for Conflict Prevention, Management and Resolution at Ambassadorial Level, 17 March 2003, Communique, Central Organ/MEC/AMB/Comm.(XC).

12   R Cornwell 'Madagascar: First Test for the African Union' (2003) 12 *African Security Review* 1.

13   'Decision on the situation in Madagascar Ass/Au/Dec. 7 (I), available at http://www.au2003.gov.mz/key_documentation/audecis1.htm (accessed on 13 May 2010).

and protection of human rights on the continent.[14] The roles and relevance of these organs in augmenting the African human rights system have been highlighted elsewhere in this book. However, in order for them to have the desired impact there is the need to equip these organs with ample resources, both material and human.

It is unfortunate that the Act has retained the OAU's infamous principle of non-interference in the internal affairs of member states.[15] This principle, in the main, accounted for the failure of the OAU to address human rights violations perpetrated by its member states.[16] However, unlike the OAU Charter which blatantly prohibited interference with the internal affairs of its member states, the Act is commendable because it permits intervention in respect of grave circumstances, namely: war crimes, genocide and crimes against humanity.[17] It also provides for the right of member states to request intervention from the AU in order to restore peace and security.[18]

The scope of the right to intervene in a member state provided for in the Act is however not satisfactory because most of the human rights violations in Africa do not reach the levels of war crimes, genocide or crimes against humanity. What the Act seems to suggest is that other forms of violations of human rights are not important to the AU, as long as they have not reached the magnitude or status of genocide, war crimes or crimes against humanity. Article 4(h) of the Act, therefore, keeps other forms of human rights violations outside the purview of the AU's intervention.[19]

The right to intervene as entrenched in the Act also presents some problems. First, it conflicts with a number of other principles

---

14   As above, art 5(1) & (2).

15   CAAU, art 4(g).

16   O Nmehielle *The African human rights system: Its laws, practice and institutions* (2001). Nmehielle observed that the notable principle that has always stood in the way of the human rights agenda in Africa is the principle of non-intervention in internal affairs of states enshrined in Article III(2).

17   CAAU, art 4(h).

18   As above, art 4(j). See 'African Union: A new opportunity for the promotion and protection of human rights in Africa' (*AI Index*: IOR 63/0002/2002).

19   See E Baimu 'The African Union: Hope for a better protection of human rights in Africa? (2001) 2 *African Human Rights Law Journal* 314.

in the Act, such as 'sovereign equality and interdependence among member states',[20] 'respect of borders existing on achievement of independence'[21], 'prohibition on the use of force or threat to use force among member states'[22], and 'non-interference by any member states in the internal affairs of another.'[23] Secondly, the right of the AU to intervene in a member state conflicts with the UN Charter, which provides that such a right can only be exercised in accordance with a resolution of the Security Council.[24]

Thirdly, the inability and unwillingness of African leaders to chastise each other for human rights violations has been proved in more than one occasion. They simply lack the political will and energy to rebuke each other for simple violations committed against their citizens. It would therefore be a draconian step, very much against the norm, for them to intervene in a situation of gross human rights violations. Besides, such intervention may be demanding, especially where a well-trained and equipped army and adequate financial and material resources, would be required. The much they could probably do is to send peace-keeping troops to restore order in warring states. In fact, this is already happening in countries like Sudan and Somalia where the AU has sent peace-keeping forces in the war-torn regions. However, it appears rather ambitious for the Union to intervene in a member state pursuant to a decision of the Assembly in respect of war crimes, genocide and crimes against humanity. This situation is not foreseeable; at least not in the near future.

4.2   HUMAN AND PEOPLES' RIGHTS UNDER THE CONSTITUTIVE ACT

As already stated, the OAU was principally a pan-continental political body motivated by the quest to end colonialism in Africa. This explains why its Charter did not afford human rights deserved attention and its activities were limited within the context of the

---

20   CAAU, art 4(a).

21   As above, art 4(b).

22   As above, art 4(f).

23   As above, art 4(g).

24   See the Charter of the United Nations, Chapter VII, arts 39-42.

right to self-determination in colonised African states and the abolition of apartheid in South Africa. Moreover, its organs, such as the Council of Ministers and the AHSG, focused almost exclusively on strengthening African unity and ensuring independence for Africans, sometimes at the expense of human rights. In other words, human rights were often detached from the mainstream OAU bodies in Addis Ababa and were relegated to the African Commission in Banjul.[25]

This should not be taken to mean that the OAU was totally out of tune with human rights issues. In all fairness, it is important to acknowledge that the organisation, to some extent, played a crucial role in the human rights agenda of the continent, particularly in the years just prior to its demise. Resolutions and decisions adopted by the former Council of Ministers and the AHSG, for example, indicated an increasing recognition of the relevance of human rights.[26] Some conferences convened by the OAU also indicated appreciation for human rights.[27] Some commissions established under the organisation's Charter equally had the mandate to consider human rights matters. These included the Labour and Social Affairs Commission, the Population Commission and the Women's Committee on Peace and Development.[28] These initiatives, as well as the adoption of regional human rights treaties, such as the African Charter on Human and Peoples' Rights (ACHPR), the African Charter on the Rights and Welfare of the Child (ACRWC), the Additional Protocol to the ACHPR on the Rights of Women in Africa, and the Convention on the Specific Aspects of Refugees in Africa, among others, evidenced the OAU's regard for human rights.

---

25   R Murray & A Lloyd 'Institutions with responsibility for human rights protection under the African Union' (2004) 48/2 *Journal of African Law* 166.

26   See, for example, Declaration on Political and Socio-Economic Situation in Africa and the Fundamental Changes taking place in the World, 11 July 1990, 26th session of AHSG; The Algiers Declaration, AHG/Decl.1 (XXXV).

27   See the Resolution on the Ministerial Conference on Human Rights in Africa, CM/Res.1673 (LXIV); Grand Bay Mauritius Declaration and Plan of Action, adopted by the Ministerial Conference on Human Rights in April 1999, CONF/HRA/DECL (I).

28   This body was a joint initiative of the OAU and UN Economic Commission for Africa, to increase the participation of women in decision making on conflict at the international level. It is composed of government representatives, NGOs and individual experts and has a task of advising on conflict and gender-related issues.

The worrisome issue about this pan-continental organisation related to the absence of clear human rights provisions in its Charter. Thus, the Constitutive Act of the AU which replaced it should be seen as a successful attempt, at least on paper, to infuse human rights in the agenda of the pan-continental political institutions created under it. This is clear in the Act's preamble, objectives and guiding principles. Whereas some of the provisions of the Act are explicit on human rights promotion and protection[29], others are implicit in the sense that they can be extrapolated to give effect to the realisation of human rights.[30]

4.2.1   HUMAN AND PEOPLES' RIGHTS IN THE OBJECTIVES OF THE CONSTITUTIVE ACT

According to the Act, one of the objectives of the AU is to promote and protect human and peoples' rights in accordance with the African Charter and other relevant human rights instruments.[31] This provision, whose effect is to concretise the relationship between the regional human rights system and its political affiliate, is an indication of AU's resolve to take human rights issues more seriously. It also sends the message that gross violations of human rights should not be permitted anywhere on the continent without serious repercussions.

It should be noted, however, that in spite of its reference to the promotion and protection of human rights in accordance with the African Charter, the Act is silent on the place of the Charter's enforcement institutions, namely, the African Commission and Court on Human and Peoples' Rights. This silence tends to undermine the intended relationship between the regional human rights institutions and their political affiliates. It further raises the pertinent question as to whether the AU seriously intended to incorporate human rights in its agenda.[32]

---

29   See, for example, art 3(h) & (g) of the Act.

30   See, for example, art 3(f), (j) & (k).

31   Art 3(h).

32   See U Udombana 'Can the leopard change its spots? The African Union treaty and human rights' (2002) 17 *American University International Law Review* 1177.

It should be recalled, when the African Charter was adopted and the Commission established, Africa was the continent with the worst human rights record in the world.[33] Hence, a good relationship between the regional human rights institutions and their political affiliates would act as an impetus for a workable human rights system. It was the place of the Act to entrench such a relationship.

Although the omission of the regional human rights institutions was subsequently addressed by the AU Assembly, this appears to be more or less an afterthought. Through a resolution, the AU decided to incorporate in its framework the African Commission and the African Committee of Experts on the Rights and Welfare of the Child.[34] However, the resolution fell short of giving details on how these institutions would be incorporated in the AU framework.

In order to encourage the promotion and protection of human and peoples' rights in accordance with Article 3(h) of the Act, the AU should urge its members to, among other things, conduct human rights education in their respective territories. The low level of consciousness of the majority of African people has contributed to the challenges in promoting and protecting human rights in the region.[35] The masses in Africa are ignorant of their human rights due to the lack of, or poor, education. As Yeshanew observed, in spite of its importance, there are only isolated efforts to conduct human rights education in Africa.[36]

The importance of human rights education is stressed under Article 25 of the African Charter, which imposes a duty on states parties to 'promote and ensure through teaching, education and publication, the respect of the rights and freedoms contained in

---

33   J Joiner 'Beyond commitments, towards practical action' in E Sall & L Wohlgemuth (eds) *Human rights, regionalism and the dilemmas of democracy in Africa* (2006) 19.

34   See 'Decision on the Interim Period', 1st Ordinary Session of the AU Assembly of Heads of State and Government, 9-10 July 2002, Durban, South Africa, AU Doc ASS/AU /Dec 1(1), para 2 (xi) & 9.

35   See these observations in J Mubangizi 'Some reflections on recent and current trends in the promotion and protection of human rights in Africa: The pains and the gains'(2006) 6 *African Human Rights Law Journal* 166.

36   S Yeshanew 'Utilising the promotional mandate of the African Commission on Human and Peoples' Rights to promote human rights education in Africa' (2007) 7 *African Human Rights Law Journal* 191.

the ... Charter and to see to it that these freedoms and rights as well as corresponding obligations and duties are understood.' This Article could be the basis on which the AU may establish and fund a comprehensive programme for human rights education, if indeed it is committed to the promotion and protection of human rights in accordance with the African Charter and its objectives.

Another objective of the Union that is stipulated in the Act is to promote democratic principles and institutions, popular participation and good governance.[37] Promotion and protection of democratic principles and institutions and good governance are important ingredients to the realisation of human rights. Democratisation and good governance in Africa are untenable without respect for human rights. In fact, human rights violations have been the main cause of the governance crises on the continent and the impediment to the much-anticipated African renaissance. It follows therefore that the prospects for democracy and good governance in the region would be bleak without their promotion and protection.

Africa is in dire need of sound democratic institutions and good governance. As stated in the previous part of this book, although the early sixties witnessed the emergence of a large number of 'independent' states, the same were devoid of democratic values and principles. Ironically, these emerging states enthusiastically adopted and ratified the UN Charter as well as other international instruments,[38] which prescribed the minimum standards for human rights, democracy and good governance. However, as Eze rightly observed:

> In spite of the adherence to and apparent commitment to the protection of human rights, the experience in most African countries ranges from anarchy to modest progress in the field of human rights protection and promotion. For the most part a gap exists between declaration and actual practice.[39]

37　CAAU, art 3(g). See also Baimu (n 19 above) 311.

38　Such as International Covenant on Civil and Political Rights (ICCPR) and International Covenant on Economic, Social and Cultural Rights (ICESCR), both adopted by General Assembly Resolution 2200 (XXI) of 16 December 1966. The former entered into force on 23 March 1976 and the later on 3 January 1976. See UNDOC. ST/HR/1 1 & 8.

39　O Eze *Human rights in Africa: Some selected problems* (1984) 23.

Although the above observation was made in the early eighties, it is still a reality in Africa today. The position is vindicated by the ongoing atrocities in some parts of the continent such as in Sudan, Democratic Republic of Congo (DRC) and Somalia, to mention but a few examples. The atrocities in most, if not all, of these countries are a culmination of the failure to observe the principles of democracy and good governance. Ironically, these countries have signed or ratified international human rights treaties, but whose provisions they have been violating with impunity. This, in a way, queries their commitment to human rights.

Other objectives of the AU that are linked to that of promoting democratic principles and good governance include to: promote peace, security, and stability on the continent;[40] promote sustainable development at the economic, social and cultural levels as well as the integration of African economies;[41] and promote cooperation in all fields of human activity to raise the living standards of African peoples.[42] All these objectives have human rights implications because they are geared towards the promotion and protection of human dignity. At the same time, these objectives cannot be realised in the absence of democracy and good governance.

4.2.2   HUMAN AND PEOPLES' RIGHTS UNDER THE PRINCIPLES OF THE CONSTITUTIVE ACT

The guiding principles of the AU that embody human rights provisions are: respect for democratic principles, human rights, the rule of law and good governance;[43] promotion of gender equality;[44] promotion of social justice to ensure balanced economic development;[45] respect for the sanctity of human life, condemnation and rejection of impunity and political assassination, acts of terrorism and subversive activities;[46] and condemnation and rejection of

---

40   CAAU, art 3(f).

41   As above, art 3(j).

42   As above, art 3(k).

43   As above, art 4(m).

44   As above, art 4(l).

45   As above, art 4(n).

46   As above, art 4(o).

unconstitutional change of government.[47] Additionally, the Act categorically stipulates that a government that shall seize power through unconstitutional means shall not be allowed to participate in the activities of the Union.[48]

Generally, there are some indications that the Union has attempted to implement some of the above stated principles. For example, the AU summit held in 2004 deliberated on the perturbing deterioration of respect for human rights in Zimbabwe. At least, this served as a strong indication that African leaders were no longer prepared to turn a deaf ear to the cries of the victims of human rights violations on the continent. The Union has also played a significant role in conflict resolution in the region. For instance, it took the initiative to send an observation mission to the Sudanese province of Darfur where militia allied to the Khartoum government were accused of grave human rights violations. Additionally, it recently deployed 7,000 peacekeepers to this war-torn country.

Further, the Union sent some soldiers to Mogadishu in Somalia in 2007, as part of a peacekeeping force. Somalia has been without a stable government since the early 1990s. A peace agreement aimed at ending the country's civil war that broke out following the fall of the regime of Siad Barre, was finally signed in 2006 after many years of peace talks. However, the new government was almost immediately threatened by further violence. Although Somaliland, in the north of Somalia, effectively operates as an independent state, the AU has refused to recognise it as such.

On the issue of unconstitutional change of government, the AU has been commended for the position adopted by its member states in relation to the recent *coup d'tat* in Togo.[49] When the former Togolese President, General Gnassimbe Eyadema, passed away in February 2005, the country's military attempted to impose Mr. Faure Gnassimbe to succeed his father. This was in violation of the country's Constitution that provided for an interim government to be headed by the Speaker of Parliament prior to the organisation

---

47   As above, art 4(p).

48   As above, art 30.

49   Mangu (n 3 above) 387.

of a fresh presidential election. The total condemnation of this unconstitutional change of government by the AU compelled Faure to resign and accept the organisation of elections within 90 days.[50]

Again, in October 2007, the AU imposed travel sanctions on Anjouan's President, Mohamed Bacar, and other officials in his government and froze their foreign assets following an unconstitutional take-over of power. Bacar, who had led a separatist government since 2001, was elected for a 5-year term as President of the country. His term expired on 14th of April 2007, and the president of the assembly, Houmadi Caambi, became acting president from 15th of April 2007 to 10th of May 2007. In the run-up to the poll, there were some irregularities and intimidation of voters. This prompted the AU and the Anjouan Union government to postpone the polls. However, Bacar printed his own ballots, held elections and claimed a landslide victory, provoking sanctions from the AU.

Likewise, the role played by the AU in Kenya's 2007 post-elections crisis cannot be ignored. The country was engulfed in months of civil unrest and political bickering following the declaration of Mr. Mwai Kibaki as the winner of the poll, contrary to the belief that the chief opposition contender, Raila Odinga, had won. During the civil unrest, at least 1,000 people were killed and 350,000 internally displaced.[51] Consequently, the AU appointed a team of international experts to mediate on the crisis. The team comprised of the former UN Secretary-General, Kofi Annan, and members of the African Panel of Eminent Persons-Graca Machel and former Tanzanian President, Benjamin Mkapa.

After prolonged negotiations, the two wrangling parties— the Party of National Unity (PNU) and the Orange Democratic Movement (ODM)— eventually signed a power-sharing agreement in February 2008, thus ending the crisis. These are just a few of the instances the AU has attempted to implement its principles enshrined in the Constitutive Act.

---

50   As above.

51   See *The Daily Nation*, 29 February 2008, available at www.nationmedia.co.ke (last accessed 12 May 2010); *The East African Standard*, 29 February 2008, available at www.eastandard.net (last accessed 12 May 2010).

While the Union should be applauded for its achievements, it should also be criticised for failing to adhere to these principles in many instances. For example, the Union's commitment to upholding some of these principles will be found wanting when tested against the background of the 2005 and 2008 Zimbabwean elections. It was largely reported that these elections fell short of the prescribed standards and guidelines of the Southern African Development Community (SADC) on democratic, free and fair elections.[52] However, the AU and SADC were all along passive until the situation in Zimbabwe went out of hand. In the country's 2008 presidential elections, opposition supporters were intimidated and killed for failing to vote for the Zimbabwe African National Union-Patriotic Front (ZANU-PF) party of President Robert Mugabe.

During the electioneering period, there was massive loss of property and lives, and the country's inflation rate was the worst in the world. Although a power-sharing agreement between the Movement for Democratic Change (MDC) and ZANU-PF parties was subsequently signed, the participation of the AU in the same is quite insignificant. Clearly, with regard to the situation in Zimbabwe, the AU assumed a passive posture, similar to that of its predecessor, the OAU. This should not be encouraged if human rights are to be a reality rather than an ideal in Africa. The Union should not be seen to be applying double standards in the implementation of its objectives and principles. Rather, in the spirit of sovereign equality of states, it should apply the same measures to all its members. By failing to chastise some states while being 'hard' on others, the Union is clearly setting a bad precedent.

The AU ought to take advantage of its position, power and influence to change the human rights situation in Africa. Its Constitutive Act already provides such an opportunity through its well crafted objectives and principles. While the full impact of the Act is yet to be seen or felt, its adoption is certainly a bold step intended to further the realisation of human rights in the region. It is also an instrument that entrenches the legitimacy of the African human rights system. It is therefore up to the Union to live to its promise to ensure the respect for human rights on the continent.

---

52   Mangu (n 3 above) 388.

CHAPTER 5

THE AFRICAN CHARTER ON HUMAN AND PEOPLES' RIGHTS

5.1 STRUCTURE AND SALIENT FEATURES OF THE AFRICAN CHARTER

The African Charter on Human and Peoples' Rights (hereafter 'the African Charter' or 'the Charter') is the main normative instrument of the African human rights system.[1] Structurally, it consists of 68 Articles and is divided into four chapters: Human and Peoples' Rights; Duties; Procedure of the Commission; and Applicable Principles. It includes all the three generations of rights: civil and political rights; economic, social, and cultural rights; and group (peoples') rights. The Charter is an innovative human rights instrument because some of its provisions distinctively depart from those in other regional human rights systems that preceded it.[2] As Umozurike correctly argued, although the Charter is different in some way from those of the other regions, it would be an overstatement to describe these differences as autochthonous.[3] The differences merely reflect the developments in international human rights law.

The first notable feature relates to the numerous 'claw-back' clauses in the Charter's provisions, which limit the enjoyment of

---

1   See the African Charter on Human and Peoples' Rights, adopted 27 June 1981, OAU Doc. CAB/LEG/67/3 rev. 5, 21 I.L.M. 58 (1982); entered into force 21 October 1986.

2   See W Benedek 'Peoples' rights and individuals' duties as special features of the African Charter on Human and Peoples' Rights' in P Kunig, W Benedek & C Mahalu (eds) *Regional protection of human rights by international law: The emerging African system* (1985) 59; U Umozurike *The African Charter on Human and Peoples' Rights* (1997) 87-96.

3   For this view and an analysis of the distinctive features of the African Charter, see U Umozurike 'The African Charter on Human and Peoples' Rights' (1983) 77 *American Journal of International Law* 911-913.

some rights to the discretion of domestic jurisdictions.[4] The issue of 'claw-back' clauses and how they limit rights under the Charter is discussed in detail elsewhere below. Notably, however, besides the 'claw-back' clauses, the Charter lacks a derogation clause that would permit the suspension of certain rights and freedoms in strictly defined circumstances.[5] This has both advantages and disadvantages. One advantage is that no emergency or special circumstances can justify the suspension of the rights enshrined in the Charter.[6] States parties are therefore obliged to uphold the rights enshrined in the Charter in good as in bad times. The disadvantage of having no derogation clause in the Charter, on the other hand, is that during emergencies or special circumstances, a state may choose to disregard the Charter in its entirety.[7]

There are numerous and significant examples of international instruments that contain an express derogation clause. These include Article 15 of the European Convention on Human Rights, Article 4 of ICCPR and Article 27 of the American Convention on Human Rights.[8] At the national level, Constitutions of some countries, such as South Africa, also have these clauses.[9]

---

4   'Claw-back' clauses are provisions in the Charter that condition the enjoyment or implementation of rights on national legislation. See M Mutua 'The African human rights system in a comparative perspective: The need for urgent reformulation' (1993) 5 *Legal Affairs* 7; E Anthony 'Beyond the paper Tiger: the challenge of a human rights court in Africa' (1997) *32 Texas International Law Journal* 518; T Buergenthal *International human rights* (1995) 234.

5   See R Murray *The African Commission on Human and Peoples' rights and international law* (2003) 123-126; D Harris O'Boyle & C Warwick *Law of the European Convention on Human Rights* (1955) 489-506.

6   In Communication 105/93, 130/94 & 152/96, *Media Rights Agenda and Constitutional Rights Project v. Nigeria*, Twelfth Annual Activity Report of the African Commission on Human and Peoples Rights (Annex V), the African Commission stated, *inter alia*, that governments should avoid restricting rights, and have special care with regard to those rights protected by constitutional or international human rights law. See also Communication 212/98, *Amnesty International v. Zambia*, Twelfth Annual Activity Report of the African Commission on Human and Peoples Rights (Annex V); G Naldi 'Limitation of rights under the African Charter on Human and Peoples' Rights: The contribution of the African Commission on Human and Peoples' Rights', (2001) 17 *South African Journal of Human Rights* 113-114.

7   R Murray 'The African Charter on Human and Peoples' Rights 1987-2000: An overview of its progress and problems' (2001) 1 *African human Rights Law Journal* 2.

8   See L Sermet 'The absence of a derogation clause from the African Charter on Human and Peoples' Rights: A critical discussion' (2007) 7 *African Human Rights Law Journal* 143.

9   See Constitution of the Republic of South Africa, 1996, art 37.

From the analysis of some of the human rights instruments, it may be concluded that at least three types of circumstances may permit states to derogate from rights:[10] (i) in the event of an exceptional public danger that threatens the existence of the nation[11], (ii) during a war or other public danger threatening the life of the nation[12] and (iii) during a war or any other crisis situation that threatens the independence or security of a state.[13] Hence, any armed conflict, whether internal or international, may be the basis for such derogation.

Because of the absence of a derogation clause in the Charter, a state is able to disregard, for political reasons, its responsibilities while ill-advisedly reducing the democratic space between the separation of powers and civil liberties.[14] The United Nations Sub-Commission on Human Rights echoed the importance of derogation clauses, by inviting all states 'whose legislation contains no explicit clause that guarantees the legality of the implementation of a state of emergency, to adopt clauses in accordance with international norms and principles...'[15] This indicates that international human rights norms attach importance to derogation clauses.

The second notable feature of the Charter relates to its social and economic rights' provisions. Arguably, the intention of incorporating this genre of rights in the Charter was to give effect to the International Covenant on Economic, Social and Cultural Rights (ICESR) at the regional level.[16] The Charter's approach, however, differs from that of the Covenant in that it avoids the incremental language of 'progressive realisation' of this category of rights. Instead, the obligations that states parties assume with respect

---

10   Sermet (n 8 above) 143.

11   ICCPR, art.

12   European Convention, art 15.

13   American Convention, art 27.

14   Sermet (n 8 above) 153.

15   Sub-Commission on Prevention of Discrimination and Protection of Minorities, Res1995/33, Question on human rights and states of exception, 35th session, 24 August 1995.

16   Adopted and opened for signature, accession and ratification by General Assembly resolution 2200 A (XXI) of 16 December 1966; entered into force 3 January 1976 in accordance with art 27.

to these rights are clearly stated as being of immediate application. Thus, the Charter places economic, social and cultural rights on the same footing as other rights.[17]

Although the African Commission acknowledged the difficulty posed by 'the present hostile economic circumstances',[18] it reminded states parties that the Charter required immediate implementation of the rights it contained.[19] Because realisation of socio-economic rights in the Charter is not subjected to availability of resources, the Charter is said to be overly ambitious and unrealistic.[20] Accordingly, it presents a challenging normative framework for the implementation of this category of rights by states parties.

It is also useful to mention that the Charter adopts a different approach to that of the European and Inter-American human rights systems by encapsulating all the three generations of rights in a single instrument. The European Convention does not contain social, economic and cultural rights. Instead, these rights were entrenched in the European Social Charter (ESC)[21] and the Organisation for Security and Cooperation in Europe (OSCE).[22] In the Americas, the American Declaration of Rights and Duties of Man[23] had elaborate provisions on economic, social and cultural rights which were, however, not recaptured in the American Convention. In

---

17   C Mbazira 'Enforcing the economic, social and cultural rights in the African Charter on Human and Peoples' Rights: Twenty years of redundancy, progression and significant strides' (2006) 6 *African Human Rights Law Journal* 339.

18   'Presentation of the Third Annual Activity Report by the then Chairman of the Commission, Professor U O Umozurike to the 26th Session of the Assembly of Heads of States and Government of the Organisation of African Unity, 9-11 July 1990', in African Commission on Human and Peoples' Rights, Documentation, Third Annual Activity Report of the African Commission on Human and Peoples' Rights; Documents of the African Commission 201.

19   As above. See also Mbazira (n 17 above) 341.

20   C Odinkalu 'Implementing economic, social and cultural rights under the African Charter on Human and Peoples' Rights' in R Murray & M Evans *The African Charter on Human and Peoples' Rights: The system in practice, 1986-2000* (2002) 196.

21   See the European Social Charter, 18 October 1961, 529 UNTS 89, entered into force on 26 February 1965.

22   See A Blored 'The human rights dimension of the OSCE: Past, present and prospects' (1995) 3 *OSCE Office for Democratic Institutions and Human Rights (ODIHR) Bulletins* 16.

23   Res. XXX, 9th International Conference of American States, Bogota, Colombia, 30 March - 2 May 1948, Final Act, 38.

1988, the General Assembly of the Organisation of American States (OAS) eventually adopted a Protocol on Economic, Social and Cultural Rights (the San Salvador Protocol) which reduced into a treaty economic, social and cultural rights recognised under the Inter-American human rights system.[24]

Thirdly, the African Charter incorporates peoples' rights in its provisions. These rights include equality of all peoples,[25] right to existence and self-determination,[26] right to sovereignty over group wealth and natural resources (including the right to dispose of the same),[27] right to development,[28] right to national and international peace and security, and the right to a general satisfactory environment favourable to development.[29] Even though the Charter recurrently refers to 'peoples', the concept is not defined anywhere in its provisions hence creating uncertainty and unnecessary speculation on the true import of the term.[30] This observation shall be revisited later when this category of rights will be discussed at length.

The Charter also imposes duties on states and individuals.[31] Thus, it is founded on the premise that rights and duties exist concomitantly.[32] Its preamble is categorical that 'the enjoyment of rights and freedoms also implies the performance of duties.' Accordingly, each of these duties embodies 'the values of African civilisation.'[33] The principle that rights reciprocate duties also forms the basis of Article 27(2), which states that rights must be 'exercised with due regard to the rights of others, collective security, morality and common interest.' This implies that rights can only make sense

---

24   Odinkalu (n 20 above) 185.

25   African Charter, art 19.

26   As above, art 20.

27   As above, art 21.

28   As above, art 22.

29   As above, art 24.

30   S Dersso 'The jurisprudence of the African Commission on Human and Peoples' Rights with respect to peoples' rights' (2006) 6 *African Human Rights Law Journal* 360.

31   Duties of states are contained in arts 20(3), 21(5), 22(2), 25 & 26. Arts 27-29 impose duties on individuals.

32   F Viljoen 'Africa's contribution to the development of international human rights and humanitarian law' (2001) 1 *African Human Rights Law Journal* 21.

33   African Charter, Preamble.

in the social and political arena when they are coupled with duties on individuals.[34]

Finally, unlike the American and European Conventions, the African Charter does not provide for the establishment of a regional human rights court. This has largely been attributed, and pretentiously so, to the supposed 'African cultural emphasis on conciliation rather than formal adversarial settlement of disputes.'[35] The drafters of the Charter were guided by the principle that the instrument 'should reflect the African conception of human rights and should take as a pattern the African philosophy of law and meet the needs of Africa.'[36]

This kind of motivation was indeed a misguided attempt to jeopardise the long awaited opportunity to craft a system that would enhance the enforcement of human rights at the regional level. It was quite pretentious for conciliation to be contemplated at the regional level while adversarial settlement of disputes took the centre stage in the domestic legal systems.[37] One would wonder whether the African culture was to be practiced only at the regional level and not the domestic one.

All the same, the absence of an African human rights court provoked heated debate and controversy that later culminated in the adoption of the Protocol to the African Charter on Human and Peoples' Rights on the Establishment of an African Court on Human and Peoples' Rights.[38] Although this is quite commendable, the impact of the continental human rights court is yet to be felt since its establishment is still at the formative stages.

---

34   Viljoen (n 32 above) 21.

35   Umozurike (n 3 above) 909.

36   See OAU CAB/LEG rev 1 at p. 1

37   M Mutua 'The African human rights court: A two-legged stool?' (1999) 21 *Human Rights Quarterly* 342.

38   See Protocol to the African Charter on Human and Peoples' Rights on the Establishment of an African Court on Human and Peoples' Rights; adopted on 8 June 1998.

5.2   INDIVIDUALS' RIGHTS UNDER THE AFRICAN CHARTER

5.2.1   CIVIL AND POLITICAL RIGHTS

The African Charter recognises the indivisibility and interrelatedness of rights. In this sense, it emphasises that the satisfaction of economic, social and cultural rights is a guarantee for the enjoyment of civil and political rights.[39] Thus, it underscores the fact that one category of rights cannot survive without the other. This relationship notwithstanding, the Charter guarantees a broad range of civil and political rights which now form the bulk of the African Commission's jurisprudence. The Commission has over the last two decades, or so, entertained numerous communications alleging violations of this category of rights. What follows therefore is a discussion of these rights and their scope in the light of the Commission's jurisprudence.

5.2.2.1   RIGHT TO NON-DISCRIMINATION

Every individual is entitled to enjoy the rights and freedoms recognised and guaranteed in the Charter without distinction of any kind such as race, ethnic group, colour, sex, language, religion, political or any other opinion, national and social origin, fortune, birth or other status.[40] The exclusion of individuals from enjoying the rights in the Charter on the basis of any of these distinctions may amount to discrimination.

'Discrimination' means any distinction, exclusion or preference that has an effect of nullifying or impairing equal enjoyment of rights.[41] Although discrimination is a particular form of differentiation, the two concepts are distinct. Discrimination refers to differentiation on subjective criteria like those mentioned in Article 2 of the Charter.[42] This does not, however, rule out affirmative action that may be undertaken to redress past inequality.

---

39   African Charter, Preamble para 8.

40   As above, art 2.

41   Communication 241/2001, *Purohit and Moore v. Gambia*, Sixteenth Annual Activity Report of the African Commission on Human and Peoples Rights (Annex VII) para 61.

42   Umozurike (n 2 above) 32.

The African Commission has had the opportunity to interpret Article 2 in a number of cases. For instance, in *Rencontre Africaine pour la Defense des Droits de l'Homme v. Zambia*[43], the Zambian government expelled West African nationals on grounds that they were living in Zambia illegally and that the African Charter did not abolish the requirements for visas and the regulation of movement over national borders between member states. The Commission held that the nature of the expulsion by the Zambian government was discriminatory on nationality basis. The Commission further stated that Zambia, by ratifying the African Charter, was committed to 'secure the rights protected in the Charter to all persons within their jurisdiction, nationals or non-nationals.'[44]

The Commission also found a violation of Article 2 in *Organisation Mondiale Contre la Torture and Association Internationale des Juristes Democrates, Commission Internationale des Juristes, Union Interafricaine des Droits de l'Homme (OMCT, AIJD, CIJ, UIDH) v. Rwanda*.[45] The communication alleged the expulsion of Burundian refugees from Rwanda as well as summary executions of Tutsis and political opponents, among other human rights violations. The Commission found that the violations of the rights of the individuals in this case were on the basis of their being Burundian nationals, members of the Tutsi ethnic group or members of opposition parties, and as such violated Article 2 of the Charter. The Commission concluded that:

> There is considerable evidence, undisputed by the government, that the violations of the rights of individuals have occurred on the basis of their being Burundian nationals or members of the Tutsi ethnic group. The denial of numerous rights to individuals on account of their nationality or membership of a particular ethnic group clearly violates Article 2.[46]

It is evident that discrimination has been practiced in many African states, more so against non-nationals. Mass expulsions, discrimination

---

43   Communication 71/92, *Rencontre Africaine pour la De'fense des Droits de l'Homme v. Zambia* (2000) *AHRLR*, (ACHPR 1996) 321.

44   As above, para 22.

45   Communication 27/89, 46/91, 49/91, 99/93, *Organisation Mondiale Contre la Torture & Others v. Rwanda,* Tenth Annual Activity Report of the African Commission on Human and Peoples' Rights (Annex X).

46   As above, para 22.

at the workplace, and subjection to unfavourable social and economic conditions, among other vices, have been experienced by foreign nationals in many African states.[47] The latest of such activities was the series of xenophobic attacks on foreigners living in South Africa. Between April and May 2008, foreigners were targeted, and some attacked and killed, by some South African nationals. As a result of the nationwide attacks, more than 30,000 people were internally displaced and another 30,000 returned to their countries of origin for fear of further attacks.

Such discriminative practices, however, have often constituted a flagrant violation of Article 2 of the Charter, among other provisions. It is appreciated that African states are generally faced with many challenges, mainly of economic nature. In the wake of such difficulties, some resort to radical legislative and other measures to protect their nationals and their economy from non-nationals. Whatever the situation, however, such measures should not be taken to the detriment of the enjoyment of human rights.[48]

Some governments have also been accused of promulgating legislation that is discriminative against some of its citizens. For instance, in *Purohit and Moore v. Gambia*[49], the communication alleged that the principal legislation governing mental health in Gambia, namely the Lunatics Detention Act of 1917, was outdated and discriminative in effect. The complainants contended, as there were no review or appeal procedures against determination or certification of one's mental state for both involuntary and voluntary mental patients, the legislation did not allow for the correction of an error assuming a wrong certification or wrong diagnosis had been made.[50] In such circumstances, they further contended, if an error was made and there was no avenue to appeal or review the medical practitioners' assessment, there would be a great likelihood that a

---

47   J Boukongou 'The appeal of the African system for protecting human rights', (2006) 6 *African Human Rights Law Journal* 278.

48   Communication 159/96, *Union Interafricaine des Droits de l'Homme & Others v. Angola*, Tenth Annual Activity Report of the African Commission on Human and Peoples' Rights (Annex X) para 16.

49   *Purohit and Moore v. Gambia* (n 41 above).

50   As above, para 27.

person could be wrongfully detained in a mental institution.[51] In finding a violation of Articles 2 and 3 of the Charter, the Commission stated:

> Clearly the situation presented above fails to meet the standards of antidiscrimination and equal protection of the law as laid down under the provisions of Articles 2 and 3 of the African Charter and Principle 1(4)[52] of the United Nations Principles for the Protection of Persons with Mental Illness and the Improvement of Mental Health Care.[53] The African Commission maintains that mentally disabled persons would like to share the same hopes, dreams and goals and have the same rights to pursue those hopes, dreams and goals just like any other human being.[54] Like any other human being, mentally disabled persons or persons suffering from mental illnesses have a right to enjoy a decent life, as normal and full as possible, a right which lies at the heart of the right to human dignity. This right should be zealously guarded and forcefully protected by all states parties to the African Charter in accordance with the well established principle that all human beings are born free and equal in dignity and rights.[55]

The African Commission's observation in this regard is quite commendable because it draws the nexus between the right to non-discrimination and human dignity. In other words, discrimination undermines a person's dignity by suggesting that he or she is inferior to the rest. Human dignity is an inherent basic right to which all human beings, regardless of their capabilities or disabilities, as the case may be, are entitled to without discrimination. It is therefore an inherent right which 'every human being is obliged to respect by

---

51   As above.

52   Principle 1(4) provides: 'There shall be no discrimination on the grounds of mental illness.' 'Discrimination' means any distinction, exclusion or preference that has an effect of nullifying or impairing equal enjoyment of rights [footnote retained].

53   GA Res 46/119, 46 UN GAOR Supp. (No. 49) at 189, UN Doc. A/46/49 (1991) [footnote retained].

54   Art 3 of the UN Declaration on the Rights of Disabled Persons, UNGA Resolution 3447(XXX) of 9   December 1975, provides 'Disabled persons have the inherent right to respect for their human dignity. Disabled persons, whatever the origin, nature and seriousness of their handicaps and disabilities, have the same fundamental rights as their fellow citizens of the same age, which implies first and foremost the right to enjoy a decent life, as normal and as full as possible.' [footnote retained].

55   Universal Declaration of Human Rights of 1948, Article 1 [footnote retained]. *Purohit and Moore v Gambia* (n 41 above) paras 35–38.

all means possible and on the other hand it confers a duty on every human being to respect this right.'[56]

It must, however, be noted that the scope of the right to non-discrimination does not exclude reasonable measures intended to protect or support individuals who are disadvantaged by reason of their race, ethnic group, colour, sex, language, religion, political or any other opinion, national and social origin, fortune, birth or other status.[57] Such measures are generally referred to as affirmative action or 'positive discrimination.' Some states, such as South Africa, have come up with concepts like 'fair discrimination' to justify affirmative action.[58] Hence, differentiation will not amount to discrimination if it is intended to redress imbalances in society and if it does not result to the violation of the right to equality and other associated rights. This essentially means that there is a very feint line between differentiation and discrimination.

Right to non-discrimination is closely linked to the right to equality. Article 3 of the Charter guarantees every individual the 'twin-rights' of equality before the law and equal protection of the law.[59] This essentially means that the law should not have regard for race, ethnic group, colour, sex, language, religion, political or any other opinion, national and social origin, fortune, birth or other status. Like the right to non-discrimination, the right to equality is not absolute, but rather recognises relative equality. Relative equality allows for a differential treatment of individuals proportionate to their circumstances.

In *Union Interafricaine des Droits de l'Homme, Federation International des Ligues des Droits de l'Homme, Rencontre Africaine des Droits de l'Homme, Organisation Nationale des Droits de l'Homme au Senegal and Association Malienne des Droits de l'Homme (UIDH, FIDH,*

---

56   As above, para 57.

57   See Umozurike (n 2 above) 32.

58   See generally chapter two of the Constitution of South Africa (1996); Promotion of Equality and Prevention of Unfair Discrimination Act (PEPUDA); and the Employment Equity Act.

59   African Charter, art 3(1) & (2).

RADDHO, ONDH and AMDH) v. Angola[60], the communication alleged the expulsion of West Africans from Angola without the opportunity to challenge the matter before the domestic courts. The African Commission held that states parties are under obligation to ensure that persons living in their territory, whether nationals or non-nationals enjoy the rights in the Charter. Thus, it found that the victims' right to equality before the law was trampled on, in violation of Article 3 of the Charter, because of their origin.[61]

The right to equality and equal protection of the law requires that no law shall be discriminatory either of itself or in its effect.[62] Hence, this right would be violated when, for example, a public authority in the performance of the functions of a public office discriminates against a person. The same could be said of a law that treats people in a discriminatory manner in respect of, for example, access to shops, hotels, lodging-houses, public restaurants or places of public entertainment or in respect of access to places of public resort maintained wholly or partly out of public funds or dedicated to the use of the general public.[63] Most communications before the African Commission that alleged the violation of Article 3 also alleged the violation of Article 2 of the Charter. Thus, it may be argued that the right to non-discrimination and the right to equality are closely related, if not intertwined.

5.2.1.2 RIGHT TO LIFE AND INTEGRITY OF THE PERSON

Article 4 of the Charter guarantees the right to life in very precise terms. It begins with affirming the inviolability of human beings then proceeds to acknowledge the entitlement to respect for life and integrity of the person.[64] The Article prohibits arbitrary deprivation of the right to life. This right has been regarded as the most

---

60   *Union Interafricaine des Droits de l'Homme & Others v. Angola* (n 48 above) (Annex II) para 1.

61   As above, para 18.

62   See section 82 of Constitution of the Republic of Kenya 1963, as amended in 1999.

63   As above.

64   Art 4 states, 'Human beings are inviolable. Every human being shall be entitled to respect for his life and the integrity of his person. No one may be arbitrarily deprived of this right.'

fundamental right on the basis of which other rights accrue.[65] As a matter of fact, a person cannot claim any other right if his or her right to life has been violated. Generally, this right is non-derogable except in certain circumstances judicially recognised or resulting from lawful acts of war or self-defence.[66] However, in some national jurisdictions, such as South Africa, this right is non-derogable even in times of emergencies.[67]

The Charter is silent on what might constitute arbitrary deprivation of the right to life. In the absence of a working definition from both the Charter and the Commission, arbitrary deprivation of the right to life could be understood to mean extra-judicial killings.[68] This reasoning is deduced from *Organisation Mondiale Contre la Torture and Association Internationale des Juristes Democrates, Commission Internationale des Juristes, Union Interafricaine des Droits de l'Homme v. Rwanda*, where the Commission observed that extra-judicial killings of Rwandan villagers by the Armed Forces violated the right to life guaranteed by the Charter.[69]

The Commission's response to the violation of the right to life has generally been unsatisfactory because it has not only failed to provide the definition of this right within the context of the Charter, but has also failed to find its violation in certain instances. For example, in *International Commission of Jurists v. Rwanda*[70], it failed to find a violation of the right even when it was informed of the extra-judicial killings that were taking place in Rwanda. Instead, it requested permission from the Rwandan government to conduct on-site investigation of the allegations.[71]

---

65 See O Nmehielle *The African human rights system: Its laws, practice and institutions* (2001) 85.

66 See S Davidson *The Inter-American human rights system* (1992) 262-263.

67 See Constitution of South Africa, art 37.

68 See R Murray 'Report on the 1996 Sessions of the African Commission on Human and Peoples' Rights- 19th and 20th Sessions: 26 March- 4 April, and 21-23 October 1996', (1997) 18 *Human Rights Law Journal* 19.

69 *Organisation Mondiale Contre la Torture & Others v. Rwanda* (n 45 above).

70 Communication 49/91, *International Commission of Jurists v. Rwanda,* Tenth Annual Activity Report of the African Commission on Human and Peoples' Rights (Annex X).

71 Nmehielle (n 65 above) 87.

Despite the quick response from the government, the Commission did not immediately send a mission to Rwanda. It was not until March 1994, after about four years from the time of its request, when it decided to send a two-person mission with the assistance of the United Nations.[72] Visiting Rwanda four years after a communication had been lodged was both unfortunate and undesirable. The Commission should have used that opportunity to elaborate on the context of the right to life as contemplated in the Charter.

In *Orton and Vera Chirwa v. Malawi*[73], the Commission also failed to clarify the scope of this right. Although the communication alleged violation of the right to fair trial, right to liberty and freedom from torture, the Commission went ahead to find the violation of the right to life. Mr. and Mrs. Chirwa, who were under political persecution from the then government of Kamuzu Banda, had their death sentences commuted to life imprisonment. They were held in solitary confinement, denied good food, adequate medical care, shackled for long periods of time in their cells and prevented from seeing each other for years. Mr. Chirwa later died in prison while the case was pending before the Commission. The Commission not only found the violation of the right to fair trial, liberty and freedom from torture, but also concluded that the right to life had been violated circumstantially.[74]

In *Interights et al (on behalf of Mariette Sonjaleen Bosch) v. Botswana*[75], the communication related to the conviction for murder and subsequent sentencing to death of Mariette Bosch in Botswana, allegedly in violation of Article 4 of the Charter. The complainants argued, among other things, that the death penalty had been imposed in breach of the Charter. While accepting Botswana's argument that the death penalty was not *per se* in breach of the Charter, the Commission cited Inter-American jurisprudence which stated that

---

72   As above.

73   Communications 64/92, 68/92 and 72/92, *Orton and Vera Chirwa v. Malawi*, Eighth Annual Activity Report of the African Commission on Human and Peoples Rights.

74   As above.

75   Communication 240/2001, *Interights et al (on behalf of Mariette Sonjaleen Bosch) v Botswana*, Seventeenth Annual Activity Report of the African Commission on Human and Peoples' Rights (Annex VII).

the death penalty should be imposed only after full consideration of the circumstances of the offence and of the offender.[76] It found that the court in respect of Mariette Bosch had looked at the circumstances fully. The Commission also observed that:

> ... it would be remiss for the African Commission to deliver its decision on this matter without acknowledging the evolution of international law and the trend towards abolition of the death penalty. This is illustrated by the UN General Assembly's adoption of the 2nd Optional Protocol to the ICCPR and the general reluctance by those states that have retained capital punishment on their Statute books to exercise it in practice. The African Commission has also encouraged this trend by adopting a 'Resolution Urging States to envisage a Moratorium on the Death Penalty' and therefore encourages all states party to the African Charter on Human and Peoples' Rights to take all measures to refrain from exercising the death penalty.[77]

It then 'strongly urged the Republic of Botswana to take all measures to comply with the Resolution Urging States to envisage a Moratorium on the Death Penalty.'[78] Despite not finding a breach of the Charter, the Commission also required the defendant state to 'report back to the African Commission when it submits its report in terms of Article 62 of the African Charter on measures taken to comply with this recommendation.'[79] This appears to be contradictory, although not dissimilar to the approach that has been adopted by other international bodies.[80] The Commission had previously held that where a trial which ordered the death penalty was not fair and so violated Article 7 of the Charter, the subsequent execution will further violate the right to life under Article 4.[81]

---

76   As above, para 52.

77   As above.

78   As above.

79   As above.

80   See in this regard the ICJ's approach in the *Legality of the Use of Force (Yugoslavia v 10 NATO States) cases*, ICJ Reports (2004) 3.

81   Communications 137/94, 139/94, 154/96 and 161/97, *International Pen, Constitutional Rights Project, Interights on behalf of Ken Saro-Wiwa Jr and Civil Liberties Organisation v. Nigeria*, Twelfth Annual Activity Report of the African Commission on Human and Peoples' Rights (Annex V).

Murray observed that although individual Commissioners have sometimes appeared to suggest that the death penalty is a violation of the guarantee of the right to life in Article 4 of the Charter, the Commission as a whole has not taken this position.[82] In the examination of state reports, Commissioners have reportedly asked states whether they have abolished the death penalty. For example, at the 31st Session of the Commission in May 2002, one Commissioner asked the delegation from Cameroon: 'the death sentence is still in the criminal code but it has been said that for more than 15 years there has been no execution. Are there any efforts to guarantee the right to life and thus abolish the death sentence?'[83] This essentially means that the Commissioner perceived the abolition of the death sentence as a guarantee to the right to life. Once again, the Commission failed to seize this moment to define the scope of the right to life as contemplated in the Charter.

In the 'Resolution Urging the State to Envisage a Moratorium on the Death Penalty'[84], the Commission urged states to review their approach and consider abolishing the death penalty. The Commission categorically stated that it:

> Urges all states parties…that still maintain the death penalty to comply fully with their obligations under the treaty and to ensure that persons accused of crimes for which the death penalty is a competent sentence are afforded all the guarantees in the African Charter…. Calls upon all states that still maintain the death penalty to: (a) limit the imposition of the death penalty only to the most serious crimes; (b) consider establishing a moratorium on executions of death penalty; (c) reflect on the possibility of abolishing death penalty.[85]

From the foregoing, it is imperative to note that the Commission is not unequivocal on the abolition of the death penalty. Rather, it gives states two options, the first being limiting the imposition of the death penalty only to the most serious crimes and the second being

---

82   Murray (n 7 above).

83   As above.

84   Adopted at 26th Ordinary Session on 15 November 1999, ACHPR/Res. 42(XXVI) 99.

85   'Resolution Urging the State to Envisage a Moratorium on the Death Penalty', ACHPR/Res.42(XXVI) 99.

considering on the possibility of abolishing the penalty. Thus, it can be said that the right to life in the context of the African human rights system does not exclude judicial executions.

The Commission still has a long way to go as far as the clarification of the right to life is concerned. For instance, it is yet to interpret Article 4 in the light of issues such as the right to life of a foetus, and other controversial components of the right to life that have come before the UN and other regional mechanisms.[86] The importance of the right to life cannot be overlooked, especially within the context of Africa. This is especially because it is one of those rights that have been violated with impunity by successive brutal regimes which have engaged in endless power struggles and extra-judicial killings.[87]

5.2.1.3 RIGHT AGAINST ALL FORMS OF SLAVERY, SLAVE TRADE, TORTURE AND CRUEL, INHUMAN OR DEGRADING TREATMENT

Article 5 of the Charter protects a number of related rights, namely: (i) the right to the respect of the dignity inherent in a person; (ii) the right to recognition of one's legal status; and (iii) the right against all forms of exploitation and degradation of people particularly slavery, slave trade, torture, cruel, inhuman or degrading punishment and treatment.[88] The right to the respect of the dignity inherent in a human being is the basis of the human rights concept. This concept, as already discussed previously, acknowledges that every individual has legal entitlements (rights) by virtue of being human.

It is on the basis of this acknowledgement that Article 5 recognises the fact that slavery is a dehumanising practice because it exploits people. Slave trade has been one of the greatest violations of human rights ever to be committed in Africa. Slave trade and slavery in their contemporary forms include practices such as: illegal

---

86   Nmehielle (n 65 above) 88.

87   As above, 85.

88   Art 5 states:'Every individual shall have the right to the respect of the dignity inherent in a human being and to the recognition of his legal status. All forms of exploitation and degradation of man particularly slavery, slave trade, torture, cruel, inhuman or degrading punishment and treatment shall be prohibited.'

sale and traffic in human beings, pledging of young girls for debts, forced marriages in exchange of dowry; use of domestic servants for extremely low pay; child labour; and forced labour.[89]

The problem presented by the provisions of Article 5 relating to slavery is that of enforcement. Slavery is a violation that cannot easily be traced to states because it is mostly perpetrated by individuals.[90] It is often rooted in traditional and religious practices.[91] The fact that this practice stems from non-state actors accounts for the few complaints the African Commission has so far received under Article 5. In *S.O.S Esclaves v. Mauritania*[92], the complainant alleged that, in some cases, the government of Mauritania supported the perpetrators of slavery, which was still a common practice in the country.[93] The communication stated, *inter alia*, that ten adults were sold and bought as slaves; children from four families were enslaved by their parents' masters; two women were married to their masters against their will; and six people and their families were dispossessed of their ancestral property by their parents' masters.[94] The communication was, however, found inadmissible for non-exhaustion of domestic remedies.[95]

In *Bah Ould Rabah v. Mauritania*[96], the complainant and his family were forcefully expelled from their ancestral home by a man named Mohamed Bah on grounds that the deceased mother of the complainant was his slave. Subsequently, the house bequeathed to her descendants and the whole estate around it became legally the property of Mohamed Bah, the alleged 'owner' of the deceased.[97]

---

89   E Ankumah *The African Commission on Human and Peoples' Rights* (1996) 119. See also Nmehielle (n 65 above) 89.

90   As above.

91   See Ankumah (n 89 above) 119, where the author discusses some of these dehumanising traditional practices.

92   Communication 198/97, *S.O.S Esclaves v. Mauritania*, Twelfth Annual Activity Report of the African Commission on Human and Peoples' Rights (Annex V).

93   As above, para 1.

94   As above, para 2.

95   As above, para 17.

96   Communication 197/97, *Bah Ould Rabah v. Mauritania*, Seventeenth Annual Activity Report of the African Commission on Human and Peoples' Rights (Annex VII).

97   As above, para 1.

The complainant therefore alleged violation of Article 5 of the African Charter.

The government of Mauritania claimed that the dispute was between two citizens who were members of the same family and that the allegations could not be justified as slavery.[98] The Commission observed that the consequences of slavery still existed in the respondent state. It therefore called on all public institutions in Mauritania 'to persevere in their efforts so as to control and eliminate all the offshoots of slavery.'[99] It then ordered the government to 'take the appropriate steps to restore the plaintiff his rights.'[100] The Commission, as has been its custom, failed to specify the 'appropriate steps' the government of Mauritania needed to take to 'restore the plaintiff's rights'. It also did not elaborate on the content of the right against slavery, especially in its contemporary application. This indeed is an overt failure on the part of the Commission.

Article 5 also provides for the prohibition of all forms of torture, cruel, inhuman or degrading punishment and treatment. Noteworthy, the term 'torture' is still highly debatable and has generated divergent views in academic circles.[101] In Article 1 of the Convention against Torture and Cruel, Inhuman or Degrading Treatment or Punishment (CAT), torture is defined as:

> any act by which severe pain or suffering, whether physical or mental, is intentionally inflicted on a person for such purposes as obtaining from him or a third person information or a confession, punishing him for an act he or a third person has committed or is suspected of having committed, or intimidating or coercing him or a third person, or for any reason based on discrimination of any kind, when such pain or suffering is inflicted by or at the instigation of or with the consent or acquiescence of a public official or other person acting in

---

98   As above, para 26.

99   As above, paras 29 & 31.

100   As above.

101   See A Cullen 'Defining torture in international law: A critique of the concept employed by the European Court of Human Rights' (2003) 34 *California Western International Law Journal* 29, where the author sees the need for a less definitive and broader view of the concept of torture. See also J Mujuzi 'An analysis of the approach to the right to freedom from torture adopted by the African Commission on Human and Peoples' Rights' (2006) 6 *African Human Rights Law Journal* 429.

an official capacity. It does not include pain or suffering arising only from, inherent in or incidental to lawful sanctions.

Torture is still a persistent problem in Africa. It has been said that this practice is usually employed by both governments and individuals, mainly to counter dissent and to impose ideas or authority on others.[102] According to Nmehielle, in Africa, 'torture, cruel, inhuman and degrading punishment are constant tools in the hands of many dictators to smother their opponents.'[103] Mujuzi notes that due to this, it is unsurprising that the African Charter puts torture in the same category as slavery and slave trade, and categorises them as 'forms of exploitation and degradation.'[104]

From the Commission's jurisprudence, it can be deduced that torture includes acts such as beatings usually carried out by security forces, long periods of detention without charge or trial, overcrowded detention cells and prisons and detention in solitary cells. In *Krishna Achuthan (on behalf of Aleke Banda), Amnesty International (on behalf of Orton and Vera Chirwa v Malawi*[105]), for example, the Commission held that conditions of overcrowding and acts of beating and torture that took place in prisons in Malawi contravened this provision of the Charter. The Commission has also found the holding of a prisoner in handcuffs, airless and dirty cells, chained by foot to the wall in the cell, and the denial of medical attention in situation of deteriorating health to be acts of torture and cruel, inhuman and degrading treatment.[106]

---

102   Statement made at an international seminar 'African cultures and the fight against torture' available at http://ww2.fiacat.org/ en/article.php3?id_article=41, (accessed 31 July 2007). See also Mujuzi (n 101 above) 429.

103   Nmehielle (n 65 above) 90.

104   Mujuzi (n 101 above) 429.

105   *Orton and Vera Chirwa v. Malawi* (n 73 above). The Commission was also seized with other communications alleging the violation of this right. However, they were dismissed for failing to meet the admissibility requirement. See, for example, Communication 8/88 *Nziwa Buyingo v. Uganda*; Communication 17/88, *Hilarie v. Benin*; and Communication 18/88, *El Hadji Boubacare v. Benin* cited in Law Reports of the African Commission Series A, Volume 1, ACHPR/LR/A1 (1997).

106   *International Pen, Constitutional Rights Project, Interights on behalf of Ken Saro-Wiwa Jr and Civil Liberties Organisation v. Nigeria* (n 81 above).

In *Curtis Francis Doebbler v. Sudan*[107], eight Muslim university students on a picnic were arrested and charged with committing, in a public place, acts contrary to public morality prohibited under Article 152 of the Sudanese Criminal Law of 1991.[108] The alleged offensive acts comprised of girls kissing, wearing trousers, dancing with men, crossing legs with men, and sitting and talking with boys.[109] They were subsequently convicted and sentenced to fines and lashes. The lashes were executed in public under the supervision of the national court. The complainant alleged that the punishment violated Article 5 of the African Charter. In finding a violation and requesting the abolition of the penalty of lashes by Sudan, the African Commission observed as follows:

> Article 5 of the Charter prohibits not only cruel but also inhuman and degrading treatment. This includes not only actions which cause serious physical or psychological suffering, but which humiliate or force the individual [to act] against his will or conscience.[110]

While ultimately whether an act constitutes inhuman degrading treatment or punishment depends on the circumstances of the case, the Commission stated that the prohibition of torture, cruel, inhuman, or degrading treatment or punishment is to be interpreted as widely as possible to encompass the widest possible array of physical and mental abuses.[111] In this regard, the Commission observed that no government has the right to apply physical violence on individuals for offences because that would be tantamount to sanctioning state sponsored torture under the Charter.[112]

---

107 Communication 236/2000, *Curtis Francis Doebbler v. Sudan*, Sixteenth Annual Activity Report of the African Commission on Human and Peoples' Rights (Annex VII). See also M Banderin 'Recent developments in the African regional human rights system' (2005) 5/1 *Human Rights Law Review* 133.

108 Art 152 of the Sudanese Criminal Law of 1991 provides as follows: "1. Whoever commits, in a public place, an act, or conducts himself in an indecent or immoral dress, which causes annoyance to public feelings, shall be punished, with whipping, not exceeding forty lashes, or with fine, or with both. 2. The act shall be deemed contrary to public morality, if it is so considered in the religion of the doer, or the custom of the country where the act occurs."

109 *Curtis Francis Doebbler v. Sudan* (n 107 above) para 3.

110 As above, para 36.

111 As above, para 37.

112 As above, para 42.

The Commission further rejected the argument by Sudan that the lashings were justified because the authors of the petition committed acts found to be criminal according to the laws in force in the country. It did not, however, address Sudan's argument that 'it was better for the victims to have been lashed rather than hold them in detention for the said criminal offences and as such deny them of the opportunity to continue with their normal lives.'[113] This is a relativist argument often advanced to establish that lashing is less cruel, inhuman or degrading than imprisonment. The argument, however, fails to appreciate that a punishment does not lose its degrading character just because it is a more effective deterrent.[114]

The Commission's jurisprudence on the violation of Article 5 of the Charter is rather scanty because it is yet to articulate on what amounts to torture, cruel, inhuman and degrading punishment in the context of the African Charter as has been done in the European and Inter-American systems.[115] This may partly be attributed to the few communications alleging the violation of this right. The fact that there are few complaints on the violation of this right, however, does not necessarily depict the situation on the ground. This is because, and sadly so to state, many practices which violate these provisions continue to persist throughout the continent.[116] Notably, corporal punishment still punctuates the criminal laws of many African states.[117] Certain religious and cultural practices such as amputation of limbs as criminal punishment are also common.

---

113   As above, para 34.

114   Banderin (n 107 above) 133.

115   See, for example, *Tyrer v. UK* (1978) 2 *ECHR* 1, where the court held that birching by order of a judicial authority in the Isle of Man amounted to degrading punishment and violated art 3 of the European Convention. Similarly, the court held in *Campbell and Cosans v. UK* (1982) 4 *ECHR* 293 that although birching in Scottish schools did not violate art 3 of the Convention *per se,* suspension of the applicants from school refusing to submit to the punishment was in breach of parental convictions against corporal punishment protected under art 2 of Protocol no. 1.

116   Nmehielle (n 65 above) 90.

117   For instance, s 18 of the Criminal Code of Southern Nigeria and s 68(i)(f) of the Penal Code of Northern Nigeria, which authorise flogging for prescribed offences. section 55(i)(d) of the Penal Code allows the reasonable chastisement of a wife by her husband, if they are married under the customary law. See Umozurike (n 2 above) 44.

Although the Commission has not evolved substantial jurisprudence on the right against torture and inhuman or degrading treatment, it has all the same taken initiatives to elaborate on, and protect this right. For instance, it adopted a 'Resolution on Guidelines and Measures for the Prohibition and Prevention of Torture, Cruel, Inhuman or Degrading Treatment or Punishment in Africa' (Robben Island Guidelines).[118] The Robben Island Guidelines (RIG) approaches the question of torture in three broad ways: prohibition, prevention, and responding to the needs of victims.[119]

Specifically, the guidelines require states to, *inter alia*: criminalise torture; combat impunity for both nationals and non-nationals who commit acts of torture; establish complaints and investigation procedures to which all persons can bring their allegations of torture; take steps to ensure that conditions of detention comply with international standards; and train and empower, among others, law enforcement officers so that they refrain from using torture.[120]

The guidelines also oblige states to ensure that all victims of torture and their dependants are offered appropriate medical care, have access to appropriate social and medical rehabilitation, and are provided with appropriate levels of compensation and support.[121] Remarkably, the guidelines recognise families and communities which have been affected by the torture and ill-treatment of one of its members as torture victims.[122]

Suffice it to state that, in spite of it being a step towards the right direction, the RIG is not binding on states, as it is a mere declaration and not a treaty. Additionally, its purported enforcement mechanism is said to be very weak.[123] This is because, the guidelines establish a follow-up committee of only five members with the mandate to

---

118   'Resolution on Guidelines and Measures for the Prohibition and Prevention of Torture, Cruel, Inhuman or Degrading Treatment or Punishment in Africa' (hereafter the 'Robben Island Guidelines' or 'RIG'); adopted by the African Commission at its 32nd ordinary session, 17-23 October 2002, Banjul, The Gambia, Sixteenth Annual Activity Report (2002-2003).

119   For a detailed discussion on these guidelines see, Mujuzi (n 101 above) 440.

120   As above.

121   RIG, Part III (49-50 a-c).

122   As above.

123   Mujuzi (n 101 above) 440.

organise seminars, to disseminate the RIG, to develop and propose to the Commission strategies to promote and implement the RIG at national and regional levels, to promote and facilitate the implementation of the RIG within member states, and to draft a progress report to the African Commission at each session.[124] This is clearly too much work for only five individuals.

In another initiative the Commission liaised with certain institutions, especially prison authorities, in some European countries in an effort to gain an insight on how, among other things, torture can be prevented in places of detention.[125] Commissioners have in the past visited countries such as France. The Commission has also granted observer status to many NGOs that deal with torture.[126] It is hoped that with time, the Commission's jurisprudence on the violation of this right will evolve to address the perturbing levels of torture, inhuman and degrading treatment or punishment on the continent.

5.2.1.4 RIGHT TO LIBERTY AND SECURITY OF THE PERSON

Article 6 of the Charter provides that 'every individual shall have the right to liberty and to the security of his person. No one may be deprived of his freedom except for reasons and conditions previously laid down by law. In particular, no one may be arbitrarily arrested or detained.' This Article guarantees individuals physical liberty by prohibiting unlawful arrests and detention. The enjoyment of this right, however, is subject to reasons and conditions laid down by law. The right to liberty and security of the person requires the state to have justifiable grounds for depriving a person of his or her liberty, and further requires such deprivation to be in accordance with stipulated procedures.[127]

---

124   As above.

125   See Thirteenth Annual Activity Report of the African Commission on Human and Peoples' Rights, para 27 & Fifteenth Annual Activity Report of the African Commission on Human and Peoples' Rights, para 30.

126   For a detailed discussion of the role of NGOs in the African human rights system, see Z Motala 'Non-governmental organisations in the African system', in Murray & Evans (n 20 above) 246-279.

127   Nmehielle (n 65 above) 92.

The Charter is not explicit on what 'law' this right should be subjected to: is it international law or domestic legislation? One might argue that the drafters intended the term 'law', as used in this Article, to mean international law. This is because there is imminent danger in subjecting the formulation of the parameters of this right to domestic legislation. The danger is to the effect that what is 'law' in a certain domestic jurisdiction may be an oppressive legislation that facilitates the violation of this right.[128] Essentially, we would agree with the proposition that the law to be relied on in limiting this right must be consistent with the standards recognised under international law.[129]

The African Commission has had the opportunity to address communications alleging violation of Article 6 of the Charter. In *Henry Kalenga v. Zambia*[130], for example, the complainant, who was detained without trial, petitioned the Commission for his release. Zambia's Ministry of Legal Affairs later informed the Commission of his release, after being in detention for three years. The Commission proceeded to declare the matter amicably resolved without consulting the victim. The conclusion of the case by the Commission without developing its jurisprudence on this right or pronouncing the appropriate relief was rather disappointing. Similarly, in *International Pen v. Burkina Faso*[131], where the victim alleged unlawful detention, a notification to the Commission of the release of the victim was enough for it to declare the matter amicably resolved.

The Commission's approach of declaring communication's amicably resolved without giving substantive reasoning was not taken lightly.[132] Subsequently, it resolved to adopt a new approach of contacting the petitioner(s) to inquire whether other forms of relief are desirable besides release from detention.[133] It also found

---

128　As above.

129　As above.

130　Communication 11/88, *Henry Kalenga v. Zambia*, ACHPR/LR/A1 (1997).

131　Communication 22/88, *International Pen v. Burkina Faso*, ACHPR/LR/A1 (1997) 7.

132　See, for example, the arguments in Ankumah (n 89 above) 123.

133　A good example is Communication 62/91, *Committee for the Defense of Human Rights (Jennifer Madike) v. Nigeria*, ACHPR/LR/A1 (1997), where despite receiving information that the detainee had been released, the Commission inquired of the petitioner if it wished to pursue the case further.

violation of Article 6 where a victim was detained for seven years without trial.[134] While this is a welcome step in the right direction, the Commission must go ahead to determine the award of compensation in cases where it finds a violation of Article 6, or any other provisions of the Charter.[135] The fact that Article 6 does not make specific provisions regarding compensation should not in any way deter the Commission from applying the standards known in international law, especially as authorised in Article 60 of the Charter.[136]

5.2.1.5 RIGHT TO A FAIR TRIAL

Article 7 guarantees the right to a fair trial in the following terms:

1. Every individual shall have the right to have his cause heard. This comprises

(a) the right to an appeal to competent national organs against acts violating his fundamental rights as recognised and guaranteed by conventions, laws, regulations and customs in force;

(b) the right to be presumed innocent until proved guilty by a competent court or tribunal;

(c) the right to defence, including the right to be defended by counsel of his choice;

(d) the right to be tried within a reasonable time by an impartial court or tribunal.

2. No one may be condemned for an act or omission which did not constitute a legally punishable offence at the time it was committed.

---

134   Communication 103/93, *Alhassan Abubaka v. Ghana*, Tenth Annual Activity Report of the African Commission on Human and Peoples' Rights (Annex X); Communication 39/90 *Annette Pagnoulle (on behalf of Abdoulaye Mazou) v. Cameroon*, Eighth Activity Report of the African Commission on Human and Peoples' Rights (Annex VI).

135   Nmehielle (n 65 above) 94.

136   As above. Art 60 provides that: 'The Commission shall draw inspiration from international law on human and peoples' rights, particularly from the provisions of various African instruments on human and peoples' rights, the Charter of the United Nations, the Charter of the Organisation of African Unity, the Universal Declaration of Human Rights, other instruments adopted by the United Nations and by African countries in the field of human and peoples' rights as well as from the provisions of various instruments adopted within the Specialised Agencies of the United Nations of which the parties to the present Charter are members.'

No penalty may be inflicted for an offence for which no provision was made at the time it was committed. Punishment is personal and can be imposed only on the offender.

This Article lays down some essential components of a fair trial, namely: (i) fair hearing; (ii) the right of appeal; (iii) presumption of innocence; (iv) defence by counsel of one's choice; (v) trial by an impartial court or tribunal; (vi) individual criminal responsibility; and (vii) prohibition of ex-post facto laws.

Article 7(1)(a) guarantees the right to an effective appeal to competent national organs against acts violating fundamental rights as recognised and guaranteed by conventions, laws, regulations and customs in force. According to the construction of the Commission, the term 'appeal' seems to refer to the right to lodge an appeal to a higher court, where one exists. In *The Constitutional Rights Project (Zamani Lekwot & 6 others) v. Nigeria*[137], the victims were convicted and sentenced to death under the Nigerian Civil Disturbances (Special Tribunal) Act. The petitioners contended, *inter alia,* that there was a violation of the right to appeal under Article 7(1)(a) of the Charter. The Commission held that to foreclose any avenue of appeal to 'competent national organs' in criminal cases violates Article 7(1)(a) of the African Charter.

The Commission had earlier held section 11(4) of the Nigerian Armed Robbery and Firearms (Special Provisions) Act[138], which restricted appeals, to be a violation of the right to appeal guaranteed under Article 7(1)(a) of the Charter.[139] The Commission has also found 'the system of executive confirmation, as opposed to appeal, provided for in the institution of special tribunals' to be contrary to Article 7(1)(a).[140] In other words, special tribunals are not entitled

---

137 Communication 87/93, *The Constitutional Rights Project (Zamani Lekwot & 6 others) v. Nigeria*, ACHPR/LR/A1 (1997) 104.

138 The sub-section provided that 'no appeal shall lie from a decision of a tribunal under this Act or from any confirmation or dismissal of such decision by the governor.'

139 Communication No. 60/91, *Constitutional Rights Project (Wahab Akunnu, G Adega & Others) v. Nigeria*, ACHPR/LR/A1 (1997) 58.

140 Communication 48/90, *Amnesty International & others v. Sudan,* Thirteenth Annual Activity Report of the African Commission on Human and Peoples' Rights (Annex V) para 69.

to substitute the right to appeal with the system of executive confirmation.

The phrase 'competent national organs' in Article 7(1)(a) has been said to envisage ingredients such as the expertise of the judges and the inherent justice of the laws under which they operate.[141] Consequently, 'to deprive a court of the personnel qualified to ensure that they operate impartially denies the right to individuals to have their case heard by such bodies.'[142] Reference to 'court or tribunal' in the subsection indicates that the Charter applies to all courts and tribunals, whether specialised or ordinary.[143]

Thus, the Commission has maintained that a military tribunal, *per se*, is not offensive to the rights in the Charter, nor does it imply an unfair or unjust process; neither is such a tribunal negated by the mere fact of being presided over by military officers.[144] However, such tribunals may present serious problems in areas of equitable, impartial and independent administration of justice. For them to be recognised, at least in the context of subsection 7(1)(a) of the Charter, they must be subject to the same requirements of fairness, openness, justice, independence, and due process as any other ordinary court.[145]

Article 7(1)(b) deals with the presumption of innocence, which is a criminal law principle that requires a person to be presumed innocent until proved guilty. In criminal cases, the burden of proof lies with the prosecution. In most military dictatorships, however, this right has always been infringed in a bid to secure quick justice.[146] The Commission has found violation of this right in a

---

141   As above.

142   As above.

143   See N Udombana 'The African Commission on Human and Peoples' Rights and the development of fair trial norms in Africa' (2006) 6 *African Human Rights Law Journal* 312.

144   Communication 151/96, *Civil Liberties Organisation v. Nigeria,* Thirteenth Annual Activity Report of the African Commission on Human and Peoples' Rights (Annex V) paras 27 & 44.

145   As above.

146   As above.

number of cases.[147] For instance, in *Annette Pagnoulle v. Cameroon*[148], the Commission held that the detention of the complainant for two years after he had served his sentence of imprisonment on the suspicion that he 'may cause problems' was a violation of his right to be presumed innocent.

In *Media Rights Agenda and others v. Nigeria*[149], Mr. Niran Malaolu and three other staff of a Nigerian newspaper, *the Diet newspaper,* were arrested by armed soldiers at the editorial offices of the newspaper in Lagos on 28 December 1997. Neither Mr. Malaolu nor his three colleagues were informed of the reasons for their arrest or shown a warrant of arrest.[150] Three of the arrestees were later released, but Mr. Malaolu continued to be held without charges until 14 February 1998, when he was arraigned before a special military tribunal for his alleged involvement in a coup. Throughout the period of his incarceration, he was not allowed access to his lawyer, doctor or family members.[151] On 28 April 1998, the tribunal, after a secret trial, found the accused guilty of concealment of treason and sentenced him to life imprisonment.[152] The African Commission held that his right to a fair trial, including the right to be presumed innocent until proven guilty, had been breached.[153]

The sub-section also requires proof of guilt to be conducted by a competent court or tribunal. To facilitate this process, the state must employ competent and qualified umpires to preside over cases. These umpires must be impartial and independent of executive influence.[154] In *Constitutional Rights Project (in respect of Zamani Lekwot and 6 others) v Nigeria*[155], the Commission found a bench composed of members of the armed forces and police to be partial

---

147   See for example, *Orton and Vera Chirwa v. Malawi* (n 43 above).

148   *Annette Pagnoulle (on behalf of Abdoulaye Mazou) v. Cameroon* (n 134 above).

149   Communication 224/98, *Media Rights Agenda and others v. Nigeria,* Fourteenth Annual Activity Report of the African Commission on Human and Peoples' Rights, (Annex V).

150   As above, para 4.

151   As above, para 7.

152   As above, para 8.

153   As above, para 43.

154   See *Rencontre Interafricaine pour la Defense des Droits de l'Homme v. Zambia* (n 43 above).

155   *The Constitutional Rights Project (Zamani Lekwot & 6 Others) v. Nigeria* (n 137 above).

and therefore in violation of Article 7(1)(b). A competent court is one whose judges (or magistrates) are duly qualified, meeting both legal and natural qualifications such as integrity.[156]

Suffice it to state that presumption of innocence, as contemplated in Article 7(1)(b), demands that the arrestee should be informed of the reasons for his being arrested. Such information must also be availed timely to avoid miscarriage of justice. This would allow the person to prepare his defence and where necessary, prove his innocence. It is unfortunate, however, that the Charter does not provide for, among other things, the right of arrestees to be informed, in a language that they understand, of reasons for their arrest and the charges against them. It was the African Commission's 'Resolution on the Right to Recourse Procedure and Fair Trial' that attempted to fill this gap. This resolution shall be revisited later.

Article 7(1)(c) guarantees every person the right to defence. The African Commission has defined this to envisage 'all sorts of elements required to prepare for one's defence.'[157] One such element that is expressly stipulated in the Charter is the right to be defended by Counsel of one's choice. Thus, trial without being defended was held to be a violation of Article 7(1)(c).[158] The guarantee of the right to be defended by 'Counsel' of one's choice is problematic if 'Counsel' is understood to mean a fully qualified and admitted lawyer.[159] It has correctly been suggested that the term 'Counsel' should be taken to mean 'legal representative' and nothing more.[160]

The Commission found a violation of the provision when Defence Counsel was harassed during a trial to the point where

---

156   Umozurike (n 2 above) 44.

157   See Communication 144/95, *William Curson (acting on behalf of Severo Moto) v Equatorial Guinea,* Eleventh Annual Activity Report of the African Commission on Human and Peoples' Rights (Annex II) para 21.

158   Communication 64/92, 68/92 & 78/92, *Krishna Achuthan (on behalf of Aleke Banda), Amnesty International (on behalf of Orton and Vera Chirwa) v. Malawi,* Seventh Annual Activity Report of the African Commission on Human and Peoples' Rights (Annex IX); Eighth Annual Activity Report of the African Commission on Human and Peoples' Rights (Annex VI).

159   See Ankumah (n 89 above) 126.

160   C Heyns 'Civil and political rights in the African Charter' in Murray & Evans (n 20 above) 158.

he withdrew from the case.[161] A similar finding was made when a Defence Counsel was allegedly assaulted by soldiers.[162] It has also been held that the right to be defended by Counsel of one's choice implies that one has the right of access to a lawyer when being detained without trial.[163] In *Media Rights Agenda and others v. Nigeria*[164], the complainant alleged, *inter alia,* that Mr. Malaolu was denied the right to be defended by lawyers of his choice and was, instead, assigned a military lawyer by the tribunal, in contravention of the right to a fair hearing.[165] The African Commission, relying on paragraph 2(e)(i) of its 'Resolution on the Right to Recourse and Fair Trial', conceded that there was a violation of the accused's basic guarantees.[166]

In *Avocats Sans Frontières (on behalf of Bwampamye) v. Burundi*[167], the African Commission was called upon to rule that, by denying Mr. Gaetan Bwampamye's Counsel the right to plead his case, the Criminal Chamber of the Ngozi Court of Appeal held a hearing which was not equitable in terms of the African Charter.[168] The communication alleged, although the Criminal Chamber of the Court of Appeal accorded the prosecution the right to make oral submissions, the Defence Counsel was denied the same.[169] The Commission recalled that the right to fair trial involves 'fulfilment of certain objective criteria, including the right to equal treatment, the right to defence by a lawyer, especially where this is called for by the interests of Justice, as well as the obligation on the part of

---

161   *International Pen, Constitutional Rights Project, Interights on behalf of Ken Saro-Wiwa Jr and Civil Liberties Organisation v. Nigeria* (n 81 above) 158.

162   As above, para 97.

163   *Media Rights Agenda and Constitutional Rights Project v. Nigeria* (n 6 above).

164   *Media Rights Agenda and others v. Nigeria* (n 149 above) para 11.

165   As above, para 11.

166   As above, para 56. Para 2(e)(i) of the 'Resolution on the Right to Recourse and Fair Trial' stipulates, 'In the determination of charges against individuals, the individual shall be entitled in particular to: (i) … communicate in confidence with Counsel of their choice.'

167   Communication 231/99, *Avocats Sans Frontières (on behalf of Bwampamye) v. Burundi,* Fourteenth Annual Activity Report of the African Commission on Human and Peoples' Rights (Annex V).

168   As above, para 11(a).

169   As above, paras 9–10.

Courts and Tribunals to conform to international standards in order to guarantee a fair trial to all.'[170] The Commission went further to elucidate the components of the right to equal treatment by stating that it means:

> ... in the first place, that both the defence and the public prosecutor shall have equal opportunity to prepare and present their pleas and indictment during the trial. Simply put, they should argue their cases before the jurisdiction on an equal footing. Secondly it entails the equal treatment of all accused persons by jurisdictions charged with trying them. This does not mean that identical treatment should be meted to all accused. The idea here is the principle that when objective facts are alike, the response of the judiciary should also be similar. There is a breach of the principle of equality if judicial or administrative decisions are applied in a discriminatory manner.[171]

The Commission's observations were indeed very constructive given that it interpreted the right to defence broadly enough to include equality of treatment of the accused persons and the prosecution. Where parties to a dispute are not afforded equal opportunities during trial, it is likely that justice would be compromised. Additionally, the Commission held that the right to defence also implies, at each stage of the criminal proceedings, the accused and his Counsel should be able to reply to indictment of the public prosecutor.[172]

Although the Charter guarantees the right to legal representation, it fails to make provision for legal aid or assistance. The European[173] and Inter-American[174] human rights systems have provisions for legal assistance. A distinction can be drawn on the circumstances under which free legal assistance is granted in the European and American systems. Under the European system, legal assistance is a

---

170   As above, para 26.

171   As above, para 27.

172   As above, para 28.

173   See European Convention art 6(3)(c), which guarantees the right of a person charged with criminal offence to: 'defend himself in person or through legal assistance of his own choosing or, if he has not sufficient means to pay for legal assistance, to be given it free when the interest of justice so requires.'

174   See art 8(2)(e) of the American Convention, which stipulates the: 'inalienable right to be assisted by Counsel provided by the state, paid or not as the domestic law provides, if the accused does not defend himself or herself personally, or engage his or her own Counsel within the time period established by law.'

right in criminal cases 'where [the accused] does not have sufficient means to pay for legal assistance' and 'when the interest of justice so requires' that the person should be granted such assistance.[175]

Under the American system, on the other hand, legal assistance is an inalienable right to be assisted by state-provided Counsel. This right accrues under two circumstances; first, if the accused does not wish to defend himself or herself personally and, secondly, if the accused fails to engage his or her Counsel within the time period established by law.[176] By extension, this means that legal assistance is granted to ensure a speedier rendition of justice to the accused person.

A combined reading of the above provisions of the European and American Conventions leads one to effectively conclude that the provision of free legal aid or assistance could be necessitated by at least two circumstances, namely that (i) the interest of justice so requires and (ii) the person is indigent, meaning that he or she does not have sufficient means to pay for legal representation. Boukongou contended, the determination of 'interest of justice' in criminal cases is based on the seriousness of the offence and the severity of the sentence, whilst in civil cases it is based on the complexity of the case and the ability of the party to adequately represent himself or herself; the rights to be affected; and the likely impact of the outcome of the case on the wider community.[177] This reasoning partly explains why free legal aid and assistance in many African countries is granted only to indigents in capital offences.

It cannot be gainsaid, the right to legal aid and assistance is an integral component of fair trial as it ensures that indigent persons are not denied fair hearing due to their insufficient, or lack of means to hire competent Counsel. However, the provision of legal aid and assistance is a capital-intensive undertaking, which many African states have found very difficult to accomplish effectively from their

---

175   European Convention, art 6(3)(c).

176   American Convention, art 8(2)(e).

177   J Boukongou (n 47 above) 290.

own resources.[178] It is not clear how the African Commission could be accessed by indigent persons, especially because no state makes provision for legal aid for the submission of cases to an international authority.

A serious thought should be given to ways and means the African human rights system, which is in an environment characterised by abject poverty, could attend to indigent complainants. Arguably, many poor people across the continent are unable to file complaints with the Commission due to inadequate financial means. Resource constraints notwithstanding, states need to commit themselves to legal assistance if the right to fair hearing is to be guaranteed.

Article 7(1)(d) guarantees the right of an accused to be tried within a reasonable time by an impartial court or tribunal. The Charter's reference to 'reasonable time' is to ensure that proceedings are not unduly prolonged. The rationale for the provision is to safeguard the speedy rendition of justice to ensure effectiveness and credibility.[179] Reasonableness of the duration of proceedings, however, depends on the particular circumstances of a case. The Commission held the detention of a victim for seven years without trial to be a violation of the right to be tried within a reasonable time under Article 7(1)(d).[180] Similarly, detention without trial was termed as a violation of this provision.[181]

The Commission has also interpreted what might reasonably constitute an impartial court or tribunal under Article 7(1)(d). In *Constitutional Rights Project (Akumu) v. Nigeria*[182], the impartiality provision was dealt with in relation to the special tribunals that had been created in Nigeria to deal with cases involving robbery and firearms. The Commission stated:

---

178   N Udombana 'The African Commission on Human and Peoples' Rights and the development of fair trial norms in Africa' (2006) 6 *African Human Rights Law Journal* 312.

179   See Nmehielle (n 65 above) 99.

180   *Alhassan Abubakar v. Ghana* (n 134 above).

181   See Communication 74/92, *Commission Nationale des Droits de l'Homme et des Libertes v. Chad*, Ninth Annual Activity Report of the African Commission on Human and Peoples' Rights (Annex VIII).

182   *Constitutional Rights Project (Wahab Akunu, G Adega &. others) v. Nigeria* (n 139 above).

The Robbery and Firearms (Special Provision) Act, Section 8 (1), describes the constitution of the tribunals, which shall consist of three persons: one judge, one officer of the Army, Navy or Air Force and one officer of the Police Force. Jurisdiction has thus been transferred from the normal courts to a tribunal chiefly composed of persons belonging to the executive branch of the government, the same branch that passed the Robbery and Firearms Decree, whose members do not necessarily possess any legal expertise. Article 7 (1) (d) of the African Charter requires the court or tribunal to be impartial. Regardless of the character of the individual members of such tribunals, its composition alone creates the appearance of, if not actual, lack of impartiality. It thus violates Article 7 (1) (d).[183]

Accordingly, it could be said that impartiality under this provision has a nexus with independence from executive interference. A court or tribunal that is not independent from executive interference is obviously not expected to be impartial, especially where the executive is a party to a case.[184]

The last of the legal protections afforded to an accused person under Article 7 of the Charter is the prohibition of ex-post facto laws. Article 7(2) prohibits retroactive punishment. The Article also provides for individual criminal responsibility. The provision prohibits the introduction of new offences with retrospective effects. Article 7(2) is, however, not confined to prohibiting the retrospective application of criminal law to an accused's disadvantage. It also embodies, more generally, the principle that only the law can define a crime and prescribe a penalty and the principle that criminal law must not be extensively construed to an accused's detriment.[185]

In *Media Rights Agenda and Constitutional Rights Project v. Nigeria*[186], the Commission stated that Article 7(2) must be read to prohibit not only infliction of punishment for acts not constituting crimes at the time they were committed, but to retroactivity itself.[187] It further observed that, 'an unjust but un-enforced law undermines . . . the

---

183   As above.

184   Nmehielle (n 65 above) 100.

185   As above, 101.

186   *Media Rights Agenda and Constitutional Rights Project v. Nigeria* (n 6 above).

187   As above, para 59.

sanctity in which the law should be held.'[188] The Commission has also been seized with communications alleging transfer of criminal liability to persons related to the accused. Members of an accused person's immediate and extended families have in certain instances allegedly been arrested, detained and even prosecuted for offences they did not commit.[189] The Commission has, however, not dealt with this issue comprehensively.

Although the Charter and the Commission seem to attach significance to the right to fair trial, certain pertinent aspects of this right have been overlooked. For instance, the Charter does not provide for public hearing. This is regrettable because some African states have been notorious in holding what Bello called 'secret proceedings', which are largely unfair to the accused person.[190] The Charter also does not provide for the right of an accused person to be assisted by an interpreter which is particularly essential in Africa because a majority of the accused are indigenous, whereas court proceedings are usually conducted in foreign languages such as English, Portuguese, Spanish, Arabic or French.[191] This limitation in language, coupled with complex court procedures emphasise the need to have interpreters for accused persons. Further, the Charter does not guarantee the right against self-incrimination or double jeopardy or compensation for miscarriage of justice.[192] These shortcomings in the Charter are discussed in detail elsewhere herein.

It is important to mention, however, that the Commission has tried to overcome some of the shortcomings and deficiencies of the Charter in relation to this right by adopting a number of resolutions. For instance, at its 11th Ordinary Session, it adopted a resolution on

---

188   As above, para 60.

189   See for example, *Alhassan Abubakar v. Ghana* (note 180 above) 116; Communication 108/93, Monja Joana v. Madagascar, Tenth Annual Activity Report of the African Commission on Human and Peoples' Rights 125; and Communication 142/94, Muthuthurin Njoka v. Kenya, Eighth Annual Activity Report of the African Commission on Human and Peoples' Rights 141.

190   See E Bello 'The African Charter on Human and Peoples' Rights: An analysis' (1985) *Recuel Des Cours* 156.

191   Nmehielle (n 65 above) 102.

192   Ankumah (n 89 above) 131.

the right to a fair trial.[193] The resolution underscores the importance that the Commission attaches to the right to fair trial. It recalled Article 7 of the African Charter and stressed that 'the right to a fair trial is essential for the protection of fundamental human rights and freedoms.'[194] In summary, the resolution amplifies Article 7 of the Charter as follows[195]:

(a) All persons shall have the right to have their cause heard and shall be equal before the courts and tribunals in the determination of their rights and obligations.

(b) Persons who are arrested shall be informed, at the time of arrest, in a language which they understand of the reason for their arrest and shall be informed promptly of any charges against them.

(c) Persons arrested or detained shall be brought promptly before a judge or other officer authorised by law to exercise judicial power and shall be entitled to trial within a reasonable time or be released.

(d) Persons charged with a criminal offence shall be presumed innocent until proven guilty by a competent court.

(e) In the determination of charges against individuals, the individuals shall be entitled in particular to—

    (i) have adequate time and facilities for the preparation of their defence and communicate in confidence with Counsel of their choice;

    (ii) be tried within a reasonable time;

    (iii) examine, or have examined, the witnesses against them and to obtain the attendance and examination of witnesses against them; and

    (iv) have the free assistance of an interpreter if they cannot speak the language used in the court.

Additionally, in 1996, the Commission, at its 19th Ordinary Session, adopted the 'Resolution on the Respect and the Strengthening of

---

193   See 'Resolution on the Right to Recourse Procedure and Fair Trial', Fifth Annual Activity Report of the African Commission on Human and Peoples' Rights, 1991–1992, ACHPR/RPT/5th (Annex VI).

194   As above, preamble.

195   As above, para 2.

the Independence of the judiciary.'[196] Among other things, it called on African countries to repeal all legislation that are inconsistent with principles of judicial independence, especially on the appointment and posting of judges; incorporate universal principles on judicial independence in their legal systems; and refrain from taking actions that could directly or indirectly threaten the independence and the security of judges and magistrates.[197]

The resolution was significant for several reasons. In the main, Judges have, on numerous occasions, been subjected to all forms of intimidation and persecution when carrying out their constitutional mandate.[198] The judiciary is particularly consigned and confounded into impotence by military regimes in many African countries. This has serious negative implications to the right to fair trial, since the harassment of judges 'makes them to look over their shoulders in the dispensation of justice.'[199]

Additionally, the 'Principles and Guidelines on the Right to a Fair Trial and Legal Assistance in Africa' were adopted by the African Commission in May 2003.[200] The Principles and Guidelines are very comprehensive, covering most of the recognised elements of the right to a fair trial and due process under international human rights law. Some of the specific elements covered are: judicial training; the right to an effective remedy; court records and public access; *locus standi*; the role of prosecutors; access to lawyers and legal services; legal aid and assistance; independence of lawyers; cross-border collaboration among legal professionals; access to judicial services; military courts; arrest and detention; criminal charges and trials; juvenile trials; victims of crime; abuse of power; and traditional courts.[201]

---

196   See 'Resolution on the Right to Recourse and Fair Trial', Ninth Annual Activity Report of the African Commission on Human and Peoples' Rights.

197   As above, para 1.

198   Udombana (n 178 above) 313. See also M Rishmawi M (ed) *Attacks on justice: The harassment and persecution of judges and lawyers* (2000) (reporting measures taken in different countries that affect judges or undermine the judiciary and the legal profession).

199   Udombana (n 178 above) 313.

200   'The Principles and Guidelines on the Right to a Fair Trial and Legal Assistance in Africa', cited in Banderin (n 107 above) 124.

201   As above.

The Principles and Guidelines therefore encompass almost all recognised pre-trial, in-trial and post-trial rights. Their adoption is a major leap towards the effective enforcement of the rights enshrined in Article 7 of the Charter. It is hoped that the Commission will articulate them in its jurisprudence whenever it is seized with communications alleging violation of Article 7 or any other relevant provision of the Charter.

5.2.1.6 RIGHT TO FREEDOM OF CONSCIENCE AND RELIGION

Article 8 guarantees the protection of two interrelated rights— right to freedom of conscience and religion. The Article stipulates that:

> Freedom of conscience, the profession and free practice of religion shall be guaranteed. No one may, subject to law and order, be submitted to measures restricting the exercise of these freedoms.

Right to freedom of conscience entitles a person to hold a belief or conviction, be it of cultural, religious, political or any other nature. The rationale of entrenching this right in the Charter is to allow an individual to hold a thought or belief that is independent of a state's or other entity's control *per se*.[202] Freedom of conscience in its broader sense envisages the right to profess and practice one's religion. This right, as contemplated under Article 8, includes the freedom to manifest one's religion or belief in public or in private, alone or with others, without the state's intervention.[203] This could be in the form of worship, teaching, practice and religious observance, among other activities.[204] Though not expressly provided in the Charter, freedom of religion could also include freedom to maintain or change one's religion or belief.

The right to freedom of conscience and religion under the Charter, however, is subject to law and order. The Charter appears to be keen to ensure the balance between freedom of conscience and religion, on the one hand, and on the other, the protection of individuals or society from religious or pseudo-religious practices,

---

202   Nmehielle (n 65 above) 104.

203   As above, 105.

204   As above. See also J Harris, *et al*, *Law of the European Convention on Human Rights* (1998) 361.

which may infringe other people's rights.[205] While states parties have the discretion to determine whether a particular religion or belief is appropriate, that discretion must not be exercised contrary to Article 8 of the Charter. In this regard, the African Commission has been faced with complaints alleging the violation of this Article.

In *Free Legal Assistance Group, Lawyers' Committee for Human Rights, Union Interafricaine des Droits de l'Homme, Les Temoins de Jehovah v. Zaire*[206], the complainants, who were Jehovah's Witnesses, were allegedly persecuted by the government of Zaire on the basis of their religious beliefs. The Commission held that such persecution violated Article 8 since the former Zaire government had presented no evidence that the practice of this religion threatened law and order.

The Commission has also held that freedom of religion has to be exercised in a way that does not violate the equal protection of the law, as guaranteed by the African Charter. Thus, it ruled against imposition of sharia trials and guaranteed the right of everyone to be tried by a secular court if they wish.[207] It is important to note, however, that in some African states, freedom of religion is limited to the practice of a certain religious faith. An example is Libya where Islam has been proclaimed to be state religion, and the Koran part of the country's laws.

The African Commission recently held that the freedom to manifest one's religion or belief does not in itself include a general right of the individual to act in accordance with his or her belief.[208] Rather, while the right to hold religious beliefs should be absolute, the right to act on those beliefs should not. In *Gareth Anver Prince v.*

---

205   Nmehielle (n 65 above) 105.

206   Communications 25/89, 47/90, 56/91 and 100/93, *Free Legal Assistance Group, Lawyers' Committee for Human Rights, Union Interafricaine des Droits de l'Homme, Les Temoins de Jehovah v. Zaire,* Ninth Activity Report of the African Commission on Human and Peoples' Rights (Annex VIII).

207   Communications 48/90, 50/91 and 89/93, *Amnesty International, Comite Loosli Bachelard, Lawyers Committee for Human Rights, Association of Members of the Episcopal Conference of East Africa v. Sudan,* Thirteenth Annual Activity Report of the African Commission on Human and Peoples' Rights (Annex V) para 73.

208   Communication 255/2002, *Gareth Anver Prince v. South Africa.*

South Africa[209], a South African citizen alleged that the Law Society of South Africa had refused to register him for practice, given his disclosure of two previous convictions for the possession of cannabis and his stated intention to continue to use it because its use was required by his Rastafarian religion. He alleged violation of, among other provisions, Article 8 of the African Charter.

The African Commission held that the restrictions on the use and possession of cannabis were reasonable and a legitimate limitation of Article 8.[210] Indeed, participating in one's religion should not be at the expense of the overall good of the society. Minorities like the Rastafarians may freely choose to exercise their religion, yet that should not grant them unfettered power to violate the norms that keep the whole nation together.[211]

5.2.1.7 RIGHT TO FREEDOM OF EXPRESSION

Article 9 guarantees the right to freedom of expression as follows:'1. Every individual shall have the right to receive information. 2. Every individual shall have the right to express and disseminate his opinions within the law.'The right to freedom of expression is the cornerstone upon which the very existence of a democratic society rests. It is indispensable for the formation of public opinion as it enables the society, when exercising its options, to be sufficiently informed.[212] The importance of freedom of expression is demonstrated by the many cases considered by the African Commission involving Article 9 violations.[213]

---

209   As above.

210   As above.

211   As above.

212   See Davidson (n 66 above) 310.

213   See, *inter alia*, Communications: *Amnesty International and others v. Sudan* (n 140 above); 102/93, *Constitutional Rights Project and Civil Liberties Organisation v Nigeria*, Thirteenth Annual Activity Report of the African Commission on Human and Peoples' Rights; 147/95, 149/96, *Sir Dawda K Jawara v. The Gambia*, Thirteenth Annual Activity Report of the African Commission on Human and Peoples' Rights; 137/94, 139/94, 154/96, 161/97, *International pen and others v. Nigeria*, Fourteenth Annual Activity Report of the African Commission on Human and Peoples' Rights; 232/93, *John D. Ouko v. Kenya*, Fourteenth Annual Activity Report of the African Commission on Human and Peoples' Rights; *Media Rights Agenda v. Nigeria* (n 149 above); *Media Rights Agenda and others v. Nigeria* (n 6 above).

The Commission observed in *Media Rights Agenda, Constitutional Rights Project, Media Rights Agenda and Constitutional Rights Project v. Nigeria*[214], that freedom of expression is a basic human right, vital to an individual's personal development, his political consciousness, and participation in the conduct of public affairs in his country.[215] The African Charter gave two aspects of this right namely: (i) the right to receive information and (ii) the right to express and disseminate one's opinion. Access to information is fundamental to encouraging transparency and accountability in the way the government and public authorities operate. Thus in *Amnesty International v. Zambia*[216], the Commission observed that the failure of the government to provide two deportees with reasons for the action taken against them 'means that the right to receive information was denied to them.'[217]

In *Constitutional Rights Project, Civil Liberties Organisation and Media Rights Agenda v. Nigeria*[218], where the communication dealt with the proscription of newspapers by the military government in Nigeria, the Commission held:

> The proscription of specific newspapers by name and the sealing of their premises, without a hearing at which they could defend themselves... amounts to harassment of the press. Such actions not only have the effect of hindering the directly affected persons in disseminating their opinions, but also pose an immediate risk that journalists and newspapers not yet affected by...the Decree will subject themselves to self-censorship... Decrees like these pose a serious threat to the public of the right to receive information not in accordance with what the government would like the public to know. The right to receive information is important: Article 9 does not seem to permit derogation, no matter what the subject of the information or opinion and no matter the political situation of a country.[219]

---

214   *Media Rights Agenda and others v. Nigeria* (n 6 above).

215   As above, para 54.

216   *Amnesty International v. Zambia* (n 6 above).

217   As above, para 33.

218   Communications 140/94, and 145/95, *Constitutional Rights Project, Civil Liberties Organisation and Media Rights Agenda v. Nigeria,* Thirteenth Annual Activity Report of the African Commission on Human and Peoples' Rights (Annex V).

219   As above, para 38.

In this regard, the Commission was emphasising the non-derogable nature of the right to receive information. The Commission's observations would, however, not have been complete had it not re-emphasised that the right was to be exercised within the confines of a pre-established law. It is clear, from the wording of Article 9(2), that the right to express and disseminate one's opinion may be restricted by law. This does not mean that national law can restrict this right to the extent that it becomes ineffective. To permit national law to take precedence over international law would defeat the purpose of codifying certain rights in international law and indeed, the whole essence of treaty making.[220] With regard to the restriction of rights through domestic legislation, the Commission has stated that restrictions should be as minimal as possible and not undermine rights guaranteed under international law.[221] Thus, any restrictions on rights should be the exception and not the rule.[222]

The Commission has expressed the importance of the right to freedom of expression by adopting resolutions to elaborate it beyond the Charter provisions. For instance, it has adopted a 'Resolution on the Right to Freedom of Expression'[223], and a 'Declaration of Principles on Freedom of Expression in Africa.'[224] While the 2002 Declaration identified freedom of expression 'as a cornerstone of democracy'[225] and stated that 'respect for freedom of expression... will lead to...the strengthening of democracy',[226] the Commission had not in its previous decisions on Article 9 specifically linked the right to freedom of expression to the strengthening of democracy in Africa.[227]

---

220   As above, para 40.

221   Communications 48/90, 50/91 and 89/93, *Amnesty International, Comite Loosli Bachelard, Lawyers Committee for Human Rights, Association of Members of the Episcopal Conference of East Africa v. Sudan,* Thirteenth Activity Report (Annex V) para 80.

222   As above.

223   Adopted at the 11th Ordinary Session of the African Commission, 2–9 March 1992.

224   Adopted at the 32nd Ordinary Session of the African Commission, 17–23 March 2002.

225   As above, first preambular paragraph.

226   As above, fourth preambular paragraph.

227   Banderin (n 107 above) 130.

The case of *The Law Offices of Ghazi Suleiman v. Sudan*[228] provided
the Commission with an opportunity to clarify its jurisprudence
on the provisions of Article 9 of the Charter and also to express
its view on the important link between freedom of expression
and the promotion and protection of democracy in Africa.[229] The
communication alleged that Mr. Ghazi Suleiman, a Khartoum based
lawyer and human rights advocate was prohibited from travelling
to deliver a public human rights lecture in Sinnar, Blue Nile State,
in the Sudan. He alleged that he had been threatened by some state
security officials that if he made the trip he would be arrested.[230]
The author complained of a violation of Article 9 of the Charter. In
upholding the complaint, the African Commission observed:

> In adopting the *Resolution on the Right to Freedom of Association*, the
> African Commission noted that governments should be especially
> careful that 'in regulating the use of this right, that the competent
> authorities should not enact provisions which would limit the exercise
> of this freedom … [and that] … the regulation of the exercise of
> the right to freedom of association should be consistent with state's
> obligations under the African Charter on Human and Peoples'
> Rights.'[231] Mr. Ghazi Suleiman's speech is a unique and important part
> of political debate in his country.[232]

The Commission went on to affirm the views of the Inter-American
Court of Human Rights to the effect that:

> Freedom of expression is a cornerstone upon which the very existence
> of a society rests. It is indispensable for the formation of public opinion.
> It is also a condition *sine qua non* for the development of political
> parties, trade unions, scientific and cultural societies and, in general,
> those who wish to influence the public. It represents, in short, the
> means that enable the community, when exercising its options, to be

---

228   Communication 228/99, *The Law Offices of Ghazi Suleiman v. Sudan*, Sixteenth
       Annual Activity Report of the African Commission on Human and Peoples' Rights
       (Annex VII).

229   See the analysis of this nexus in Banderin (n 107 above) 130.

230   *The Law Offices of Ghazi Suleiman v. Sudan* (n 228 above) para 3.

231   See 'Resolution on the Freedom of Association', adopted at the 11th Ordinary
       Session in Tunis from 2 to 9 March 1992. [Footnote retained].

232   *The Law Offices of Ghazi Suleiman v. Sudan* (n 228 above) para 46.

sufficiently informed. Consequently, it can be said that a society that is not well informed is not a society that is truly free.[233]

The Commission could therefore be taken to mean that when an individual's freedom of expression is unlawfully restricted, it is not only the right of that individual to disseminate information that is being violated but also the corresponding right of others to receive information and ideas. Hence, speech that contributes to political debate must be respected and protected.[234] In light of the important role of the right to freedom of expression in the fledging democracies in Africa today, these observations and findings by the Commission must be welcomed as landmark pronouncements.

5.2.1.8 RIGHT TO FREEDOM OF ASSOCIATION

According to Article 10(1), every individual is entitled to the right to free association.[235] This right envisages a number of components. For example, it contemplates the freedom of individuals to come together for the protection of their interests by forming a collective entity which represents them. These interests may be of a political, economic, religious, social, cultural, professional or labour union nature.[236] However, this does not mean that such an individual has an absolute right to become a member of a particular association. An association may decide not to admit or continue the membership of an individual without necessarily infringing on his right to freedom of association.[237]

Equally, an individual cannot be compelled to become a member of an association nor disadvantaged if he or she chooses not to do so. This right therefore precludes compulsion to join an association, but subject to Article 29 of the Charter.[238] Article 29(4) imposes

---

233 As above, para 49, quoting from *Compulsory Membership in an Association Prescribed by Law for the Practice of Journalism* (arts 13 & 29 American Convention on Human Rights) Advisory Opinion OC-5/85, Series A. N.5, November 1985 at para 70.

234 *The Law Offices of Ghazi Suleiman v. Sudan* (n 228 above) para 50.

235 Art 10(1) states: 'Every individual shall have the right to free association provided that he abides by the law.'

236 Nmehielle (n 65 above) 110.

237 As above.

238 Art 10(2) provides: 'Subject to the obligation of solidarity provided for in 29 no one may be compelled to join an association.'

duties on individuals 'to preserve and strengthen social and national solidarity, particularly when the latter is threatened.' This provision, read together with Article 10(2), limits the right to freedom of association to the effect that an individual could be forced into association in order to strengthen social and national solidarity.[239]

In *International Pen, Constitutional Rights Project, Interights on behalf of Ken Saro-Wiwa Jr and Civil Liberties Organisation v. Nigeria*[240], the Commission found that the tribunal which had convicted Saro-Wiwa and his fellow accused of murder did so because they were members of a political group. Their freedom of association as expressed through their membership in that group was thus violated.[241] The right to freedom of association has also been interpreted to include the right to disassociation.[242]

The Commission has cited many instances where the right to freedom of association may be violated. These include: banning of political parties[243], being arrested as a result of one's political belief[244] and the prohibition of any assembly for a political purpose in a private or a public place.[245] With regard to laws limiting the right to freedom of association, the Commission has held that they should include an objective description that makes it possible to determine the criminal nature of an organisation.[246]

---

239   See Heyns (n 160 above) 169.

240   *International Pen, Constitutional Rights Project, Interights on behalf of Ken Saro-Wiwa Jr and Civil Liberties Organisation v. Nigeria* (n 81 above).

241   As above, para 108.

242   Communication 101/93, *Civil Liberties Organisation in Respect of the Nigerian Bar Association v. Nigeria,* Eighth Annual Activity Report of the African Commission on Human and Peoples' Rights (Annex VI).

243   *Sir Dawda K. Jawara v. The Gambia* (n 213 above) para 68.

244   Communication 205/97, *Kazeem Amitu v. Nigeria,* Thirteenth Annual Activity Report of the African Commission on Human and Peoples' Rights (Annex V) para 22.

245   *Amnesty International, Comite Loosli Bachelard, Lawyers Committee for Human Rights, Association of Members of the Episcopal Conference of East Africa v. Sudan* (n 221 above) para 82.

246   Communications 54/91, 61/91, 98/93, 164/97-196/97 and 210/98, *Malawi African Association, Amnesty International, Ms Sarr Diop, Union Interafricaines des Droits de l'Homme and RADDHO, Collectif des Veuves et Ayants-droits, Association Mauritanienne des Droits de l'Homme v. Mauritania,* Thirteenth Annual Activity Report of the African Commission on Human and Peoples' Rights (Annex V) para 107.

Apart from its jurisprudence, the Commission has also adopted a resolution on the right to freedom of association with a view to strengthening the provisions of Article 10 of the Charter.[247] The resolution provides, *inter alia*, that:

> competent authorities should not override constitutional provisions or undermine fundamental rights guaranteed by the constitution and international human rights standards; ... in regulating the use of the right to association, the competent authorities should not enact provisions which will limit the exercise of the freedom and such a regulation should be consistent with state obligations under the Charter.[248]

Though the resolution may not be seen as dramatic in clarifying the provisions of the Charter on the right to freedom of association, it serves the purpose of emphasis. What is important, however, is that the Commission interprets the right bearing in mind the emphasis it has given to it in the resolution.

5.2.1.9 RIGHT TO FREEDOM OF ASSEMBLY

The right to freedom of assembly complements the right to freedom of association. Article 11 of the Charter provides that:

> Every individual shall have the right to assemble freely with others. The exercise of this right shall be subject only to necessary restrictions provided for by law in particular those enacted in the interest of national security, the safety, health, ethics and rights and freedoms of others.

The right to freedom of assembly allows individuals to engage in meetings, picketing, protest marches and demonstrations, as long as the assemblers aim to express a common opinion. In *Commission Internationale de Juristes v. Togo*[249], the African Commission found that the shooting at peaceful demonstrators by the Togolese military was a violation of the right to assembly. Since the purpose of the right is to protect assembly as a means of communicating opinion, the

---

247   'Resolution on the Right to Freedom of Association, adopted by the African Commission on Human and Peoples' Rights', at its 11 Ordinary Session, See *Documents of the African Commission* 225.

248   As above.

249   Communication 91/93, *Commission Internationale de Juristes v. Togo.*

assembly must be 'peaceful' and unarmed. Actions or laws aimed against armed or violent assemblies will therefore not constitute an infringement of the right to assemble.[250]

5.2.1.10 RIGHT TO FREEDOM OF MOVEMENT

Article 12 of the Charter stipulates as follows:

1.   Every individual shall have the right to freedom of movement and residence within the border of a state provided he abides by the law.
2.   Every individual shall have the right to leave any country including his own, and to return to his country. This right may only be subject to restrictions, provided for by law for the protection of national security, law and public order, public health or morality.
3.   Every individual shall have the right, when persecuted, to seek and obtain asylum in other countries in accordance with the laws of those countries and international conventions.
4.   A non-national legally admitted in a territory of a state party to the present Charter, may only be expelled from it by virtue of a decision taken in accordance with the law.
5.   The mass expulsion of non-nationals shall be prohibited. Mass expulsion shall be that which is aimed at national, racial, ethnic or religious groups.

The provisions of Article 12 could be divided into three main classes of rights: (i) freedom of movement within and freedom to return to an individual's country of origin or residence; (ii) the right to seek and obtain asylum; and (iii) the right not to be expelled extra-judicially or en mass.[251] Freedom of movement in the context of the Charter applies to 'every person', including aliens or stateless persons. This freedom is, however, subject to the sovereign power of a state to regulate and control the entry of aliens into its territory. This means in effect that an alien does not *per se* have an unqualified right to

---

250   See the Constitution of the Republic of South Africa art 17. See also Nmehielle (n 65 above) 113.

251   Nmehielle (n 65 above) 114.

enter, reside or remain in a particular country.[252] The Charter is silent on the expulsion of a person from the territory of a state which he or she is a citizen or national. This is rather strange given that many Africans have over the years been sent to exile by their countries, for holding or perpetuating divergent political views.

With regard to the rights of asylum seekers, Article 12(3) is quite an unusual provision in the sense that it provides that one has the right not only to seek but also to obtain asylum. Nmehielle correctly observed that, while a person may not be prevented from seeking asylum, the granting of asylum is entirely a different matter dependent upon the will of a state.[253] Whether or not a person should obtain or be granted asylum rests with the law of the territory in which asylum is sought and international law.[254] Further, the Charter gives persecution as a condition for the exercise of the right to seek and obtain asylum but does not indicate the grounds for the persecution. Generally, a person is afforded refugee status if he or she has been persecuted or has a well founded fear of persecution on account of race, religion, nationality, membership of a particular social group or political opinion.[255]

Article 12(4) and (5) prohibits two forms of expulsion of persons from the territory of a state party to the Charter. First, an alien lawfully admitted to any such territory may only be expelled pursuant to a decision reached in accordance with the law; Secondly, the mass expulsion of non-nationals. The Charter goes on to define mass expulsion as one aimed at national, racial, ethnic, or religious groups. Unlike the prohibition of the expulsion of lawfully resident non-nationals in member states, the prohibition of mass expulsion aims to protect groups of persons based on nationality, ethnicity, race and religion, whether or not such groups of persons are lawfully residing in the expelling state.[256] Mass expulsion has been an issue of

---

252   As above.

253   As above.

254   See art 12(3) of the African Charter.

255   See art 1(2) of the 1951 Geneva Convention Relating to the Status of Refugees.

256   Ankumah (n 89 above) 140.

concern in Africa. A notable example was the expulsion of Nigerians from Ghana in 1969.[257]

5.2.1.11 RIGHT TO PARTICIPATE IN THE GOVERNMENT OF ONE'S COUNTRY

Article 13 guarantees the right to participate in the government of one's country in the following terms:

1.   Every citizen shall have the right to participate freely in the government of his country either directly or through freely chosen representatives in accordance with the provisions of the law.

2.   Every citizen shall have the right of equal access to the public service of his country;

3.   Every individual shall have the right of access to public property and services in strict equality of all persons before the law.

Article 13 presents different facets in which the right to participate in the government of one's country may be enjoyed. Article 13(1), for example, provides that citizens may enjoy this right either directly or through freely chosen representatives. This seems to guarantee participation in decision making through a legislative body such as parliament. Essentially, this means that, subject to relevant electoral laws, citizens of a state party to the Charter are entitled to participate in periodic elections either as candidates or voters.[258]

The purpose of Article 13(1) is therefore to allow an individual, without apparent legal disability, to participate in periodic elections, exercise his or her voting rights, and participate in the conduct of public affairs directly or through freely chosen representatives.[259] By extension, the provision requires state authority to be based on the sovereignty of the people. Hence, this right is infringed when

---

257   As above.

258   See M Mbondenyi 'The right to participate in the government of one's country: An analysis of Article 13 of the African Charter on Human and Peoples' Rights in the light of Kenya's 2007 political crisis' (2009) 9 *African Human Rights Law Journal* 185-186.

259   Umozurike (n 2 above) 32.

any group or person seizes the reigns of government and imposes themselves on the rest of the population.[260]

Article 13(1) should be read in tandem with Article 20(1) which recognises the right to self-determination. This nexus was recognised by the African Commission in a case concerning an attempted secession from Zaire by Katanga.[261] Although the Commission held that there was no violation of Article 20, it could be inferred, from its observations, that massive human rights violations as well as the denial of the right to political participation under Article 13(1) could constitute transgressions of the Charter on such a scale that it would justify secession.[262]

In another case, the Commission held that to participate freely in government entails, among other things, the right to vote for the representative of one's choice and to have the results of free expression of the will of voters respected.[263] The Commission has also found a ban on members of a former government and parliament after a coup to be in violation of their Article 13(1) rights.[264]

The right to participate in the government of one's country cannot be fully enjoyed unless citizens have the right to equal access to, for example, public services and property.[265] The drafters of the Charter, in recognition of this fact, incorporated these important rights under Article 13(2) and (3). These two provisions resonate the importance of democratic governance in which citizens have unfettered rights to participate, as well as a reasonably unrestrained right of access to public property and services. Unfortunately, the issue of equal access to public services and property in many African states has remained very controversial and complicated for reasons

---

260   As above.

261   As above. See also Communications 75/92, *Katangese Peoples' Congress v. Zaire*, Eighth Annual Activity Report of the African Commission on Human and Peoples' Rights (Annex VI).

262   As above, para 6.

263   *Constitutional Rights Project v. Nigeria* (n 213 above) para 50.

264   *Sir Dawda K. Jawara v. The Gambia* (n 213 above) para. 67.

265   Mbondenyi (n 258 above).

ranging from legal complexities, political involvement, corruption and extreme poverty.[266]

This situation is exacerbated by the fact that some states still largely rely on laws and policies promulgated in the colonial era, which in many cases prevent the most disadvantaged groups from accessing public services and property that they need to survive. Due to such policies and laws, equitable land allocation and distribution, for example, have not as yet been achieved in most post-colonial African states.[267] Political contests in most African states have therefore become all the more charged because of what is at stake; those who achieve political power benefit from widespread abuses, including theft and misappropriation of public resources.[268]

Many African states have not taken heed of the citizens' right to participate in their government despite its fundamental importance to nation building. Consequently, Africans have been victims of governments of exclusion such as dictatorships, military rule, or single-party autocracies. Ethnicity, corruption and vote rigging have also had a hand in derailing the democratic process on the continent. It is encouraging to note that the importance of this right is resonated in the Constitutive Act of the African Union (hereafter 'CAAU' or 'the Act'). The Act condemns and rejects unconstitutional change of government.[269] In fact, it categorically states that a government that seizes power through unconstitutional means shall not be allowed to participate in the activities of the Union.[270]

The Union has a variety of options on how to deal with an unconstitutional government, including imposition of sanctions.[271] In 2008, Zimbabwe and Kenya were wallowing in political crises following disputed presidential elections which brought to question

---

266   J Achieng 'Protests against land reforms in Kenya' available at http://www.afrol.com/News/ken008_landreform2.htm (accessed 15 March 2010).

267   Mbondenyi (n 258 above).

268   As above.

269   See Constitutive Act of the African Union, art 4(p).

270   As above, art 30.

271   Art 23 provides as follows: '2. …any member state that fails to comply with the decisions and policies of the Union may be subjected to other sanctions, such as the denial of transport and communications links with other member states, and other measures of a political and economic nature to be determined by the Assembly.'

the legitimacy of their governments. In Kenya, the African Union initiated a mediation process that led to the signing of a power-sharing agreement between the warring political factions.[272] Months later, a similar move was undertaken in Zimbabwe. The AU's initiative in this regard is welcomed.

5.2.1.12 RIGHT TO PROPERTY

Article 14 provides for the right to property, stating that 'the right to property shall be guaranteed. It may only be encroached upon in the interest of public need or in the general interest of the community and in accordance with the provisions of appropriate laws.' The right to property guaranteed under this provision is the right to own property, hold it and to dispose of it. It should be noted, however, 'property' is not limited to land. Rather, the term should be taken to mean movable and immovable property. In *UIDF, FIDH, FADDHO, ONDH, AMDH v. Angola*[273], the Commission observed that the deportation of the non-nationals in this case called into question rights guaranteed under the Charter such as property rights. It concluded that the deportation of victims, thus separating them from their property constituted a violation of Article 14 of the Charter.

From the wording of Article 14, it can correctly be concluded that the enjoyment of the right to property is subject to encroach upon 'in the interest of public need or in the general interest of the community and in accordance with the provisions of the law.' The Charter, however, does not define what constitutes public or community interests. Additionally, it does not provide for compensation of state encroachment (acquisition) victims. The fact that state acquisition should be in accordance with appropriate laws is not sufficient enough to indicate whether the Charter subscribes to compensation of victims.[274] However, 'in accordance with

---

272   For a detailed account see Mbondenyi (n 258 above).

273   Communication 159/96, *UIDF, FIDH, FADDHO, ONDH, AMDH v. Angola*, Eleventh Annual Activity Report of the African Commission on Human and Peoples' Rights (Annex II).

274   Nmehielle (n 65 above) 119.

appropriate laws' could be construed to mean 'in accordance with international standards on state acquisition.'[275]

Thus, when interpreting Article 14 of the Charter, regard could be had to corresponding provisions of other human rights systems. Contextually, the Article is narrower than the corresponding provision of the American Convention, which is more progressive in the recognition of the right to property than any other regional human rights instrument.[276] Its Article 21(2) stipulates that 'no one shall be deprived of their property except upon payment of just compensation, for reasons of public utility or social interest...'

The African Commission and the Court can thus ensure that the power of the state to encroach upon private property for public or community interest is not abused, by requiring states to adhere to the international law principles of payment of just and adequate compensation. The amount of the compensation and the time and manner of the payment must reflect an equitable balance between the public interest and the interests of those affected, with due regard to all relevant circumstances.[277] Such circumstances should include, for example, the current use of the property; the history of the acquisition and use of the property; the market value of the property; the extent of direct state investment and subsidy in the acquisition and beneficial capital improvement of the property; and the purpose of the encroachment.[278] It would be more expedient if the time and manner of the payment is agreed to by those affected or in the alternative, decided or approved by a competent court of law.

In wrapping-up the above discussion on civil and political rights under the African Charter, it is inevitable to note that the jurisprudence of the Commission is yet to attain the standards of other international judicial mechanisms, such as the Inter-American and European human rights systems. As Murray noted, this may be partly because the Commission is faced with the difficult task of

---

275   As above.

276   As above. See the American Convention, art 21.

277   See art 25(3) of the Constitution of the Republic of South Africa.

278   As above.

overcoming the shortcomings in the way in which the Charter has been drafted.[279] In all fairness though, it is important to note that the Commission, as of recent, has shown some willingness to be creative in its interpretation of the Charter provisions.[280] There are certain instances, however, where it miserably failed to expound on certain rights even when the opportunity arose.

This is not very encouraging especially given that the substantive rights in the Charter are not elaborate. It is hoped that the establishment and operationalisation of the African Court on Human and Peoples' Rights will reverse this trend. The inadequacies of the civil and political rights provisions of the Charter, their possible reform, as well as the failure of the Commission to amplify them shall be discussed extensively in subsequent chapters of this book.

5.2.2   Economic, Social and Cultural Rights

The Charter guarantees the protection of a number of economic, social and cultural rights. As noted earlier in this chapter, the approach of the Charter with regard to this category of rights is a marked departure from that of other regional human rights systems. The Charter puts economic, social and cultural rights at par with other rights such as civil and political rights. Its Preamble categorically provides that:

> ...Civil and political rights cannot be disassociated from economic, social and cultural rights in their conception as well as universality and ... the satisfaction of economic, social and cultural rights is a guarantee for the enjoyment of civil and political rights.[281]

Whether or not the Charter purports to give more priority to economic, social and cultural rights than to civil and political rights is an issue that is debatable. Gittleman feared that giving priority to this category of rights over others would 'undoubtedly grant a state greater latitude to restrict or violate civil and political rights.'[282] This

---

279   Murray (n 7 above) 1.

280   As above, p. 3.

281   African Charter, preamble para 8.

282   See R Gittleman 'The African Charter on Human and Peoples' Rights: A legal analysis' (1982) 22 *Virginia Journal of International Law* 687.

sentiment reflects the prevalent misunderstanding and suspicion of the nature of economic, social and cultural rights and their place in the human rights paradigm. Whatever the Charter purports, it must be understood that human rights are interrelated and indivisible. Perhaps, what the drafters of the Charter wanted to emphasise is the importance of economic, social and cultural rights in the human rights discourse.

The most contentious issue on the Charter's economic, social and cultural rights provisions relates to their enforceability.[283] For many decades, socio-economic rights have been regarded as secondary rights. Mbazira rightly noted that, 'civil and political rights are thought to be 'absolute' and 'immediate', whereas economic, social and cultural rights are held to be programmatic; to be realised gradually and therefore not to be 'real' rights.'[284] The argument that socio-economic rights are not justiciable is based on the conception that these rights require vast resources for their implementation. This view, however, is blind to the fact that not all socio-economic rights need to be implemented immediately.[285]

Indeed, the International Covenant on Economic, Social and Cultural Rights (ICESCR) attests to this fact by requiring states to 'take steps to the maximum of [their] available resources, with a view to progressively achieving the full realisation of the rights ...'[286] Although the UN Committee on Economic, Social and Cultural Rights has said that some of the obligations are of immediate effect, this does not necessarily mean that states are compelled to do the impracticable.[287] The argument on impracticability of enforcement of socio-economic rights is also blind to the fact that the enforcement

---

283   See for example, Nmehielle (n 65 above) 124; Ankumah (n 89 above) 144.

284   See C Mbazira 'A path to realising economic, social and cultural rights in Africa? A critique of the New Partnership for Africa's Development' (2004) 4 *African Human Rights law Journal* 36. See also A Eide 'Economic, social and cultural rights as human rights' in E Eide, C Krause & A Rosas (eds) *Economic social and cultural rights: A text book* (2001) 10; K Arambulo *Strengthening the supervision of the International Covenant on Economic, Social and Cultural Rights* (1999) 58.

285   As above.

286   ICESCR, art 2(1).

287   Mbazira (n 284 above) 38. See also General Comment No:3 (Fifth session, 1990) [UN doc E/1991/23] 'The nature of the states' obligations' (art 2, para 1 of the Covenant).

of some civil and political rights may be equally impracticable. The right to life, for example, imposes an obligation on the state to provide security to its citizens. But this does not mean that murders are not committed. It is impracticable to provide every citizen with a policeman at his or her guard.[288]

One would therefore agree with Ankumah that economic, social and cultural rights are justiciable under the Charter, but there is the need for their progressive realisation, taking into consideration the circumstances faced by the states parties.[289] This aspect of the argument as well as the obstacles to the enforcement of this category of rights under the African human rights system is discussed elsewhere. It is expedient, however, to examine their normative framework under the Charter.

5.2.2.1 RIGHT TO EQUITABLE AND SATISFACTORY CONDITIONS OF WORK

Article 15 of the Charter guarantees the right to equitable and satisfactory work conditions as follows: 'Every individual shall have the right to work under equitable and satisfactory conditions, and shall receive equal pay for equal work.' According to Ankumah, this provision obligates states to adopt programmes and other measures to create job opportunities for every person.[290] This interpretation should, however, be faulted in as far as it construes the 'right to work' to mean the imposition of an obligation on the state to create job opportunities, more so, for every person. Umozurike argued, and rightly so, that the Charter does not guarantee the right to work *simpliciter* because that would have been an impossible task, given the economic situation of most African states.[291] Faced with the scarcity of industries and a limited wage system, a majority of Africans are peasant farmers and petty traders.[292]

---

288   As above.

289   See Ankumah (n 89 above) 144.

290   As above.

291   Umozurike (n 2 above) 65.

292   As above.

Arguably, this provision obligates states parties to adopt measures and programmes that would ensure a conducive work environment. One would think in terms of measures such as: fair and equitable wages; the right to promotion where appropriate; the right to follow one's vocation and to change employment; reasonable working hours; right to paid vacation (leisure and rest); safe working conditions; and non-discrimination of individuals in their place of work.[293]

The right to work under satisfactory conditions also precludes sexual harassment at the work place. States parties to the Charter are therefore obligated to come up with suitable legislation and policies to prohibit such vices that may render work conditions un-equitable and unsatisfactory. It should be noted, the Charter, unlike Article 7 of both the ICCPR and ICESCR, does not expressly guarantee the right to rest, leisure, limited working hours and paid holidays. It has been argued that a broad interpretation of the phrase 'equitable and satisfactory conditions' would encompass all these aspects of the right.[294]

The African Commission found a violation of Article 15, among other provisions, in *Annette Pagnoulle (on behalf of Abdoulaye Mazou) v. Cameroon*.[295] The victim in this case was a Magistrate who had been tried and sentenced to 5 years' imprisonment. Upon his release, the government of Cameroon refused to reinstate him to his position as a Magistrate. Under an Amnesty law of 23 April 1992, persons granted amnesty and who had public employment were to be reinstated. The Commission held that by not reinstating Mr. Mazou to his former position, the government was in violation of Article 15.[296]

5.2.2.2 Right to Health

Article 16 of the Charter guarantees everyone the right to enjoy the best attainable state of physical and mental health. States parties to the Charter are obliged to take the necessary measures to protect

---

293   See in this regard, the ICESCR and the European Social Charter (ESC), which clearly define the parameters of this right.

294   Nmehielle (n 65 above). 125.

295   *Annette Pagnoulle (on behalf of Abdoulaye Mazou) v. Cameroon* (n 134 above).

296   As above, p. 56.

the health of their people and to ensure that they receive medical attention when they are sick.[297] The measures contemplated in this Article include, but are not limited to: elimination of epidemics; availing health services to the people through construction of adequate hospitals and health centres; promulgation of appropriate health policies; establishing appropriate legal standards that empower people to demand action against the violation of their right to health; and provision of free vaccinations, drugs and other healthcare services.[298] Arguably, this provision also prohibits the denial of emergency medical treatment to indigent persons.

In *Free Legal Assistance Group, Lawyers' Committee for Human Rights, Union Interafricaine des Droits de l'Homme, Les Temoins de Jehovah v. Zaire*,[299] the Commission found that the failure of the government of Zaire to provide the complainants with basic services such as safe drinking water and electricity constituted a violation of the right to health. It also held that the shortage of medicines was a breach of the duty to protect the health of the people under Article 16 of the Charter.

While it was innovative to link the provision of basic services to the right to health, the interpretation of the right by the Commission in this case is somewhat overbroad. Not all basic services are linked to health. It would be appropriate for the Commission to specify that the failure by the government to provide basic services is a violation of the right to health only to the extent to which the failure violates this right.[300]

5.2.2.3 RIGHT TO EDUCATION

Article 17 of the Charter guarantees the right to education.[301] This right envisages a number of components, such as the right to

---

297   See Article 16(1) & (2).

298   Umozurike (n 2 above) 65.

299   *Free Legal Assistance Group, Lawyers' Committee for Human Rights, Union Interafricaine des Droits de l'Homme, Les Temoins de Jehovah v. Zaire* (n 206 above).

300   Nmehielle (n 65 above) 127.

301   The Article provides: '1. Every individual shall have the right to education. 2. Every individual may freely take part in the cultural life of his community. 3. The promotion and protection of morals and traditional values recognised by the community shall be the duty of the state.'

primary education, the right to secondary education, the right to higher education, the right to fundamental education and the right to choice of schools. While Article 17 does not elaborate on the content of the right to education, other international instruments can be consulted in this regard. Under the European Convention, for example, the right is treated as a civil and political right.[302] This gives it more force in terms of the obligation imposed on states to enforce it. Under the Inter-American system, it is one of the economic, social and cultural rights which are subject to the individual complaint procedure under Article 44 of the American Convention.

In the American and European systems, as well as the ICESCR, the right is guaranteed more elaborately than in the African Charter. The Charter provisions overlook aspects such as the right to choice of education. The right to choice of education is important because it allows parents to decide the kind of education they think is appropriate for their children.[303] It corresponds with the right of parents to have their children educated in conformity with their own religious, cultural, moral and philosophical convictions. Article 17(2) and (3) could thus be read to mean that education is intended to facilitate the promotion of cultures, morals and traditions of communities.[304]

The African Commission emphasised on the importance of the right to education in *Free Legal Assistance Group, Lawyers' Committee for Human Rights, Union Interafricaine des Droits de l'Homme, Les Temoins de Jehovah v. Zaire*[305], when it stated that the closure of universities and secondary schools, as alleged in the communication, constituted a violation of Article 17. The Commission has also taken the initiative to strengthen the provisions of Article 17 by defining the scope of the right to education in its guidelines for state reporting.[306] The guidelines indicate that the right to education comprises the

---

302   See art 2, First Protocol to the European Convention.

303   Nmehielle (n 65 above) 130.

304   As above.

305   *Free Legal Assistance Group, Lawyers' Committee for Human Rights, Union Interafricaine des Droits de l'Homme, Les Temoins de Jehovah v. Zaire* (n 206 above).

306   See Old Guidelines for National Periodic Reports, section II(B) (42)- (59).

right to primary education, secondary education, post-secondary education, fundamental education, the right to choice of schools and the principle of free and compulsory education for all.[307]

In order to ensure the effective realisation of this right, the state must consider all reasonable educational alternatives. This means that possibilities should be explored on how people can receive education in the language of their choice, rather than the foreign languages that were instituted during the colonial era. Education must also be practicable, equitable and non-discriminative. Therefore, whereas the right to education gives individuals the freedom to establish and maintain, at their own expense, independent educational institutions, the same should not be used as a basis to discriminate people on racial, social status, political or religious grounds. Such institutions should also not be allowed to maintain standards that are inferior to those of comparable public educational institutions.

5.3   COLLECTIVE AND PEOPLES' RIGHTS UNDER THE CHARTER

The African Charter provides for collective and peoples' rights. These rights, also known as 'solidarity', 'group' or 'third generation' rights, because they can be realised only through the concerted efforts of all the actors on the social scene, are the latest to be recognised by the international community.[308] Accordingly, they cannot be claimed by any person in an individual capacity. They are rights that belong to individuals as a community, be it ethnic or national.[309] While this may be the case, it should be noted, however, the African Charter does not subordinate individual rights to collective rights. Instead, it establishes a link between the inalienable rights of the individual and of the group in a contextual manner.[310] Thus, it recognises the importance of the co-existence of both categories of rights.

---

307   Nmehielle (n 65 above) 129.

308   K Vasak 'For the third generation of human rights: The rights of solidarity', (Inaugural Lecture, 10th Study of the International Institute of Human Rights, Strasbourg, July 1979).

309   Umozurike (n 2 above) 70.

310   See the argument in this regard in T Boven 'The relations between peoples' rights and human rights in the African Charter' (1986) 2/4 *Human Rights Law Journal* 191.

Indeed, one of the paragraphs in its preamble emphasises this relationship by stating that member states of the OAU/AU recognise, 'on the one hand, that fundamental human rights stem from the attributes of human beings, which justifies their national and international protection, and on the other hand, that the reality and respect of peoples' rights should necessarily guarantee human rights.'[311] This paragraph emphasises the need to look at human rights holistically, meaning, from both the individual and collective perspectives.

Ironically, despite the fact that it recognises collective rights, the Charter is silent on the definition of the term 'peoples', which has repeatedly been used to give credence to this category of rights. The absence of a working definition of the term has solicited different interpretations and responses from scholars.[312] Consequently, there is uncertainty on the application and enforceability of the collective rights provisions of the Charter since the term embodies many different facets. One of the facets relates to peoples subject to colonial or alien domination. Seen from this perspective, the Charter uses the term to underscore the struggle for the eradication of colonialism in Africa.[313] Heyns regards some of the provisions on peoples' rights as a reflection of the reaction to the continental experience of slavery and colonialism.[314]

The term also refers to the population of a state as a whole.[315] Murray cited different occasions when the African Commission mentioned, for example, the protection of the 'people of Rwanda', 'people of Togo', 'people of Liberia' and 'people of South Africa.'[316] Another interpretation of the term as employed in the Charter signifies the people of Africa in general. The Preamble to the Charter mentions the awareness of African states of their duty to 'achieve the

---

311   African Charter, Preamble, para 5.

312   Dersso (n 30 above) 360.

313   As above.

314   C Heyns 'The African regional human rights system: The African Charter' (2004) 108 *Pennsylvania State Law Review* 679.

315   Dersso (n 30 above) 361. See in this regard art 23(2)(b) of the African Charter.

316   See R Murray & S Wheatley 'Groups and the African Charter on Human and Peoples' Rights' (2003) 25 *Human Rights Quarterly* 231.

total liberation of Africa, the peoples of which are still struggling for their dignity and genuine independence.'[317] Similarly, the African Commission has on several occasions spoken of 'African peoples.'[318] Finally, 'peoples' is also used to refer to the distinct communities within a state. In this sense, the subjects of peoples' rights are the different ethnic groups or inhabitants of a particular territory within a state, who on account of historical, cultural and/or existing patterns of discrimination have come to form a sense of separate identity.[319]

The African Commission has contributed to the uncertainty of the meaning of the term 'people', owing to the different interpretations and divergent opinions from its members. During one of the Commission's sessions, for example, Commissioner Nguema commented: '... I think that according to the interpretation and even the principles which are enforced in the OAU at the level of the states it is admitted that we do not have to take account of the rights of various ethnic groups to consider them as peoples' rights.'[320] Conversely, Commissioner Umozurike retorted: '... there is no way that people here simply means all the people of the country— it is people that have an identifiable interest, and this may be carpenters, may be tribes, may be fishermen or whatever.'[321]

The fact that even the Commissioners seem not to agree on the definition of 'peoples' in the context of the Charter indicates that so far there is no standard to determine the working definition of the term for purposes of the African human rights system. In other words, it is not as yet very clear how and when a group qualifies to be a 'people', and hence a subject of peoples' rights. The attribution of the term to any group of persons, such as 'fishermen' or 'carpenters',

---

317   See the African Charter, para 8 to preamble.

318   See 'Resolution on the Celebration of African Day of Human Rights', Second Annual Activity Report of the African Commission on Human and Peoples' Rights (Annex VII); 'Resolution on the African Commission on Human and Peoples' Rights', Sixth Annual Activity Report of the African Commission on Human and Peoples' Rights.

319   Art 19 of the Charter stipulates: 'All peoples shall be equal; they shall enjoy the same respect and shall have the same rights. Nothing shall justify the domination of a people by another.'

320   African Commission, Examination of State Reports (Libya-Rwanda-Tunisia) General Discussions (9th session March 1991) http://www1.umn.edu/humanrts/achpr/sess9-generaldiscussions.htm (accessed 15 May2010).

321   As above.

certainly emphasises the need to clarify the meaning of the concept in the African context.[322]

Although there is no general consensus on the definition of 'peoples', some working characteristics of the term have emerged from studies made under the auspices of UNESCO.[323] Such characteristics include: common historical traditions; ethnic group identity; cultural homogeneity; linguistic unity; religious or ideological affinity; territorial connection; and common economic life.[324] In addition, the group as a whole must have the will to be identified as a people or the consciousness of being a people.[325] What follows, therefore, is a discussion of the nature and scope of this category of rights as reflected in the African Charter's provisions and the Commission's jurisprudence.

5.3.1   RIGHT TO THE PROTECTION OF THE FAMILY AND OTHER RELATED RIGHTS

Article 18 of the Charter provides for a number of group rights. The groups envisaged therein are: the family, children, women, the aged and the disabled. It states that:

1. The family shall be the natural unit and basis of society. It shall be protected by the state which shall take care of its physical and moral health.

2. The state shall have the duty to assist the family which is the custodian of morals and traditional values recognised by the community.

3. The state shall ensure the elimination of every discrimination against women and also ensure the protection of the right of the women and the child as stipulated in international declarations and conventions.

4. The aged and the disabled shall also have the right to special measures of protection in keeping with their physical and moral needs.

---

322   Dersso (n 30 above) 364.

323   See UNESCO, 'Meeting of Experts on International Law', Paris, February, 1990.

324   As above.

325   As above.

The Article identifies the family as the custodian of the moral and traditional values recognised by the community. The rights guaranteed to the family may include the rights to found a family, to marry and to have a family. It may also include the right not to get married without one's consent and equality in marriage.[326] The rationale for incorporating this provision is to ensure the peaceful existence of the family. In *UIDH, FIDH, RADDHO, ONDH and AMDH v. Angola*[327] it was held that deportation of the victims leading to separation from their families was a violation of Article 18 of the Charter which guarantees the right to the protection of the family.

Other than promoting its physical and moral health, the Charter does not specify ways in which the state could assist the family. It is not enough for the state to create a legislative framework to secure family rights. It must, in addition, strive to create social conditions that would enable families to flourish. It has been proposed that the state could, for example, undertake special programmes geared towards training of families in order to help create a stable and positive environment in which children will be imparted with virtues and values.[328]

In addition to the promotion and protection of the family, Article 18 also obliges states to protect the rights of women and children. In addressing women's rights, states are required to ensure the elimination of every form of discrimination against women and also to ensure the protection of their rights as stipulated in international declarations and conventions. This provision of the Charter has attracted mixed reactions arising from the juxtaposition of women with the rather complex and controversial notions of the family, tradition and morality.[329]

---

326   Nmehielle (n 65 above) 132.

327   *UIDH, FIDH, RADDHO, ONDH and AMDH v. Angola* (n 273 above).

328   Nmehielle (n 65 above) 132.

329   See, for example, C Beyani 'Towards a more effective guarantee of women's rights in the African human rights system' in R Cook (ed) *Human rights of women: National and international perspectives* (1994) 285; F Butengwa 'Using the African Charter on Human and Peoples' Rights to secure women's access to land in Africa' in Cook, *op cit*, 503; L Kois 'Article 18 of The African Charter on Human and Peoples' Rights: A progressive approach to the women's human rights' (1997) 3 *East African Journal of Peace and Human Rights* 92.

One view is that Article 18(3) consigns women's rights to a 'legal comma'.[330] It has also been argued that it protects women in the context of the family and that outside this arena there is not much protection afforded to women.[331] It has also been criticised for failing to address numerous issues affecting the rights of women such as Female Genital Mutilation (FGM), inheritance by women, and forced marriages.[332] In spite of these observations, some of which are true, it has now been established that the intention of the drafters of the Charter was not to suppress women's rights in Africa. This fact is vindicated by the adoption of a Protocol on the rights of women.[333] The Protocol is comprehensive enough to address some of the concerns raised by the critics of Article 18(3) of the Charter.

The second part of Article 18(3) guarantees the protection of the rights of the child in accordance with international declarations and conventions. Children are usually vulnerable and need special support in order to fully enjoy their rights. They need family care and protection from abuse, neglect, forced labour, forced marriages, detention, among other concerns. The rights of the Africa Child have indeed been addressed more comprehensively in a separate instrument.[334] The African Charter on the Rights and Welfare of the Child, apart from providing for substantive rights, sets up a supervisory organ, the African Committee of Experts on the Rights and Welfare of the Child to monitor its enforcement.[335]

With regard to the rights of the aged and disabled, Article 18(4) stipulates that this category of persons shall have the right to special measures of protection in keeping with their physical

---

330   K Elmadmad 'The rights of women under the African Charter on Human and Peoples' Rights' in W Benedek & W Heinz (eds) *Regional systems of human rights in Africa, America and Europe: Proceedings of the conference* (1992) 17.

331   M Nsibirwa 'A brief analysis of the Draft Protocol to the African Charter on Human and Peoples' Rights on the Rights of Women' (2001) 1 *African Human Rights Law Journal* 41.

332   As above.

333   Protocol to the African Charter on Human and Peoples' Rights on the Rights of Women in Africa; adopted by the 2nd Ordinary Session of the Assembly of the African Union in Maputo (11 July 2003).

334   African Charter on the Rights and Welfare of the Child; OAU Doc. CAB/LEG/24.9/49 (1990); entered into force 29 November 1999.

335   African Charter on the Rights and Welfare of the Child, art 44.

or moral conditions. Like many other rights in the Charter, the rights of the aged and disabled have not received adequate attention from the African Commission. The protection afforded this class of people must go beyond providing suitable facilities, food and specialised medical care, to providing them with opportunities to engage in productive activities, commensurate with their abilities and consistent with their vocations or desires.[336]

Additionally, states should ensure that disabled and old persons are able to access public places such as buildings and other social infrastructure. This is essential because, most public offices have not been designed to allow, for example, people on wheel-chairs to access them. Public lavatories and streets in most African towns and cities do not have rumps which may ease the movement of such persons. As a result, many rights civil and political as well as socio-economic of such persons are violated. For instance, their right to freedom of movement is significantly limited. The same could be said of their right to freedom of association in as far as they are impaired by such factors to associate with other members of the society. The African Commission should look for ways of facilitating the enjoyment of all the rights contained in the Charter by this category of persons to the fullest possible extent, without necessarily waiting for communications alleging violation of their rights.

5.3.2   RIGHT TO SELF-DETERMINATION

Article 19 of the Charter defines the content of the right to self-determination by providing that 'all peoples shall be equal; they shall enjoy the same respect and shall have the same rights. Nothing shall justify the domination of a people by another.' Article 20 expounds this provision by providing that:

> 1.   All peoples shall have the right to existence. They shall have the unquestionable and inalienable right to self-determination. They shall freely determine their political status and shall pursue their economic and social development according to the policy they have freely chosen.

---

336   Nmehielle (n 65 above) 137.

2.   Colonised or oppressed peoples shall have the right to free themselves from the bonds of domination by resorting to any means recognised by the international community.

3.   All peoples shall have the right to the assistance of the states parties to the present Charter in their liberation struggle against foreign domination, be it political, economic or cultural.

From the wording of the Article, it can be concluded that self-determination under the African human rights system entails the following components: (i) the right to existence; (ii) the right of all peoples to freely determine their political status and to pursue their economic and social development according to the policy they have freely chosen; (iii) the right of colonised or oppressed peoples to free themselves from the bonds of dominion by resorting to any means recognised by the international community; and (iv) the right of all peoples to get assistance of the states parties in their liberation struggle against foreign domination, be it political, economic or cultural.

The Charter is categorical that the right to self-determination is unquestionable and inalienable. It is difficult, therefore, for one to agree with the argument that Article 20 of the Charter could only have been intended to underscore the colonial experience and domination of Africa.[337] The fact that Article 20(1) guarantees all peoples the right to freely determine their political status and to pursue their economic and social development according to the policy they have freely chosen, clearly indicates that this provision was also intended for post-colonial Africa.

This essentially means that people have the right to form a government, establish and exercise control over their own institutions, and work towards their self-development. Such a government can only subsist where like-minded people with a common ideology and political belief come together.[338] Where a group within a state fundamentally disagrees with other groups on issues pertaining to governance, such a group should be allowed,

---

337   As above, 142.

338   As above.

under the principle established in Article 20(1), to secede and form their own government. Unfortunately, this has not been the interpretation given to Article 20 of the Charter.

In *Katangese Peoples' Congress v. Zaire*[339], the people of Katanga wanted to secede from the former Zaire. The Commission agreed that self-determination may be exercised in a number of ways, such as independence, self-government, local government, federalism, confederalism, unitarism or any other form of relations that accords with the wishes of the people. The Commission, however, observed that this must be fully cognisant of other recognised principles, such as sovereignty and territorial integrity.[340] It vehemently maintained that it was obliged to uphold the sovereignty and territorial integrity of Zaire as a member of the former OAU and a party to the African Charter.

It further ruled that in the absence of concrete evidence of violations of human rights to the point that the territorial integrity of Zaire is called to question, and in the absence of evidence that the people of Katanga were denied the right to participate in government as guaranteed by Article 13(1) of the African Charter, Katanga could only exercise a variant of self-determination that is compatible with the sovereignty and territorial integrity of Zaire.[341] From the foregoing, one could conclude that, under the African human rights system, the right to self-determination is recognised within the limits of the territorial integrity of a state.

The Commission also considered the issue of peoples' right to self-determination in relation to the separatist movement of Casamance in Senegal.[342] After analysing the positions of both the government and the separatist movement, the Commission rejected the claim of the separatists for the independence of Casamance

---

339 Communication 75/92, *Katangese Peoples' Congress v. Zaire*, ACHPR/LR/A/1 (1997) 91-92.

340 As above, para 5.

341 As above, para 26.

342 'African Commission Report on the Mission of Good Offices to Senegal of the African Commission on Human and Peoples' Rights', Tenth Annual Activity Report of the African Commission on Human and Peoples' Rights (Annex VIII)(hereinafter the 'Casamance case').

from Senegal as lacking 'pertinence.'[343] Although it criticised the Senegalese state because it 'had a mechanical and static conception of national unity', the Commission recommended that the issue must be addressed within the framework of 'the cohesion and continuity of the people of the unified Senegalese state in a community of interest and destiny.'[344] This clearly indicates the Commission's preference for national unity over and above the right to secede.

From the analysis, Article 20(1) of the Charter seems to guarantee the right to secede in exceptional circumstances. Be that as it may, not to recognise that there can be cases of well founded secessionist pleas is not only to turn a deaf ear to living reality, but also a blind eye to the conceptual deficiency of the old normative framework on the issue of secession.[345] The African Commission should adopt certain prescriptive measures, which would ensure that neither frivolous claims are allowed to dent its competence, nor is the right to secede denied to genuine claimants.[346]

Article 20(2) explicitly intended to block foreign domination. It has correctly been argued that the provision has not yet been overtaken by events, even though all African states have now attained independence.[347] The provision guarantees 'colonised and oppressed' people the right to free themselves from the bonds of domination. 'Oppressed people', it is observed, could well be within sovereign states because oppression manifests itself in different forms–social, economic, political *etcetera.*[348] Thus, the application of this provision should not be confined to freedom from colonial domination, but may be extended to contemporary forms of oppression. Finally, Article 20(3) obligates states parties to the Charter to assist people in the liberation struggle against foreign domination, politically, economically or culturally. This provision seems to have outlived

---

343   As above.

344   As above.

345   See in this regard, C Okeke 'A note on the right of secession as a human right' (1996) III *Annual Survey of International and Comparative Law* 35.

346   Nmehielle (n 65 above) 145.

347   As above.

348   As above.

its purpose and therefore it is not any relevant to the contemporary African society.

5.3.3   RIGHT OVER WEALTH AND NATURAL RESOURCES

Article 21 guarantees the right over wealth and natural resources. This right is a component of self-determination, and has been so regarded since the adoption of the 'UN Resolution on Permanent Sovereignty Over Natural Resources.'[349] In the resolution, the UN General Assembly recognised 'that the under-developed countries have the right to determine freely the use of their natural resources… in order to be in a better position to further the realisation of their plans of economic development in accordance with their national interests.'[350]

A distinction may be drawn in the way Article 21 of the Charter guarantees this right to the 'peoples' and states. While it is the right of all peoples to freely use, exploit, and dispose of their natural wealth and resources[351], states are under obligation to exercise control over the same.[352] The obligations of the state in this regard are two-fold: (i) to individually and collectively exercise the right to freely dispose of their wealth and natural resources with a view to strengthening African unity and solidarity[353]; and (ii) to eliminate all forms of foreign economic exploitation particularly that practiced by international monopolies so as to enable their peoples to fully benefit from the advantages derived from their national resources.[354]

It is not clear why international monopolies were seen as the possible foreign economic exploiters in the context of Article 21(5). States are also known to have participated in foreign exploitation, particularly during colonialism. As Umozurike observed, the drafters of the Charter seemed to have forgotten this fact too soon,

---

349   G.A res. 1803 (XVII), 17 UN GAOR Supp (no:17) 15, UN Dec. A/5217 (1952), cited in Nmehielle (n 65 above) 146.

350   As above.

351   African Charter, art 21(1), (2) & (3).

352   Art 21(4) & (5).

353   Art 21(4).

354   Art 21(5).

especially given that many African states were barely two decades into independence at the time the Charter was adopted.[355]

The findings and recommendations of the African Commission in *Social and Economic Rights Action Centre (SERAC) & another v. Nigeria*[356] (otherwise known as the '*Ongoni case*' or '*SERAC case*') bring out very pertinent issues on Article 21 of the Charter. The communication was brought on behalf of the Ongoni people, alleging that the military government of Nigeria had, among other provisions, violated Article 21 of the Charter by virtue of being directly involved in oil production through the state oil company, the Nigerian National Petroleum Company (NNPC), the majority shareholder in a consortium with Shell Petroleum Development Corporation (SPDC).[357]

It was the complainants' contention that, by disposing toxic wastes into the environment and local waterways, the oil consortium exploited oil reserves in Ongoniland with no regard for the health or environment of the local communities. The consortium also allegedly neglected and/or failed to maintain its facilities causing numerous avoidable spills in the proximity of villages. The resulting contamination of water, soil and air had serious short and long-term health impacts, including skin infections, respiratory ailments, and increased risk of cancers, and neurological and reproductive problems.[358] The African Commission found a violation of the right to free disposal of one's wealth and natural resources under Article 21. It noted that:

> … despite its obligation to protect persons against interferences in the enjoyment of their rights, the Government of Nigeria facilitated the destruction of the Ongoniland. Contrary to its Charter obligations and despite such internationally established principles, the Nigerian Government has given the green light to private actors, and the oil Companies in particular, to devastatingly affect the well-being of

---

355   Umozurike (n 2 above) 68.

356   Communication 155/96, *Social and Economic Rights Action Centre (SERAC) & another v. Nigeria,* Fifteenth Annual Activity Report of the African Commission on Human and Peoples' Rights (Annex V).

357   As above, para 1.

358   As above, para 2.

the Ogonis. By any measure of standards, its practice falls short of
the minimum conduct expected of governments, and therefore, is in
violation of Article 21 of the African Charter.[359]

With regard to the violation of Article 21(5) of the Charter, which
imposes a duty on states parties to undertake to eliminate all forms
of foreign exploitation particularly that practised by international
monopolies, the Commission stated:

> Governments have a duty to protect their citizens, not only through
> appropriate legislation and effective enforcement, but also by protecting
> them from damaging acts that may be perpetrated by private parties.
> This duty calls for positive action on the part of governments in
> fulfilling their obligations under human rights instruments.[360]

The Commission seemed to suggest that, although the Nigerian
government had the right to produce oil to fulfil the economic
and social rights of Nigerians as a whole, it equally had the duty to
protect the interests of the Ongonis who were being affected by its
activities. Hence, when a state allows private persons or groups to act
freely and with impunity to the detriment of the rights recognised
in the Charter, it would be in violation of its obligations to protect
the human rights of its citizens.[361] There is, therefore, an obligation
on governmental authorities to take steps to make sure that private
persons do not interfere with the enjoyment of the rights in the
Charter.

5.3.4   RIGHT TO ECONOMIC, SOCIAL AND CULTURAL DEVELOPMENT

Article 22 of the Charter encapsulates the controversial right to
development. This right, which is relatively new, was first enunciated
by Keba M'Baye.[362] At the request of the UN Commission on
Human Rights, the UN Secretary-General made a study in which
he concluded that a large number of principles based on the UN

---

359   As above, para 58.

360   As above, para 57.

361   As above.

362   See K M'Baye 'Le droits development comme un droits de l'homme' (1982) 5 *Review Droit de l'Homme* 623.

Charter and human rights texts and declarations confirm the existence of the right to development.[363]

The right to development, considered holistically, includes political, economic, social and cultural processes aimed at the constant improvement of the well-being of all individuals.[364] This right guarantees all people free participation in the economic, social and cultural processes of their states and the fair distribution of the proceeds. Owing to its broad spectrum, the right to development should be construed in the light of other related rights contained in the Charter, *inter alia,* the right to self-determination, the right to exercise sovereignty over wealth and natural resources, the right to a general satisfactory environment and the right to peace and territorial integrity.[365] Although the Charter imposes a duty on the state, either individually or collectively, to ensure the exercise of the right to development, it fails to be precise on the scope of the duty and on how this right could be exercised. It is therefore up to the state to be innovative to ensure the enjoyment of this right.

The emergence of the New Partnership for Africa's Development (NEPAD) has revived hopes for the realisation of Article 22 of the Charter, which has all along been a dead letter. As already stated, NEPAD is a strategic framework for Africa's renewal, designed to support the vision and goals of the AU.[366] Although it is an economic development programme, in many ways it emphasises the fact that human rights, peace and development are inter-dependent matters.[367] Through this initiative, African leaders have set an agenda for the renewal of the continent. This agenda is based on national and regional priorities and development plans that must be prepared through a participatory process involving the people of

---

363   As above. See also UN Doc. E/CN/4/1334 (1979) para 305.

364   J Swanson 'The emergence of new rights in the African Charter' (1991) 12 *New York Law School Journal of International & Comparative law* 317.

365   As above.

366   See 'NEPAD in brief' available at http://www.nepad.org/2005/files/inbrief.php (accessed 1 March 2010).

367   See W Nagan 'Implementing the African renaissance: Making human rights comprehensive for the new millennium' available at http://www.cha.uga.edu/CHA-CITS/Nagan_paper.pdf (accessed 1 March 2010).

Africa.[368] NEPAD is therefore a framework intended, among others, to define the nature of the interaction between Africa and the rest of the world, including the industrialised countries and multilateral organisations.[369]

It is needless to emphasise that the protection and respect for human rights are *sine qua non* for development, peace and African renaissance. Similarly, there is a close nexus between justice and development. For instance, it is not often easy for justice to be realised in a context of poorly developed social and economic institutions, sparse resources, and countless competing needs. In Africa, for example, armed conflicts and humanitarian disasters negatively affect development, and transitional states usually find it difficult to dispense justice due to unavailability of resources that would sustain the relevant institutions.

5.3.5 RIGHT TO PEACE

The Charter guarantees all peoples the right to national and international peace and security. Accordingly, the principle of solidarity and friendly relations implicitly affirmed by the Charter of the United Nations are to govern the relationship between African states.[370] Article 23(2) of the African Charter obliges states to strengthen peace, solidarity and friendly relations by ensuring that:

(a)   Any individual enjoying the right of asylum under Article 12 of the present Charter shall not engage in subversive activities against his country of origin or any other state party to the present Charter;

(b)   Their territories shall not be used as bases for subversive or terrorist activities against the people of any other state party to the present Charter.

---

368   NEPAD Document, para 47.

369   As above, para 48.

370   Art 32(1) of the Charter stipulates: 'All peoples shall have the right to national and international peace and security. The principles of solidarity and friendly relations implicitly affirmed by the Charter of the United Nations and reaffirmed by that of the Organization of African Unity shall govern relations between states.'

The concept of peace as a human right is entirely novel and began with the African Charter.[371] The Charter intends to promote the principle of good and peaceful co-existence among states. Thus, a state which collaborates with terrorists or militia groups against another state tends to jeopardise the purport and intention of Article 23 of the Charter. The continent has experienced gross violations of this provision of the Charter in recent times. For example, The DRC has been accused of harbouring Ugandan and Rwandese rebels who have been attacking their governments from time to time.[372] Similarly, Uganda and Rwanda have been said to be the bases and training grounds for Congolese rebels.[373] This has compromised the good relationships these countries might have otherwise enjoyed by being neighbours.

The Charter provisions regarding the right to peace have some shortcomings. For example, it is difficult to countenance how Article 23(1) can be enforced.[374] It is true that in Africa, peace and security have become increasingly of grave concern. However, the Charter does not contain enough contents to aid the realisation of this right. The two situations in which states are obliged to ensure the achievement of peace— solidarity and friendly relations— are not adequate, especially in the absence of political will of states parties to the Charter.[375] It should suffice to note that the elements and the scope of the right to peace are yet to be determined. Additionally, no effort has as yet been made to elevate the concept beyond the level of generalities.[376]

This partly explains why, in spite of there being a regional human rights Charter that seeks to protect and promote the rights of individuals, some African countries still experience massive human

---

371   Nmehielle (n 65 above) 152.

372   See generally, Human Rights Watch, *World Report 2007* (2007).

373   See 'Act to end Congo war, UN boss tells leaders' *Saturday Nation,* available at www.nationmedia.com (accessed 08 March 2010), where Rwandan President Paul Kagame, DRC's Joseph Kabila and Uganda's Yoweri Museveni were said to be on the spot at the 'Great Lakes Conference' held in Nairobi, in which leaders urged an to end hostilities between the neighbouring countries.

374   Nmehielle (n 65 above) 153.

375   As above.

376   As above.

rights violations. Others are engulfed in endless wars and civil strife between pro-government and rebel forces. Some of these wars are instigated by external forces, mainly from Western countries. It is obviously impracticable for a country that is in the middle of a civil or political strife to contribute to the advancement of the regional human rights system given that during crises, human rights are either being violated or are derogated from. Moreover, the socio-political instability of many African countries has led to poverty and loss of human and material resources which could otherwise be useful in strengthening the regional human rights system.

5.3.6 RIGHT TO A GENERAL SATISFACTORY ENVIRONMENT

In terms of Article 24 of the Charter, all peoples have the right to a general satisfactory environment favourable to their development. This right is concerned with maintaining an environment fit for human habitation that poses no, or minimum, threat to human life. Environmental conservation is very important in this respect. It is important to note that the right has both individual and collective dimensions.[377] The individual dimension is the right of any victim or potential victim of an environmentally damaging activity to obtain reparation for harm suffered, while the collective dimension imposes a duty on individuals and states to cooperate to resolve environmental problems.[378] The issue of environmental rights in Africa did not begin with the adoption of the African Charter. Rather, it was engrafted into the African human rights system in 1968 when African Heads of States and Governments adopted the African Convention on the Conservation of Nature and Natural Resources.[379]

Despite the inaction on the violation of the right to a general satisfactory environment, the right has become very important and relevant to Africa. The importance culminated from the toxic waste dumping of 1988 in some African countries by international corporations.[380] After discovering the dumping, the former OAU

---

377   Umozurike (n 2 above) 75.

378   As above.

379   See (1989) 28 *International Legal Materials* 649.

380   Nmehielle (n 65 above) 157.

took quick action to forestall future occurrences. The same year, the OAU Council of Ministers passed a resolution condemning the import of toxic wastes to Africa, and emphasised that toxic dumping is a crime against Africa.[381] This resolution was followed by the adoption of the convention banning the importation of toxic waste into Africa.[382]

When interpreting Article 24 of the Charter, it is imperative to note that the primary responsibility lies with states to adopt measures that will effectively address environmental degradation. On the other hand, individuals ought to have the right in domestic law to institute private action against any violation of the right to a general satisfactory environment. Unfortunately, many states in Africa do not have adequate national environmental laws or policies, if at all. Thus, the realisation of this provision of the Charter is impeded.

To conclude this discussion, it must be pointed out that the African Charter is a challenging, ambitious and innovative document in the area of group or collective rights.[383] It fails to take note that these rights are weak in their content and in the manner of their enforcement. Perhaps, by making provision for these rights, the drafters of the Charter intended to respond to human rights concerns in the context of African realities, given that Africans are more group-oriented than individualistic.[384] Be that as it may, there is still a lot to be desired in as far as these rights are concerned. It is therefore not surprising that the African Commission has handled only a handful of communications alleging the violation of this category of rights.

---

381   'OAU Council of Ministers Resolution on Dumping of Nuclear and Industrial Waste in Africa', adopted at Addis Ababa, 23 May 1998. CM/Res. 1153 (XLVIII); (1989) 28 *International Legal Materials* 567.

382   Bamako Convention on the Ban of Importation into Africa and the Control of Transboundary Movement and Management of Hazardous Waste Within Africa; concluded at Bamako, 29 January 1991. (1991) 30 *International Legal Materials* 775.

383   See generally Dersso (n 30 above) 358-381.

384   See generally O Eze *Human rights in Africa: Some selected problems* (1984) 9; M Mutua 'The Banjul Charter and the African Cultural Fingerprint: An evaluation of the language of duties' (1995) 35 *Virginia Journal of International Law* 349.

5.4　LIMITATION OF RIGHTS UNDER THE AFRICAN CHARTER

It is the nature of human rights that, except in exceptional circumstances, they are subject to limitations.[385] However, the African Charter is not explicit on how rights could be limited. Thus, it is interesting to note that it does not have a derogation clause that would permit the suspension of certain rights and freedoms in strictly defined circumstances.[386] The absence of a derogation clause could therefore result in the Charter being ignored, in its entirety, in times of emergency or national disaster.

There are numerous and significant examples of international instruments that contain an express derogation clause. These include Article 15 of the European Convention on Human Rights, Article 4 of the ICCPR and Article 27 of the American Convention on Human Rights.[387] At the national level, Constitutions of some countries, such as South Africa, also have these clauses.[388]

The African Commission has interpreted the absence of a derogation clause to mean that the Charter 'does not allow for states parties to derogate from their treaty obligations during emergency situations. Thus, even a civil war ... cannot be used as an excuse by the state violating or permitting violations of rights in the African Charter.'[389] It further observed that the lack of a derogation clause 'can be seen as an expression of the principle that the restriction of human rights is not a solution to national difficulties: the legitimate exercise of human rights does not pose dangers to a democratic state governed by the rule of law.'[390]

The Commission's observation may have been instigated by the fact that, despite the lack of a derogation clause, the Charter

---

385　Heyns (n 160 above) 139.

386　See Murray (n 5 above) 123-126; Harris (n 5 above) 489-506.

387　See Sermet (n 8 above) 143.

388　See Constitution of the Republic of South Africa, art 37.

389　*Commission Nationale des Droits de l'Homme et des Libertes v. Chad* (n 181 above) Para 21.

390　*Amnesty International, Comite Loosli Bachelard, Lawyers Committee for Human Rights, Association of Members of the Episcopal Conference of East Africa v. Sudan* (n 207 above).

limits rights in other ways. For example, the Charter limits rights through imposition of duties on the individual and through internal qualifications.[391] These ways are discussed below. It should be noted, however, that these forms of limitation of rights are mostly applicable in normal circumstances but not during emergency situations.

5.4.1   LIMITATION OF RIGHTS THROUGH IMPOSITION OF DUTIES

One of the ways the Charter tends to limit rights is through the imposition of duties on individuals. Duties under the African Charter have been discussed below in detail. Important at this stage is the fact that the Charter imposes duties to limit rights by stating that 'the enjoyment of rights and freedoms also implies the performance of duties on the part of everyone.'[392] According to Heyns, this statement has two possible interpretations: (i) the performance of duties could be seen as a precondition for attaining rights; or (ii) rights are naturally limited by duties.[393] The latter would appear to be more appropriate. For example, the duties of solidarity imposed by Article 29 could be used to justify certain forms of community services that could otherwise have constituted violations of civil and political rights, such as freedom of association or movement.[394]

In tandem with this argument, the Commission has stated that 'the only legitimate reasons for limitations to the rights and freedoms of the African Charter are to be found in Article 27(2).'[395] Article 27(2) is categorical that the rights and freedoms of each individual are to be exercised with due regard to the rights of others, collective security, morality and common interest. In essence, the enjoyment of a right by a person entails the observance of a duty by another. The Commission also appears to require limitations to be absolutely necessary:

---

391   See this argument in Heyns (n 160 above) 139.

392   See African Charter, Preamble.

393   Heyns (n 160 above) 139.

394   See generally, C Heyns 'Extended medical training and the constitution: Balancing civil and political rights and socio-economic rights' (1997) *De Jure* 1-17.

395   *Media Rights Agenda and Constitutional Rights Project v. Nigeria* (n 6 above) para 68.

The reasons for possible limitations must be founded in a legitimate state interest and the evils of limitations of rights must be strictly proportionate with and absolutely necessary for the advantages which are to be obtained.[396]

On the basis of the above observations, it may be argued that the Commission would permit limitations of rights if: (i) there is a legitimate state interest for the limitation; (ii) the consequences of the limitations are strictly proportionate with the advantages which are to be obtained; and (iii) the limitation is absolutely necessary. It is conceivable that a legitimate state interest to limit a right may be justified if the limitation is not overbroad and therefore unnecessary. In other words, limitation of a right may be said to be absolutely necessary only after taking into account all relevant factors, including: the nature of the right; the importance of the purpose of the limitation; the nature and the extent of the limitation; the relation between the limitation and its purpose; and the availability of less restrictive means to achieve the purpose.[397]

Limitation of rights through imposition of duties has some shortcomings, the main one being that the duties in the African Charter are unenforceable. Most, if not all, of the duties in the Charter are mere moral obligations on the state and individuals. Hence, a state may not proceed to court to compel an individual to perform a duty. For duties to be enforceable there ought to be a clear separation of mandatory provisions from hortatory ones. The imprecision of some provisions of the Charter therefore makes limitation of rights through the imposition of duties impossible, at least at the moment.[398]

5.4.2 LIMITATION OF RIGHTS THROUGH INTERNAL QUALIFICATIONS (CLAW-BACK CLAUSES)

The Charter also limits rights through internal qualifications or modifiers. Internal qualifications or modifiers are phrases within the provisions of a legal instrument that subject the enjoyment of

---

396   As above, para 69 & 70. See also *Constitutional Rights Project, Civil Liberties Organisation and Media Rights Agenda v. Nigeria* (n 218 above) para 42.

397   See in this regard, art 36(1) of the Constitution of the Republic of South Africa.

398   Heyns (n 160 above) 141.

rights to certain conditions. Those conditions could be international standards or principles, or relevant domestic laws.[399] Thus, some of the internal qualifications assume the form of 'claw-back clauses' in the sense that they subject the enjoyment of certain rights to domestic laws.

Whereas internal limitations are permissible in human rights instruments, the Charter may be said to be very liberal in this regard as many of its provisions contain loosely-worded claw-back clauses. For instance, Article 8 guarantees freedom of conscience and religion 'subject to law and order.' Article 9(2) states: 'Every individual shall have the right to express and disseminate his opinions within the law.' Additionally, Article 10 guarantees the enjoyment of the right to freedom of association, provided an individual 'abides by the law.' An individual's freedom of movement under Article 12 is guaranteed 'provided he abides by the law.' Article 13(1) guarantees citizens the right to participate freely in their governments 'in accordance with the provisions of the law.' The same is evident in Article 14 which permits the encroachment upon property 'in accordance with the provisions of appropriate law.'

These clauses have deservedly been criticised by many commentators. For instance, Ankumah observed that they 'could render previously granted rights meaningless.'[400] D'sa was of the view that the Charter provides 'no external control over state behaviour where such suspensions have occurred in accordance with domestic law.'[401] Gittleman contended that the Charter is 'incapable of supplying even a scintilla of external restraint upon a government's power to create laws contrary to the spirit of the rights granted.'[402] Kunig remarked that since 'there are no provisions to ensure that a core of the human rights guarantees prevails against legislative restrictions, this represents a considerable structural defect.'[403] Murray contributed

---

399   As above.

400   Ankumah (n 89 above) 176.

401   R D'sa 'The African Charter on Human and Peoples' Rights: Problems and prospects for regional action' (1981/83) 10 *Australian Yearbook of International Law* 110.

402   Gittleman (n 282 above) 694.

403   P Kunig 'The Protection of human rights by international law in Africa' (1982) 25 *German Yearbook of International Law* 155.

to this debate by adding that 'the limitations are not defined exactly in the Charter, arguably leaving it purely to the discretion of states and thus, in effect, allowing rights to be denied.'[404]

On the *prima facie,* claw-back clauses seem to insubordinate the relevant Charter provisions to domestic legislation. In effect, they seriously undermine the intended usefulness of the Charter as they inhibit its uniform application and enforcement by states. This is because instead of the Charter having primacy, the various national laws of states parties actually assume a primary place. In any case, such domestic laws could be legislations that are made to validate violations of human rights.

Nonetheless, the African Commission has played a crucial role to water-down the effects and implication of these clauses. For instance, it has sought to interpret arguments on claw-back clauses, that have been raised before it, in accordance with international law principles. Thus, it is now settled that the phrase 'subject to law', which is predominant in some of the Charter provisions should be understood to refer, not to domestic, but instead to international law.[405] The Commission has emphasised that:

> Government(s) should avoid restricting rights, and take special care with regard to those rights protected by constitutional or international human rights law. No situation justifies the wholesale violation of human rights. In fact, general restrictions on rights diminish public confidence in the rule of law and are often counterproductive.[406]

By adopting such an approach, the Commission augmented the fact that internal qualifications generally do not necessarily permit states to set aside the rights guaranteed in the Charter. Instead, they require states to employ international standards when limiting rights. In the event of a conflict between national laws and international standards, the latter should prevail.[407] In *Amnesty International v. Zambia,*[408] the

---

404   Murray (n 5 above) 127.

405   *Civil Liberties Organisation in respect of the Nigerian Bar Association v. Nigeria* (n 242 above) para 16.

406   *Constitutional Rights Project and Civil Liberties Organisation v Nigeria* (n 213 above) para 57 & 58.

407   *Media Rights Agenda and Constitutional Rights Project v. Nigeria* (n 6 above) para 66.

408   *Amnesty International v. Zambia* (n 6 above) para 50.

Commission stated as follows in relation to the claw-back clause in Article 12 (2):

> The Commission is of the view that the 'claw-back' clauses must not be interpreted against the principles of the Charter. Recourse to these should not be used as a means of giving credence to violations of the express provisions of the Charter. ... it is important for the Commission to caution against a too easy resort to the limitation clauses in the African Charter. The onus is on the state to prove that it is justified to resort to the limitation clause.

In this case, the Commission was able to neutralise claw-back clauses by referring to its duty to interpret the Charter in light of international human rights jurisprudence as required by Articles 60 and 61. This effectively compels any state, purporting to be acting under legislation 'previously laid down by law', to show that such law is consistent with its obligations under the Charter.[409]

In *Amnesty International v. Sudan*[410], the Commission had to consider, among other things, allegations of arbitrary arrests which the state claimed were lawful under powers given to the president in a state of emergency. The Commission stated that Article 6 of the Charter 'must be interpreted in such a way as to permit arrests only in the exercise of powers normally granted to the security forces in a democratic society. In these cases, the wording of this decree allows for individuals to be arrested for vague reasons, and upon suspicion, not proven acts, which conditions are not in conformity with the spirit of the African Charter.'[411]

While it must be acknowledged that the wording of the Charter in terms of claw-back clauses leaves much to be desired, it is encouraging to observe that the Commission has through its case law to date confounded the pessimistic predictions of many commentators. However, more still needs to be done to redress the negative impacts of these clauses.

---

409   See Communications 27/89, 46/91 and 99/93, *Organisation Mondiale Contre La Torture and the Association Internationale des Juristes Democtates and others v. Rwanda* (1999) 6 *IHRR* 816 Para 30.

410   (n 140 above) para 59.

411   As above.

5.5   DUTIES UNDER THE AFRICAN CHARTER

The African Charter prescribes duties for both the state and the individual. Duties under international human rights law owe their origin to the 1948 Universal Declaration of Human Rights (UDHR).[412] However, they are absent in the European Convention and barely mentioned in the American Convention.[413] A distinction can be drawn between duties under the Inter-American and African human rights systems. While in the former the duties are entrenched in a non-binding declaration (the American Declaration on the Rights and Duties of Man), in the latter they are provided for in a legally binding instrument. Thus, duties under the African system are intended to be legally binding and therefore enforceable. Whereas this is the position, there is doubt about the enforceability of these duties.

5.5.1   STATE'S DUTY TO PROMOTE AND RESPECT THE RIGHTS IN THE CHARTER

States parties have the duty to promote and ensure through teaching, education and publication, the respect of the rights and freedoms contained in the Charter.[414] The rationale of this provision is to ensure that the freedoms, rights and corresponding obligations in the Charter are understood. This duty is in line with the undertaking by states to take legislative or other measures to give effect to the rights and freedoms enshrined in the Charter.[415] Thus, Article 25 goes further to list some of the possible ways this could be achieved. States can promote the Charter's provisions by prescribing human rights studies in school curricula and also conduct seminars, conferences and publication of necessary human rights literature.

In Africa, there are only isolated efforts to educate the public on human rights. There are, for instance, ongoing thematic human

---

412   See art 29 of the UDHR.

413   Art 33(1) of the American Declaration on the Rights and Duties of Man provides that 'every person has responsibilities to his community and mankind.'

414   African Charter, art 25.

415   As above, art 1.

rights conferences, workshops and ad hoc training programmes.[416] In some states, human rights are regarded as nothing more than a subject in law, or as a component of interdisciplinary courses.[417] In other words, such states do not see the need for more extensive and rigorous human rights education programmes.[418] Even in countries where human rights education programmes have been launched, they are often flawed because they are sometimes used as means of legitimising the ruling political party.[419]

Unfortunately, the great opportunity created by the 'Declaration of the United Nations Decade for Education on Human Rights'[420] has not been fully utilised since only a handful of African states responded to its valuable Plan of Action for 1994-2004.[421] The failure by most African states to implement it clearly indicates the place of human rights in their agenda. It is needless to state that the same indolence has been slow in the promotion of education on the African Charter provisions. It is regrettable that states have either refused or ignored to give human rights the publicity they deserve through education and other relevant means.

---

416   M Addo 'Implementation by African states of the plan of action for the United Nations Decade for Human Rights' (2000) 44 *Journal of African Law* 104.

417   See 'Report of the United Nations High Commissioner for Human Rights on the mid-term global evaluation of the progress made towards the achievement of the objectives of the United Nations Decade for Human Rights Education (1995-2004)', adopted at the 55th session of General Assembly, UN Doc A/55/360 (2000) paras 31 & 32.

418   As above, para 129(a). See also S Yeshanew 'Utilising the promotional mandate of the African Commission on Human and Peoples' Rights to promote human rights education in Africa' (2007) 7 *African Human Rights Law Journal* 191; L Gearon *The human rights handbook: A global perspective for education* (2003) 160-161.

419   P Martin *et al* 'Promoting human rights education in a marginalised Africa' in G Andreopoulos & P Claude (eds) *Human rights education for the twenty-first century* (1997) 446.

420   Res. 1993/56 of 9 March 1993.

421   See UN Doc A/51/506 and UN Doc A/52/469. Algeria, Chad, Ghana, Sudan and Tunisia were the only countries that responded on the establishment of a national focal point and centre for human rights education which was required by the Plan of Action.

5.5.2 STATE'S DUTY TO GUARANTEE THE INDEPENDENCE OF THE JUDICIARY

States parties to the Charter also have the duty to guarantee judicial independence.[422] This duty calls them to establish and improve national institutions entrusted with the promotion and protection of the rights and freedoms guaranteed in the Charter. Such institutions include national human rights commissions, human rights institutions of learning, and non-governmental organisations concerned with human rights. Through the encouragement of the African Commission many African states have now established national human rights commissions to help ensure that their obligations under the Charter are effectively carried out.

Article 26 takes cognisance of the fact that the whole notion of human rights protection will become useless in a society where the judiciary is not independent. Judicial independence demands for separation of powers because the state (or executive arm of the government) is usually the chief violator of human rights and would not always like to be called to account for its actions. In tandem with this Article, the African Commission adopted the 'Resolution on the Respect and the Strengthening of the Independence of the Judiciary.'[423] The resolution noted that justice is an integral part of human rights and a necessary condition for democracy. It further called on African countries to repeal all legislation that are inconsistent with principles of judicial independence, especially on the appointment and posting of judges.

The resolution also urged states to provide the judiciary with sufficient resources to fulfil its functions; provide judges with decent living and working conditions for them to maintain their independence and realise their full potential; incorporate universal principles on judicial independence in their legal systems, especially with regard to security of tenure; and refrain from taking actions that could directly or indirectly threaten the independence and

---

422   As above, art 26.

423   See 'Resolution on the Respect and the Strengthening on the Independence of the Judiciary (ACHPR/Res.21(XIX) 96).

the security of judges and magistrates.[424] It is hoped that states will implement the tenets of this resolution to the fullest possible extent.

5.5.3   INDIVIDUAL'S DUTY TO RESPECT THE RIGHTS OF OTHERS

Article 27 of the Charter provides:

1.   Every individual shall have duties towards his family and society, the state and other legally recognised communities and the international community.

2.   The rights and freedoms of each individual shall be exercised with due regard to the rights of others, collective security, morality and common interest.

This Article requires the individual to utilise his or her ability and potential for the benefit of their family, society, state and the international community. It may be presumed that an individual is expected to play an active role in his field of competence and work towards the development of his or her family, society, state and international community. Further, as stated earlier, the Article serves as a limitation clause as it limits the enjoyment of rights and freedoms contained in the Charter. Accordingly, a person is entitled to enjoy the rights and freedoms in the Charter, as long as the rights and freedoms of others, as well as their collective security, morality and common interest are not infringed. This emphasises the point that rights are not absolute and that their enjoyment is subject to the fulfilment of prescribed duties.

5.5.4   INDIVIDUAL'S DUTY TO PROMOTE AND SAFEGUARD RESPECT AND TOLERANCE

Article 28 re-echoes the provisions of Article 27, stating that 'every individual shall have the duty to respect and consider his fellow beings without discrimination and to maintain relations aimed at promoting, safeguarding and reinforcing mutual respect and tolerance.' While Article 27 focuses more on respecting others, Article 28 leans towards tolerance. Thus, just as the individual has the right not to be discriminated against by the state, as guaranteed in Article

---

424   As above, para 1.

2 of the Charter, he or she has the duty not to discriminate against others either. As already stated earlier in this chapter, discrimination is differentiation on illegal grounds such as race, ethnic group, colour, sex, religion, political or other opinion, national and social origin, fortune, birth or other status.

5.5.5   INDIVIDUAL'S DUTY TO THE FAMILY AND OTHER RELATED DUTIES

According to Article 29, the individual shall have the duty:

1. to preserve the harmonious development of the family and to work for the cohesion and respect of the family; to respect his parents at all times, to maintain them in case of need;

2. to serve his national community by placing his physical and intellectual abilities at its service;

3. not to compromise the security of the state whose national or resident he is;

4. to preserve and strengthen the national solidarity, particularly when the latter is threatened;

5. to preserve and strengthen the national independence and the territorial integrity of his country and to contribute to its defence in accordance with the law;

6. to work to the best of his abilities and competence, and to pay taxes imposed by law in the interest of the society;

7. to preserve and strengthen positive African cultural values in his relation with other members of the society, in the spirit of tolerance, dialogue and consultation and, in general, to contribute to the promotion of the moral well-being of society; 8. to contribute to the best of his abilities, at all times and at all levels, to the promotion and achievement of African unity.

This article imposes duties on the individual towards his family, his society, and the state as a whole. The individual's duty to his family includes respecting his or her parents at all times and caring for them as necessary. The inclusion of this cluster of duties in the Charter resonates the African communitarian values founded on respect, harmonious co-existence and morality. It is a tenet of the African society that an individual preserves and strengthens social solidarity. Thus, the duties enumerated under Article 29 are solely geared to ensure peace, love and harmony in society, on the one hand, and African unity, on the other.

Generally, the entrenchment of duties in the African Charter has come under scathing criticism from a number of scholars. Some are of the view that their formulation could be a basis for states parties to the Charter to perpetrate human rights violations.[425] Others, like Okoth-Ogendo, see the language of duties as 'little more than the formulation, entrenchment, and legitimation of state rights and privileges against individuals and peoples.'[426] The fear is frequently expressed that emphasis on duties may lead to the 'trumping' of individual rights.[427]

Some of these criticisms are unfounded because the duties in the Charter more or less emphasise the point that the realisation of human rights calls for joint efforts between the individual and the state. As already elaborated above, they serve as limitations to the enjoyment of the rights in the Charter. It is therefore not a plausible argument that individuals should not owe any duties to the state. In fact, they do, in tax, criminal, and other laws.[428] As Mutua urged, a valid criticism of the language of duties should focus on their precise meaning, content, conditions of compliance, and application. In this sense, more needs to be done in terms of clarifying the status of the duties in the Charter, as well as establishing their moral and legal dimensions and implications for enforcement.[429]

---

425   See Mutua (n 4 above) 10.

426   See H Okoth-Ogendo 'Human and peoples' rights: What point is Africa trying to make?' in R Cohen, *et al, Human Rights and Governance in Africa* (1993) 78-79.

427   R Cohen 'Endless teardrops: Prolegomena to the study of human rights in Africa' (1990) *Human rights and governance* 15.

428   See Mutua (n 4 above) 33.

429   As above.

CHAPTER 6

THE AFRICAN CHARTER ON THE RIGHTS AND WELFARE OF THE CHILD

The African Charter on the Rights and Welfare of the Child[1] (hereafter 'Children's Charter' or 'the Charter') was the first regional treaty for the promotion and protection of the rights of children. Its adoption was necessitated by a number of factors. To begin with, there was the recognition of the fact that everyone, without distinction of any kind, is entitled to all the rights and freedoms guaranteed in the African Charter on Human and Peoples' Rights (hereafter the 'ACHPR' or 'African Charter').[2] To this end, the former Organisation of African Unity (OAU) decided to take appropriate measures to promote and protect the rights and welfare of the African children, due to their vulnerability.

The member states of the OAU noted with concern that 'the situation of most African children remains critical due to the unique factors of their socio-economic, cultural, traditional and developmental circumstances, natural disasters, armed conflicts, exploitation and hunger, and on account of the child's physical and mental immaturity....'[3] Children occupy a unique and privileged position in the African society. For the full and harmonious development of their personality, they need to grow up in an atmosphere of happiness, love and understanding.[4] Moreover, due to their physical, mental, moral and social development needs, they require special care. They also require legal protection for their freedom, dignity and security.[5]

---

1   African Charter on the Rights and Welfare of the Child; adopted 11 July 1990; entered into force 29 November 1999. OAU Doc CAB/LEG/24 9/49 (1990).

2   As above, preamble para 2.

3   As above, preamble para 4. See also the Declaration on the Rights and Welfare of the African Child, AHG/ST.4 Rev.l; adopted by the Assembly of Heads of State and Government of the Organization of African Unity, at its Sixteenth Ordinary Session in Monrovia, Liberia, from 17-20 July 1979.

4   Children's Charter, preamble para 5.

5   As above, para 6.

Secondly, the adoption of the Charter was necessitated by the need to take into consideration the values of African civilisation 'which should inspire and characterise their reflection on the concept of the rights and welfare of the child.'[6] In this sense, the OAU member states wanted to underscore the fact that the protection of children's rights is not a concept alien to traditional African cultures, and that international human rights principles on childhood find support within the African cultural conception of human rights.[7]

The adoption of the Children's Charter was also motivated by events in the international circles, such as, the promulgation of the UN Convention on the Rights of the Child (UNCRC) in 1989.[8] Although this Convention received overwhelming global support[9], its provisions were thought not to be adequate to protect the African child who was exposed to unique circumstances that required additional measure of protection, more so, from an African perspective.[10] It has been contended, for example, that the drafters of the UNCRC ignored important socio-cultural and economic realities of the African child.[11]

It cannot be gainsaid, therefore, that the adoption of the Children's Charter is a major contribution to the advancement of regional protection and promotion of international human rights law. As Sloth-Nielsen and Mezmur observed, in their vulnerability and in their need for protection and justice, African children now have a place on the international legal platform.[12] As such, they cannot be

---

6   As above, para 7.

7   T Kaime 'The Convention on the Rights of the Child and the cultural legitimacy of children's rights in Africa: Some reflections' (2005) 5 *African Human Rights Law Journal* 225.

8   (1989) 28 *International Legal Materials* 1448. See also G Naldi 'Future trends in human rights in Africa: the increased role of the OAU? M Evans & R Murray *The African Charter on Human and Peoples' Rights: The system in practice, 1986-2000* (2002) 14.

9   Somali is so far the only African state that has not ratified the Convention.

10   J Arts 'The international protection of children's rights in Africa: The 1990 OAU Charter on the Rights and Welfare of the Child' (1993) 5 *RADIC* 141-143.

11   D Olowu 'Protecting Children's Rights in Africa: A Critique of the African Charter on the Rights and Welfare of the Child' (2002) 10 *International Journal of Children's Rights* 128; F Viljoen 'The African Charter on the Rights and Welfare of the Child' in C Davel (ed) *Introduction to Child Law in South Africa* (2000) 222.

12   J Sloth-Nielsen & B Mezmur 'Surveying the research landscape to promote children's legal rights in an African context' (2007) 7 *African Human Rights Law Journal* 331.

regarded merely as subjects of their national legal systems but also of the African human rights system. In an apparent recognition of this fact, some African countries have now begun to take children more seriously by legislating on matters affecting their rights. There appears to be a paradigm shift from the archaic colonial legislation to modern, more accessible and comprehensive children's statutes. Countries like Ghana, Kenya, Madagascar, Nigeria and Uganda now have comprehensive legislation on children's rights, structured in line with the Children's Charter and the UNCRC.[13]

6.1   GENERAL STRUCTURE AND FEATURES OF THE CHILDREN'S CHARTER

The Children's Charter is divided into a substantive part containing a catalogue of rights and duties[14] and a procedural part providing for the establishment and organisation of the Committee on the Rights and Welfare of the Child.[15] It guarantees a number of civil, political, economic, social and cultural rights, akin to those in the UNCRC. However, while upholding the universal standards contained in the UNCRC, the Children's Charter goes further to address a number of problems that specifically affect African children.[16] For example, it seeks to protect the African child from harmful cultural practices,[17] provides for the rights of refugee children[18] and accords priority to the special needs of children living under Apartheid and in states subject to military destabilisation by the Apartheid regime.[19]

Like the African Charter, the Children's Charter does not seem to give civil and political rights pre-eminence over social, economic and cultural rights. Rather, it dispenses with the traditional approach of 'progressive realisation' of socio-economic rights and requires their 'immediate implementation.' A number of its provisions attest to this position. For example, under Article 11(3), the Children's

---

13   As above.

14   See Children's Charter, part 1.

15   As above, part 2.

16   Sloth-Nielsen & Mezmur (n 12 above) 331.

17   Children's Charter, art 1(3).

18   As above, art 23.

19   As above, art 26.

Charter requires states parties to 'take all appropriate measures with a view to achieving the full realisation' of the right to education.

Similarly, states parties undertake to pursue 'the full implementation' of the right to health and health services entrenched in Article 14 of the Charter. With regard to the rights of the children of imprisoned mothers, Article 30(1) requires states parties to '... undertake to provide special treatment to expectant mothers and to mothers of infants and young children who have been accused or found guilty of infringing the penal law.' Thus, a cursory glance of these provisions would make one to conclude that socio-economic rights under the Charter are of immediate implementation.

Due to its 'equal treatment' of all categories of human rights, the Charter has been hailed as 'the most progressive of the treaties on the rights of the child.'[20] This is certainly because the UNCRC clearly distinguishes between socio-economic rights and civil and political rights in terms of their mode of enforcement. Under its Article 4, the Convention provides that '... with regard to economic, social and cultural rights, states parties shall undertake such measures to the *maximum extent of their available resources* and, where needed, within the framework of international co-operation ....' [emphasis supplied]. This therefore means that the UNCRC does not require the 'immediate implementation' of this category of rights since the obligation of states parties is subject to 'the maximum extent of their available resources'.

Another notable feature of the Children's Charter relates to its construction of childhood within the African cultural context. The Charter evolves a normative framework based on the African conception of human rights and guarantees the enjoyment of children's rights within African cultural values.[21] It is within this context that the Charter provides for the responsibilities (duties) of children to their parents, communities and society as a whole, proportionate to their age and ability.[22] This is in line with the African notion that every right comes with corresponding duties.

---

20   G Van Bueren *The International Law on the Rights of the Child* (1995) 402.

21   Children's Charter, preamble para 7.

22   As above, art 31.

In a similar vein, the Charter imposes obligations on states parties. Some of the obligations require states parties: to recognise the rights, freedoms and duties enshrined in the Charter and to adopt such legislative or other measures as may be necessary to give effect to its provisions;[23] and to discourage any custom, tradition, cultural or religious practice that is inconsistent with the rights, duties and obligations contained in the Charter.[24]

Another notable feature of the Charter concerns the interpretation and application of its rights and duties. Generally, the Charter, like the UNCRC, embodies four principles that would assist with the interpretation and application of its substantive provisions.[25] The first is the 'best interests principle' which requires that 'in all actions concerning the child undertaken by any person or authority, the best interests of the child shall be the primary consideration.'[26] The second principle, that of 'non-discrimination', entitles every child the enjoyment of the rights and freedoms recognised and guaranteed in the Charter, irrespective of the child's or his/her parents' or legal guardians' race, ethnic group, colour, sex, language, religion, political or other opinion, national and social origin, fortune, birth or other status.[27]

Thirdly, the 'principle of participation' requires states parties to ensure the participation of children in any matter affecting them.[28] Article 4(2) of the Children's Charter expounds this principle by stating that:

> In all judicial or administrative proceedings affecting a child who is capable of communicating his/her own views, an opportunity shall be provided for the views of the child to be heard either directly or through an impartial representative as a party to the proceedings, and

---

23   As above, art 1(1).

24   As above, art 1(3).

25   For a detailed discussion on these principles, see S Rosa & M Dutschke 'Children rights at the core: The use of international law on South African Cases on Children's Socio-economic rights' (2006) 22 *South African Journal of Human Rights* 231-233.

26   Children's Charter, art 4(1).

27   As above, art 3.

28   Rosa & Dutschke (n 25 above) 232.

those views shall be taken into consideration by the relevant authority in accordance with the provisions of appropriate law.

The final principle is that of 'maximum survival and development' which deals with the actual protection of life and the holistic development of the child.[29] As shall be shown below, all the above principles are essential when interpreting and giving effect to the various rights entrenched in the Charter.

6.2   RIGHTS UNDER THE CHILDREN'S CHARTER

6.2.1   CIVIL AND POLITICAL RIGHTS

The Charter guarantees the enjoyment of a number of civil and political rights. Pursuant to Article 3, every child is entitled to the enjoyment of the rights and freedoms recognised and guaranteed in the Charter irrespective of the child's or his/her parents' or legal guardians' race, ethnic group, colour, sex, language, religion, political or other opinion, national and social origin, fortune, birth or other status.

Whereas Article 3 seeks to protect children from discrimination based on the above stated grounds, it could also be interpreted to mean that vulnerable or disadvantaged children should be afforded special protection in order to bring them to par with their colleagues. These include children who are temporarily or permanently deprived of their family environment, children living in poverty, children with disabilities, children living and/or working on the streets and those subjected to discriminatory cultural practices. Examples of discriminatory cultural practices are son–preference and female circumcision. Such discrimination manifests itself in the unequal allocation of family resources between the girl-child and her brothers.[30] This disparity translates to the further violation of the girl-child's rights such as access to health services, educational opportunities and ultimately her career choices.

To alleviate discrimination on the basis of disability, the Charter provides for special protection to handicapped children. According

---

29   Children's Charter, art 5.

30   Kaime (n 7 above) 229.

to Article 13(1), every mentally or physically disabled child has the right to special measures of protection in keeping with his physical and moral needs and under conditions which ensure his dignity, promote his self-reliance and active participation in the community. This places a duty on states parties to ensure:

> ... assistance for which application is made and which is appropriate to the child's condition and in particular shall ensure that the disabled child has effective access to training, preparation for employment and recreation opportunities in a manner conducive to the child achieving the fullest possible social integration, individual development and his cultural and moral development.[31]

Mental and physical disabilities have been one of the major impediments to the growth and development of some children in Africa. It is rather unfortunate that, in some communities, disabled children are regarded as social out-casts and are normally rejected by their parents and the community at large. Such children are subjected to traumatising experiences, which make them lonely and withdrawn. By being forced to beg in the streets and other public places, some of them are nothing but 'economic objects' to their families. They rarely benefit from the proceeds of their begging, since the same are diverted to support their 'able-bodied' siblings to continue with schooling.

Moreover, most African countries have failed to facilitate disabled children's free movement and access to public places. This is contrary to their obligation to ensure 'the full convenience of the mentally and physically disabled person to movement and access to public highway, buildings and other places to which the disabled may legitimately want to have access to.'[32] Consequently, such children have been deprived of the enjoyment of, among other things, their right to freedom of movement and association, due to their inability to access public facilities.

At another level, the Charter intends to avert discrimination by emphasising that the child's best interest should be taken into

---

31   Children's Charter, art 13(2).

32   As above, art 13(3).

consideration in all actions undertaken by any person or authority. Article 4 provides:

1.   In all actions concerning the child undertaken by any person or authority the best interests of the child shall be the primary consideration.

2.   In all judicial or administrative proceedings affecting a child who is capable of communicating his/her own views, an opportunity shall be provided for the views of the child to be heard either directly or through an impartial representative as a party to the proceedings, and those views shall be taken into consideration by the relevant authority in accordance with the provisions of appropriate law.

The 'best interests principle' guarantees children the right to take part in decisions that would affect them. In effect, the principle waters-down the 'paternalistic' or 'know-it-all' attitude that has traditionally been embraced by parents, guardians or any other decision-maker.[33] Instead of imposing their views or opinions on children, Article 4 requires decision-makers to carefully balance the values and interests 'competing for the core of best interests.'[34] These interests include, but are not limited to, the opinions of the child, the needs of the child and the risk of harm. Consequently, any decision that may threaten or harm the growth and development of the child cannot be said to be in conformity with this principle.[35]

The Charter also guarantees every child the inherent right to life.[36] Accordingly, states parties are to ensure, to the maximum extent possible, the survival, protection and development of the child.[37] Thus, the Charter outlaws the imposition of capital punishment on children.[38] The provisions of the Children's Charter on the right to life appear to be more progressive than those of the African Charter

---

33   Van Bueren (n 20 above) 47.

34   As above.

35   Kaime (n 7 above) 232.

36   Children's Charter, art 5(1).

37   As above, art 5(2).

38   As above, art 5(3).

because the latter prohibits the 'arbitrary deprivation of life'[39] but fails to define the scope of the rights to life. The Children's Charter is clear that the right to life prohibits any kind of execution, whether judicial or extra-judicial. The African Commission on Human and Peoples' Rights (hereafter 'the African Commission' or 'the Commission') has stated that the death penalty could be imposed 'only after full consideration of the circumstances of the offence and of the offender.'[40]

Article 6 of the Children's Charter guarantees the right to a name and nationality.[41] This right imposes a duty on a state to register every child immediately after birth.[42] In order to ensure the protection of this right, the Charter obligates states parties to 'ensure that their constitutional legislation recognise the principles according to which a child shall acquire the nationality of the state in the territory of which he has been born if, at the time of the child's birth, he is not granted nationality by any other state in accordance with its laws.'[43] The intention of the Charter is to prevent situations where a child living in a foreign country is deprived of nationality by reason of his or her parents not being citizens of that country. The legislation in some African countries allows nationality to be conferred only to children whose parents are citizens of those particular countries. Children born to foreign nationals in such countries are therefore deprived of this right.

The Children's Charter also guarantees freedom of expression. Accordingly, every child who is capable of communicating his or her own views is assured the right to express his opinions freely in all matters and to disseminate his opinions subject to such restrictions as are prescribed by laws.[44] Additionally, Article 8 affords every child the right to free association and freedom of peaceful assembly

---

39   As above, art 4.

40   Communication 240/2001, *Interights et al (on behalf of Mariette Sonjaleen Bosch) v. Botswana*, Seventeenth Annual Activity Report of the African Commission on Human and Peoples' Rights (Annex VII) para 52.

41   Children's Charter, art 6(1).

42   As above, art 6(2).

43   As above, art 6(3).

44   As above, art 7.

in conformity with the law. Like in the African Charter, the two rights are subject to claw-back clauses. In other words, the scope of enjoyment of these rights can be regulated by states parties to the Charter through legislation. However, while regulating the scope of enjoyment of these rights, the state should be careful to ensure that they are not unreasonably limited.

Article 9 of the Charter guarantees the enjoyment of the right to freedom of thought, conscience and religion by stipulating that:

1.   Every child shall have the right to freedom of thought, conscience and religion.
2.   Parents, and where applicable, legal guardians shall have a duty to provide guidance and direction in the exercise of these rights having regard to the evolving capacities, and best interests of the child.
3.   States parties shall respect the duty of parents and where applicable, legal guardians to provide guidance and direction in the enjoyment of these rights subject to the national laws and policies.

From the wording of the above provisions, it can be deduced that a child's freedom of thought, conscience and religion is subject to the guidance and direction of his or her parents or legal guardians. This essentially means, until a certain age is attained, a child may not exercise the discretion, for example, to choose his or her religion. In other words, at a certain phase of childhood, a child's religion is subject to the discretion of the parent or guardian. The exercise of such discretion, however, may be limitation by national laws or policies.

Article 10 of the Charter protects the right to privacy. It prohibits arbitrary or unlawful interference with a child's privacy, family home or correspondence. It also prohibits attacks on a child's honour or reputation. However, it appears that the Charter authorises parents or guardians to supervise the conduct of their children, as long as the same does not amount to unreasonable interference or personal attacks on the children. In line with the prohibition of personal attacks, Article 16 imposes an obligation on states parties to take special legislative, administrative, social and educational measures to protect the child from all forms of torture, inhuman or degrading treatment.[45] The forms of inhuman or degrading treatment contemplated under this provision include physical or mental injury or abuse, neglect or maltreatment including sexual abuse.

Child abuse and torture are rampant practices in Africa. For example, some parents or guardians use excessive force to discipline their children by resorting to measures, which normally lead to their physical or mental harm. Such abhorrent practices have also been reported in some institutions of learning where children are 'unreasonably chastised' in the name of imparting discipline. Further, some cultural practices, such as circumcision of children without their consent, also amount to torture and abuse. Traditional circumcision exposes children to untold psychological suffering and often ends in physical torture. In this time and age of anaesthetics, it is perturbing that children are still exposed to painful and horrific experiences in the name of traditional circumcision rites.

In order to give effect to the right against child abuse, torture and other forms of cruel and inhuman treatment, states must therefore undertake some protective measures, including, the establishment of special monitoring units to provide necessary support and protection to endangered children.[46] Additionally, they can initiate other measures such as identification, reporting, investigation and follow-up of instances of child abuse, torture and related vices.

The Charter also affords protection against child labour. Although the term is not expressly defined in the Charter, constructive interpretation of Article 15(1) could lead to the conclusion that child labour refers to subjecting a child to all forms of economic exploitation, including the performance of work 'that is likely to be hazardous or to interfere with their physical, mental, spiritual, moral, or social development.' In order to ensure protection from child labour, the Charter imposes obligations on states parties to, among other things: provide, through legislation, minimum ages for admission to every employment; provide for appropriate regulation of hours and conditions of employment; provide for appropriate

---

45   As above, art 16(1).

46   As above, art 16(2).

penalties or other sanctions to ensure the effective enforcement of Article 15 of the Charter; and promote the dissemination of information on the hazards of child labour to all sectors of the community.[47]

In poverty-stricken Africa, child labour is a common practice. Children are usually forced to work in farms, industries and other formal and informal sectors in order to help their parents or guardians to raise an income that would sustain their families' livelihood. As a result, such children are exposed to precarious conditions, are deprived other rights, such as the right to education, and end up being exploited.

Article 17 guarantees children the right to a fair trial. In effect, every child accused or found guilty of having breached penal laws has the 'right to special treatment in a manner consistent with the child's sense of dignity and worth and which reinforces the child's respect for human rights and fundamental freedoms of others.'[48] In order to avail this right, states parties are under obligation to[49]:

(a)   ensure that no child who is detained or imprisoned or otherwise deprived of his/her liberty is subjected to torture, inhuman or degrading treatment or punishment;

(b)   ensure that children are separated from adults in their place of detention or imprisonment;

(c)   ensure that every child accused in infringing the penal law:

(i)   shall be presumed innocent until duly recognised guilty;

(ii)   shall be informed promptly in a language that he understands and in detail of the charge against him, and shall be entitled to the assistance of an interpreter if he or she cannot understand the language used;

(iii)   shall be afforded legal and other appropriate assistance in the preparation and presentation of his defence;

---

47   As above, art 15(2)(a)-(d).

48   As above, art 17(1).

49   As above, art 17(2)(a)-(d).

>   (iv)   shall have the matter determined as speedily as possible by an impartial tribunal and if found guilty, be entitled to an appeal by a higher tribunal;
>
> (d)   prohibit the press and the public from trial.

The Children's Charter has adopted a broader approach to the protection of the right to a fair trial than the African Charter.[50] In fact, it even goes further to emphasise that the essential aims of juvenile justice should be reformation, re-integration into family and social rehabilitation.[51] The Charter also requires the prescription of a minimum age limit for criminal capacity for children.[52] Article 22 provides for the protection of children in armed conflicts. Accordingly:

> 1.   States parties to this Charter shall undertake to respect and ensure respect for rules of international humanitarian law applicable in armed conflicts which affect the child.
>
> 2.   States parties to the present Charter shall take all necessary measures to ensure that no child shall take a direct part in hostilities and refrain in particular, from recruiting any child.
>
> 3.   States parties to the present Charter shall, in accordance with their obligations under international humanitarian law, protect the civilian population in armed conflicts and shall take all feasible measures to ensure the protection and care of children who are affected by armed conflicts. Such rules shall also apply to children in situations of internal armed conflicts, tension and strife.

The above provision provides two kinds of protection to children. The first relates to the protection during armed conflicts, while the second prohibits their recruitment as soldiers. With regard to the first scenario, the Charter obliges states to comply with the rules of international humanitarian law applicable in armed conflicts. The

---

50   See the African Charter on Human and Peoples' Rights (hereafter the 'African Charter' or 'Charter') art 7.

51   Children's Charter, art 17(3).

52   As above, art 17(4).

1949 Geneva Conventions[53] and their two Additional Protocols[54] of 1977 set out in detail the general rules of international humanitarian law dealing with, *inter alia,* the rights and obligations in respect of children in situations of armed conflict.

Specifically, Article 77 of Additional Protocol I (which deals with international armed conflicts) requires the parties to a conflict to take 'all feasible measures in order that children who have not attained the age of 15 years do not take a direct part in hostilities and, in particular, they shall refrain from recruiting them into their armed forces.' Similarly, Article 4(c) of Additional Protocol II (which covers non-international armed conflict) prohibits the recruitment of children under the age of 15 years in hostilities, whether as members of the armed forces or militia groups. It appears therefore that according to the rules of international humanitarian law, the minimum age limit in which a child is permitted to take part in hostilities or armed conflicts is 15 years.

Unfortunately, many hostilities and armed conflicts in Africa ignore this age restriction. Statistics indicate that the number of child soldiers worldwide is a staggering 300,000,[55] of which about 120,000 are from Africa.[56] Whereas the majority of the children recruited into armed service are between 15 and 18 years, there are reports indicating that children as young as seven years are also recruited.[57] Consequently, this has impacted on the children's growth and development. Without immediate attention to the ensuing

---

53   The Conventions, signed at Geneva on 12 August 1949, are: Convention I for the Amelioration of the Condition of the Wounded and Sick in Armed Forces in the Field; Convention II for the Amelioration of the Condition of Wounded, Sick and Shipwrecked Members of Armed Forces at Sea; Convention III Relative to the Treatment of Prisoners of War, including Annexes; Convention IV Relative to the Protection of Civilian Persons in Time of War.

54   Protocol I Additional to the Geneva Conventions of 12 August 1949, and Relating to the Protection of Victims of International Armed Conflicts, 8 June 1977; entered into force 7 December 1978; Protocol II Additional to the Geneva Convention of 12 August 1949, and Relating to the Protection of Victims of Non-International Armed Conflicts, June 1977; entered into force 7 December 1978.

55   R Brett 'Child soldiers: Causes, consequences and international responses' in E Bennett, *et al* (eds) *ACT against child soldiers in Africa: A reader* (2000) 18.

56   A Twum-Danso *Africa's young soldiers: The co-option of childhood* (2003) 12.

57   D Singh 'When a child is not a child: The scourge of child soldiering in Africa' (2007) 7 *African Human Rights Law Journal* 208.

problem of child soldiering, the plausible reality for Africa will be the creation of a brutalised, violent generation of people who know nothing except sadism and aggression.[58]

The Children's Charter also seeks to protect the rights of refugee children.[59] It obliges states parties to take all appropriate measures to ensure that a child who is either seeking or granted refugee status receives appropriate protection and humanitarian assistance.[60] States are required to cooperate with refugee organisations in their efforts to protect and assist such children. The nature of the cooperation contemplated in this provision includes the efforts to trace the parents or other close relatives of an unaccompanied refugee child in order to obtain information necessary for reunification with the family.[61] Where no parents, legal guardians or close relative is found, the child is to be accorded the same protection as any other child permanently or temporarily deprived of his family environment for any other reason.[62]

Article 26 guarantees protection from apartheid and other forms of discrimination. It is an undertaking by states parties to individually and collectively accord the highest priority to the special needs of children living under apartheid and other forms of discrimination and in states subject to military destabilisation caused by these inhumane practices.[63] Thus, states are expected to provide material assistance to such children and to direct efforts towards the elimination of all forms of discrimination and apartheid on the continent.[64] One may question the relevance of this provision in as far as it relates to apartheid, a practice that was phased out of Africa by the early 1990s. Apartheid was mainly practised in colonised African states and it is no longer an issue of concern in independent Africa. What seems to be of great concern in many African countries in

---

58   As above.

59   Children's Charter, art 23.

60   As above, art 23(1).

61   As above, art 23(2).

62   As above, art 23(3).

63   As above, art 26(1) & (2).

64   As above, art 26(3).

this time and age is the issue of discrimination based on, particularly, one's religious, tribal, ethnic and gender affiliation.

The Children's Charter also guarantees protection from some of the worst practices that threaten to stifle the growth and development of the modern day child. These practices include sexual exploitation,[65] drug abuse[66] and child trafficking, sale and abduction.[67] Additionally, the Charter guarantees special treatment to expectant mothers and to mothers of infants and young children who have been accused or found guilty of infringing the penal law. Towards this end, states parties are required to ensure that a non-custodial sentence is first considered when sentencing such mothers. Additionally, they are to come up with forms of punishment other than institutional confinement for such mothers. However, where confinement is inevitable, it is advisable for states to establish special alternative institutions for such mothers. The Charter prohibits the imprisonment of a mother together with her child as well as the imposition of a death sentence on such mothers. Finally, it obliges states to ensure that the essential aim of the penitentiary system will be the reformation, integration of the mother to the family and social rehabilitation.

6.2.2   Economic, Social and Cultural Rights

Many of the economic, social and cultural rights in the Children's Charter are similar in content and substance to those in the African Charter, although they specifically relate to children. These rights were discussed extensively in the Chapter dealing with the African

---

65   Art 27 provides: '1. States parties to the present Charter shall undertake to protect the child from all forms of sexual exploitation and sexual abuse and shall in particular take measures to prevent: (a) the inducement, coercion or encouragement of a child to engage in any sexual activity; (b) the use of children in prostitution or other sexual practices; (c) the use of children in pornographic activities, performances and materials.'

66   According to art 28, 'States parties to the present Charter shall take all appropriate measures to protect the child from the use of narcotics and illicit use of psychotropic substances as defined in the relevant international treaties, and to prevent the use of children in the production and trafficking of such substances.'

67   Art 29 states that 'States parties to the present Charter shall take appropriate measures to prevent: (a) the abduction, the sale of, or traffic in children for any purpose or in any form, by any person including parents or legal guardians of the child; (b) the use of children in all forms of begging.'

Charter and it is needless to repeat the discussion in this section. However, it is important to underscore some of them in order to elucidate how the Children's Charter guarantees the enjoyment of this category of rights. Some of the economic, social and cultural rights contained in the Charter are the right to education; leisure, recreation and cultural activities; health and health services; parental care; and family. It also guarantees protection from harmful social and cultural practices.

With regard to the right to education, the Charter is categorical that education of the child shall be directed to[68]:

(a)   the promotion and development of the child's personality, talents and mental and physical abilities to their fullest potential;

(b)   fostering respect for human rights and fundamental freedoms with particular reference to those set out in the provisions of various African instruments on human and peoples' rights and international human rights declarations and conventions;

(c)   the preservation and strengthening of positive African morals, traditional values and cultures;

(d)   the preparation of the child for responsible life in a free society, in the spirit of understanding tolerance, dialogue, mutual respect and friendship among all peoples' ethnic, tribal and religious groups;

(e)   the preservation of national independence and territorial integrity;

(f)   the promotion and achievements of African unity and solidarity;

(g)   the development of respect for the environment and natural resources;

(h)   the promotion of the child's understanding of primary health care.

The full realisation of this right requires states parties to the Charter to take appropriate measures, which will include to[69]:

(a)   provide free and compulsory basic education;

---

68   Children's Charter, art 11(2)(a)-(h).

69   As above, art 11(3).

(b)   encourage the development of secondary education in its different forms and to progressively make it free and accessible to all;

(c)   make higher education accessible to all on the basis of capacity and ability by every appropriate means;

(d)   take measures to encourage regular attendance at schools and the reduction of drop-out rates;

(e)   take special measures in respect of female, gifted and disadvantaged children, to ensure equal access to education for all sections of the community.

As stated in our discussion on this right in the context of the African Charter, the right to education includes the right to determine one's school or institution of learning, and the further right to establish such institutions. The Children's Charter goes further to grant parents and legal guardians the right to choose their children's schools, which would ensure 'the religious and moral education of the child in a manner with the evolving capacities of the child.'[70] The Charter appears to suggest that the right to education includes 'schools' or parental discipline.' In this regard, Article 11(5) stipulates that:

> States parties to the present Charter shall take all appropriate measures to ensure that a child who is subjected to school's or parental discipline shall be treated with humanity and with respect for the inherent dignity of the child and in conformity with the present Charter.

In other words, within the context of the Charter, a child's right to education does not preclude school's or parental discipline. Parental discipline was an integral component of education in many traditional African societies and the Charter seems to underscore this fact. It is rather strange that this component of the right to education is now being ignored in many countries. There is an emerging trend where school's or parental discipline is being outlawed in some countries. Accordingly, neither parents nor school teachers are allowed to chastise children or undertake any other form of disciplinary measure that may be appropriate to the child's upbringing. This is not in line with African cultural values, whose tenets have influenced the content of the Charter. Indiscipline in

---

70   As above, art 11(4).

schools, especially among teenage children, is a growing concern in the contemporary African society and states can only turn a blind eye to this vice to their own peril.

The Charter also safeguards the girl-child's right to education by ensuring that she is not discontinued from school in the event she falls pregnant. Towards this end, states parties are required to put in place appropriate measures to ensure that girls who become pregnant before completing their education shall have an opportunity to continue with their education based on their individual ability.[71]

While the Charter has laid a good foundation on the right to education, it is now incumbent on states parties to ensure the realisation of all the components of this right. States should, for example, provide incentives to encourage school entrance; regular school attendance and school retention; the purchase of uniforms and school books, at least for children from poor families; transportation; school meals; payments for extracurricular activities; and the responsibility for building and maintaining schools.[72]

The Charter also guarantees the right to leisure, recreation and cultural activities. This envisages a child's right to rest, engage in play and recreational activities appropriate to his or her age, and to participate freely in cultural life and the arts.[73] It is the duty of the state to respect and promote the child's right to participate in cultural and artistic life. This may be through the provision of equal opportunities for cultural, artistic, recreational and leisure activity.[74] Some countries have annual cultural events and music festivals where schools compete and the best performers rewarded. Such activities should be encouraged in order to promote the realisation of this and other related rights.

Article 14 of the Charter guarantees the right to health and health services. Accordingly, every child has the right to enjoy the

---

71   As above, art 11(6).

72   Sloth-Nielsen & Mezmur (n 12 above) 343.

73   Children's Charter, art 12(1).

74   As above, art 12(2).

best attainable state of physical, mental and spiritual health.[75] For this right to be realised, certain measures must be taken[76]:

(a)   to reduce infant and child mortality rate;

(b)   to ensure the provision of necessary medical assistance and health care to all children with emphasis on the development of primary health care;

(c)   to ensure the provision of adequate nutrition and safe drinking water;

(d)   to combat disease and malnutrition within the framework of primary health care through the application of appropriate technology;

(e)   to ensure appropriate health care for expectant and nursing mothers;

(f)   to develop preventive health care and family life education and provision of service;

(g)   to integrate basic health service programmes in national development plans;

(h)   to ensure that all sectors of the society, in particular, parents, children, community leaders and community workers are informed and supported in the use of basic knowledge of child health and nutrition, the advantages of breastfeeding, hygiene and environmental sanitation and the prevention of domestic and other accidents;

(i)   to ensure the meaningful participation of non-governmental organisations, local communities and the beneficiary population in the planning and management of a basic service programme for children;

(j)   to support through technical and financial means, the mobilisation of local community resources in the development of primary health care for children.

To ensure that a child grows in a conducive social setting, the Charter dedicates a number of provisions to the protection and recognition of family relationships.[77] It is within this context that parental care, protection and responsibility are promoted and protected. Article 18(1), which recognises the family as the natural unit and basis of

---

75   As above, art 14(1).

76   As above, art 14(2)(a)–(j).

77   See generally arts 18, 19, 20, 24 & 25.

society, entrusts the state with the protection and support of the family. Hence, the state is obliged to facilitate the establishment and development of the family. States parties are also encouraged to take appropriate steps to ensure equality of rights and responsibilities of spouses with regard to children during marriage and in the event of its dissolution.[78] There is the need for legislation to protect children during the subsistence and dissolution of marriages. Such legislation should cater for issues such as child maintenance.[79]

With regard to parental care and protection, it is the intention of the Charter that, whenever possible, every child should reside with his or her parents. However, where separation is unavoidable, the same has to be determined by a judicial authority in accordance with the appropriate laws and with due consideration of the best interests of the child.[80] Even then, such a child has the right to maintain personal relations and direct contact with both parents and on a regular basis.[81] Where separation results from the action of a state party, the concerned state ought to inform the child of the whereabouts of the member(s) of his or her family.[82]

Concerning the upbringing and development of the child, the Charter entrusts such responsibilities to parents and 'other responsible persons.'[83] This is essential because parents are important channels through which social and cultural values can be passed over to the next generation. Parental responsibility is an important human rights concept in the sense that, while it imposes certain duties on parents, it confers certain rights and freedoms on children. The duties it imposes on parents include to: (a) ensure that the best interests of the child are their basic concern at all times; (b) to secure, within their abilities and financial capacities, conditions of living necessary to the child's development; and (c) to ensure that domestic discipline is administered with humanity and in a

---

78   As above, art 18(2).

79   As above, art 18(3).

80   As above, art 19(1).

81   As above, art 19(2).

82   As above, art 19(3).

83   As above, art 20(1).

manner consistent with the inherent dignity of the child.[84] From the children's perspective, these duties translate to rights that promote their growth and development.

In acknowledging the relevance and significance of parental responsibility, the Charter requires states parties to assist parents and other persons responsible for the child by providing material assistance and support programmes particularly with regard to nutrition, health, education, clothing and housing.[85] Additionally, states are to assist in child-rearing and ensure the development of institutions responsible for providing care to children;[86] and to ensure that the children of working parents are provided with care services and facilities.[87]

Article 21 of the Charter guarantees children protection against harmful social and cultural practices. Accordingly:

1.   States parties to the present Charter shall take all appropriate measures to eliminate harmful social and cultural practices affecting the welfare, dignity, normal growth and development of the child and in particular:

     (a)   those customs and practices prejudicial to the health or life of the child; and

     (b)   those customs and practices discriminatory to the child on the grounds of sex or other status.

2.   Child marriage and the betrothal of girls and boys shall be prohibited and effective action, including legislation, shall be taken to specify the minimum age of marriage to be 18 years and make registration of all marriages in an official registry compulsory.

The term 'culture' refers to 'customs and beliefs, art, way of life and social organisation of a particular society or group' and 'beliefs and attitudes about something that people in a particular group or organisation share.'[88] According to Article 21, therefore, harmful

---

84   As above, art 20(1)(a)-(c).

85   As above, art 20(2)(a).

86   As above, art 20(2)(b).

87   As above, art 20(2)(c).

88   *Oxford advanced learners' dictionary, 6th edition.*

cultural practices are those that would ordinarily affect the welfare, dignity, normal growth and development of the child. Whereas the concept of 'growth' connotes the physical aspects of a child, 'development' is a holistic concept referring to the physical, mental, spiritual, psychological and social advancement, aimed at preparing the child for an adult lifestyle.[89]

As argued elsewhere above, African traditional cultural values emphasise on the respect for human dignity. This perception views children as a valuable component of society, entitled to special protection.[90] Whereas this is the general rule in as far as ideals are concerned, there are several exceptions when it comes to reality. It cannot be gainsaid that there are some African cultural practices which militate against the implementation of children's rights. A frequently cited example of such practices is female circumcision, otherwise known as 'Female Genital Mutilation' (FGM).[91] It is rather unfortunate that most of the harmful cultural practices are gender-biased, some of which include female excision, bride burning, female infanticide, sex slavery and servile marriage. These mundane practices are usually discriminative both in their application and effect.

It has been argued, and correctly so, that some of these practices are too deeply entrenched to be eradicated by a simple legislative process.[92] The situation is even worse in countries where customary law co-exists with statutory law. In countries like Swaziland, for example, civil and criminal courts have the mandate to apply customary law and this may impact negatively on children's rights.[93] There is the need therefore for a re-evaluation, reformulation and replacement of some of the African cultural values that have a negative impact on children. However, this process must be done in a manner which is neither culturally offensive nor results in the

---

89   R Hodgkin & P Newell 'The child's right to life and maximum survival and development', in R Hodgkin & P Newell (eds) *An implementation handbook on the United Nations Convention on the Rights of the Child* (1998) 94.

90   Sloth-Nielsen & Mezmur (n 12 above) 347.

91   As above, 348.

92   Kaime (n 7 above) 237.

93   Sloth-Nielsen & Mezmur (n 12 above) 348.

loss of African cultural integrity. Towards this end, states could, for example, undertake extensive educational and training programmes that would sensitise people on human rights generally and children's rights in particular.

6.3   DUTIES (RESPONSIBILITIES) UNDER THE CHILDREN'S CHARTER

The Children's Charter, like its older sibling, the African Charter, bestows duties on children towards their families, society, state and other legally recognised communities and the international community.[94] However, these duties are imposed subject to a child's age, ability and 'such limitations as may be contained in the ... Charter.' The rationale for imposing duties on children could be to prepare and equip them for adulthood, so that they gradually acquire the capacity to assume adult responsibilities.[95] Hence, one of the duties of the child is to work for the cohesion of the family, to respect his or her parents, superiors and elders at all times and to assist them when in need.[96] Gross disobedience may therefore be a breach of this duty and may attract some form of discipline from the parents or family members of the child.

Secondly, it is the duty of a child to serve his national community by placing his physical and intellectual abilities at its service.[97] This duty may require a child to participate in community service such as a clean-up exercise. It may also mean that a child should refrain from those activities that could deter the development of his national community, such as joining a militia group that intends to jeopardise national security. Thirdly, children are expected to preserve and strengthen social and national solidarity.[98] In this sense, they ought to be loyal to their country. Fourthly, they have the duty to preserve and strengthen African cultural values in their relations

---

94   Children's Charter, art 31.

95   J Sloth-Nielsen & B Mezmur 'Win some, lose some: The 10th ordinary session of the African Committee of Experts on the Rights and Welfare of the Child' (2008) 8 *African Human Rights Law Journal* 216.

96   Children's Charter, art 31(a).

97   As above, art 31(b).

98   As above, art 31(c).

with other members of the society, in the spirit of tolerance, dialogue and consultation and to contribute to the moral well-being of society.[99] Arguably, this duty aims at cultural continuity, reason being, preservation of subsisting cultural values would ensure they are handed-down to the next generation.

Finally, children have the duty to preserve and strengthen the independence and integrity of their country and to contribute, to the best of their abilities, at all times and at all levels, to the promotion and achievement of African unity.[100] As argued in our discussion on the African Charter, the problem with the concept of duties under the African human rights system relates to their enforceability. Duties under both the African Charter and Children's Charter are loosely worded and cannot be judicially enforced.

In the case of the Children's Charter, the duties of a child are more or less moral obligations without any legal force. At least, the duties of states parties to the Charter are more precise and enforceable. States appear to be the primary duty bearers under the Children's Charter because almost all the rights guaranteed therein require their input, either through legislative or other appropriate measures. This therefore means, states must take the lead in ensuring that the rights in the Charter are realised. Generally, the Charter is comprehensive enough to ensure the protection of the rights of the African child. However, it is not just enough to have a comprehensive normative instrument whose enforcement is not taken seriously. Concerted efforts must therefore be directed to encourage its enforcement, both at the national and international levels.

---

99   As above, art 31(d).

100   As above, art 31(e) & (f).

CHAPTER 7

THE PROTOCOL TO THE AFRICAN CHARTER ON HUMAN AND PEOPLES' RIGHTS ON THE RIGHTS OF WOMEN IN AFRICA

Women's rights are an integral component of the African system on human and peoples' rights. The African Charter on Human and Peoples' Rights[1] (hereafter 'the Charter' or 'the African Charter') was the first normative instrument under the system to provide for the protection and promotion of these rights. It imputes an obligation on states to 'ensure the elimination of every discrimination against women and also ensure the protection of the rights of the woman ... as stipulated in international declarations and conventions.'[2] This provision, however, has attracted mixed reactions from scholars and women's rights activists, a majority of them stressing its inadequacy in protecting the rights of women on the continent.[3] Following this disquiet, the Protocol to the African Charter on Human and Peoples' Rights on the Rights of Women in Africa[4] (hereafter 'the Women's Protocol' or 'the Protocol') was subsequently adopted. The Protocol is the first regional human rights treaty to specifically and comprehensively provide for the protection and promotion of women's rights.[5]

---

1   See the African Charter on Human and Peoples' Rights, OAU Doc. CAB/LEG/67/3 rev. 5; adopted 27 June 1981; entered into force 21 October 1986.

2   As above, art 18(3).

3   See, for example, K Elmadmad 'The rights of women under the African Charter on Human and Peoples' Rights' in W Benedek & W Heinz (eds) *Regional systems of human rights in Africa, America and Europe: Proceedings of the conference* (1992) 17; F Butengwa 'Using the African Charter on Human and Peoples' Rights to secure women's access to land in Africa' in R Cook (ed) *Human right of women: National and international perspective* (1996) 503; L Kois 'Article 18 of The African Charter on Human and Peoples' Rights: A progressive approach to the women's human rights' (1997) 3 *East African Journal of Peace and Human rights* 92.

4   Protocol to the African Charter on Human and Peoples' Rights on the Rights of Women in Africa; adopted by the 2nd Ordinary Session of the Assembly of the Union Maputo, 11 July 2003.

5   M Banderin 'Recent developments in the African Regional Human Rights System' (2005) 5/1 *Human Rights Law Review* 118.

The initiative to promulgate a regional human rights treaty on women began in 1995 at a seminar held in Lome Togo, organised by the African Commission in conjunction with Women in Law and Development in Africa (WILDAF).[6] During this seminar, proposals were made for the formulation and adoption of a protocol that would specifically address the rights of women in Africa. Affirming the need for such a normative instrument, the former Organisation of African Unity (OAU) consented to the appointment of experts to spearhead the process.[7] Within three years, 'the Draft Protocol to the African Charter on the Rights of Women in Africa' (hereafter 'the Draft Women's Protocol') was approved by the African Commission on Human and Peoples' Rights (hereafter 'the African Commission' or 'the Commission') and was subsequently tabled before the OAU for its comments.[8]

Meanwhile, the Women's Unit of the OAU was busy working on the 'Draft OAU Convention on the Elimination of All Forms of Harmful Practices (HPs) Affecting the Fundamental Human Rights of Women and Girls' (hereafter 'the Draft OAU Women's Convention').[9] To avoid unnecessary duplication, the OAU urged the African Commission and the Women's Unit to work together and come up with an integrated normative instrument embodying various aspects of women's rights.[10] It also recommended that the Draft OAU Women's Convention should be integrated in the Draft Kigali Protocol. The integrated document was finalised in September 2000.[11] After lengthy negotiations, the Women's Protocol was eventually adopted by the Assembly of the African Union (AU) in Maputo on 11 July 2003 and subsequently came into force on 25

---

6   See WILDAF 'The African Charter on Human and Peoples' Rights and the Additional Protocol on Women's Rights' available at <http://www.wildaf.org.zw/news4.html> (accessed 21 April 2010).

7   See 31st Ordinary Session Resolution AHG/Res 240 (XXXI).

8   26th Ordinary Session of the African Commission on Human and Peoples' Rights 1-15 November 1999 'Final Communique' available at <http://www1.umn.edu/humanrts/africa/african charter26f.html> (accessed 2 April 2010) para 16.

9   M Nsibirwa 'A brief analysis of the Draft Protocol to the African Charter on Human and Peoples' Rights on the Rights of Women' (2001) 1 *African Human Rights Law Journal* 42.

10   As above.

11   As above.

November 2005, 30 days after the fifteenth instrument of ratification was deposited by Togo.

Other than the inadequacy of the African Charter's provisions relating to the rights of women, the promulgation of the Women's Protocol was motivated by many factors. First, it was borne out of the fact that women's rights are recognised and guaranteed in several international human rights instruments.[12] Most notable of these instruments are the Universal Declaration of Human Rights (UDHR),[13] International Covenant on Civil and Political Rights (ICCPR),[14] International Covenant on Economic, Social and Cultural Rights (ICESCR)[15] and the Convention on the Elimination of All Forms of Discrimination Against Women (CEDAW) and its Optional Protocol.[16]

Further, the Protocol's adoption was in recognition of the fact that women's rights and the essential role of women in development have been reaffirmed in many United Nations (UN) plans of action, including that on Environment and Development in 1992, on Human Rights in 1993, on Population and Development in 1994 and on Social Development in 1995.[17] African states did not therefore want to be left out of these global trends touching on women and their rights.

Moreover, events within the AU circles also inspired the promulgation of the Protocol. For instance, the Constitutive Act of the African Union (hereafter 'CAAU' or 'the Act') and the New Partnership for Africa's Development (NEPAD) Document embody the promotion of gender equality as one of their principles.[18] In

---

12   Women Protocol, preamble para 5.

13   See Universal Declaration on Human Rights, G.A Res. 217 (III); adopted on 10 December 1948.

14   Adopted 16 December 1966, G.A Res. 2200 (XXI); entered into force 23 March 1976.

15   Adopted 16 December 1966, G.A Res. 2200 (XXI); entered into force 23 March 1976)

16   The United Nations General Assembly adopted the Optional Protocol in October 1999 (A//res/54/4). It entered into force on 22 December 2000, after ten states had become parties thereto.

17   Women's Protocol, preamble para 6.

18   As above, para 8.

order to underscore the commitment of the African states to ensure the full participation of African women as equal partners in Africa's development, it was therefore necessary to reinforce their rights.

Lastly, the Protocol was also motivated by the need to recognise the crucial role of women in the preservation of African values, based on the principles of equality, peace, freedom, dignity, justice, solidarity and democracy.[19] Despite the ratification of the African Charter and other international human rights instruments by a majority of African states, African women have continued to be victims of all forms of discrimination and harmful practices.[20] This necessitates not only the condemnation, but also the elimination of any practice that hinders or endangers the normal growth and development of women and girls.[21]

7.1   GENERAL STRUCTURE AND FEATURES OF THE PROTOCOL

The Women's Protocol is divided into 32 Articles, guaranteeing both individual and group rights. Unlike other international human rights instruments on women's rights (such as CEDAW), the Protocol provides some unique rights for women. These include special protection of women in armed conflicts,[22] widows' rights,[23] with disabilities,[24] and in distress.[25]

Moreover, the scope and content of some of the rights in the Protocol could be distinguished from that of the CEDAW. For instance, the definition of 'discrimination' in the former is much broader than that of the latter. Whereas in the CEDAW the term is limited to 'any distinction, exclusion or restriction', the Protocol broadens it to include 'any differential treatment based on sex and whose objectives or effects compromise or destroy the recognition, enjoyment or the exercise by women, regardless of their marital

---

19   As above, para 10.

20   As above, para 12.

21   As above, para 13.

22   As above, art 11.

23   As above arts 20 & 21.

24   As above, art 23.

25   As above, art 24.

status, of human rights and fundamental freedoms in all spheres of life.'[26] This clears the apparent grey area between 'differentiation' and 'discrimination'.[27] Further, the Protocol extends the definition of violence against women from mere 'acts that could cause physical, sexual and psychological harm', to the realm of 'economic harm'.[28]

Again, the Protocol departs from the UN treaty bodies' position on the issue of polygamy. According to the UN Human Rights Committee (HRC), for example, 'equality of treatment with regard to the right to marry implies that polygamy is incompatible with this principle ... violates the dignity of women ... is an inadmissible discrimination against women ... [and] should be definitely abolished wherever it continues to exist.'[29] Additionally, the CEDAW Committee has maintained:

> Polygamous marriage contravenes a woman's right to equality with men, and can have such serious emotional and financial consequences for her and her dependants that such marriages ought to be discouraged and prohibited. The Committee notes with concern that some states parties, whose constitutions guarantee equal rights, permit polygamous marriage in accordance with personal or customary law. This violates the constitutional rights of women, and breaches the provisions of Article 5(a) of the Convention.[30]

Conversely, the Women's Protocol requires states parties to enact appropriate legislation to guarantee that 'monogamy is encouraged as the preferred form of marriage and that the rights of women in marriage and family, including in polygamous marital relationships are promoted and protected.'[31] In this sense, the Protocol appears to be non-committal on the prohibition of polygamy. While this is the case, it is definitely difficult to reconcile this position with

---

26   As above, art 1(f).

27   Banderin (n 5 above) 121.

28   Women's Protocol, art 1(j).

29   HRC General Comment 28, 'Equality of Rights between Men and Women (Article 3)', 29 March 2000, CCPR/C/21/Rev.1/Add.10.

30   CEDAW General Recommendation 21, 'Equality in Marriage and Family Relations' HRI/- GEN/1/Rev.1 (1994) 90.

31   Women's Protocol, art 6(c).

the principle of non-discrimination and equality between men and women under Article 2 of the Protocol.[32]

The Protocol, unlike the African Charter on the Rights and Welfare of the Child, does not provide for the establishment of an independent body to ensure its interpretation, implementation and monitoring. Instead, states parties are required to submit periodic reports to the African Commission pursuant to Article 62 of the African Charter.[33] Article 32 of the Protocol maintains, 'pending the establishment of the African Court on Human and Peoples' Rights, the African Commission on Human and Peoples' Rights shall be seized with matters of interpretation arising from the application and implementation of this Protocol.' This could as well be taken to mean that individual communications alleging a breach of the Protocol's provisions may also be lodged with the Commission. Ultimately, the mandate to interpret the Protocol is vested on the African Court.[34]

7.2   INDIVIDUALS' RIGHTS UNDER THE PROTOCOL

7.2.1   CIVIL AND POLITICAL RIGHTS

The Protocol guarantees civil and political rights which in many respects are similar to those enlisted in the African Charter, but with slight modifications intended to address the peculiar circumstances affecting women. The main intention of such modifications could be to eliminate gender-based discrimination and to promote gender equality on the continent. Accordingly, Article 2 of the Protocol prohibits discrimination against women by stating as follows:

1.   States parties shall combat all forms of discrimination against women through appropriate legislative, institutional and other measures. In this regard, they shall:

   a)   Include in their national constitutions and other legislative instruments, if not already done, the

---

32   Banderin (n 5 above) 121.

33   Women's Protocol, art 26(1).

34   As above, art 27.

> principle of equality between women and men and ensure its effective application;
>
> b) Enact and effectively implement appropriate legislative or regulatory measures, including those prohibiting and curbing all forms of discrimination particularly those harmful practices which endanger the health and general well-being of women;
>
> c) Integrate a gender perspective in their policy decisions, legislation, development plans, programmes and activities and in all other spheres of life;
>
> d) Take corrective and positive action in those areas where discrimination against women in law and in fact continues to exist;
>
> e) Support the local, national, regional and continental initiatives directed at eradicating all forms of discrimination against women.

Discrimination against women in many African societies is mainly perpetuated by the tendency to uphold certain mundane socio-cultural beliefs and practices. In fact, some practices, such as female circumcision, are harmful and pose a threat to the health of women and the girl-child. Women are also denied equal opportunities when it comes to participation in governance and other public activities. They are mostly expected to ratify decisions made by their male counterparts without registering any reservations.

In order to reverse this trend, states parties are expected to spearhead the initiative to modify those social and cultural patterns that are discriminative against women. This could be achieved by, for example, conducting public education, information and communication strategies, 'with a view to achieving the elimination of harmful cultural and traditional practices and all other practices which are based on the idea of the inferiority or the superiority of either of the sexes, or on stereotyped roles for women and men.'[35]

It appears that gender equality is the golden thread that cuts across a number of provisions in the Protocol. Article 8, for example, guarantees equal access to justice and protection before the law.

---

35   As above, art 2(2).

Towards this end, states parties are enjoined to take all appropriate measures to ensure, among other things, the effective access by women to judicial and legal services. This includes the provision of legal aid to indigent litigants.[36] Sensitisation of people on the rights of women,[37] equipping law enforcement organs to effectively interpret and enforce gender equality rights[38] and ensuring gender-balance in the judiciary and law enforcement organs,[39] are also enlisted among the measures states are to undertake to avail this right.

Further, the Protocol guarantees gender equality in political and decision-making processes.[40] Over the years, women have been precluded from participating in the political life and decision-making processes of their countries. Ironically, even the self-styled 'mothers of democracy and human rights', such as the United States of America (US), have also been guilty of excluding women from holding key governance positions. The Protocol therefore places a moratorium on this trend by urging states parties to adopt affirmative action, enact enabling national legislation and other measures to ensure that women participate without any discrimination in all elections.[41] Additionally, states are to regard women as equal partners with men at all levels of development and implementation of state policies and development programmes.[42] Not only so, they are also to ensure increased and effective representation and participation of women at all levels of decision-making.[43]

The Protocol also guarantees every woman the right to dignity and to the recognition and protection of her human and legal rights.[44] These include the right to be respected as a person and to the free development of one's personality.[45] Arguably, by referring

---

36   As above, art 8(a).

37   As above, art 8(b).

38   As above, art 8(c).

39   As above, art 8(d).

40   As above, art 9(1).

41   As above, art 9(1)(a).

42   As above, art 9(1)(c).

43   As above, art 9(2).

44   As above, art 3(1).

45   As above, art 3(2).

to the right to 'the recognition and protection of her human and legal rights', the Protocol guarantees women the enjoyment of other rights that are not expressly mentioned in it. Such rights may include those enumerated in the African Charter or any other international human rights instrument designed to guarantee women's rights.

The right to dignity may effectively be guaranteed through the prohibition of any form of exploitation or degradation,[46] and the protection of women from all forms of violence, particularly sexual and verbal violence.[47] Noteworthy, the scope of violence against women in the Protocol is not limited to actual physical, sexual and psychological harm, but also envisages the mere threat to commit such acts.[48] It can be contended that in effect, the Protocol outlaws domestic violence in all its forms and facets.[49]

It is pitiful to note that prohibition of violence against women is conspicuously lacking in the CEDAW. However, the CEDAW Committee has attempted to remedy this omission through some of its general recommendations.[50] Specifically, General Recommendation number. 19 partly provides:

> ... The definition of discrimination includes gender-based violence, that is, violence that is directed against a woman because she is a woman or that affects women disproportionately. It includes acts that inflict physical, mental or sexual harm or suffering, threats of such acts, coercion and other deprivations of liberty. Gender-based violence may breach specific provisions of the Convention, regardless of whether those provisions expressly mention violence.[51]

---

46 As above, art 3(3).

47 As above, art 3(4).

48 As above art 1(h).

49 See generally E Curran & E Bonthuys 'Customary law and domestic violence in rural South African societies' (2005) 21 *South African Journal of Human Rights* 607-635; R Murray 'A feminist perspective on reform of the African human rights system' (2001) *African Human Rights Law Journal* 205.

50 These efforts began with the adoption of General Recommendation nuomber 12 on violence against women, UN Doc A/44/38 (1990). See this observation in F Banda 'Building on a global movement: Violence against women in the African context' (2008) 8 *African Human Rights Law Journal* 5.

51 See General Recommendation 19, para 6.

It is therefore clear, according to the CEDAW Committee, there is a close nexus between violence against women and gender-based discrimination. This partly explains why the international community has lately embarked on concerted efforts to prohibit violence against women. For instance, after the 1993 World Conference on Human Rights held in Vienna, the UN Assembly adopted the 'Declaration on the Elimination of Violence Against Women' (DEVAW).[52] The declaration recognised that women experience violence, not only in the family and community, but also through the state and its agencies.[53] The declaration envisages the adoption of a multi-agency approach to tackling violence against women, involving both states and Non-Governmental Organisations (NGOs).[54]

Another remarkable initiative by the international community was the appointment of the Special Rapporteur on violence against women in 1994.[55] The rapporteur has done a tremendous job in documenting instances and causes of violence against women.[56] Further, in 1995, the 'Beijing Declaration and Platform for Action' was adopted, identifying violence against women as one of the 12 areas of gross concern.[57] The document enjoined states in the strategy to prevent violence against women within their respective societies.[58] A subsequent review conducted on the implementation of the 'Beijing Declaration and Platform for Action' revealed that

---

52   Declaration on the Elimination of Violence against Women, GA Res 48/104 of 20 December 1993. See H Charlesworth & C Chinkin *The boundaries of international law* (2000) 12-14.

53   Declaration on the Elimination of Violence against Women (note 52 above) art. 2.

54   As above, art 4.

55   See United Nations Commission on Human Rights Resolution 1994/45 on the question of integrating the rights of women into human rights mechanisms of the UN and the elimination of violence against women, adopted on 4 March 1994.

56   See, for example, Special Rapporteur on Violence Against Women in the Family E/CN 4/1996/53 and E/CN 4/1999/68; Special Rapporteur on Violence Against Women Violence against women perpetrated or condoned by the state during times of armed conflict (1997-2000) E/CN4/2001/73; and Special Rapporteur on Violence Against Women Cultural practices in the family that are violence towards women E/CN 4/2002/83.

57   'Beijing Declaration and Platform for Action' para 44, Fourth World Conference on Women, 15 September 1995, A/CONF.177/20 (1995).

58   As above, Strategic Objective D1.

commendable progress had since been made in recognising violence against women as a form of human rights violation.[59]

Africa, as a region, has also attempted to address the issue of violence against women. For instance, in 2004, the AU adopted the 'Solemn Declaration on Gender Equality in Africa', which proscribes violence and abuse against women and girls, particularly during armed conflicts.[60] The declaration, save for the fact that it has no binding legal force, is a pointer towards the right direction in tackling sexual assault committed in the context of armed conflicts. It is sad to note that during armed conflicts, sexual violence against women is usually perpetrated, 'either as an encouragement for soldiers or as an instrument of policy.'[61] However, little has been done over the years to curtail the rising incidences of war-related sexual violations. It was not until the creation of the International Criminal Tribunal for the former Yugoslavia (the ICTY) and later, the International Criminal Tribunal for Rwanda (the ICTR), that these crimes received international attention.[62] At least, the two tribunals have sent a signal that wartime abuses against women will henceforth be rigorously prohibited, prosecuted and punished.[63]

Be that as it may, cases of violence against women are still prevalent in Africa, in times of peace as in times of war. This is a clear indication that a colourful normative framework on this subject is not any meaningful if the same is not diligently implemented to the letter. Perhaps, possibilities should be explored towards crafting a regional instrument to enable the prosecution of perpetrators of violence against women, especially in wartime. The instrument

---

59   See Beijing + 5 Outcome Document reproduced in United Nations *Beijing to Beijing + 5: Review and appraisal of the implementation of the Beijing Platform for Action* (2001) 195, section D para 13.

60   'Solemn Declaration on Gender Equality in Africa', Assembly/AU/Decl 12 & 13 (III), Assembly of Heads of State and Government 3rd ordinary session 6-8 July 2004, Addis Ababa.

61   T Meron 'Rape as a crime under international humanitarian law' (1993) 87 *American Journal of International Law* 424.

62   See K Askin 'Sexual violence in decisions and indictments of the Yugoslav and Rwandan Tribunals: Current status (1999) 93 *American Journal of International Law* 101.

63   N Pillay 'The advancement of women's rights' (2002) 16 *Occasional Paper* Centre for human rights University of Pretoria.

should also provide for the rehabilitation and reparation of the victims of violence. Article 4 of the Women's Protocol seems to give force to the prohibition of violence against women by stating that:

> Every woman shall be entitled to respect for her life and the integrity and security of her person. All forms of exploitation, cruel, inhuman or degrading punishment and treatment shall be prohibited.[64]

It is interesting to note that the Protocol enlists 'unwanted or forced sex' as a form of violence against women.[65] However, it is not clear whether the drafters had 'marital rape' in mind when framing this provision. This has led to the contention that, since the provision suggests that violence may take place 'in private or public', there is a strong indication that unwanted or forced sex may as well be committed between spouses in the privacy of their homes.[66] Accordingly, this implies that states parties to the Protocol are expected to introduce the crime of 'marital rape' in their statute books.[67] However, it is generally difficult to prosecute this crime, especially because it involves the privacy and sanctity of the marriage institution. It has therefore not been easy for legal systems to formulate water-tight legislation on this crime, without being seen to be interfering with the privacy of the marriage institution.

All the same, the Protocol obligates states parties to enact and enforce laws prohibiting all forms of violence against women, including unwanted or forced sex.[68] Apart from undertaking legislative measures, states are also expected to 'actively promote peace education through curricula and social communication in order to eradicate elements in traditional and cultural beliefs, practices and stereotypes which legitimise and exacerbate the persistence and tolerance of violence against women.'[69] Other measures they are expressly required to undertake include:

---

64   Women's Protocol, art 4(1).

65   Art 4(2)(a). This provision requires states parties to take appropriate and effective measures to 'enact and enforce laws to prohibit all forms of violence against women including unwanted or forced sex whether the violence takes place in private or public.'

66   Banda (n 50 above) 13.

67   As above.

68   Women's Protocol, art 4(2)(b).

69   As above, art 4(2)(d).

- Punishment of perpetrators of violence against women and implementation of programmes for the rehabilitation of women victims;[70]
- Establishment of mechanisms and accessible services for effective information, rehabilitation and reparation for victims of violence against women;[71]
- Prevention and condemnation of trafficking in women, prosecute the perpetrators of such trafficking and protect those women most at risk;[72]
- Prohibition of all medical or scientific experiments on women without their informed consent;[73]
- Providing adequate budgetary and other resources for the implementation and monitoring of actions aimed at preventing and eradicating violence against women;[74]
- Ensuring that, in those countries where the death penalty still exists, not to carry out death sentences on pregnant or nursing women;[75] and
- Ensuring that women and men enjoy equal rights in terms of access to refugee status determination procedures and that women refugees are accorded the full protection and benefits guaranteed under international refugee law, including their own identity and other documents.[76]

Generally, the Protocol's provisions on violence against women are remarkably comprehensive in that they not only cover the elimination of violence but also provide ways of catering for the victims. Consequently, they act both as a deterrent to perpetrators of the offence and also as an aid to the victims to normalise their lives.[77] Ultimately, this will ensure that victims of violence, who are normally ignored in pursuit of the perpetrators, shall be afforded greater attention. In most legal systems, focus is usually on the

---

70   As above, art 4(2)(e).
71   As above, art 4(2)(f).
72   As above, art 4(2)(g).
73   As above, art 4(2)(h).
74   As above, art 4(2)(i).
75   As above, art 4(2)(j).
76   As above, art 4(2)(k).
77   Nsibirwa (n 9 above) 45.

prosecution of the perpetrators of violence, without taking heed of the need to rehabilitate or compensate the victims.[78]

In line with the prohibition of violence against women, the Protocol also guarantees them protection from harmful practices. According to Article 5:

> States parties shall prohibit and condemn all forms of harmful practices which negatively affect the human rights of women and which are contrary to recognised international standards. States parties shall take all necessary legislative and other measures to eliminate such practices ...

Harmful practices include 'all behaviour, attitudes and/or practices which negatively affect the fundamental rights of women and girls, such as their life, health, dignity, education and physical integrity.'[79] The list of harmful practices perpetrated against women is endless. In recognition of the fact that law in itself is not sufficient to curtail such practices, the Protocol has adopted a multi-pronged approach to this issue. The envisaged approaches necessitate states to, among other things, conduct public awareness on harmful practices,[80] provide necessary support to victims,[81] and protect women who are at risk of being subjected to such practices or other forms of violence, abuse and intolerance.[82]

Noteworthy, the Protocol totally outlaws Female Genital Mutilation (FGM), notwithstanding the fact that it is conducted under medical supervision. Article 5(b) is categorical that states parties should ensure the 'prohibition, through legislative measures backed by sanctions, of all forms of female genital mutilation, scarification, medicalisation and para-medicalisation of female genital mutilation and all other practices ...' Banda correctly observed, the Protocol incorporates an important innovation that brings to rest the argument that FGM is only a problem if performed under unsafe or

---

78   As above.

79   Women's Protocol, art 1(g).

80   As above, art 5(a).

81   As above, art 5(c). The services listed under this provision include health services, legal and judicial support, emotional and psychological counselling as well as vocational training to victims.

82   As above, art 5 (d).

unsanitary conditions.[83] It is now an established fact, no matter the socio-cultural reasons advanced to justify it, FGM is both abhorrent and a threat to the health of the girl-child.

Like the African Charter, the Protocol guarantees the right to peace.[84] Within this context, it affords women two-intertwined rights, namely the right to a peaceful existence and the right to participate in the promotion and maintenance of peace.[85] On the other hand, it places an obligation on the state to ensure the increased participation of women in realising this set of rights.[86] It is encouraging to note that the Protocol also urges states to take the necessary measures to reduce military expenditure significantly in favour of spending on social development in general, and the promotion of women in particular.[87] As stated elsewhere in this book, military expenditure consumes a large portion of the national budgets of many African states, which would otherwise be channelled to support other constructive activities, such as the promotion and protection of human rights.

7.2.2 ECONOMIC, SOCIAL AND CULTURAL RIGHTS

The Protocol guarantees the enjoyment of economic, social and cultural rights, including the right to marriage, education and training, economic and social welfare, health and reproduction, food security, adequate housing, positive cultural context, healthy and sustainable environment and the right to sustainable development.

It underscores the right to equality in marriage between men and women in no uncertain terms. Article 6, for example, emphasises certain marriage-related rights which are more or less a pointer to the intended equality.[88] The rights envisaged therein relate to, among other issues, the full and free consent of both parties to a marriage, the minimum age of marriage for women,

---

83   Banda (n 50 above) 17.

84   Women's Protocol, art 10.

85   As above, art 10(1).

86   As above, art 10(2)(a)-(e).

87   As above, art 10(3).

88   See As above, art 6(a)-(j).

encouragement of monogamous marriages, protection of women in polygamous marriages, matrimonial property and nationality. Additionally, Article 7 guarantees protection to women in the event of separation, divorce and annulment of marriages.

As stated previously, the Protocol appears to be non-committal on the prohibition of polygamy because it casually states, '... monogamy is encouraged as the preferred form of marriage ...'[89] Arguably, the drafters ought to have been aware that the encouragement of monogamy does not necessarily mean the prohibition of polygamy. It will equally be gullible for one to attribute the imprecision of this provision to poor drafting because it goes on to urge states to ensure that, '... the rights of women in marriage and family, including in polygamous marital relationships are promoted and protected.' Visibly, the drafters wanted to retain the institution of polygamy, an age-long practice that is prevalent across the continent. Hence, polygamy seems to be permissible under the African human rights system, but only to the limited extent that it does not infringe on the rights of women.

The Protocol also guarantees the right to education and training, of course, within the context of equality and non-discrimination. In this regard, states are to take all appropriate measures to eliminate all forms of discrimination against women and guarantee equal opportunity and access in the sphere of education and training.[90] They are also to eliminate all stereotypes in textbooks, syllabuses and the media, that perpetuate such discrimination.[91] Gender stereotyping has taken a central stage in depicting women or the girl-child as inferior, while their male counterparts as superior. School textbooks and other educational materials have all along conveyed the impression that certain influential professions and careers are a preserve for men. This has played a significant role in entrenching gender-based discrimination and inequality.

The right to education and training also includes the protection of women, especially the girl-child, from all forms of abuse, including

---

89   As above, art 6(c).

90   As above, art 12(1)(a).

91   As above, art 12(1)(b).

sexual harassment in schools and other educational institutions.[92] Sexual harassment in schools has been one of the major hurdles to equality between boys and girls. In many instances, girls succumb to pressure from their school teachers, who solicit 'sexual-favours' in exchange for good grades. Those who resist such advances are usually 'punished' with poor grades, while those who comply sometimes fall pregnant and are expelled from school. Despite the attendant trauma, women and girls who suffer abuses and sexual harassment rarely have access to counselling and rehabilitation services.

With regard to economic and social welfare rights, the Protocol obliges states parties to adopt and enforce legislative and other measures to guarantee women equal opportunities in work and career advancement. Such measures include the promotion of equality of access to employment;[93] promotion of the right to equal remuneration for jobs of equal value for women and men;[94] and ensuring transparency in recruitment, promotion and dismissal of women from the workplace.[95] While the Protocol guarantees women the right to choose their occupation, it also affords them diverse forms of protection.[96] The protection relates to the prohibition of exploitation by employers,[97] social insurance for women working in the informal sector,[98] introduction of minimum working age,[99] and adequate and paid pre and post-natal maternity leave in both the private and public sectors.[100]

On health and reproductive rights of women, states are to promote and protect, among other things, the right to control their fertility;[101] the right to decide whether to have children, the

---

92   As above, art 12(1)(c).

93   As above, art 13(a).

94   As above, art 13(b).

95   As above, art 13(c).

96   For a catalogue of these protections, see generally, art 13(d)– (m).

97   As above, art 13(d).

98   As above, art 13(f).

99   As above, art 13(g).

100   As above, art 13(i).

101   As above, art 14(1)(a).

number of children and the spacing of children;[102] and the right to choose any method of contraception.[103] Women also have the right to self-protection and to be protected against sexually transmitted infections, including HIV/AIDS.[104] Reproductive rights of women also entail the authorisation of medical abortion in cases of sexual assault, rape, incest, and where the continued pregnancy endangers the mental and physical health of the mother or the life of the mother or the foetus.[105]

Women also have the right to food security, which encompasses access to clean drinking water, sources of domestic fuel, land, and the means of producing nutritious food.[106] They also have the right to adequate housing and to acceptable living conditions in a healthy environment.[107] The parameters of this right under the Protocol are closely related to those of the right to a healthy and sustainable environment[108] and the right to sustainable development.[109] As already emphasised, although the contents of these rights resonate those of similar provisions under the African Charter, the Protocol intends that these rights be construed from a feminist perspective.

7.3   RIGHTS OF SPECIAL GROUPS

The Protocol has provisions specifically tailored to protect the rights of women falling within at least five groups, namely, women in armed conflicts, widows, elderly women, women with disabilities and women in distress. These could be said to be special groups of women who require preferential treatment owing to the uniqueness of their circumstances.

In order to protect women in armed conflicts, states parties to the Protocol undertake to promote and ensure respect for the rules of international humanitarian law applicable in armed conflict

---

102   As above, art 14(1)(b).

103   As above, art 14(1)(c).

104   As above, art 14(1)(d).

105   As above, art 14(2)(c).

106   As above, art 15(a).

107   As above, art 16.

108   As above, art 18.

109   As above, art 19.

situations.[110] International humanitarian law has two sets of rules. The first comprises of rules that protect persons who do not, or no longer, participate in hostilities, namely, the sick and wounded members of the armed forces, prisoners of war and civilians. The second set prescribes the conduct of hostilities.[111] These rules 'are based on the fundamental principle that a distinction must be made at all times between the civilian population and military objectives.'[112] The main treaties of humanitarian law are the four Geneva Conventions of 1949[113] and their two Additional protocols of 1977.[114]

It cannot be gainsaid that the greatest casualties in armed conflicts are civilians, particularly women, children, the disabled and the elderly. It is little wonder, therefore, that the Women's Protocol obligates states to undertake to protect asylum seeking women, refugees, returnees and internally displaced persons, against all forms of violence, rape and other forms of sexual exploitation.[115] It goes further to instruct that such acts should be considered war crimes, genocide and/or crimes against humanity and that their perpetrators be brought to justice before a competent criminal jurisdiction.[116]

Under international law, crimes against humanity are committed as part of a widespread or systematic attack against any civilian population, on national, political, ethnic, racial or religious grounds.[117]

---

110   As above, art 11(1)-(2).

111   See J Lavoyer 'Implementation of international humanitarian law and the role of the International Committee of the Red Cross' in J Carey, *et al*, (eds) *International Humanitarian Law: Challenges* (2004) 213.

112   As above.

113   The Conventions, signed at Geneva on 12 August 1949, are: Convention I for the Amelioration of the Condition of the Wounded and Sick in Armed Forces in the Field; Convention II for the Amelioration of the Condition of Wounded, Sick and Shipwrecked Members of Armed Forces at Sea; Convention III Relative to the Treatment of Prisoners of War; Convention IV Relative to the Protection of Civilian Persons in Time of War.

114   Protocol I Additional to the Geneva Conventions of 12 August 1949, and Relating to the Protection of Victims of International Armed Conflicts, 8 June 1977, entered into force 7 December 1978; Protocol II Additional to the Geneva Convention of 12 August 1949, and Relating to the Protection of Victims of Non-International Armed Conflicts, June 1977, entered into force 7 December 1978.

115   Women's Protocol, art 11(3).

116   As above.

117   See Rome Statute for the International Criminal Court, 1998 UN Doc A/CONF 183/9 (17 July 1998), arts 7 & 8.

These crimes could be in the form of murder, extermination, imprisonment, torture, rape, forced pregnancy and any other form of sexual violence. Other forms include persecution on political, racial, ethnic or religious grounds and other inhumane acts. However, these offences will amount to crimes against humanity only if they are part of a widespread or systematic practice. Isolated offences of this nature may only constitute grave infringements of human rights, but may fall short of being crimes against humanity.[118]

Related to crimes against humanity are genocide and war crimes. Genocide refers to acts committed with intent to destroy, in whole or in part, an ethnic, racial, religious, or national group. According to the 1948 'United Nations Convention on the Prevention and Punishment of the Crime of Genocide'[119] (hereafter 'the Genocide Convention'), the crime comprises of acts such as, 'killing members of the group; causing serious bodily or mental harm to members of the group; deliberately inflicting on the group conditions of life, calculated to bring about its physical destruction in whole or in part; imposing measures intended to prevent births within the group; and forcibly transferring children of the group to another group.'[120] War crimes are violations of established 'laws of war', which are mainly entrenched in the Geneva Conventions.

It is important to point out that, since the early 1990s, a number of tribunals have been established globally to prosecute people for various crimes under international law. These include the International Criminal Tribunal for Rwanda (ICTR), International Criminal Tribunal for the former Yugoslavia (ICTY), International Criminal Court (ICC), Special Court for Sierra Leone (SCSL), Crimes Panels of the District Court of Dili (of East Timor) and 'Regulation 64' Panels in the Courts of Kosovo. Although these tribunals have roundly been criticised for failing to prosecute sexual

---

118   See this position in *Prosecutor v. Tadic* Case IT-94-1, opinion and judgment (7 May 1997) paras 646–647.

119   The Convention on the Prevention and Punishment of the Crime of Genocide; adopted 9 December 1948, UNGA Res 260 (III) A.

120   As above, art 42.

crimes perpetrated against women in armed conflicts,[121] recent developments indicate a commendable shift from this trend.

For example, the ICTR made a landmark pronouncement in *The Prosecutor v. Jean-Paul Akayesu,*[122] when it construed rape as an international crime. The Tribunal observed that rape, as far as it is committed with the intention to destroy a particular group either in whole or in part, amounts to genocide. Akayesu's indictment alleged that he knew of and encouraged the commission of sexual violence against displaced Tutsi women.[123] On this basis, the Tribunal found him guilty of genocide and crimes against humanity by observing that:

> Sexual violence was an integral part of the process of destruction, specifically targeting Tutsi women and specifically contributing to their destruction and to the destruction of the Tutsi group as a whole.[124]

Magnarella commented, and rightly so, that the Akayesu judgement is of immense factual and jurisprudential importance.[125] This stems from the fact that it is the first decision where rape has been construed as an act of genocide. On the same note, the judgement stresses the point that it is possible for African states to ensure the prosecution of perpetrators of sexual violence in armed conflicts, and that there is no reasonable excuse for failing to do so. Arguably, the major impediment to domestic prosecution of such crimes has been the lack of adequate legislation, funds and political will.

Most states rely solely on their criminal statutes, which are at best suitable for the prosecution of domestic crimes that are 'petty', compared to international crimes. This therefore leaves them with one of two options when it comes to crimes committed during armed conflicts: either to form special tribunals to prosecute alleged

---

121   See, for example, J Gardham & H Charlesworth 'Protection of women in armed conflict' (2000) 22 *Human Rights Quarterly* 148.

122   ICTR 96-4-T, judgment of 2 September 1998, <http://www.ictr.org> (last accessed 8 May 2010).

123   As above, paras 10A, 12A & 12B.

124   As above, paras 731 & 734.

125   P Magnarella 'Some milestones and achievements at the International Criminal Tribunal for Rwanda: The 1998 Kambanda, Akayesu cases' (1998) 11 *Florida Journal of International Law* 537.

perpetrators or defer jurisdiction to a competent international court or tribunal. In order to effectively protect the rights of women in armed conflicts, states should therefore strive to enact comprehensive legislation to enable the effective prosecution of war-related crimes.

Regarding the rights of widows, the Protocol requires states parties to take appropriate legal measures to ensure that this group enjoys all human rights. Specifically, it emphasises that a widow should not be subjected to inhuman, humiliating or degrading treatment;[126] should automatically become the guardian and custodian of her children, after the death of her husband, unless this is contrary to the interests and welfare of the children;[127] and shall have the right to remarry, and in that event, to marry the person of her choice.[128] Additionally, the Protocol guarantees widows the right to an equitable share in the inheritance of their deceased husbands' property.[129] In terms of Article 22, elderly women are guaranteed special protection as follows:

> The states parties undertake to:
>
> a)   provide protection to elderly women and take specific measures commensurate with their physical, economic and social needs as well as their access to employment and professional training;
>
> b)   ensure the right of elderly women to freedom from violence, including sexual abuse, discrimination based on age and the right to be treated with dignity.

Article 22(a) is ambiguous and could therefore resort to misinterpretation. First, it could be understood to mean, when assisting elderly women, states should consider, among other things, their previous employment and professional training. This interpretation is sensible, if the specific measures contemplated in this provision would involve giving elderly women some form of 'old-age grants.' Definitely, retired professional women, who probably

---

126   Women's Protocol, art 20(a).

127   As above, art 20(b).

128   As above, art 20(c).

129   As above, art 21(1).

held well-paying jobs, deserve attractive retirement packages or any other form of 'old-age grants' in keeping with their previous status.

The second interpretation of this provision is to the effect that, 'access to employment and professional training', should be taken to mean that states parties are to provide elderly women with jobs. If this is the case, this provision could be said to be overly ambitious, especially when one takes into consideration the job scarcity and the attendant rate of unemployment in Africa. Many qualified youngsters find it exceptionally difficult to secure employment in Africa. Under such circumstances, one would be eager to see how this provision will be effected. In fact, it makes more sense when the Protocol extends this right to young women with disabilities,[130] than to retired elderly women.

Lastly, the Protocol affords protection to women in distress. However, although it refers to 'women in distress', it is not categorical on the nature or composition of this group. The mere fact that Article 24 mentions poor women, female heads of families, pregnant or nursing women, and women from marginalised population groups[131] is not sufficient for one to construct a proper definition of this category of persons. It would have been expedient if a composite definition of the term were provided. In the absence of such a definition, chances are that this provision will remain a dead letter, without any meaning or effect in legal parlance.

It is clear from the above discussion that the Women's Protocol is a marked departure from the African Charter, as it provides women in Africa a wider range of protection. Whereas the Charter has scanty provisions specifically touching on the rights of women, the Protocol dedicates a whole catalogue of rights to this category of vulnerable persons. It is hoped that states parties will effect these rights in their domestic legal systems. Similarly, aggrieved women ought to play an active role in ensuring that they are afforded adequate redress to any violation of their rights. After all, states parties have expressly undertaken to provide appropriate remedies to any woman whose

---

130   As above, art 23(a).

131   As above, art 24(a).

rights or freedoms have been violated.[132] It is equally hoped that the African Court shall, in accordance with its mandate under Article 27 of the Protocol, evolve an admirable body of jurisprudence relating to the rights of the African woman.

---

132   See art 25(a). According to art 25(b), states parties undertake to ensure that such remedies are determined by competent judicial, administrative or legislative authorities, or by any other competent authority provided for by law.

Part III

Institutional Mechanisms of the African System on Human and Peoples Rights

CHAPTER 8

THE AFRICAN UNION AND ITS ORGANS

In line with the 'political' and 'legal' compartmentalisation of the African human rights system, it is notable that the institutional mechanisms of the legal component of the system[1] are designed to operate within the African Union (political) institutional framework. The Constitutive Act of the African Union (hereafter 'CAAU', 'Constitutive Act' or 'the Act') provides for the establishment of a number of organs within the framework of the African Union (AU), most of which have a direct bearing on regional human rights protection and promotion.

Moreover, the AU has also adopted programmes and initiatives that cement its role in human rights enforcement in the region. These are, for example, the New Partnership for Africa's Development (NEPAD), African Peer Review Mechanism (APRM) and the Conference on Security, Stability, Development and Cooperation in Africa (CSSDCA). What follows, therefore, is a brief discussion of the importance and relevance of AU's organs and programmes (initiatives) to the African human rights system. Noteworthy, however, because an in-depth discussion of each of these organs and programmes is beyond the scope of this book, a brief highlight would suffice.

8.1 AFRICAN UNION'S ORGANS INVOLVED IN REGIONAL HUMAN RIGHTS ENFORCEMENT

Article 5 of the CAAU provides for the establishment of a number of organs within the AU framework. These include the: Assembly of the Union; Executive Council; Pan-African Parliament; Court of Justice; Commission; Permanent Representatives Committee; Specialised Technical Committees; Economic, Social and Cultural Council; and Financial Institutions.[2] Each of these organs has its

---

1   These are the African Commission and Court on Human and Peoples' Rights and the African Committee of Experts on the Rights and Welfare of the Child.

2   See the CAAU, art 5(1)(a)-(i).

own composition, power, sphere of operation, and procedures. The Assembly of the Union is also permitted to establish other organs as and when it may deem proper.[3] This is crucial due to the fact that the Act is apparently devoid of sufficient mechanisms to enforce its ambitious objectives and principles.[4]

The Assembly serves as the supreme organ of the Union vested with the ultimate political authority. In other words, it is to the AU what the General Assembly is to the UN, or the European Council is to the EU. The Assembly is comprised of the Heads of State and Government of member states or their representatives.[5] Among other functions, it is mandated to: (i) receive, consider and take decisions on reports and recommendations from the other organs of the Union[6]; and (ii) monitor the implementation of policies and decisions of the Union as well as to ensure their compliance by all member states.[7] Additionally, the Assembly performs other functions that are not enumerated in the Act. These include the: appointment of members of the African Commission;[8] replacement of a member of the African Commission in the event of death or resignation;[9] appointment of judges to the African human rights Court;[10] and replacement of any member of the Court in the event of any vacancy.[11] It also receives and adopts annual activity reports from both the Commission and Court.

In line with the functions stipulated in the Act, the Assembly could effectively encourage the efficiency of the African human rights system. For example, it could choose to be more serious and

---

3   As above, art 5(2).

4   See in this regard, N Udombana 'The institutional structure of the African Union: A legal analysis' (2002) 33 *California Western International Law Journal* 84.

5   CAAU, art 6 (1).

6   As above, art 9(1)(b).

7   As above, art 9(1)(e).

8   See art 33 of the African Charter on Human and Peoples' Rights, OAU Doc. CAB/LEG/67/3 rev. 5; adopted 27 June 1981; entered into force 21 October 1986.

9   As above, art 39(3).

10   See Protocol to the African Charter on Human and Peoples' Rights on the Establishment of the African Court on Human and Peoples' Rights, OAU/LEG/MIN/AFCHPR/PROT (III), art 14(1).

11   As above, art 20(2).

act on the reports submitted to it by the African Commission in tandem with Articles 52-54 and 58-59 of the African Charter. It could also play a more active role in ensuring the implementation of the recommendations and resolutions of the African Commission and the decisions and judgements of the African Court on Human Rights. After all, the Protocol establishing the African Court mandates the Assembly to receive annual reports detailing the work of the Court.[12] Such reports are to specify, *inter alia,* the cases in which a state has not complied with the Court's judgements.[13]

Article 9(1)(e) of the CAAU could also be invoked by the Assembly to punish any member state that fails to respect its decisions on matters relating to human rights. In such cases, the recalcitrant state may be subjected to sanctions such as 'the denial of transport and communications links with other member states, and other sanctions of a political and economic nature that may be determined by the Assembly.'[14] The AU has so far issued a number of declarations, decisions and resolutions.[15] It is unfortunate that most of them are a mere rhetoric without any binding force. For the Assembly to be a useful organ to human rights promotion and protection in the region, it needs to be more aggressive and forceful; not just a 'toothless bull-dog'.

Another AU organ of relevance to regional protection and promotion of human rights is the Executive Council (EC).[16] The EC, comprising of Foreign Affairs Ministers, has two principal functions. First, it coordinates and takes decisions on policies in areas

---

12   As, above, art 31.

13   As above.

14   CAAU, art 23(2).

15   See, for examples, Declarations and decisions adopted by the Thirty-Sixth Ordinary Session of the Assembly of Heads of States and Government, AHG/ Decl.1-6 (XXXVI) AHG/Dec. 143-159 (XXXVI) AHG/OAU/AEC/Dec.1 (IV); Declaration on the Resolution of the Land Question in Zimbabwe, AHG/Decl.2 (XXXVII); Decision on the Pan African Forum on the Future of Children, AHG/ Dec.11 (XXXVII); Declaration on the Review of the Millennium Declaration and the Millennium Development Goals (MDGs), Assembly/AU/Decl. 1 (V); Sirte Declaration on the Reform of the United Nations, Assembly/AU/Decl. 2 (V); Declaration on the Inter-Sudanese Peace Talks in Darfur, Assembly/AU/Decl. 3(V); and Resolution on the United Nations Reform: Security Council, Assembly/AU/ Resolution.1 (V).

16   See CAAU, arts 10-13.

of common interest to member states including, among other things, foreign trade; energy, industry and mineral resources; education, culture, health and human resource developments; and social security.[17] Secondly, it considers issues referred to it and monitors the implementation of policies formulated by the Assembly.[18]

Of the two functions, the latter could be pursued to further the human rights agenda of the continent. This function puts the EC in a better position to ensure the enforcement of the recommendations of the African Commission and the decisions of the African Court. Specifically, the Protocol establishing the African Court mandates the EC to monitor execution of the Court's judgments on behalf of the Assembly.[19]

The Pan-African parliament is also potentially at the core of human rights enforcement in the region. The Parliament has been established to ensure the full participation of African peoples in the development and economic integration of the continent.[20] In accordance with Article 17(2) of the CAAU, a Protocol was adopted that defines the composition, functions, powers and organisation of the Parliament.[21] It can be deduced from the wording of the Protocol that the promotion and protection of human rights are in the purview of the Parliament. For instance, it is within the remits of the Parliament to facilitate the effective implementation of the policies and objectives of the AU.[22] As stated earlier, human rights protection and promotion are embodied in some of the objectives of the AU.[23] It follows therefore that the Parliament can play an instrumental role in bringing these objectives to fruition, hence contribute to the advancement of the regional human rights system.

---

17   As above, art 13(1).

18   As above, art 13(2).

19   See the Protocol Establishing the African Court, art 29(2).

20   CAAU, art 17(1).

21   The Protocol relating to the Treaty establishing the African Economic Community relating to the Pan-African Parliament was adopted by the 5th Ordinary Summit of the OAU in Sirte, Libya, on 2 March 2001.

22   As above, art 3(1).

23   Art 3(h) of the CAAU states one of the objectives of the AU as to: 'Promote and protect human and peoples' rights in accordance with the African Charter on Human and Peoples' Rights and other relevant human rights instruments.'

More expressly, Article 11 of the Protocol empowers the Parliament to 'examine, discuss or express an opinion on any matter, either on its own initiative or at the request of the Assembly or other policy organs and make any recommendations it may deem fit relating to, *inter alia*, matters pertaining to respect of human rights, the consolidation of democratic institutions and the culture of democracy, as well as the promotion of good governance and the rule of law.'[24] Additionally, the Parliament may make recommendations aimed at contributing to the attainment of the objectives of the AU, particularly those touching on human rights.[25] Such recommendations may include, for example, ways of curbing impunity, how to sanction a member state that perpetrates human rights violations unabatedly, among others. Further, the Parliament may promote the human rights programmes and objectives of the AU in the member states[26], as well as perform such other functions as it deems appropriate to achieve the objectives set out in Article 3 of its Protocol.[27]

Another organ in the AU institutional framework that is relevant to human rights enforcement in the region is the Court of Justice.[28] According to the Protocol establishing it,[29] the Court shall have jurisdiction over the interpretation and application of the CAAU; the interpretation, application or validation of the Union's treaties and all subsidiary legal instruments adopted within the framework of the Union; any question of international law; all acts, decisions, regulations and directives of the organs of the Union; breach of an obligation by a state party and the nature and extent of the reparation to be made for the breach of an obligation.[30] The Assembly of the Union may also confer jurisdiction on the Court over any other

---

24   Protocol on the Pan-African Parliament, art 11(1).

25   As above, art 11(4).

26   As above, art 11(6).

27   As above, art 11(9).

28   Created under art 5(d) of the CAAU.

29   Adopted by the Assembly of the Union in Maputo on 11 July 2003.

30   Art 19(1) of the Protocol establishing the African Court of Justice.

dispute.[31] Arguably, such disputes may include matters involving violations of human rights.

The jurisdiction of the Court is to be exercised in accordance with the CAAU, international treaties, international customs, the general principles of law recognised universally or by African states, judicial decisions and writings of highly qualified publicists of various nations as well as directives, regulations and decisions of the Union.[32] It may be argued that the African Charter also embodies 'principles of law recognised by African states' and therefore the Court must have regard to it in determining issues of human rights that may be brought before it. This presents the Court the opportunity to adjudicate over human rights matters.

There have been initiatives to merge the Court of Justice and the African Court on human and peoples' rights.[33] This may be a welcome idea towards the realisation of effective enforcement of human rights in the region. In the main, the merger will help to facilitate the much desired institutional mainstreaming and rationalisation of the regional human rights system. At the moment, the system is faced with the challenge of proliferation of institutions that tend to overlap or duplicate each others' functions. The issue of institutional proliferation and overlapping is discussed comprehensively below in the chapter that deals with mainstreaming and rationalisation of the African human rights system.

Other organs of the AU that are, or could be, useful in the regional enforcement of human rights are the Commission (Secretariat), the Permanent Representatives Committee, Specialised Technical Committees, Economic, Social and Cultural Council and Financial Institutions. The Commission is instrumental in coordinating the activities of the Union and could be used as the springboard to the realisation of human rights promotion and protection in the

---

31   As above, art 19(2).

32   As above, art 20(1).

33   At the 5th Ordinary Session of the Union held in Sirte, Libya in July 2005, the AU Assembly made a decision to merge the African Court on Human and Peoples' Rights and the African Court of Justice of the African Union. See Assembly Decision no. Assembly/AU/Dec.83 (V).

region.[34] The same could be said of the Permanent Representatives Committee which is charged with the responsibility of preparing the work of, and acting on the Executive Council's instructions.[35]

The Specialised Technical Committees (STCs), could be relevant in, for example, assessing states' compliance with their human rights obligations. These Committees are mandated to 'submit to the Executive Council, either on its own initiative or at the request of the Executive Council, reports and recommendations on the implementation of the provisions of this Act.'[36] These could of course include reports on states' compliance with their human rights obligations under the Act.

The financial institutions listed in the CAAU are also needful in the human rights agenda of the continent. Their role in financing other institutions and organs, particularly those concerned with human rights enforcement, cannot be overlooked. The effective enforcement of human rights in the region has always been hampered by the limited financial resources allocated towards this course. As will be stressed elsewhere below, there is the need to ensure adequate funding if the African human rights system is to function properly.

Apart from the various organs highlighted above, some of the AU's Directorates are also involved in human rights promotion and protection.[37] The Political Affairs Directorate, for example, is involved in matters to do with democratisation, governance, the rule of law and human rights. Its core functions include, among others, to monitor the implementation of international humanitarian law by member states, the situation and flow of refugees and displaced persons in Africa, and to collaborate with the CSSDCA and NEPAD to ensure harmonisation of activities.[38]

Within the Political Affairs Directorate there are various branches concerned with human rights issues. These include the:

---

34   See art 20 of the CAAU for the functions of the Commission.

35   As above, art 21.

36   As above, art 15(d).

37   Visit www.africa-union.org.

38   As above.

Democracy, Governance, Human Rights and Elections Division; and Humanitarian Affairs, Refugees and Displaced Persons Division.[39] The Humanitarian Affairs, Refugees and Displaced Persons Division (HARDP) has been involved in monitoring the situations of refugees and other displaced persons on the continent. Its activities include conducting visits to member states, participating in meetings as well as regularly monitoring the humanitarian crises on the continent.

The Democracy, Governance, Human Rights and Elections Division is principally involved in strengthening the African Commission and Court on Human and Peoples' Rights.[40] Furthermore, it is mandated to promote and strengthen co-operation between member states, civil society organisations and Regional Economic Communities (RECs)[41] on human rights issues and to promote transparency, accountability and the rule of law.

Another directorate that is concerned with human rights is the Women, Gender and Development Directorate. This directorate was established because one of the principles of the AU is the promotion of gender equality.[42] The Directorate is currently building on the activities began by the former OAU, such as the policy Framework on Ageing and the Addis Ababa Declaration on the Eradication of Harmful Traditional Practices.[43]

The AU also has the Peace and Security Council (PSC). Among the aims of the PSC is to develop a common defence policy and to 'promote and encourage democratic practices, good governance

---

39   As above.

40   R Murray & A Lloyd 'Institutions with responsibility for human rights protection under the African Union' (2004) 48/2 *Journal of African Law* 174.

41   Such as the Community of Sahel-Saharan States (CEN-SAD), Economic Community of Central African States (ECCAS), Common Market for Eastern and Southern Africa (COMESA), Economic Community of West African States (ECOWAS), Intergovernmental Authority for Development (IGAD), Southern African Development Community (SADC), Union du Maghreb Arabe (UMA).

42   CAAU, art 4 (l).

43   Other programmes and policies are the African Women Committee on Peace and Development; the Plan of Action on Enhancing the Participation of Refugee, Returnee and Internally Displaced Women and Children in Post-Conflict Reintegration, Rehabilitation, Reconstruction and Peace Building; and the Kampala Declaration and Plan of Action on the Empowerment of Women Through Functional Literacy and Education of the Girl-Child. www.africa-union.org.

and the rule of law, protect human rights and fundamental freedoms, respect for the sanctity of human life and international humanitarian law, as part of efforts for preventing conflicts.'[44]

Despite these initiatives, concerns have been raised on the AU's failure to mainstream, consolidate and rationalise the many institutions and organs created under it.[45] This has been one of the main challenges to effective enforcement of human rights in the region. This argument shall be revisited later.

8.2 AFRICAN UNION'S PROGRAMMES (INITIATIVES) WITH HUMAN RIGHTS IMPLICATIONS

The AU embodies two initiatives (programmes) that are relevant to the regional human rights agenda. These initiatives are the New Partnership for Africa's Development (NEPAD) and the African Peer Review Mechanism (APRM). The historical origins and parameters of these initiatives were discussed in detail in part I of this book. However, their roles in promoting and protecting human rights in the region need to be underscored.

8.2.1 HUMAN RIGHTS UNDER NEPAD

As already stated, NEPAD is a vision and strategic framework for Africa's renewal.[46] It is an initiative designed to support the vision, objectives and principles of the AU. Although it is principally an economic development programme, it emphasises the fact that human rights, peace and development are interdependent matters.[47]

---

44   Protocol Relating to the Establishment of a Peace and Security Council of the African Union, 9 July 2002, art 3(f).

45   See, for example, P Mistry 'Africa's record of regional co-operation and integration' (2000) 99 *African Affairs* 553–573. See also O Quist-Arcton 'From OAU to AU: Whither Africa?' available at http://www.allafrica.com (accessed on 13 April 2010); 'High cost of change', *The Sowetan, Johannesburg*, 19 July 2001, available at http://www.allafrica.com (accessed on 13 April 2010).

46   See 'NEPAD in brief' available at http://www.nepad.org/2005/files/inbrief.php (accessed 1 March 2010).

47   See W Nagan 'Implementing the African renaissance: Making human rights comprehensive for the new millennium' available at http://www.cha.uga.edu/CHA-CITS/Nagan_paper.pdf (accessed 1 March 2010). See also, C Heyns 'The African regional human rights system: The African Charter' (2004) 108/3 *Penn State Law Review* 684.

It underscores the commitment of African leaders to: strengthening the mechanisms for conflict prevention, management and resolution; promoting and protecting democracy and human rights; restoring and maintaining micro-stability through fiscal and monetary policies; regulating financial markets and private companies; promoting the role of women in social and economic development by reinforcing their capacity in the domains of education and training, revitalising health training and education with high priority to HIV/AIDS; maintaining law and order; and promoting the development of infrastructure.[48]

NEPAD consists of three initiatives: the Peace and Security Initiative,[49] Economic and Corporate Governance Initiative and Democracy and Political Governance Initiative. It is the latter which is relevant to human rights. Through it, 'Africa undertakes to respect the global standards of democracy, the core components of which include political pluralism, allowing for the existence of several political parties and workers unions, and fair, open and democratic elections periodically organised to enable people to choose their leaders freely.'[50]

In July 2002, the Heads of State and Government of the AU agreed to the NEPAD Declaration on Democracy, Political, Economic and Corporate Governance.[51] In the particular context of human rights, paragraph 15 of the Declaration states as follows:

> To promote and protect human rights, we have agreed to:
>
> • facilitate the development of vibrant civil society organisations, including strengthening human rights institutions at the national, sub-regional and regional levels;

---

48   NEPAD Document, para 49.

49   Comprising development and security, early warning and prevention, management and resolution of conflicts.

50   NEPAD Document, para 79.

51   Declaration on Democracy, Political, Economic and Corporate Governance, AHG/235(XXXVIII), Annex 1, adopted by the HSIC at its Third Meeting in June 2002; Communiqué Issued at the end of the third Meeting of the Heads of State and Government Implementation Committee of the New Partnership for Africa's Development (HSIC), Rome, Italy on 11 June 2002, available at www.nepad.org (accessed 11 May 2010).

- support the Charter, African Commission and Court on Human and Peoples' Rights as important instruments for ensuring the promotion, protection and observance of human rights;
- strengthen co-operation with the UN High Commission for Human Rights; and
- ensure responsible free expression, inclusive of the freedom of the press.

There is therefore a strong indication that NEPAD's agenda on human rights is based on national and regional priorities and plans. These priorities and plans must, however, be prepared through a participatory process involving the people of Africa.[52] Moreover, the framework should endeavour to, among other things, define the nature of the interaction between Africa and the rest of the world. Indeed, the continued marginalisation of Africa from the globalisation process and the social exclusion of the vast majority of its people constitute a serious threat. NEPAD should therefore be seen more as a process than just a programme that is intended to reverse this situation.

NEPAD is also designed to engage in the prevention, management and resolution of conflicts, peacemaking and peace enforcement, post-conflict reconciliation, rehabilitation and reconstruction, and combating the illicit proliferation of small arms, light weapons and landmines.[53] To further these objectives, a sub-committee on peace and security has been established within NEPAD.[54] If these commitments are fulfilled, then it will promote peace and security and reduce the occurrence of conflicts in the region. Income previously spent on wars and conflicts may perhaps be diverted to the realisation of human rights.

Implementation of the NEPAD is envisaged through a number of mechanisms. First, there is the Heads of States and Governments

---

52   NEPAD Document, para 47.

53   NEPAD Document, para 74.

54   See Communiqué issued at the end of the first meeting of the HSGIC, Abuja, 23 October 2001.

Implementation Committee (HSGIC) composed of 20 states,[55] which meets every four months. Secondly, its Secretariat based in South Africa assists in administrative work. The third mechanism is the African Peer Review Mechanism (APRM).[56]

8.2.2   HUMAN RIGHTS UNDER THE APRM

Paragraph 28 of the NEPAD Declaration on Democracy, Political, Economic and Corporate Governance (DDPECG) acknowledges the establishment of the APRM on the basis of voluntary accession. The mandate of the APRM is to ensure that the policies and practices of the participating states conform to the agreed political, economic and corporate governance values, codes and standards contained in the Declaration.[57] The primary purpose of the mechanism is to:

> foster the adoption of policies, standards and practices that lead to political stability, high economic growth, sustainable development and accelerated sub-regional and continental economic integration through sharing of experiences and reinforcement of successful and best practice, including identifying deficiencies and accessing the needs of capacity building.[58]

In this regard, the mechanism intends to ensure that all participating countries adopt and implement the priorities and programmes of NEPAD and achieve the mutually agreed objectives in compliance with the best practices in respect of each of the areas of governance and development. Accordingly, APRM is executed through four types of reviews, three of which are compulsory and periodically mandated, and an optional one.

The compulsory reviews include: (i) the initial country review which is carried out within 18 months of the accession to the APRM; (ii) the periodic review that takes place every two to four years; and

---

55   This was expanded from 15. They are: Nigeria, Senegal, Algeria, Egypt and South Africa as the five founding states; as well as the central African states of Cameroon, Gabon, Sao Tome and Principe; East African states of Ethiopia, Kenya, Mauritius and Rwanda; North African states including Libya and Tunisia; Southern African states of Angola, Botswana and Mozambique, and West African states of Ghana and Mali.

56   African Peer Review Mechanism, Doc AHG/235(XXXVIIII), Annex II.

57   As above, para 2.

58   As above, para 3.

(iii) a review that can be decided by participating Heads of State and Government, prompted by an 'impending political or economic crisis.'[59] The optional review may be solicited by a participating state for its own reasons and is not part of the periodical reviews.[60]

The reviews are undertaken by a Panel of Eminent Persons comprised of Africans who have distinguished themselves in careers that are considered relevant to the work of the APRM and who are 'persons of high moral stature and demonstrated commitment to the ideals of Pan-Africanism.'[61] The Panel has between five and seven members, appointed by Heads of State and Government of the participating countries. The members exercise the oversight function over the review process to ensure its integrity.[62] They serve for a maximum period of four years but the Chairperson of the Panel could serve for a maximum of five years.[63] The Panel may engage the services of African experts and institutions that it considers competent and appropriate to act as its agents in the peer review process.[64]

The review process per country is expected not to take more than six months from the date of the inception stage or up to the date the report is submitted for consideration by the Heads of State and Government.[65] Procedurally, the review is conducted in five stages. The first stage involves the study of the political, economic and corporate governance and development environment of the country being reviewed.[66] It entails the preparation of a comprehensive background document (Country Background Document) and the Country Issue Paper (CIP) by the APRM Secretariat on the basis of materials provided by national, sub-regional, regional and international institutions.[67] The CIP identifies areas that require

---

59   As above, para 13.
60   As above, para 14.
61   As above, paras 5 & 6.
62   As above, paras 6 & 7.
63   As above, para 8.
64   As above, paras 11 & 12.
65   As above, para 26.
66   As above, para 18.
67   As above, para 18.

further information, as well as major shortcomings and deficiencies and areas for capacity building for further investigation by the Country Review Mission (CRM). This is done through collecting and collating pertinent information on the governance and development status of the country to be reviewed.

Meanwhile, a questionnaire on the four focus areas of APRM is forwarded by the Secretariat to the country to be reviewed. The country establishes a Focal Point and constitutes an independent National Governing Council (NGC) or a National Commission, consisting of all the stakeholders, to conduct the self-assessment on the basis of the questionnaire, and with the assistance, if necessary, of the Secretariat and/or relevant partner institutions. Where the need arises, a Country Support Mission (CSM) is sent to assist in the preparation of a Country Self-Assessment Report (CSAR) and a preliminary Programme of Action (POA). The stage is concluded when the Memorandum of Understanding (MOU) for Technical Assessment and the Country Review Visit are signed between the government of the participating country and the review Team led by a member of the Panel.

The second stage is conducted in the country being reviewed. During this stage, the review team consults with, among others, government officials, political parties, parliamentarians and representatives of civil society organisations.[68] In the third stage, the team prepares its report which is measured against the state's adherence to the applicable political, economic and corporate governance standards.[69] A draft report is first prepared and discussed with the government concerned in order to ascertain the accuracy of the information and also present the government the opportunity to respond to the findings of the review team. The response is then appended to the team's report.[70]

During the fourth stage, the report is submitted to the participating Heads of State and Government for their final report

---

68   As above, para 19.

69   As above, para 20.

70   As above, para 21.

and decision.[71] At this stage, the Heads of State and Government are expected to offer technical and other appropriate assistance to the government under review in order to help it to improve its standards. They may also engage in constructive dialogue or request donor governments and agencies to intervene as best as they can. As a last resort, however, they may put the government on notice to proceed with appropriate measures, should dialogue prove to be unavailing.[72]

The fifth and final stage entails the presentation of the final report to organs such as the Pan-African Parliament, the African Commission, the Peace and Security Council and the Economic, Social and Cultural Council of the AU.[73] It is rather unfortunate that there are no sufficient instructions on what these institutions should do with the report. It is therefore difficult to tell whether, for example, they are allowed to take any solid stance against a government that fails to comply with its commitment to the prescribed standards and values.

So far, the APRM process has been completed for Ghana, Kenya, Rwanda, South Africa and Algeria. Because the leaders of Algeria, Nigeria, Senegal and South Africa championed the NEPAD and APRM initiatives, it was anticipated that their countries would be the first to be reviewed. Unfortunately they were not, and this raised the question of their commitment to the process.[74] Instead, Ghana set the precedent in this regard, thus earning the reputation of being a 'country of firsts'.[75] It was then followed by Rwanda, which is still grappling with post-genocide reconstruction, and Kenya, a country still embroiled in a constitutional dilemma. Be that as it may, from the reviews so far conducted, it can be ascertained that APRM, just like NEPAD, is encumbered with a number of problems and

---

71 As above, para 23.

72 As above, para 24.

73 As above, para 24

74 See A Mangu 'Assessing the effectiveness of the APRM and its impact on the promotion of democracy and good political governance' (2007) 7 *African Human Rights Law Journal* 367.

75 See Country Review Report (CRR) of the Republic of Ghana (Ghana Report) 4 para 14, available at http://www.polity.org.za/article.php?a_id=99408 and http://www.nepad.org/aprm (accessed 4 May 2010).

challenges that need to be addressed to ensure their efficacy in the promotion and protection of human rights in the region.

8.2.3   A Critique of the NEPAD and APRM

Generally, the NEPAD and APRM initiatives can innovatively be used to come up with uniform human rights standards across the continent. Through them, African states could be persuaded to ratify the treaties that they have not, in order to encourage uniformity of human rights practices in the region. This way, the initiatives may provide a platform for the development of Africa's regional human rights system within the AU framework. The initiatives, however, have some overt shortcomings which must first be addressed for them to have the desired impact on the continent's human rights agenda.

To begin with, NEPAD is an 'over-crowded programme' with so many activities ranging from political, social to economic. With such a heavy programme of activities, it is inconceivable that the initiative would produce the desired impact in the long run. As the Bible notes, a divided house will not stand. This apparent lack of focus in the initiative can be deciphered from its superficial approach to human rights promotion and protection. For example, it is easy to note that economic, social and cultural rights are vaguely referred to in terms of greater access to services instead of as concrete, inherent rights.[76] The NEPAD document also fails to concretise the relationship between human rights and development, although it is evident that it was intended to do so.[77] This is contrary to the understanding that, if human rights are to be realised, they have to be streamlined in all activities, including development.

To make matters worse, NEPAD has had to grapple with a legitimacy crisis due to its dubious origins.[78] Its proponents were just a handful of African leaders who were then perceived either to have

---

76   Rights & Democracy, 'Human rights and democratic development in Africa: Policy considerations for Africa's development in the new millennium' available at http://www.ichrdf.ca (accessed 27 May 2010).

77   E Baimu 'Human rights in NEPAD and its implications for the African human rights system' (2002) 2 *African Human Rights Law Journal* 303.

78   As above.

strong ties with, or to be seeking the favour of, the Western world. This could possibly be the reason why NEPAD has contemptuously been dismissed as dubious economic globalisation.[79] It is also important to note that, despite its commitment to human rights, the NEPAD document did not in any material sense establish a direct nexus between the initiative and the African human rights system. Although this nexus was subsequently established through the Declaration on Democracy, Political, Economic and Corporate Governance, in practice there is still not much interaction between the initiative and the human rights system.

The APRM could also be faulted. In the main, because its membership is voluntary, states can withdraw without any severe consequences.[80] The initiative also lacks definite elements of compulsion. The reviewing body has no clearly defined ways of compelling deviant states to reform. This rather loose setup with its attendant lack of serious internal coercive mechanisms may have contributed to the general reluctance of many African countries to subscribe to the project. A further source of concern is the tendency of African leaders to shy away from condemning their peers even in cases where the APRM produces damning reports.[81]

The continental silence on human rights violations, including the range of grotesque human rights abuses in, for example, Sudan, Rwanda, Cameroon, Liberia, Somalia, Kenya and Burundi have amply demonstrated African leaders' lack of moral courage to chastise each other. This lack of 'tough stance' by African leaders on human rights violations, even in countries across their borders, is a clear sign that it is extremely dangerous to place undue expectation on the APRM in its bid to police or prevent human rights abuses.[82] Moreover, the country review process under the APRM is lengthy and over-broad and gives room to political manoeuvres. As Mangu noted:

---

79   As above.

80   As above.

81   J Akokpari 'Policing and preventing human rights abuses in Africa: the OAU, the AU & the NEPAD Peer Review' (2004) 32/2 *International Journal of Legal Information* 468.

82   As above.

APRM is cabinet-driven and centred. The procedure for the selection of stakeholders to sit on NGCs is unclear. Civil society organisations that are soft on governmental policies are more likely to be selected than those which take a hard stance or are close to the opposition. Universities, research institutions and academics are marginalised.[83]

NGCs are 'politicised' because countries want to use the review reports to showcase 'their good credentials' in order to get the much needed external financial support. This kind of attitude should not be condoned, for if African countries had already achieved democracy and good political governance, as they tend to purport during the reviews, there would be no need for the APRM.[84]

In line with the politicisation of the process is the apparent lack of credibility and independence of the Panel. There is the temptation of the Cabinet, which already dominates the self-assessment process, to manipulate the process and to undermine the independence of members of the Panel. In the event of adverse findings against their countries, Cabinets resort to the use of tactics such as disputing the accuracy of the information or pressurising the Panel members to reverse their position.[85] At another level, politicisation of the APRM process could be seen from the mode of appointment of the members of the Panel.

First, the positions on the Panel are never advertised. Secondly, the mandate of the eminent persons as well as the criteria for their appointment is unclear. In fact, they seem to serve at the whims of the participating countries because they are appointed and may also be dismissed by the Heads of State and Government. Accordingly, they are accountable to them and cannot be said to be immune to political pressure. This may affect their independence and integrity if their status is not secured in a binding instrument.[86]

The reports of the Panel have also been faulted for providing partial findings and recommendations. For example, whereas the Panel commended Kenya as a 'model' of best practice in organising

---

83   Mangu (n 74 above) 382.

84   As above.

85   As above, 383.

86   As above.

the review process,[87] this position was contradicted by many findings in the CSAR and the CRM. Civil society organisations in the country also complained that the CRR had focused on the delivery of services and did not tackle the more challenging task of institutional reform that was vital for the country's democratic transition.[88] The same goes for Rwanda where the Panel made no recommendation as to the role the country could play in preventing or reducing interstate conflicts in the Great Lakes region. The findings and recommendations made in the CSAR and CRR on the issues of separation of powers, independence of the judiciary, and political pluralism were also disputed.[89]

Despite the above shortcomings, NEPAD and the APRM cannot be dismissed as having no positive influence in the advancement of human rights in Africa. There is no doubt that under the umbrella of the AU, through the inspiration of the NEPAD and APRM, African leaders have developed their own strategies for meeting the continent's pressing challenges, including extreme poverty, illiteracy, HIV/AIDS, war, environmental degradation and, most importantly, human rights abuses. Moreover, the initiatives have made a major contribution to international human rights law in the world. Arguably, for the first time in the history of international law, states that were more or less intoxicated with the controversial principles of state sovereignty, independence and non-interference in their respective national affairs, agreed to subject their governance to reviews by their peers. This is indeed a commendable achievement, indicative of the fact that Africa is also keen to ensure the realisation of human rights.

---

87   Country Review Report (CRR) of the Republic of Kenya's Report (Kenya Report) 16, available at http://www.polity.org.za/article.php?a_id=99422 and http://www.nepad.org/aprm (last accessed 4 May 2010) 38.

88   Mangu (n 74 above) 383-384.

89   As above.

CHAPTER 9

THE AFRICAN COMMISSION ON HUMAN AND PEOPLES' RIGHTS

9.1 STRUCTURE AND COMPOSITION

The African Commission on Human and Peoples' Rights (hereafter the 'African Commission' or 'Commission') was established in 1987, a year after the African Charter entered into force.[1] The Commission consists of eleven members (Commissioners) chosen from amongst African personalities of the highest reputation, 'known for their high morality, integrity, impartiality and competence in matters of human and peoples' rights; particular consideration being given to persons having legal experience.'[2]

The eleven Commissioners are elected by secret ballot by the Assembly of Heads of State and Government (AHSG) (now the African Union Assembly) from a list nominated by states parties to the African Charter.[3] The Commissioners, who serve in their personal capacity,[4] are elected for a six-year term and are eligible for re-election.[5] During proceedings, they elect the Chairman and Vice-Chairman of the Commission for an initial tenure of two years subject to re-election.[6] In carrying out their functions, they enjoy diplomatic privileges and immunities.[7] Their emoluments and allowances are provided for in the regular budget of the AU.

A Commissioner's office becomes vacant due to death or resignation, or if, in the opinion of other members of the Commission,

---

1   See art 30, The African Charter on Human and Peoples' Rights, OAU Doc. CAB/
     LEG/67/3 rev. 5; adopted 27 June 1981; entered into force 21 October 1986.

2   As above, art 31.

3   As above, art 33.

4   As above, art 31(2).

5   As above, art 36.

6   As above, art 42.

7   As above, art 43.

the member has stopped discharging his or her functions.[8] The issue of incompetence is unfortunately not mentioned in the Charter. A Commissioner may be incompetent or fall short of the required standards and yet still be willing to serve. The power of the Commissioners to sanction each other should have related to unavailability, incompetence or inability to maintain the necessary standard, rather than the unwillingness to serve.[9] A Commissioner can be removed by either his own action or that of his colleagues and not by the Assembly or his own national state. This strengthens his independence from those that nominate or elect him.[10]

There is a general dissatisfaction on a number of issues regarding the composition of the African Commission, ranging from the mode of election, impartiality of its members, gender representation, and equitable geographic and legal cultural representation.[11] These issues are discussed in detail in the chapter that deals with the challenges to effective enforcement of human rights in Africa.

9.2   MANDATE OF THE COMMISSION

The Commission's mandate is stipulated in Chapter II of the Charter. Specifically, Article 45 entrusts it with four broad functions:

- Promotion of human and peoples' rights;
- Protection of human and peoples' rights under conditions laid down by the Charter;
- Interpretation of the African Charter at the request of a state party, an institution of the AU or an African organisation recognised by the AU; and
- Performance of any other tasks that may be entrusted to it by the AU Assembly.

In its promotional functions, the Commission is expected to, among other things, engage in: information collection; formulation

---

8   As above, art 39.

9   U Umozurike *The African Charter on Human and Peoples' Rights* (1997) 51.

10   As above.

11   See, for example, O Nmehielle *The African human rights system: Its laws, practice and institutions* (2001) 172; S Rembe *The system of protection of human rights under the African Charter on Human and Peoples' Rights: Problems and prospects* (1991) 25; E Ankumah *The African Commission on Human and Peoples' Rights* (1996) 18-19.

and development of principles relating to human rights to guide legislative actions by African governments; and, collaboration with other African and international institutions concerned with the promotion and protection of human rights.[12] Arguably, evaluation of periodic reports submitted by states parties is also a promotional function of the Commission. This is because the main purpose of state reporting is to determine the extent to which the Charter has been implemented at the domestic level.[13]

The Commission performs its protection functions in terms of Articles 47 to 60 of the Charter. In particular, Articles 47 to 54 make provision for inter-state complaints while Articles 55 to 60 establish the machinery for the receipt and handling of individuals' complaints.[14] What follows is a more detailed discussion of the practice of the Commission in its endeavour to fulfil its mandate concordant to Chapter II of the Charter.

9.2.1   THE COMMISSION'S PROMOTIONAL MANDATE

9.2.1.1   GENERAL PROMOTIONAL ACTIVITIES

Article 45(1) of the African Charter spells out the promotional functions of the Commission to include:

(a)   to collect documents, undertake studies and researches on African problems in the field of human and peoples' rights, organise seminars, symposia and conferences, disseminate information, encourage national and local institutions concerned with human and peoples' rights, and should the case arise, give its views or make recommendations to governments.

(b)   to formulate and lay down, principles and rules aimed at solving legal problems relating to human and peoples' rights and fundamental freedoms upon which African governments may base their legislations.

---

12   African Charter, art 45(1)(a)-(c).

13   As above, art 62 states in part: 'each state party shall undertake to submit every two years, from the date the present Charter comes into force, a report on the legislative or other measures taken with a view to giving effect to the rights and freedoms recognised and guaranteed by the present Charter…'

14   As above, art 56.

(c)   co-operate with other African and international institutions concerned with the promotion and protection of human and peoples' rights.

To execute its promotional mandate, the Commission has over the years come up with several programmes of action and activities touching on the areas outlined above. For example, at its Second Session in Dakar, Senegal in 1988, it spelt out its first programme of action, outlining its research and information dissemination, quasi-legislative and cooperation activities.[15]

Again, the Commission at its Eleventh Session in March 1992 finalised and adopted another programme of action for the years 1992-1996. The programme contained, as its main components, the establishment of the information and documentation centre; convening seminars, workshops and training courses; promotional activities by Commissioners; translation and distribution of public documents of the Commission, including state reports and relevant summary records; publication of Annual Reports of the Commission: the Review Bulletin, brochure and other publications; and convening inter-session working groups.[16]

The Commission has also been progressive on information dissemination and publication. For example, it has so far produced and circulated several human rights documents, including the 'Review of the African Commission on Human and Peoples' Rights', its 'Annual Activity Reports', the African Charter and its Rules of Procedure.[17] Additionally, the Commission has adopted a number of resolutions, declarations and recommendations in the course of exercising its promotional mandate. The resolutions, some of which were discussed in the previous chapters of this book, address various human rights issues affecting the continent. Sadly, they have received little publicity and there are no indications that states take them seriously.

---

15   See Doc. AHG/155 (XXIV) Annex VIII.

16   E Badawi 'The African Commission on Human and Peoples' Rights: A call for justice' in K Koufa (ed) *International Justice* (1997) 283.

17   As above. See in this regard, 'African Commission on Human and Peoples' Rights, Establishment' (Information Sheet no. 1) 11.

The Commission has also developed a procedure by which each Commissioner is assigned a number of member states for promotional activities.[18] The Commissioners visit these states and organise lectures, seminars, and other activities in collaboration with various institutions. They then report on their promotional activities at each session of the Commission. Moreover, the Commission has initiated the internationally recognised Special Rapporteurs mechanism that is not specifically provided for in the African Charter.

So far there are five Special Rapporteurs: the Special Rapporteur on Summary, Arbitrary and Extrajudicial Executions (appointed in 1994)[19]; the Special Rapporteur on Prisons and Conditions of Detention in Africa (appointed in 1996)[20]; the Special Rapporteur on Women's Rights in Africa (appointed in 1999)[21]; the Special Rapporteur on Human Rights Defenders (appointed in 2004)[22]; and the Special Rapporteur on Refugees, Asylum Seekers and Displaced Persons in Africa (appointed in 2004).[23]

In terms of Article 45(1)(c), the Commission is also mandated to cooperate with other African and international institutions concerned with the promotion and protection of human and peoples' rights. Towards this end, cooperation has been sought with organisations such as the Inter-American Commission and Court on Human Rights and other international and national human rights organisations. The Commission has improved its working relations with Non-Governmental Organisations (NGOs)[24] and National

---

18   R Murray 'Report of the 1996 Sessions of the African Commission on Human and Peoples' Rights' (1997) 18 *Human Rights Law Journal* 16.

19   Eighth Annual Activity Report of the African Commission, Annex VII.

20   Tenth Annual Activity Report of the African Commission, Annex VII.

21   Eleventh Annual Activity Report of the African Commission, Annex VII.

22   Seventeenth Annual Activity Report of the African Commission, Annex IV.

23   Eighteenth Annual Activity Report of the African Commission.

24   By the 39th Ordinary Session of the African Commission, 339 NGOs had been granted observer status before the Commission. See the Twentieth Annual Activity Report of the African Commission on Human and Peoples' Rights, para 20.

Human Rights Institutions.[25] In terms of the Rules of Procedure, these organisations can attend the Commission's sessions.[26]

Generally, there are a number of problems connected with the Commission's efforts to execute its promotional mandate that need to be mentioned here.[27] From the catalogue of activities listed above, it is evident that the promotional mandate of the Commission is enormous. However, promotional activities are only carried out during the inter-session period. Even so, the Commissioners have restricted themselves to visiting universities and other institutions of higher learning in the countries assigned to them, giving lectures on the African Charter, African human rights issues and the work of the Commission.[28] While this is happening, an average African is ignorant, not only of his or her rights, but also of the work of the Commission.

Human rights promotion requires sustained activities tailored to suit the ages and vocations of the target audience. Additionally, it requires publicity in the media-radio, television, newspapers-which in many African countries are still controlled by governments.[29] It follows that the efforts to promote the Charter are impeded by the prevalent political climate in a country.[30] The problems highlighted herein shall be discussed in detail later on.

9.2.1.2 THE STATE REPORTING MECHANISM

State reporting is more of a promotional activity of the Commission than it is a protective one. Article 62 of the African Charter requires member states to submit reports every two years. Such reports are to indicate the legislative or other measures taken by states to give effect to the rights and freedoms recognised and guaranteed

---

25   By the 39th Ordinary Session of the Commission at least seven National Human Rights Institutions had affiliate status.

26   African Commission's Rules of Procedure, rules 75 & 76.

27   For a detailed discussion on the shortcomings of the promotional activities of the Commission, see Part IV of this book, which deals with challenges and reforms to the African human rights system.

28   Nmehielle (n 11 above) 179.

29   As above.

30   As above.

under the Charter. However, the Charter did not designate the responsibility to receive and review the reports to any competent organ. Consequently, at its Third session, the African Commission adopted a resolution requesting the OAU Assembly to entrust it with the task of reviewing state reports.[31] The Commission rightly noted that 'it [was] the only appropriate organ of the OAU capable not only of studying the said periodic reports, but of making pertinent observations to states parties.'[32]

In response to this request, the OAU Assembly, as it then was, entrusted the Commission with the task.[33] Unfortunately, through the request, which was meant to mandate it with the task of 'examining' the periodic reports, the Commission limited its own scope and by extension the effectiveness of the reporting mechanism.[34] Nothing is specifically stated in relation to what is to be done with the 'conclusions' or 'observations' arising from the examination, as is the case, for instance, under the European Social Charter system.[35] This, notwithstanding, the importance of state reporting in the promotion of human rights cannot be ignored. The Commission has spelt out the importance or benefits of the reporting mechanism to include the following[36]:

- Through the reporting system the implementation of the African Charter by states within their domestic systems is monitored.
- Through the examination of state reports, the African Commission is afforded the opportunity to understand the problems encountered by states in transforming the

---

31   First Annual Activity Report of the African Commission on Human and Peoples' Rights, 28. See also Q Kofi 'The African Charter on Human and Peoples' Rights: Towards a more effective reporting mechanism' (2002) 2 *African Human Rights Law Journal* 263.

32   As above.

33   Second Annual Activity Report of the African Commission on Human and Peoples' Rights, 20.

34   Kofi (n 31 above) 263.

35   As above.

36   The African Commission on Human and Peoples' Rights 'State reporting procedure Information Sheet no. 4', 6-7. See also G Mugwanya 'Examination of state reports by the African Commission: A critical appraisal' (2001) 2 *African Human Rights Law Journal* 274.

Charter into reality, and the Commission may make recommendations which may be taken by states to address the problems and promote effective realisation.

- The reporting system enables states to constantly check the whole government machinery as it requires all relevant government institutions and departments to evaluate their legal regulations, procedures and practices in terms of the provisions of the Charter.

- State reporting permits the African Commission to collect information on common experiences, both good and bad, from state parties so that states may learn from each other.

On the basis of the above, state reporting should be seen as a non-contentious mechanism that allows states to present a comprehensive picture of the human rights situation in their countries.[37] The mechanism gives states the opportunity to engage in constructive dialogue with the Commission with a view to enhance their human rights standards. Through this dialogue the difficulties to the realisation of human rights and possible ways to address them could be identified.[38]

In the formative years of state reporting, the Commission did not have clearly laid down procedures. Thereafter, at its Fourth ordinary session in October 1991, it adopted the 'General Guidelines for National Periodic Reports'.[39] The initial guidelines were divided into seven parts, each dealing with different aspects of rights and duties contained in the Charter.[40] The guidelines were, nevertheless, found not to be very useful because they were too detailed and complex,

---

37   R Murray 'Report on the 1997 sessions of the African Commission on Human and Peoples' Rights— 21st and 22nd sessions: 15-25 April and 2-11 November 1997' (1998) 19 *Human Rights Law Journal* 181.

38   The African Commission on Human and Peoples' Rights (n 36 above) 5-7.

39   See 'Guidelines on national periodic reports', Second Annual Activity Report of the African Commission on Human and Peoples' Rights (Annex XII).

40   These parts were: civil and political rights; economic and social rights; peoples' rights; duties under the Charter; elimination of all forms of racial discrimination; suppression of apartheid; and elimination of all forms of discrimination against women.

making it difficult for member states to follow.[41] The Commission, realising the problems associated with the old guidelines, proceeded to amend them. These amendments were intended to aid state parties to submit reports that are clear, organised, adequate in scope and sufficient in detail.[42]

Although the initial guidelines had shortcomings, they assisted in clarifying some ambiguous provisions of the Charter. Mugwanya succinctly captured this achievement as follows:

> ... while the Charter has no derogation clause, the guidelines require states to report on whether there is a provision in their laws for derogation and under what circumstances derogations are possible. Moreover, the guidelines are detailed on the information states must furnish to demonstrate that they have taken appropriate measures to give effect to individual and group rights. For instance, as regards peoples' rights to equality under Article 19, they require states to state the constitutional framework which protects the different sections of national community.[43]

The amended guidelines highlight eleven areas to be addressed in the reports.[44] On the basis of these guidelines, the Commission has evolved the procedure and practice of examining state reports. Procedurally, examination of state reports is conducted in the

---

41   See Mugwanya (n 36 above) 275; Nmehielle (n 11 above) 189; F Viljoen 'State reporting under the African Charter on Human and Peoples' Rights: A boost from the South' (1999) 44 *Journal of African Law* 112.

42   Nmehielle (n 11 above) 189.

43   Mugwanya (n 36 above) 275.

44   These areas are: (i) the initial report should contain a brief history of the state, its form of government, the legal system and the relationship between the arms of government; (ii) basic legislation of the state, such as the Constitution and criminal codes; (iii) the major human rights instruments to which the state is party and the steps taken to internalise them; (iv) how the state is implementing the rights protected by the Charter; (v) what the state is doing to improve the condition of women, children and the disabled; (vi) what steps are being taken to protect the family and encourage its cohesion; (vii) what is being done to ensure that individual duties are observed; (viii) what problems are encountered in implementing the Charter having regard to the political, economic or social circumstances of the state; (ix) how the state is carrying out its obligations under Article 25 of the Charter on human rights education; (x) how the state as an interested party is using the Charter in its international relations, particularly in ensuring respect for it and; (xi) any other information relevant to the implementation and promotion of the Charter.

Commission's open sessions. However, only Commissioners are allowed to pose questions to state representatives.[45]

Normally, the state's representative is first given the opportunity to present the report, after which the Commission's designated Rapporteur poses questions to him or her. Additional questions are posed to the representative by other Commissioners and are generally not limited to the line of questions prepared by the Secretariat.[46] After the question-and-answer session, the Rapporteur sums up the discussion, and the Chairman of the Commission concludes the session.

In the past, the Commission had adopted the practice of not considering a report in the absence of the state's representative. The Commission, however, changed its approach during its 23rd Ordinary Session. In the new approach, it first requests the state concerned to send a representative, failure to which it goes ahead to examine the report and forward its comments to the state.[47] In the case of non-submission of reports, the Commission may authorise the Secretary to send to the state concerned a report or reminder on the submission of the report or additional information.[48] Where the state concerned does not respond to the reminder, the Commission is obliged to point it out in its Annual report to the AHSG.[49]

It is disturbing to note that there have been unwarranted delays and defaults in the submission of state reports, which at best depict the lack of political will to ensure the success of this process. In an apparent move to curb such delays and defaults, the Commission recommended to the AHSG to adopt a resolution on overdue

---

45   See the African Commission on Human and Peoples' Rights, 'Rules of Procedure of the African Commission on Human and Peoples' Rights', revised and adopted on 6 June 1995, rule 3 (hereafter 'Rules of Procedure of the African Commission').

46   The African Commission on Human and Peoples' Rights (n 36 above) 9.

47   Nmehielle (n 11 above) 192.

48   Rules of Procedure of the Commission (n 45 above) rule 84(1).

49   As above, rule 84(2).

reports.[50] Thus, at its 29th Ordinary Session in Cairo, the Assembly adopted a resolution that *inter alia*[51]:

> (2) Urges the states parties to the African Charter on Human and Peoples' Rights which have not yet submitted their reports to submit them as soon as possible;
>
> (3) Requests that states should report not only on the legislative or other measures taken to give effect to each of the rights and freedoms recognised and guaranteed by the African Charter on Human and Peoples' Rights but also on the problems encountered in giving effect to these rights and freedoms;
>
> (4) ...;
>
> (5) Encourages states parties which encounter difficulties in preparing and submitting their periodic reports to seek help as soon as possible from the African Commission on Human and Peoples' Rights which will arrange for assistance in this task through its own or other resources.

This resolution is commendable in as far as it seeks to redress the shortcomings of irregular or non-reporting by member states. The mere adoption of resolutions, however, is not enough to change the ingrained negative attitudes of African governments to human rights reporting.[52] Rather, a radical system of sanctions and monitoring involving the organs of the AU would be a more effective and meaningful approach.

9.2.2 THE COMMISSION'S PROTECTIVE MANDATE

Although Article 45(2) of the Charter does not specifically state how the Commission may exercise its protective mandate, Chapter III provides for the 'communications' ('complaints') procedure, which has been the main way this mandate is executed. As already stated, this procedure is conducted in terms of Articles 47 to 60 of the Charter and involves the consideration of both inter-state and individual communications.

---

50   Fifth Annual Activity Report of the African Commission on Human and Peoples' Rights, (Annex VII).

51   AHSG/Res (XXVIII), 1993.

52   Kofi (n 31 above) 266.

9.2.2.1 INTER-STATE COMMUNICATIONS PROCEDURE

The African human rights system makes provision for the settlement of human rights disputes arising between states. However, neither the African Charter nor the Rules of Procedure of the African Commission indicate the type of disputes or violations of the Charter that are contemplated under the inter-state complaints procedure. As Nmehielle suggested, violation of Article 20 dealing with the general question of the right to self-determination and Article 23, which deals with the right to national and international peace and security, would probably fall within the purview of this procedure.[53] Additionally, the procedure could be used where a state chooses to claim on behalf of its nationals whose rights may have been violated by another state party to the Charter.[54] The Charter provides for two approaches to redress inter-state complaints. Pursuant to Article 47:

> If a state party to the present Charter has good reasons to believe that another state party to this Charter has violated the provisions of the Charter, it may draw, by written communication, the attention of that state to the matter. This communication shall also be addressed to the Secretary-General of the OAU and to the Chairman of the Commission. Within three months of the receipt of the communication, the state to which the communication is addressed shall give the enquiring state, written explanation or statement elucidating the matter. This should include as much as possible relevant information relating to the laws and rules of procedure applied and applicable, and the redress already given or course of action available.

The procedure under Article 47 therefore contemplates a situation where the contending states want to resolve a dispute in a friendly manner without involving the Commission. However, where the contending states fail to settle the dispute through negotiation or any other peaceful procedure, the matter may be brought before the Commission for resolution.[55] The second procedure, which

---

53   Nmehielle (n 11 above) 203.

54   As above.

55   Art 48 of the Charter states, 'If within three months from the date on which the original communication is received by the state to which it is addressed, the issue is not settled to the satisfaction of the two states involved through bilateral negotiation or by any other peaceful procedure, either state shall have the right to submit the matter to the Commission through the Chairman and shall notify the other states involved.'

is stipulated under Article 49 of the Charter, allows a state party to proceed directly with a communication to the Commission. Accordingly:

> Notwithstanding the provisions of [Article] 47, if a state party to the present Charter considers that another state party has violated the provisions of the Charter, it may refer the matter directly to the Commission by addressing a communication to the Chairman, to the Secretary-General of the Organisation of African Unity and the state concerned.

The two inter-state procedures may be distinguished in more than one way. The most obvious distinction is that the first procedure (hereafter 'Article-47 procedure') permits the amicable settlement of a dispute between contending states before they proceed to the Commission, while this is not required in the second procedure (hereafter 'Article-49 procedure'). The second distinction is that, while Article-47 procedure requires three months of exchange of information before the Commission is seized of the complaint, Article-49 procedure does not require such.

One would wonder why the Charter provides for two approaches under the inter-state communications procedure. The drafters of the Charter should rather have made one provision in which a time limit for bilateral peaceful resolution of the dispute is specified before a communication is filed with the Commission.[56] Another issue concerning the inter-state communications procedure relates to the role of the OAU/AU Secretary-General. Under both Article-47 and Article-49 procedures, states parties are required to address their communications to the Commission and the Secretary-General of the OAU/AU. One would think that the Commission should have been the only and proper institution to receive such communications.[57] This would avert any potential interference from the political institutions of the African human rights system. Perhaps, the input of the AU's organs could be solicited afterwards, especially during the enforcement of the Commission's recommendations.

---

56   Nmehielle (n 11 above) 201.

57   As above.

The African Commission has attempted to expedite the complaints procedure by adopting guidelines for the submission of inter-state communications.[58] These guidelines require the complaining state to: (i) state in writing, *inter alia*, its name, official language, and the year in which it ratified the African Charter; (ii) state the name of the accused state, its official language and the year it ratified the Charter; (iii) state the facts constituting the violation; (iv) indicate measures that have been taken to resolve the matter amicably; why the measure, if any, failed, or why no measure was used at all. Along this line the state must also indicate measures taken to exhaust local remedies; (v) state domestic legal remedies not yet pursued, giving reasons why this has not yet been done; (vi) state whether the case has also been referred to other international avenues, such as referral to other international settlement body like the UN or within the OAU system; and (vii) show complaints submitted to the Secretary-General of the OAU/AU and to the accused state, accompanied by any response from these two sources.[59] The guidelines for the inter-state complaints are similar in many respects to the requirements under the individual communications procedure.

9.2.2.2 Individuals ('Non-state') Communications Procedure

In addition to determining inter-state disputes, the Charter mandates the African Commission to receive 'other communications.' Although neither the Charter nor the Rules of Procedure of the Commission define the phrase, Article 55(1) appears to suggest that 'other communications' connotes communications that are not from a state party because it provides that:

> Before each Session, the Secretary of the Commission shall make a list of the communications other than those of states parties to the present Charter and transmit them to the members of the Commission, who shall indicate which communications should be considered by the Commission.

---

58   See African Commission on Human and Peoples' Rights, 'Guidelines on the Submission of Communications: Information Sheet no. 2', 14 (hereafter 'Information sheet no. 2).

59   As above.

An analytical reading of this provision suggests that the Charter does not restrict or limit access to the Commission by non-state complainants. This would essentially mean, therefore, that any person, group of persons or Non-Governmental Organisation, is allowed to lodge a complaint or petition alleging violation of the Charter. Hence, the Charter has been said to be more liberal in granting access to its non-state complainant's procedure than other regional and international human rights systems.[60] For example, whereas the Inter-American system allows only NGOs legally recognised in the member states of the OAS to lodge complaints before the Inter-American Commission[61], the African system does not have such regulations. Thus, NGOs from all over the world, with or without observer status with the Commission, have enjoyed unlimited access to the Commission on behalf of complainants. In the same vein, the African Charter does not contain any primary requirement that petitioners be the victims of the alleged violation, neither does it require that the complainants or petitioners be within the jurisdiction of the respondent state.[62]

It is therefore expedient to examine the individuals (non-state) communications procedure in detail, in order to highlight its ramifications under the African human rights system. The examination shall be conducted sequentially by discussing the procedure from the point a complaint is lodged before the Commission to when redress is offered. For purposes of clarity and consistency, the non-state complaints procedure shall herein be referred to as 'the individual communications procedure'.

9.2.2.2.1 SUBMISSION OF INDIVIDUAL COMMUNICATIONS

Before a communication is lodged with the Commission, certain issues must be ascertained. First, according to Rule 102(2) of the

---

60   Nmehielle (n 11 above) 204.

61   See art 44 of the American Convention on Human Rights, Signed at the Inter-American Specialized Conference on Human Rights, San Josi, Costa Rica, 22 November 1969.

62   Old rule 114(2), deleted in amended Rules. See also R Murray 'Decisions by the African Commission on individual communications under the African Charter on Human and Peoples' rights', (1997) 46 *International and Comparative Law Quarterly* 420.

Rules of Procedure, a communication submitted against a non-party state cannot be entertained because the Commission is mandated to only receive individual communications against a state party to the African Charter. Additionally, one cannot bring a communication against a non-state entity such as a supra-national organisation or an NGO.[63]

The starting point of the individual communications procedure is the submission of a complaint (communication). The Secretary of the Commission is required to make a list of all individual communications and transmit them to the Commissioners.[64] A communication will only be considered by the Commission upon the decision of a simple majority of the Commissioners.[65] It is not clear whether Article 55(2) of the Charter, which provides for a simple majority decision of the Commissioners prior to the determination of a communication, could be taken to mean that the Commission could decline to consider a communication that meets all admissibility requirements just because a simple majority of its members so decide. One would agree with Murray that this provision could only be applicable in cases where admissibility requirements have not been met because anything to the contrary may give the Commission unfettered discretion which could eventually be abused.[66]

9.2.2.2.2 ADMISSIBILITY OF INDIVIDUAL COMMUNICATIONS

Once an individual communication has been received, it is incumbent upon the Commission to decide whether or not the communication meets the admissibility requirements stipulated in Article 56 of the Charter. It may set up working groups, comprising a maximum of three Commissioners, to recommend on the admissibility of a communication.[67] The Commission or its working groups is at liberty to request additional information relating to the

---

63   See Communication 12/88, *Mohamed El-Nekheily v. OAU*, Seventh Annual Activity Report of the African Commission on Human and Peoples' Rights.

64   African Charter, art 55(1).

65   As above, art 55(2).

66   Murray (n 62 above) 420.

67   Rules of Procedure (n 45 above) rule 115.

issue of admissibility from either the complainant or the respondent state.[68] The decision on admissibility can only be taken after the communication or its brief summary has been transmitted to the state party concerned to make its observations.[69] The Commission is mandated to give the state party three months within which to submit its comments.[70]

Unless the Commission is compelled by exceptional circumstances to review its position, a decision on admissibility is final. Thus, if a communication is declared inadmissible its consideration will automatically come to a close. A decision on inadmissibility may, however, be reconsidered if the Commission is requested to do so.[71] Sometimes the Commission invites the author to do so, as in *Alberto T. Capitao v. Tanzania,*[72] where it observed that the 'case can be resubmitted when the local remedies have been properly exhausted or if the complainant proves that local remedies are unavailable, ineffective or unreasonably prolonged.' Where a communication is declared admissible, the parties will be informed before the case proceeds to the 'merits stage'.[73]

The principle that communications have to comply with certain admissibility requirements serves as an important screening or filtering mechanism between national and international institutions.[74] Viljoen correctly argued that, by requiring disputes between nationals and their states to be resolved, in the first instance, at the national level, the principle emphasises the divide between sovereignty of states and international supervision.[75] Article 56 of the

---

68   As above, rule 117.

69   As above.

70   As above, rule 117(4).

71   As above, rule 118(2).

72   Communications 53/90 and 53/91, *Alberto T. Capitao v. Tanzania,* Seventh Annual Activity Report of the African Commission on Human and Peoples' Rights (Annex IX); Eighth Annual Activity Report of the African Commission on Human and Peoples' Rights (Annex VI).

73   Rules of Procedure (n 45 above) rule 118(1).

74   F Viljoen 'Admissibility under the African Charter' in M Evans & R Murray *The African Charter on Human and Peoples' Rights: The system in practice, 1986-2000* (2002) 62.

75   As above.

African Charter, therefore, provides such a filter by outlining seven admissibility requirements as follows:

> Communications relating to human and peoples' rights referred to in Article 55 received by the Commission shall be considered if they:
>
> 1.   Indicate their authors even if the latter request anonymity,
> 2.   Are compatible with the Charter of the Organisation of African Unity or with the present Charter,
> 3.   Are not written in disparaging or insulting language directed against the state concerned and its institutions or to the Organisation of African Unity,
> 4.   Are not based exclusively on news disseminated through the mass media,
> 5.   Are sent after exhausting local remedies, if any, unless it is obvious that this procedure is unduly prolonged,
> 6.   Are submitted within a reasonable period from the time local remedies are exhausted or from the date the Commission is seized of the matter, and
> 7.   Do not deal with cases which have been settled by these states involved in accordance with the principles of the Charter of the United Nations, or the Charter of the Organisation of African Unity or the provisions of the present Charter.

1.   THE COMMUNICATIONS MUST INDICATE THEIR AUTHORS EVEN IF THEY REQUEST ANONYMITY.

Article 56(1) stipulates that communications must 'indicate their authors even if the latter request anonymity.' This should be understood to mean that the authors ought to furnish the Commission with their full particulars.[76] According to the Commission, this includes the authors' full identity[77] and contact addresses.[78] It was the

---

76   As above, 62.

77   Communication 70/92, *Ibrahim Diomessi, Sekou Kande, Ousmane Kabe v. Guinea,* Seventh Annual Activity Report of the African Commission on Human and Peoples' Rights (Annex IX); Ninth Annual Activity Report of the African Commission on Human and Peoples' Rights (Annex VIII).

78   In Communication 57/91, *Tanko Bariga v. Nigeria,* Seventh Annual Activity Report of the African Commission on Human and Peoples' Rights (Annex IX), the Commission made it clear that an address is required because 'for practical reasons it is necessary that the Commission is able to contact the author.'

Commission's position that, although Article 56(1) does not expressly require authors to provide their addresses, the same is necessary to expedite communication.[79] Moreover, the fact that authors may request anonymity does not preclude them from providing their names and other relevant particulars to the Commission.[80]

It has been contended, and rightly so, that anonymity will be difficult to maintain, especially when the respondent state has to be briefed on the nature and content of the complaint against it.[81] The Charter and the Rules of Procedure are also not clear on the scope and nature of anonymity that may be requested; whether it is in respect of the respondent state or the general public or even to some Commissioners.[82] It is therefore necessary for complainants to specify how they prefer to remain anonymous.[83] Anonymity could be enhanced by a party being represented by, for example, an NGO and the Commission could use the name of the NGO in the title of the case.[84] Alternatively, the Commission could choose to use a pseudonym. But either way, it may be difficult to maintain anonymity in the event the respondent state is called upon to vindicate its position and counter the complainant's allegations.

2.　　THE COMMUNICATIONS MUST BE COMPATIBLE WITH BOTH THE AFRICAN CHARTER AND THE CHARTER OF THE ORGANISATION OF AFRICAN UNITY (OR THE CAAU).

The essence of Article 56(2) is that the Commission considers communications only if they are 'compatible with' the African Charter. Compatibility with the African Charter has various connotations. First, the communication must provide *prima facie* evidence that a right set out in the Charter has been violated.[85] In

79　　Communication 57/91, *Tanko Bariga v. Nigeria* (n 78 above).

80　　Rules of Procedure (n 45 above), rule 104.

81　　Viljoen (n 74 above) 67.

82　　As above.

83　　S Gumedze 'Bringing communications before the African Commission on Human and Peoples' Rights' (2003) 3 *African Human Rights Law Journal* 129.

84　　As above.

85　　Viljoen (n 74 above) 69.

Frederick Korvah v. Liberia[86]*, where the complainant alleged, among other things, the lack of discipline in the Liberian Security Police and corruption, the communication was declared inadmissible because the allegations did not 'amount to violations of human rights under the provisions of the Charter.'[87] The Commission has also stated that although it is not necessary to mention specific provisions of the Charter, there must be sufficient indication of the factual basis of the violation.[88]

Secondly, the communication must be directed at a state party to the Charter and must be submitted by someone who is competent to do so.[89] Observing that numerous petitioners in the early years of the Commission overlooked this requirement, Viljoen stated:

> In the first few years, this requirement was the cause of most findings of inadmissibility: twenty-three of the fifty-four cases found to be inadmissible until May 1999. There are four categories of countries against whom these communications were directed: non-African states, OAU member states that had not yet become states parties of the Charter; the only African non-OAU member, Morocco and the OAU itself.[90]

Thirdly, the communication must be based on events that have occurred within the period of the Charter's application.[91] This stems from the general principle of international law that treaties 'do not bind a party in relation to any act or fact which took place in any situation which ceased to exist before the date of the entry into force of the treaty in respect of that party.'[92] Thus, the Commission is competent only to consider violations that are alleged to have occurred from the date of entry into force of the Charter. In relation

---

86   Communication 1/88, *Frederick Korvah v. Liberia,* Seventh Annual Activity Report of the African Commission on Human and Peoples' Rights (Annex IX).

87   As above.

88   See communication 162/97, *Mouvement des Refugies Mauritaniens au Senegal v. Senegal,* Eleventh Annual Activity Report of the African Commission on Human and Peoples' Rights (Annex II), which was found inadmissible on ground that the facts do not reveal a *prima facie* violation of the Charter.

89   See Viljoen (n 74 above) 72.

90   As above, 72-73.

91   As above.

92   Vienna Convention on the Law of Treaties, art 28.

to states that became parties after the entry into force of the Charter, the Commission has the competence to consider communications that have originated after the date of entry into force for a particular state. The date of entry into force is three months after the deposit by that state of its instrument of adherence.[93] Thus, in Communication 39/90, *Annette Pagnoulle v. Cameroon*[94], the Commission reiterated that it 'cannot pronounce on the quality of court proceedings that took place before the African Charter entered into force in Cameroon', but was quick to point out that: 'if, however, irregularities in the original sentence have consequences that constitute a continuing violation of any of the Articles of the African Charter, the Commission must pronounce on these.'[95]

Fourthly, the communication must be based on events that took place within the territorial sphere in which the Charter applies.[96] The territorial requirement is to the effect that states parties to the Charter are in principle only responsible for violations that occur within their territory.[97]

It should be noted, however, that the requirement that a communication must be compatible with both the African Charter and the OAU Charter (or the Constitutive Act of the African Union) raises some controversy. It is obvious that the Constitutive Act which succeeded the OAU Charter is not a source of substantive rights in the African human rights system.[98] It is understandable that a complaint pursuant to the provisions of the Charter should show a violation because the Charter contains substantive rights. What still

---

93   African Charter, art 65.

94   Communication 39/90, *Annette Pagnoulle v. Cameroon*, Eighth Annual Activity Report of the African Commission on Human and Peoples' Rights (Annex VI); Tenth Annual Activity Report of the African Commission on Human and Peoples' Rights (Annex X).

95   As above, para 15.

96   Viljoen (n 74 above) 78.

97   As above.

98   A Odinkalu & C Christensen 'The African Commission on Human and Peoples' Rights: Development of its non-State communications procedure' (1998) 20 *Human Rights Quarterly* 253.

needs to be demystified is the requirement for compatibility with the OAU Charter (or CAAU).[99]

3.   The Communications must not be Written in Disparaging or Insulting Language Directed against the State Concerned and its Institutions or to the OAU/AU.

The Charter disqualifies communications that are written in disparaging or insulting language directed at the state complained against and its institutions, or the OAU (AU).[100] No other international or regional human rights instrument contains this 'non-disparaging language' requirement for purposes of admissibility. One would agree with Ankumah that 'even if this provision did not exist, it would not be prudent for a litigant to write a communication in disparaging or insulting language as it would tend to detract from the issues.'[101] Apparently, the requirement seeks to ensure respect for state parties and their institutions as well as the AU. It is, however, unfortunate that the phrase 'disparaging or insulting' language is not defined in the Charter. Thus, whether or not the language is disparaging is exclusively for the Commission to decide.

The Commission has found a communication inadmissible on this ground. In *Ligue Camerounaise des Droits de l'Homme v. Cameroon*[102], the communication alleged violations of human rights in Cameroon between 1984 and 1989. It contained statements such as 'Paul Biya must respond to crimes against humanity', '30 years of the criminal neo-colonial regime incarcerated by the duo Ahidjo/Biya', 'regime of torturers', and 'government barbarism'. The Commission held these statements to be insulting language. As Odinkalu and Christensen observed, the decision of the Commission in this regard

---

99   Nmehielle (n 11 above) 215.

100   African Charter, art 56(3).

101   Ankumah (n 11 above) 64.

102   Communication 65/92, *Ligue Camerounaise des Droits de l'Homme v. Cameroon*, Tenth Annual Activity Report of the African Commission on Human and Peoples' Rights (Annex X).

sets a dangerous precedent in as far as it tends to make Article 56(3) subject to the feelings of state parties.[103]

4.   THE COMMUNICATIONS MUST NOT BE BASED ON NEWS
        DISSEMINATED THROUGH THE MASS MEDIA.

This is another provision that is unique to the African Charter as no other human rights instrument provides for a similar admissibility requirement. It appears that the provision is aimed at ensuring that authors of the communication are able to investigate and ascertain the truth of the facts before requesting for the Commission's intervention.[104] In *Jawara v. The Gambia*[105], for example, the Commission resonated that:

> It would be damaging if the Commission were to reject a communication because some aspects of it are based on news disseminated through the mass media. This is borne out of the fact that the Charter makes use of the word 'exclusively'. There is no doubt that the media remains the most important if not the only source of information…The issue therefore should not be whether the information was gotten from the media, but whether the information is correct.[106]

Thus, while it is important that allegations contained in communications be verifiable, there would be situations where authors of communications may not gain the requisite information access and therefore must depend on the news disseminated through the mass media. After all, the mass media has from the past played an instrumental role in ensuring respect for human rights.[107]

5.   THE COMMUNICATIONS MUST BE SENT AFTER ALL EXISTING
        LOCAL REMEDIES HAVE BEEN EXHAUSTED.

The rule on exhaustion of domestic remedies is paramount in that it provides the respondent state the opportunity to redress, within

---

103   Odinkalu & Christensen (n 98 above) 255.

104   Nmehielle (n 11 above) 217.

105   Communications 147/95, 149/95, *Sir Dawda K Jawara v The Gambia*, Thirteenth
        Annual Activity Report of the African Commission on Human and Peoples' Rights
        (Annex X).

106   As above, para 24.

107   Nmehielle (n 11 above) 218.

the framework of its own domestic legal system, the wrongs alleged to be done to the individual.[108] Besides giving the state the first opportunity to redress alleged violations, the rule also ensures respect for state sovereignty.[109] Accordingly, Article 56(5) requires admissibility of communications that 'are sent after exhausting local remedies, if any, unless it is obvious that this procedure is unduly prolonged.' The use of 'if any' in this sub-Article connotes that exhaustion of domestic remedies is predicated on their availability.

From the Commission's jurisprudence, Viljoen cited four possible categories of situations in which remedies may be said to be unavailable.[110] These are: (i) where a decree or other measure has ousted the jurisdiction of the courts, making judicial recourse impossible[111]; (ii) where pursuing a remedy is dependent on extrajudicial considerations, such as a discretion or some extraordinary power granted to an executive state official[112]; (iii) where a situation of serious massive violations of human rights exists[113]; and (iv) where complainants are detained without trial.[114] Arguably, the Charter does not waive the rule where remedies are inadequate or when it can be established that the due process of law is not tenable.[115]

The Commission has on many occasions ensured that communications complied with the exhaustion of domestic

---

108   C Odinkalu 'The role of case and complaints procedures in the reform of African regional human rights system' (2001) 2 *African Human Rights Law Journal* 227.

109   Murray (n 62 above) 422.

110   F Viljoen 'Review of the African Commission on Human and Peoples' Rights: 21 October 1986 to 1 January 1997' in C Heyns (ed) *Human rights law in Africa 1997* (1999) 72.

111   See Communications 137/94, 139/94, 154/96 & 161/97, *International PEN, Constitutional Rights Project, Interights on behalf of Ken Saro-Wiwa jr and Civil Liberties Organisation v. Nigeria,* Twelfth Annual Activity Report of the African Commission on Human and Peoples' Rights (Annex V) para 76.

112   Communication 87/93, *Constitutional Rights Project (in respect of Zamani Lekwot and 6 others v. Nigeria),* Eighth Annual Activity Report of the African Commission on Human and Peoples' Rights (Annex VI).

113   Communications 48/90, 50/91, 52/91, 89/93 *Amnesty International, Comite Loosli Bachelard, Lawyers Committee for Human Rights, Association of members of the Episcopal Conference of East Africa v. Sudan,* Thirteenth Annual Activity Report of the African Commission on Human and Peoples' Rights (Annex V).

114   Viljoen (n 110 above) 72.

115   See Ankumah (n 11 above) 67.

remedies requirement. Thus, communications based on claims pending in national courts have been declared inadmissible for non-exhaustion of domestic remedies.[116] Similarly, the Commission has held that exhaustion of local remedies does not preclude exhaustion of appellate procedures.[117] With regard to effectiveness of remedies, the Commission found a 'discretionary' and 'extraordinary' remedy of a non-judicial nature to be both inadequate and ineffective.[118] Hence, in *Civil Liberties Organisation v. Nigeria*[119], the Commission held that the rule does not apply in cases where national legislation or decree ousts the jurisdiction of the court to entertain claims for breaches of fundamental rights.[120]

The 'unduly prolonged' criterion, upon which the exhaustion of domestic remedies rule could be waived, has also received the attention of the Commission. In communication 59/91, *Louis Emgba Mekongo v. Cameroon,* for example, the Commission decided that the fact that the complainant's case had been pending in a Cameroonian court for twelve years was sufficient proof that procedures for exhaustion of domestic remedies had been unduly prolonged.[121] The Commission is yet to define the phrase 'unduly prolonged' under Article 56(5) of the Charter.

It has correctly been argued that the question of whether or not local remedies have been exhausted is that of fact whose burden of proof rests upon the author or applicant of the communication.[122] This may be the reason why Rule 104(1)(f) of the Rules of Procedure authorises the Commission to request the author to furnish clarifications regarding measures taken to exhaust local remedies or

---

116   Communication 151/96, *Civil Liberties Organisation v. Nigeria,* Thirteenth Annual Activity Report of the African Commission on Human and Peoples' Rights (Annex V) 44.

117   Communication 90/93 *Paul Haye v. The Gambia,* ACHPR/LR/1 105.

118   See Communication 60/91, *Constitutional Rights Project (Wahab Akumu, G Adega & others v. Nigeria),* ACHPR/LR/A1 57.

119   Communication 151/96, *Civil Liberties Organisation v. Nigeria,* Thirteenth Annual Activity Report of the African Commission on Human and Peoples' Rights (Annex V) 71.

120   As above.

121   Communication 59/91, *Louis Emgba Mekongo v. Cameroon,* Eighth Annual Activity Report of the African Commission on Human and Peoples' Rights.

122   Nmehielle (n 11 above) 225.

to give an explanation of why local remedies would be futile, if it is so alleged. It must, therefore, be shown that an attempt had been made to have recourse to national procedures.[123] In communication 8/88, *Buyingo v. Uganda*, the Commission failed to get a response from the complainant on whether or not he had recourse to local remedies as required by Article 56 of the Charter.

It needs to be observed that the practice of the African Commission in demonstrating the burden of proof for the exhaustion of domestic remedies has not been consistent.[124] In some cases, when the state party refused to provide a response to allegations, the Commission accepted the facts as alleged in the complaints and made a decision thereon. In other cases, the Commission appeared to be more reluctant towards the complainant's allegation.[125] Rather than request for additional information from the complainant in such cases, the Commission declared the communications inadmissible on the grounds that the complainants failed to provide information as to the exhaustion of domestic remedies. In developing its jurisprudence, the Commission should avoid double standards and maintain consistency in the determination of communications.

6.   THE COMMUNICATIONS MUST BE SUBMITTED WITHIN A
      REASONABLE PERIOD FROM THE TIME LOCAL REMEDIES
      ARE EXHAUSTED OR FROM THE DATE THE COMMISSION IS
      SEIZED WITH THE MATTER.

Article 56(6) requires communications to be submitted within a reasonable period from the time local remedies are exhausted or from the date the Commission is seized of the matter. However, the Charter does not state the time limit within which communications must be submitted. The determination of a 'reasonable period' is therefore a task left to the Commission. This position can be contrasted with that of the European and Inter-American systems, where a maximum period of six months after the date the 'final decision

---

123   See Communication 92/93 *International Pen v. Sudan (in respect of Kemal al-Jazouli)* Eighth Annual Activity Report of the African Commission on Human and Peoples' Rights.

124   Nmehielle (n 11 above) 225.

125   As above. See also Odinkalu & Christensen (n 98 above) 265.

was taken'[126] or 'after the notification of the final judgement',[127] is expressly prescribed.

The fact that the Charter requires communications to be submitted within a reasonable period, without specifying the time limit, has both negative and positive implications. On the one hand, it may prejudice valid claims because what is 'reasonable period' to one member of the Commission may not be likewise to another. On the other hand, this provision has positive implications in the sense that many Africans are ignorant of the Commission's procedures and if a time limit was to be imposed, many communications would be declared inadmissible due to non-compliance.[128] Additionally, this less stringent requirement takes account of the communication difficulties in many African countries.[129]

Some communications dealing with the exhaustion of domestic remedies have impliedly addressed circumstances that may be used to determine what a reasonable time is. For example, in *Mekongo v. Cameroon*[130], the Commission declared the complaint admissible even though the complainant had spent over twelve years pursuing a discretionary presidential remedy after the conclusion of domestic proceedings. This could be taken to mean that twelve years after the exhaustion of domestic remedies was reasonable time, especially because the complainant could not lodge a communication for reason of his pursuit of a discretionary remedy. Similarly in *John Modise v. Botswana*[131], the Commission admitted a communication that was submitted nearly fifteen years from the time judicial proceedings were concluded.

---

126   European Convention, art 35.

127   Inter-American Convention, art 46(1)(b).

128   Viljoen (n 74 above) 91.

129   As above.

130   *Louis Emgba Mekongo v. Cameroon* (n 121 above).

131   Communication 97/93, *John Modise v. Botswana,* Tenth Annual Activity Report of the African Commission on Human and Peoples' Rights (Annex X).

7.   THE COMMUNICATION MUST NOT RELATE TO CASES
WHICH HAVE BEEN SETTLED IN ACCORDANCE WITH THE
PRINCIPLES OF THE CHARTER OF THE UNITED NATIONS OR
THE CHARTER OF THE ORGANISATION OF AFRICAN UNITY
OR THE PROVISIONS OF THE AFRICAN CHARTER.

According to Article 56(7), a communication is inadmissible if it
has already been 'settled' under the African Charter. In other words,
the *ne bis in idem* rule applies.[132] This rule prohibits 'double jeopardy'
by protecting a state from being found in violation twice for one
violating act or conduct. Its effect is similar to that of *autrefois acquit*
and *autrefois convict* principles of criminal law, which prohibit the
re-trial of an accused person for an offence for which he or she had
already been either acquitted or convicted.[133]

    While the African Charter allows for the simultaneous
submission of communications to both the African Commission and
a UN treaty body such as the UN Human Rights Committee, the
complainant has to abide by the first decision or finding.[134] This was
enunciated in *Bob Ngozi Njoku v. Egypt*[135] where, before submitting
the communication to the African Commission, the complainant
approached the UN Sub-Commission on Human Rights with the
same matter. The latter decided not to entertain it or to make any
pronouncement on it and the African Commission found that the
inaction by the UN Sub-Commission 'does not boil down to a
decision on the merits of the case and does not in any way indicate
that the matter' has been 'settled', as required by Article 56(7).[136] The
communication was consequently declared admissible.

9.2.2.2.3 PROCEDURE AFTER A COMMUNICATION HAS BEEN DECLARED ADMISSIBLE

Once the communication passes the admissibility test under Article
56 of the Charter, it proceeds to the substantive consideration stage

---

132   Viljoen (n 74 above) 91.

133   As above.

134   As above.

135   Communication 40/90, *Bob Ngozi Njoku v. Egypt*, Eleventh Annual Activity Report
of the African Commission on Human and Peoples' Rights (Annex II).

136   As above.

('merit stage').The admissibility decision is made known to the state party as soon as possible by the Secretary of the Commission.[137] At this stage, Rule 119(2) requires the state party concerned to 'submit in writing within three months to the Commission, its explanations or statements, elucidating the issues under consideration and indicating, if possible, measures taken to remedy the situation.' The Commission, however, has the discretion to extend the period if such extension serves the interests of justice. The author is also given the opportunity to comment on what the state submits.[138] It is interesting to note that no time limit has been set within which the author's comments should be received by the Commission.This may be an oversight on the part of the drafters.

The Commission considers the communication in the light of information submitted to it by parties in writing.[139] During this stage, hearing takes place; a brief presentation of the case is made by the complainant or an NGO and the respondent state is then given the opportunity to respond to the allegations.The complainant or NGO is then asked to reply to the state's response. After careful deliberations based on the facts and arguments put forward by the parties, the Commission retires in private to make its decision on whether it finds a violation of the Charter or not.Where the Commission finds a violation, it issues recommendations to the state party concerned.[140] In effect, the Commission's decisions are recommendations.

There are occasions where the respondent state party completely ignores or refuses to respond to allegations made by a complainant, or to respond to the request for information by the Commission. In such situations, the Commission would rely on the facts presented by the complainant and treat them as given.[141] The Commission is,

---

137   Rule 119(1).This Rule requires the Secretary of the Commission to submit, as soon as possible, the decision of admissibility and text of relevant documents to the state party concerned.The Rule further mandates the secretary to inform the author of the decision about the admissibility of the communication.

138   Rule 119(3).

139   Rule 120(1).

140   For a more detailed discussion on the Commission's procedure in determining a communication, see Nmehielle (n 11 above) 230-232.

141   As above. See also *Louis Emgba Mekongo v. Cameroon* (n 121 above) 26-27.

however, cautious when applying this rule. It has therefore warned that, the fact that the complainant's allegations are not contested, or are partially uncontested by the state, does not mean the Commission would blindly accept their veracity.[142] Thus, the Commission could invoke the power vested in it under Article 46 to get information from alternative sources and from third parties.[143] Alternatively, the Commission may set up a working group of three of its members to whom it would refer the communication and which would submit final recommendations to it.[144]

9.2.2.2.4 THE COMMISSION'S RECOMMENDATIONS ON COMMUNICATIONS

There is no provision in the Charter that mandates the Commission to make recommendations to states on every individual communications it considers. Rather, the term, 'recommendation', is mentioned in the context of special cases revealing the existence of serious or massive violation of human rights. Article 58 of the Charter stipulates that:

1. When it appears after deliberations of the Commission that one or more communications apparently relate to special cases which reveal the existence of a series of serious or massive violations of human and peoples' rights, the Commission shall draw the attention of the Assembly of Heads of State and Government to these special cases.
2. The Assembly of Heads of State and Government may then request the Commission to undertake an in-depth study of these cases and make a factual report, accompanied by its findings and recommendations.
3. A case of emergency duly noticed by the Commission shall be submitted by the latter to the Chairman of the Assembly of Heads of State and Government who may request an in-depth study.

From the foregoing provisions, it is obvious that the Commission has no enforcement powers and its recommendations, unless the

---

142   As above.

143   As above.

144   Rule 120(1).

state agrees, are not capable of being executed in the national jurisdiction.[145] Worst still, the implementation of its reports and recommendations solely depends on the political will of the Assembly of Heads of States and Government. In this regard, the Commission functions at the mercy of states parties. It has, therefore, rightly been observed that Article 58 'would appear to suggest that not only does the Commission have no jurisdiction in separate individual cases unless they are of an urgent nature, it also has no formal power to take the initiative itself.'[146]

It is rather unfortunate that the Charter is silent on how the Commission should deal with communications not revealing the existence of a series of serious or massive violations of human and peoples' rights.[147] As a result of this overt weakness in the Charter's provisions, some governments have in the past declined to comply with the Commission's recommendations and decisions. For example, during the period of military dictatorship in Nigeria, the Commission adopted resolutions and gave recommendations condemning both ouster clauses and special tribunals in the country.[148] However, the government of Nigeria contended, among other things, that the Commission lacked the competence to issue such recommendations.[149] Similarly, in another communication, Gambia insisted that 'the Commission is allowed under the Charter

---

145   C Odinkalu 'Proposals for review of the Rules of Procedure of the African Commission on Human & Peoples' Rights' (1992) 21/2 *Human Rights Quarterly* 543.

146   Murray (n 62 above) 46.

147   In communications 27/89, 46/90, 99/93 (Joined), *Organization Mondiale Contre la Torture and three others v. Rwanda*, Tenth Annual Activity Report of the African Commission on Human and Peoples' Rights (Annex X), the Commission joined four communications, which made reference to the expulsion from Rwanda of Burundi nationals who had been in Rwanda for many years for allegedly being a national risk due to their 'subversive activities', as well as the arbitrary arrest and extra-judicial executions of Rwandans, mostly from the Tutsi ethnic group. In this communication, the Commission held that the facts constituted serious or massive violations of the Charter, namely of arts 4, 5, 6, 12(3) & 12(5).

148   See, for example, 'Account of Internal Legislation of Nigeria and the Dispositions of the Charter of African Human and Peoples' Rights', Second Extraordinary Session, Kampala, 18-19 December 1995 DOC. II/ES/ACHPR/4. See also the analysis in F Viljoen & L Louw 'The status of the findings of the African Commission: From moral persuasion to legal obligation' (2004) 48/1 *Journal of African Law* 5.

149   As above.

to take action only in cases that reveal a series of serious or massive violations of human rights.'[150]

While this position is true in relation to the Charter's provisions, the Commission's Rules of Procedure and its practice vehemently refute these arguments. The Commission developed its own Rules of Procedure in such a way as to enable it to accept communications from individuals alleging human rights violations that are not necessarily serious or massive.[151] In responding to Nigeria's arguments, the Commission justified its competence to issue recommendations by stating that:

> It is true that the communications procedure, as set out in Article 55 of the Charter, is quasi-judicial, in that communications are necessarily adversarial. Complainants are complaining against some act or neglect of a government and the Commission must ultimately, if it is unable to effect a friendly settlement, decide for one side or the other. These actions of the Commission are clearly required by the stipulations of Articles 55-59 of the Charter....This charge to ensure protection clearly refers to the Commission's duties under Articles 55-59 to protect the rights in the Charter through the communications procedure. The Commission therefore cannot take the government's contention that in deciding communications it has acted outside its capacity.[152]

As for the argument by Gambia, the Commission dismissed the proposition as 'erroneous'.[153] It is now settled that the Commission has the mandate to consider communications and give recommendations, whether or not massive or serious violations of human and peoples' rights have occurred. Not only has it become a norm for the Commission to make recommendations; over the years, the recommendations have become more detailed than they were initially.[154] Unfortunately, states do not always put

---

150   See *Sir Dawda K Jawara v The Gambia* (n 105 above) para 41. See also Viljoen & Louw (n 148 above) 5.

151   Viljoen & Louw (n 148 above) 5. See also old Rule 114 replaced by 1995 Rules of Procedure.

152   'Account of Internal Legislation of Nigeria and the Disposition of the Charter of African Human and Peoples' Rights' (n 148 above).

153   See *Sir Dawda K Jawara v The Gambia*, para 42.

154   A Ayinla 'The African Union (AU) human rights agenda: The panacea to the problem of non- compliance with human rights norms in Africa?' (2003) *LLM Thesis Makerere University* 26.

the recommendations into effect. This, of course, is one of the main challenges to human rights enforcement in Africa and has been described as 'one of the major factors of the erosion of the Commission's credibility.'[155] This issue shall be revisited later when the challenges to effective enforcement of human rights under the African human rights system shall be explored.

9.2.2.2.5 PROVISIONAL (INTERIM) MEASURES AND REMEDIES

Provisional (interim) measures and remedies under the African human rights system are intended to provide some form of relief to victims of human rights violations, albeit at different stages of the proceedings. Interim or provisional measures are normally issued to avoid irreparable damage to victims, or sometimes, complainants, while a communication or petition is still under consideration.[156] Remedies, on the other hand, are awarded to redress a violation of human rights after a communication is fully determined. Notably, however, whereas interim measures provide temporary relief to the victims, remedies are of a more permanent nature.

The African Charter does not specifically provide for interim measures. Consequently, the Commission decided to make provision for these measures under its Rules of Procedure. According to Rule 111:

1. Before making its final views known to the Assembly on the communication, the Commission may inform the state party concerned of its views on the appropriateness of taking provisional measures to avoid irreparable damage being caused to the victim of the alleged violation. In so doing, the Commission shall inform the state party that the expression on its views on the adoption of those provisional measures does not imply a decision on the substance of the communication.

---

155 'Non-Compliance of state parties to adopted recommendations of the African Commission: A legal approach' 24th Ordinary Session, 22-31 October 1998, DOC/OS/50b para 2, cited in I Österdahl 'Implementing human rights in Africa: The African Commission on Human & Peoples' Rights and individual communications' (2002) *Swedish Institute of International Law Studies in International Law* 15.

156 Nmehielle (n 11 above) 232.

2.   The Commission, or when not in session, the Chairman, in consultation with other members of the Commission, may indicate to the parties any interim measure, the adoption of which seems desirable in the interest of the parties or the proper conduct of the proceedings before it.

3.   In case of urgency [sic] when the Commission is not in session, the Chairman, in consultation with other members of the Commission, may take any necessary action on behalf of the Commission. As soon as the Commission is again in session, the Chairman shall report to it any action taken.

Rule 111 does not specify at what stage of the proceedings provisional measures may be granted. This leaves one to wonder whether these measures should be granted only where a communication has passed the admissibility stage, or even prior thereto.[157] While the Commission is yet to state its position on this issue, it may be argued that the circumstances of a given case, irrespective of its admissibility, would determine whether or not a request for provisional measures should be granted. This is actually the position adopted under the Inter-American human rights system. In the words of Pasqualucci:

> such precautionary measures may be requested [under the Inter-American system] even when the admissibility of a case has not yet been defined by the Commission pursuant to Article 46 of the Convention, since, by their very nature, provisional measures arise from a reasonable presumption of extreme and urgent risk of irreparable damage to persons.[158]

Under the African human rights system, the African Commission has invoked Rule 111 of its Rules of Procedure in very few instances. For example, in *Constitutional Rights Project (Zamani Lekwot and 6 others) v. Nigeria*[159], a Nigerian NGO submitted a complaint on behalf of Zamani Lekwot and six other people who were awaiting execution after being sentenced to death by a military tribunal. The Commission requested the Nigerian government not to execute

---

157   As above.

158   M Pasqualucci 'Provisional measures in the Inter-American human rights system: Innovative development in international law' (1993) 26 *Vanderbuilt Journal of Transnational Law* 803.

159   *Constitutional Rights Project (in respect of Zamani Lekwot and 6 others) v. Nigeria* 102.

the victims until it considered the substance of the case. With this request for provisional measures the NGO instituted an action in Lagos High Court to stay the execution of the death sentences.[160]

The government responded by filing a preliminary objection on the grounds that the court had no jurisdiction to entertain the suit, the same having been ousted by decree. The court, however, held that it had jurisdiction to hear the case and issued an injunction against carrying out the execution pending the determination of the complaint before the African Commission.[161] The death sentence was later commuted to five years' imprisonment. This indeed is a landmark achievement on the part of the African Commission that needs to be applauded.

On the issue of remedies, it should be recalled that an aggrieved state or individual, whose rights have been violated, has recourse for redress. This may take the form of an apology, reparations, or damages for alleged wrongdoing, condemnation of the acts of the violators, injunction in the case of a continuing violation, or the removal of the sources of violation, for example, the repeal of legislation or the enactment of a new one.[162] Neither the African Charter nor the Rules of Procedure of the African Commission explicitly provides for any forms of remedies to redress violations of human rights. The fact that the Commission has no express powers to grant remedies has correctly been viewed as an 'important reason for [its] inability... to attain its principal objective of protecting human rights in Africa.'[163]

---

160   *Registered Trustees of the Constitutional Rights Project v. The President of Federal Republic of Nigeria and Two others* (Unreported judgement of the High Court of Lagos State, Suit no. m/102/93) cited in Nmehielle (n 11 above) 236.

161   As above.

162   As above.

163   N Enonchong 'The African Charter on Human and Peoples' Rights: Effective remedies in domestic law?' (2002) 46 *Journal of African Law* 197.

Nevertheless, the Commission has in several cases attempted to recommend some forms of remedies to victims of violations.[164] At one time it was accused of assaulting the sovereignty of Nigeria for ordering 'the annulment of decrees found to be in violation of the Charter.'[165] Nigeria questioned the competence of the Commission to issue remedies, to which the latter responded:

> ...Nigeria is bound by the African Charter. The Commission is likewise bound by the Charter, to consider communications fully, carefully, and in good faith. When the Commission concludes that a communication describes a real violation of the Charter's provisions, its duty is to make that clear and indicate what action the government must take to remedy the situation. Naturally, the Commission could not make such judgements with regard to states outside its jurisdiction. But in ratifying the Charter without reservation, Nigeria voluntarily submitted itself to the Commission's authority in this regard.[166]

Regardless of the apparent lack of normative basis from which the Commission derives its authority to recommend remedies, the fact still remains that the pronouncement of remedies is now an established practice within its remits. However, the Commission, unlike its counterparts, has been very reluctant to recommend certain forms of remedies, such as damages or reparations, even where it finds massive or serious violations of the Charter.[167] For example, in *Louise Emgba Mekongo v. Cameroon*[168], it found that the complainant was entitled to reparations for the prejudice he had suffered, but left the valuation of the amount of such reparation to be determined in accordance with the legal system of Cameroon. The Commission ought to have been bold enough to pronounce

---

164   See, for example, *Louis Emgba Mekongo v. Cameroon* (n 121 above) and joint communications 54/91, 61/91, 98/93, 164/97-196/97 & 210/98 *Malawi African Association v. Mauritania, Amnesty International v. Mauritania, Ms Sarr Diop v. Mauritania;* communication 101/93, *Civil Liberties Organisation v. Nigeria;* communication 60/91, *Constitutional Rights Projects v. Nigeria;* communication 87/93, *Constitutional Rights Project (in respect of Zamani Lekwot and 6 others) v. Nigeria;* and Joint communications 54/91, 61/91, 98/93, 164/97-196/97 & 210/98, *Malawi African Association v. Mauritania, Amnesty International v. Mauritania, Ms Sarr Diop v. Mauritania.*

165   See 'Account of internal legislation of Nigeria and the disposition of the Charter of African Human and Peoples' Rights' (n 148 above).

166   As above.

167   Nmehielle (n 11 above) 236.

168   *Louis Emgba Mekongo v. Cameroon* (n 121 above).

the value of such reparation instead of delegating the task to the same government that had perpetrated the violations.

States' compliance with recommendations for remedies is also another area of great concern. Although the Commission has in the past recommended some forms of remedies, the recommendations have largely gone unheeded. The Charter is silent on follow-up to communications, thus, confining the enforcement of the Commission's recommendations to the goodwill of states. Noteworthy, the Commission has embarked on the practice of requiring states to 'report back to the Commission when it submits its next country report in terms of Article 62 on measures taken to comply with' the remedies stated in the recommendations.[169]

It may be argued that this is not an effective follow-up approach because not all state parties to the Charter are faithfully committed to the reporting exercise.[170] Undoubtedly, the African Commission's inability to pronounce effective remedies and the lack of proper follow-up procedures has negatively affected the effectiveness of the African human rights system. It is in this regard that the creation of the African Court on Human and Peoples' Rights is seen as a welcome idea. At least with the Court in place, litigants are assured of binding and enforceable decisions against the respondent states.

---

169   See, for example, communication 211/98, *Legal Resources Foundation v. Zambia*, Fourteenth Annual Activity Report of the African Commission on Human and Peoples' Rights, concluding para. See also communication 241/2001, *Purohit and Moore v. The Gambia*, Sixteenth Annual Activity Report of the African Commission on Human and Peoples Rights (Annex VII), concluding para.

170   The Commission set a good follow-up precedent in communication 87/93, *Constitutional Rights Project v. Nigeria* (n 112 above), where it found a violation of the Charter and recommended that the government of Nigeria should free the complainants. At its 17th Session, the Commission decided to bring the file to Nigeria for a planned mission for purposes of making sure that the violation of rights had been redressed.

CHAPTER 10

THE AFRICAN COURT ON HUMAN AND PEOPLES' RIGHTS

Within less than ten years after the African Charter and Commission came into existence, there was mounting pressure to consider appropriate ways of improving the African human rights system. Several possibilities were mooted, particularly on how the efficiency of the Commission could be enhanced.[1] It was suggested that the Commission be strengthened, complemented, or altogether be replaced by a court. The option of strengthening the Commission was rather a theoretical one because, among other shortcomings, it is not independent of its political parent, the African Union (AU).[2] The option of replacing the Commission with a court was also found not to be very noble because a court is not well-suited to promote human rights by conducting studies or organising conferences. Thus, the 'complementarity' option, comprising of a dual system was most preferable.[3]

The upsurge of the clamour for the creation of an African human rights court cannot solely be attributed to the ineffectiveness of the African Commission. It also has to be viewed against the background of changing world affairs. Between the late 1980s and 1990s, for example, 'African states, having outlived their purpose as proxies during the Cold War era, came under fresh scrutiny, with the protection of human rights increasingly being mandated as a pre-condition for the granting of Western development aid.'[4] There was therefore the need to look for ways of putting straight the already crooked human rights record that was haunting the continent. One

---

1   G Bekker 'The African Court on Human and Peoples' Rights: Safeguarding the Interests of African States' (2007) 51/1 *Journal of African Law* 152.

2   A Van Der Mei 'The new African Court on Human and Peoples' Rights: Towards an effective human rights protection mechanism for Africa?' (2005) 18 *Leiden Journal of International Law* 118.

3   Bekker (n 1 above) 153.

4   As above.

of those ways was through the creation of a robust regional human rights court.

As noted before, some African governments contested the idea of establishing a powerful regional court that would challenge their sovereignty, alleging that African cultures preferred reconciliation over adjudication of disputes.[5] Thus, the idea of a regional human rights court was trapped between two schools of thought; one in favour of a wholesale transfer of the Commission's jurisdiction to the court, the other insisting on a complementary relationship between the two institutions. Eventually, the African Court on Human and Peoples' Rights ('the Court' or 'the African Court') emerged as a compromise, complementing and reinforcing the functions of the Commission.

The adoption of its Protocol on 9 June 1998 and its entry into force on 25 January 2004 heralded the beginning of a new era in the history of the African human rights system.[6] The process of establishing the Court has, however, been very slow and somewhat encumbered with some challenges. These challenges shall be discussed later in detail but at least two of them need to be mentioned here.

First, it took until 25 January 2004 (that is, longer than five years) to ensure the fifteen ratifications required for the entry into force of the Protocol.[7] This is not very encouraging, given the fact that its creation was mooted for more than thirty years.[8] Secondly, while preparations were underway to make the Court operational, the AU decided to merge it with its Court of Justice[9], and suspend

---

5   A Dieng 'Introduction to the African Court on Human and Peoples' Rights' (2005) 15 *INTERIGHTS Bulletin* 3.

6   Protocol to the African Charter on Human and Peoples' Rights on the Establishment of an African Court on Human and Peoples' Rights, OAU Doc OAU/LEG/EXP/ AFCHPR/ PROT (III), available at http://www.achpr.org (accessed 28 May 2010). The Protocol was signed in June 1998 and entered into force on 25 January 2004, 30 days after the requisite 15th ratification (art 34(3) of the Protocol) by the Union of the Comoros.

7   F Viljoen (ed) *The African human rights system: Towards the co-existence of the African Commission on Human and Peoples' Rights and the African Court on Human and Peoples' Rights* (2006) iii.

8   The quest for a regional human rights Court began in the 1961 Lagos Conference that was organised by the International Commission of Jurists.

9   Decision on the Seats of the Organs of the African Union, Assembly/AU/Dec.45 (III).

the process until the modalities of the merger had been considered. Obviously, there are several legal and practical implications of such a merger. With the upsurge of atrocities and other violations taking place across the continent, it is rather disturbing that the court has taken too long to be operationalised. It is therefore commendable that the AU eventually decided to continue with the 'operationalisation' of the Court despite the fact that the complexities of the merger are still being considered.[10] Thus in July 2006, the first eleven Judges of the African Court were sworn in. What follows below is a critical examination of the Court. However, due to the fact that it has not yet begun its proceedings, nor has it formulated its Rules of Procedure, discussions shall be confined to the provisions of the Protocol establishing it.

10.1 ESTABLISHMENT AND COMPOSITION OF THE COURT

The African Court is established to operate within the AU framework, in accordance with Article 1 of its Protocol.[11] As already stated, the Court was established when the Protocol to the African Charter on Human and Peoples' Rights on the Establishment of an African Court on Human and Peoples' Rights (hereafter the 'Court's Protocol' or 'Protocol'), came into force in January 2004. The Protocol consists of thirty-five Articles, addressing various issues pertaining to the Court's composition and operation. It provides for the appointment of eleven judges, nationals of member states of the AU, elected in an individual capacity from among jurists of high moral character and of recognised practical, judicial or academic competence and experience in the field of human and peoples' rights.[12]

The AU correctly noted that the 'moral authority, credibility, and reputation of the ... Court ... will, to a large extent, depend on

---

10   Decision on the Merger of the African Court on Human and Peoples' Rights and the Court of Justice of the African Union, Doc. EX.CL/162(VI).

11   Art 1 of the Protocol reads: 'There shall be established within the Organisation of African Unity an African Court on Human and Peoples' Rights hereinafter referred to as "the Court", the organisation, jurisdiction and functioning of which shall be governed by the present Protocol.'

12   Art 11(1) of the Protocol.

the composition of its first bench.'[13] This is indeed true because all eyes are on the first bench, which is expected to begin the transition from the tradition of the Commission. The Commission has set the tradition of incompetence, lack of motivation and laxity in the way it conducts its activities. Additionally, Amnesty International rightly observed that the 'effectiveness and efficiency of the Court will, to a large extent, depend on the personal and professional capacities of the judges, their skills and experience as well as their commitment and integrity.'[14] It therefore proposed a Checklist to ensure the nomination of the highest qualified candidates for judges as required under Article 11 of the Protocol.[15] Article 14 of the Protocol stipulates that:

1.   The judges of the Court shall be elected by secret ballot by the Assembly from the list referred to in Article 13 (2) of the present Protocol.

2.   The Assembly shall ensure that in the Court as a whole there is representation of the main regions of Africa and of their principal legal traditions.

3.   In the election of the judges, the Assembly shall ensure that there is adequate gender representation.

From the above provisions, it is evident that the Protocol addresses the issue of nomination of judges in a comprehensive manner to avert the possibility of regional and gender imbalance. In tandem with Article 14, the AU has recommended that 'states parties should ensure that at least one (1) of the candidates they nominate is a female and that they give preference to candidates with experience in more than one of the principal legal traditions of Africa (Civil Law, Common Law, Islamic Law, Custom and African Customary Law).'[16] This would allow the Court to greatly harmonise the different interpretations of the Charter provisions based on religious or traditional convictions that might have contributed to its violation in some states.

---

13   *Note Verbale* 5 April 2004, BC/OLC/66.5/8/Vol V para 3.

14   Amnesty International *African Court on Human and Peoples' Rights: Checklist to ensure the nomination of the highest qualified candidates for Judges* AI Index: IOR 63/001/2004.

15   As above, 5.

16   *Note Verbale* (n 13 above) para 2.

The AU proposed a 'geographical representation formula' of the Bench as follows: West Africa—three, Central Africa—two, East Africa—two, Southern Africa—two and North Africa—two.[17] However, this 'formula' was not strictly adhered to in the appointment of the first bench, given that three judges were appointed from North Africa while only one was appointed from East Africa. Generally, however, the distribution is fair since all the geographic regions of the continent were represented. While geographic distribution should be encouraged, the criterion should nonetheless not be used to compromise the competence and moral integrity of the Bench.[18]

The judges are elected for a period of six years and may be re-elected only once.[19] For purposes of continuity, the terms of four judges elected on the first bench expires at the end of two years, and the terms of four other judges expires at the end of four years.[20] Article 15(4) provides that 'all judges except the President shall perform their functions on a part-time basis. However, the Assembly may change this arrangement as it deems appropriate.' This may partly be attributed to the financial constraints facing the AU and the African human rights system. Viewed critically, this is a significant deficiency in comparison with, for example, the European system, whose judges serve on a full-time basis.[21]

As the African Court is an attempt to remedy the weaknesses of the African Commission, it would be better for its judges to serve on full-time basis. The Assembly should therefore exercise its discretion under Article 15(4) of the Protocol to 'change this arrangement' and appropriately provide for a full-time bench.[22] This discretion may be exercised as soon as the court is seized with a reasonable number of cases.

---

17   As above.

18   See Viljoen (n 7 above) iii.

19   Art 15(1) of the Protocol.

20   As above. Art 15(3) provides that: 'A judge elected to replace a judge whose term of office has not expired shall hold office for the remainder of the predecessor's term.'

21   Under the Inter-American human rights system, judges also serve on part-time basis. See Amnesty International (n 14 above).

22   M Banderin 'Recent developments in the African regional human rights system' (2005) 5/1 *Human Rights Law Review* 143.

Independence of the judges of the Court is also guaranteed under the Protocol. Article 17 provides that independence of the Judges shall be fully ensured in accordance with international law.[23] It also restrains a judge from hearing cases in which he or she may have previously taken part as agent, Counsel, advocate for one of the parties, or as a member of a national or international court, or a commission of inquiry, or in any other capacity.[24] The Protocol expressly excludes the participation of judges in cases involving nationals from their country.[25] This is quite contrary to the practice under the Inter-American system which permits judges who are nationals of member states to preside over cases involving their own states.[26]

The position taken by the African system is indeed noble because it gives room for transparency and accountability. A judge who presides over a case involving a national of his or her country may be accused of being biased in the event he or she makes an unpopular decision.[27] Further, this position minimises the likelihood of states nominating judges, not on merit, but on ulterior motives aimed at securing their personal interests.

In the course of their duties, judges of the Court 'shall enjoy, from the moment of their election and throughout their term of office, the immunities extended to diplomatic agents in accordance with international law.'[28] Hence, a judge cannot be held liable for any decision or opinion issued in the exercise of his or her functions.[29] Whereas judges enjoy immunity, they are also prohibited from engaging in any activity that might interfere with their independence or impartiality.[30] This provision of the Protocol accords with the recommendation by the United Nations to the effect that 'state parties to human rights treaties should refrain from nominating

---

23   Art 17(1) of the Protocol.

24   Art 17(2) of the Protocol.

25   Art 22 of the Protocol.

26   See Arts 55 & 41 of the American Convention.

27   Amnesty International (n 14 above) 5.

28   Art 17(3) of the Protocol.

29   Art 17(4) of the Protocol.

30   Art 18 of the Protocol.

or electing to treaty bodies persons performing political functions or occupying positions which were not readily reconcilable with obligations of independent experts under the given treaty.'[31]

Additionally, judges enjoy security of tenure so that they may dispense their duties without any influence, fear or favour instigated by, for example, the state that nominated them. Pursuant to Article 19 of the Protocol, a judge cannot be suspended or removed from office unless by the unanimous decision of the other judges of the Court. Such a decision can only be made on grounds that the judge concerned has been 'found to be no longer fulfilling the required conditions to be a judge of the Court.'[32] This provision is not so clear and it leaves more questions than answers. One may wonder whether the 'requirements' to be fulfilled relate to competence or integrity.

The AU Assembly is empowered by the Protocol to set-aside the decision to suspend or remove a judge.[33] However, the Protocol does not state the grounds upon which the Assembly could decide to reverse such a decision. It is therefore hoped that this provision will be implemented with caution, when the need arises, so as to avert the subordination of the Court to the whims of the Assembly. It should also be made clear, perhaps in the Court's Rules of Procedure, when, how and on what grounds a suspended or removed judge can seek the intervention of the Assembly, in order to avoid unnecessary interference with the Court by the Assembly.

The AHSG is mandated to determine the seat of the Court, within the territory of one of the state parties to the Protocol.[34] Although the Protocol does not specify the location of the Court, it has been proposed that it will be situated in Arusha, Tanzania.[35] In light of the complementary roles between the Court and Commission,

---

31   Report of 8th Meeting of Chairpersons of the UN Treaty Bodies UN General Assembly UN Doc.A/52/507 para 68.

32   Art 19(1) of the Protocol.

33   Art 19(2) of the Protocol.

34   Art 25(1) of the Protocol.

35   Activity Report of the Court for 2006, Assembly/AU/8(VIII). The meetings held dealt with drafting the Court's Rules of Procedure, discussing its budget and the seat of the Court.

it would have been expedient for the two institutions to be located in the same country. Currently, the Secretariat of the Commission is in Banjul, The Gambia, although it also holds sessions in other member states. The location of the Court in relation to that of the Commission is one issue that requires very serious consideration if regional enforcement of human rights is to be meaningful. Arusha being more centrally located, it would be proper for the AHSG to consider the possibility of moving the Commission's Secretariat to this venue for the two institutions to work closely.

Article 25 allows the Court to convene its sessions in the territory of any member state of the AU and for its seat to be changed by the Assembly after due consultation with the Court. This is important because the operations and proceedings of the Court will be impeded in the event its seat is engulfed in war or other related calamities.[36]

Finally, the issue of funding of the Court has also been addressed in the Protocol. According to Article 32, the 'expenses of the Court, emoluments and allowances for judges and the budget of its registry shall be determined and borne by the AU, in accordance with the criteria laid down by the AU, in consultation with the Court.' This is a marked departure from Article 44 of the African Charter, which merely states, 'provision shall be made for the emoluments and allowances of the members of the Commission in the regular budget of the Organisation of African Unity.'

10.2   ACCESS AND JURISDICTION OF THE COURT

10.2.1   ACCESS TO THE COURT

Access to the African Court is regulated by Article 5 of the Protocol, which stipulates as follows:

1.   The following are entitled to submit cases to the Court:

     a)   The Commission
     b)   The state party which had lodged a complaint to the Commission

---

36   Amnesty International (n 14 above).

c) The state party against which the complaint has been lodged at the Commission

d) The state party whose citizen is a victim of human rights violation

e) African Intergovernmental Organisations.

2. When a state party has an interest in a case, it may submit a request to the Court to be permitted to join.

3. The Court may entitle relevant Non-Governmental Organisations (NGOs) with observer status before the Commission, and individuals to institute cases directly before it, in accordance with Article 34 (6) of this Protocol.

Article 34(6) requires states parties to make a declaration accepting the competence of the Court to receive cases under Article 5(3). It reads:

> At the time of the ratification of this Protocol or any time thereafter, the state shall make a declaration accepting the competence of the Court to receive cases under Article 5(3) of this Protocol. The Court shall not receive any petition under Article 5(3) involving a state party which has not made such a declaration.

From the above provisions it is clear that the Court grants two kinds of access: direct (automatic) and indirect (optional). Direct or automatic access is granted to the potential litigants listed under Article 5(1)(a)-(e), while indirect or optional access may be granted to individuals and relevant NGOs with observer status, subject to a state's declaration to that effect. The main reason for the inclusion of Article 34(6) is thought to have been a strategy to encourage states to ratify the Protocol.[37] This is because the Draft Protocol had provided for direct access by individuals and NGOs to the Court in 'urgent cases or serious, systematic or massive violation of human rights', but this was omitted in the final Protocol.[38]

The inclusion of a provision requiring a declaration by states to allow access by individuals is not unique to the African Court. Other human rights instruments have similar provisions. These include: the First Optional Protocol to the International Covenant on Civil and Political Rights[39]; the Optional Protocol to the Convention on the Elimination of All Forms of Discrimination against Women[40]; the Convention against Torture and Other forms of Cruel, Inhuman or Degrading Treatment or Punishment[41]; and the International Convention on the Elimination of All Forms of Racial Discrimination.[42]

Indirect (optional) access is also adopted by the Inter-American system. Under this system, individuals lodge their cases with the Inter-American Commission, which then determines which cases would proceed to the Court.[43] Individuals or NGOs interested in taking part in the proceedings are allowed to act as advisors to the Inter-American Commission. Victims and their representatives also play a crucial role in making arguments on reparations and legal

---

37   M Mutua 'The African human rights court: A two-legged stool?' (1999) 21 *Human Rights Quarterly* 355.

38   Art 6 of the Draft (Nouakchott) Protocol to the African Charter on Human and People's Rights on the Establishment of an African Court on Human and People's Rights 1997, OAU/LEG/EXP/AFCHPR/PROT (2), provided that: 'The Court may entitle NGOs with observer status before the Commission, and individuals to institute directly before it, urgent cases or serious, systematic or massive violations of human rights.' See Baderin (n 22 above) 144.

39   Art 1. See also art 41 of the International Covenant on Civil and Political Rights (ICCPR).

40   Arts 1 & 2.

41   Art 22.

42   Art 14.

43   W Kaguongo 'The questions of *locus standi* and admissibility before the African Court on Human and Peoples' Rights' in Viljoen (n 7 above) 85.

costs.[44] That is why, in both the Inter-American and African systems, no special declaration is required to access the Commissions. As Padilla observed, the Commissions could be seen as 'sieves' to weed out frivolous and unnecessary communications that might find their way to the Courts if direct access were allowed.[45]

The European system, during the co-existence of the European Commission and Court, also made provision for a declaration by states to allow individuals and NGOs to access the Court.[46] Prior to the coming into force of Protocol 11, Articles 25(1) and 46(1) of the European Convention required the High Contracting Parties to make separate declarations to allow the European Commission and Court, respectively, to entertain communications from individuals and NGOs.[47] Under the new arrangement, however, the European Human Rights Court may receive applications from any person, NGO or group of individuals claiming to be victims of a violation by one of the High Contracting Parties.[48]

The rationale for limiting individual and NGOs' access to the African Court, however, needs to be queried. First, one may argue that Article 5, as read together with Article 34(6), grants the state undue protection from proceedings from individuals and NGOs on matters relating to human rights violations.[49] It is needless to re-emphasise that human rights violations are mostly perpetrated by states against individuals. Thus individuals, or human rights NGOs, are more likely to be the complainants.

As a matter of fact, states rarely initiate cases against each other for human rights violations.[50] This argument is vindicated by the

---

44   D Padilla 'An African human rights court: Reflections from the perspective of the Inter-American system' (2002) 2 *African Human Rights Law Journal* 185.

45   As above.

46   See Baderin (n 22 above) 143-144 for a brief discussion on the proactiveness of the European Court of Human Rights in enabling individuals to participate in proceedings before it.

47   R Murray 'A comparison between the African and European Courts of Human Rights' (2002) 2 *African Human Rights Law Journal* 201.

48   As above. See also art 34 of Protocol 11 to the European Convention.

49   A O'Shea 'A critical reflection on the proposed African Court on Human and Peoples' Rights' (2001) 2 *African Human Rights Law Journal* 287-288.

50   Banderin (n 22 above) 145.

records of the African Commission, which has received only a handful inter-state communications since its inception.[51] This is despite grave human rights violations in some African states, such as the Rwandan genocide, crisis in the DRC and the ongoing Darfur crisis in Sudan, just to mention a few examples. Most of the communications before the African Commission have been initiated either by individual victims or NGOs.

Secondly, it is doubtful that many states will be considerate enough to make the declaration contemplated under Article 34(6) of the Protocol.[52] States are generally reluctant to expose themselves to international scrutiny. Again, there has been an ongoing notion that the African human rights system prefers an amicable rather than adversarial dispute resolution mechanism. In view of the foregoing, the motive behind the agitation for a regional human rights court would have been better fulfilled if individuals and NGOs had been allowed automatic or direct access to the Court.[53]

It is true that granting limited access would make the Court appear as a 'forum that evolves human rights jurisprudence aimed at enhancing the realisation of rights by states' and not as a 'court of first instance or an appeal court for all cases.'[54] However, as it stands, the Court could end up serving as an appeal forum for states against unfavourable decisions from the Commission rather than a forum for individuals to obtain legally binding judicial decisions and remedies for the violation of their human rights by their states. The latter is a more dangerous position because the Court would have failed to serve one of the key purposes that led to its establishment, namely, redressing human rights violations perpetrated by the state.

Thus, the failure of a state to make the declaration under Article 34(6) would frustrate the *raison d'être* of the Protocol.[55] One would also argue that nearly all the rights entrenched in the African Charter

---

51   So far, less than five inter-state communications have been presented before the Commission. For the list of these cases visit: http://www1umn.edu/humanrts/Africa/comcases/allcases.html.

52   O'Shea (n 49 above) 288.

53   As above.

54   Kaguongo (n 43 above) 83.

55   As above.

are enforceable against the state and not individuals. Why the state would be the complainant before the Court, as the Protocol seems to suggest, is therefore a legal paradox.

Thirdly, access by NGOs is further restricted to 'relevant NGOs with observer status before the Commission.' While it is possible to determine which NGOs have observer status before the Commission, the term 'relevant' is not so clear. What constitutes a 'relevant NGO' is not known.[56] The wording of this provision therefore generates more questions than answers. Determination of a 'relevant NGO' is a mystery which only the Commission could probably demystify.

It may also be contended that the statement 'the Court *may* entitle...' (emphasis added) in Article 5(3) gives the Court the discretion to either allow or deny access to a 'relevant NGO with observer status'. This imposes a further, and unnecessary, restriction to access to the Court by NGOs.[57] Generally, this provision is very restrictive when compared to what exists under the Inter-American system, where any NGO legally recognised in one or more member states of the OAS may lodge petitions with the Inter-American Commission.[58] It is hoped that the African system will follow this precedent, especially when drafting its Rules of Procedure.

Fourthly, it is not clear whether Article 34(6) places an obligation on states to make the declaration contemplated therein.[59] The Article seems to suggest that states must, at one point or the other, make such a declaration because it uses the word 'shall'. Accordingly, this provision fails to impose a time limit within which the declaration is to be made.[60] Article 14(1) of the International Convention on the Elimination of all Forms of Racial Discrimination and Article 21 of the Convention Against Torture and Other Cruel, Inhuman or Degrading Treatment, which have similar provisions, use the term 'may'. Hence, this provision should be read in the strict sense to

---

56   As above.

57   F Ouguergouz *The African Charter on Human and Peoples' Rights: A comprehensive agenda for human dignity and sustainable democracy in Africa* (2003) 724.

58   See art 44 of the American Convention.

59   Kaguongo (n 43 above) 83.

60   As above.

require states to make a declaration to that effect.[61] It is suggested
that the Rules of Procedure of the Court should address these issues
in a very comprehensive manner in order for the Court to operate
efficiently. Preferably, the Rules should state the time limit within
which a state should make the declaration contemplated in Article
34(6) of the Protocol.

10.2.2   Jurisdiction of the Court

In legal parlance, the term 'jurisdiction' refers to the power of a
court, tribunal or other judicial body to entertain a matter brought
before it. Every judicial mechanism or organ possesses jurisdiction
over matters only to the extent granted to it by the enabling legal
provisions. It follows therefore that the African Court has the
power to entertain cases to the extent the Protocol permits it. The
jurisdictional provisions of the Protocol are very important as they
determine who will have access to the Court, under what conditions,
and what types of violations it can entertain.

In the broader sense, the Protocol grants the Court the following
heads of jurisdiction: personal jurisdiction (*ratione personae*); subject
matter jurisdiction (*ratione materiae*); temporal jurisdiction (*ratione
temporis*); contentious jurisdiction; advisory jurisdiction and;
conciliatory jurisdiction. In the narrower sense, the jurisdiction
of the Court could be categorised into three, namely, contentious
(adjudicatory), advisory and conciliatory.

10.2.2.1 Contentious (Adjudicatory) Jurisdiction

The Court's contentious or adjudicatory powers are conferred
to it by Article 3(1) of the Protocol. In terms of this Article, the
jurisdiction of the Court extends to 'all cases and disputes submitted
to it concerning the interpretation and application of the Charter,
this Protocol and any other relevant human rights instrument
ratified by the states concerned.' When read together with Article
7, the material scope of the contentious jurisdiction seems to be
remarkably broad. Article 7 provides that 'the Court shall apply

the provisions of the Charter and any other relevant human rights instruments ratified by the states concerned.'

These provisions, it has been argued, give the Court a wider adjudicatory jurisdiction than the other regional human rights systems.[62] Accordingly, whereas the European[63] and Inter-American[64] human rights courts' jurisdiction is limited to the conventions under which they were established, the African Court can consider cases brought before it under any human rights treaty ratified by the states concerned. Naldi and Magliveras, for example, described Article 3(1) as 'innovative', and said that the Article:

> would appear to extend the jurisdiction of the Court over any treaty which impinged on human rights in Africa, e.g., the OAU Convention on Refugees, and the African Charter on the Rights and Welfare of the Child, but also UN instruments such as the International Covenants on Human Rights . . . .[65]

Whereas some scholars have insisted that Articles 3(1) and 7 of the Protocol should be interpreted widely enough to allow the Court to adjudicate on human rights instruments other than the African Charter[66], others have advocated for a narrower interpretation because, according to them, these two provisions afford the Court excessively broad jurisdiction.[67] Some of those advocating for a narrower interpretation argue that if the Court exercises its jurisdiction under these provisions, *stricto sensu,* 'jurisprudential chaos' might occur.[68] This, according to the argument, might occur in two ways. First, the

---

62   G Naldi & K Magliveras 'Reinforcing the African system of human rights: The Protocol on the establishment of a regional court of human and peoples' rights' (1998) 16 *Netherlands Quarterly of Human Rights* 435.

63   European Convention, arts 32–34.

64   American Convention, art 62(1).

65   Naldi & Magliveras (n 62 above) 435.

66   See, for example, Mutua (n 37 above) 354; N Udombana 'Toward the African Court on Human and Peoples' Rights: Better late than never' (2000) 3 *Yale Human Rights and Development Law Journal* 90 and W Eno 'The Jurisdiction of the African Court on Human and Peoples' Rights' (2002) 2 *African Human Rights Law Journal* 227–228.

67   See, for example, C Heyns 'The African regional human rights system: In need of reform?' (2001) 2 *African Human Rights Law Journal* 166–168; I "Osterdahl 'The Jurisdiction *Rationae Materiae* of the African Court of Human and Peoples' Rights: A Comparative Critique' (1998) 7 *Revue Africaine des Droits de l'Homme* 138.

68   See, for example, Heyns (n 67 above) 167.

application of treaties other than the Charter would 'creep into' the jurisdiction of other human rights organs and could possibly lead to inconsistent interpretations and applications of those treaties.[69] Secondly, it has been contended that, because this broad jurisdiction exceeds the competence of the African Commission as provided in the African Charter, it would permit the African Court to intrude into 'a faculty the African Commission itself does not possess.'[70]

This latter argument is predicated on the fact that Article 7 of the Protocol goes beyond Article 60 of the African Charter, which mandates the African Commission to:

> draw inspiration from international law on human and peoples' rights, particularly from the provisions of various African instruments on human and peoples' rights, the Charter of the United Nations, the Charter of the Organisation of African Unity, the Universal Declaration of Human Rights, other instruments adopted by the United Nations and by African countries in the field of human and peoples' rights as well as from the provisions of various instruments adopted within the Specialised Agencies of the United Nations of which the parties to the present Charter are members.

Clearly, while the African Commission is expected to draw inspiration from the sources listed in Article 60, its mandate is limited to the interpretation of the African Charter. There is therefore the fear that the apparent jurisdictional asymmetry between the Court and the Commission could give rise to problems in future.[71] Heyns foresees the possibility of states being deterred not only from ratifying the Protocol, but also from the ratification of other human rights treaties.[72]

Some of the arguments for a narrow interpretation of Articles 3(1) and 7 of the Protocol are both exaggerated and unfounded. As Udombana argued, although it is true that the wording of Article 3(1) could deter some states from ratifying other treaties in future, it is rather simplistic to deny the Court substantial jurisdiction purely

---

69   As above.
70   Padilla (n 44 above) 193.
71   Heyns (n 67 above) 167.
72   As above.

on the basis of this argument.[73] If the jurisdiction conferred to the Court by these provisions would scare any state from ratifying a particular treaty, the state's commitment to the promotion and protection of human rights should be queried. The argument on 'jurisprudential chaos' on the basis of different interpretations is also a bit far stretched. Differences in interpretations will obviously occur whenever various organs apply the same instruments, but this may not necessarily result to 'jurisprudential chaos.'[74]

Some of those advocating for a broader interpretation of the above provisions insist that the Court does not deserve to limit itself to the spirit and letter of the African Charter. Instead it must refer to other treaties ratified by the states, including UN treaties, bilateral and multilateral treaties at regional and sub-regional levels. According to Udombana, an aggrieved person who is not adequately covered by the African Charter may bring a case in terms of the Protocol under 'any other international treaty' that provides a higher level of protection, including sub-regional treaties, such as the ECOWAS treaty.[75] Thus, the argument goes on, conferring a wider jurisdiction on the Court would expose those states that took ratification as a public relations exercise. After all, it is further contended, the Court has the discretion either to consider or transfer cases to the African Commission.[76] This should allow the Court to avoid overload and to hear only those cases which have the potential to advance human rights protection in a meaningful way.[77]

The above observations cannot go uncontested. In the main, it is acknowledged that the purpose of a regional mechanism such as the African Court is to interpret and give effect to the norms and instruments promulgated at the regional level. It would, therefore, be highly unusual for an institution from one system (AU) to enforce the treaties of another system (for example UN). Reference to 'any other relevant human rights instrument ratified by the states

---

73   Udombana (n 66 above) 90.

74   As above. See also J Charney 'Is International law threatened by multiple international tribunals?' (1998) 271 *Recueil des cours* 101.

75   Udombana (n 66 above) 90. See also Mutua (n 37 above) 354.

76   Art 6(3) of the Protocol.

77   Eno (n 66 above) 228.

concerned' could therefore mean instruments promulgated within the African region. The use of the word 'relevant' justifies this position.[78] It is inevitable to note, however, that the phrasing of these Articles needs to be revisited and their meaning made clear. As they stand, Articles 3(1) and 7 are ambiguous and confusing.

10.2.2.2 ADVISORY JURISDICTION

In addition to its contentious jurisdiction, the Court is also vested with advisory powers. In this sense, it has the discretionary competence to give advisory opinions 'on any legal matter relating to the Charter or any other relevant human rights instruments, provided that the subject matter of the opinion is not related to a matter being examined by the Commission.'[79] A request for an opinion can be made by the AU, one of the AU organs, an AU member state, or an African organisation recognised by the AU. Like its adjudicatory jurisdiction, the Court possesses an advisory jurisdiction that exceeds that of any other regional human rights system in the sense that it can express itself not only on the Charter but also on 'any other human rights instrument'. The European Convention only entitles the Council of Europe's Committee of Ministers to ask for an opinion,[80] while the American Convention allows the OAS member states and, within their spheres of competence, the OAS organs to do so.[81]

Some aspects of the advisory jurisdiction provisions of the Protocol need further clarification. For example, the inclusion of the AU in Article 4(1) of the Protocol does not seem to add any value to the provision because the AU, by definition, will have to be represented by one of its organs, which in their own right enjoy

---

78   Heyns (n 67 above) 168.

79   See art 4(1) which reads: 'At the request of a member state of the OAU, the OAU, any of its organs, or any African organisation recognised by the OAU, the Court may provide an opinion on any legal matter relating to the Charter or any other relevant human rights instruments, provided that the subject matter of the opinion is not related to a matter being examined by the Commission.'

80   European Convention, art 47.

81   See J Pasqualucci 'Advisory Practice of the Inter-American Court of Human Rights: Contributing to the Evolution of International Human Rights Law' (2002) 38/2 *Stanford Journal of International Law* 241; and T Buergenthal 'The Advisory Practice of the Inter-American Human Rights Court' (1985) 79 *American Journal of International Law* 1.

the right to seek an advisory opinion from the Court.[82] Further, the Protocol is not clear as to whether NGOs having observer status before the African Commission can request for an advisory opinion from the Court.[83]

One might think that the phrase 'any African organisation recognised by the OAU (AU)', under Article 4(1), could be taken to include NGOs with observer status before the Commission. If this is the case, such NGOs might invoke Article 4(1) to apply for an advisory opinion.[84] It could also be argued, to the contrary, that because NGOs in principle have no direct access to the Court in contentious cases, they have no right to request an opinion since they could use this opportunity to argue a case against a member state that has not accepted the Court's jurisdiction in cases brought by NGOs and individuals.

It is evident that the power of the African Court to render advisory opinions is purely discretionary. By allowing NGOs to participate, the opinions of the Court could serve as a reference for a dynamic and progressive interpretation of the African Charter and other human rights treaties.[85] Like in the case of the Inter-American Court, the Protocol should have made it possible for the African Court to give opinions on the compatibility of national legislation or practices with international human rights law.[86] This is significant because the possibility of these organs obtaining clarification from the African Court could contribute to the objective application of human rights treaties and the development of universal human rights jurisprudence on the continent.[87]

---

82   Van Der Mei (n 2 above) 121.

83   As above.

84   As above.

85   As above.

86   See American Convention, art 64(2).

87   K Hopkins 'The effect of the African Court on the domestic legal orders of African states' (2002) 2 *African Human Rights Law Journal* 234.

10.2.2.3 Conciliatory Jurisdiction

In the course of its proceedings, the Court may try to reach an amicable settlement in a case pending before it.[88] As already stated, the Charter and the African human rights system at large, favours the amicable settlement of disputes approach. Article 9 is discretionary in the sense that it uses the word 'may'. It is not known whether the contending parties will be allowed to request for an amicable settlement of a pending case or the Court would do so at its own volition.[89] It is important that cases be allowed to proceed to a completion so that the human rights jurisprudence of the African system may be developed. An amicable settlement may not allow for such development.[90]

There is an apparent dilemma in conferring both conciliatory and adjudicatory powers on a single body. This has been one of the causes of disquiet in the African Commission, whose practice has leaned more towards conciliation than adjudication. The Court should give a careful thought on this arrangement when drafting its rules of procedure. This, however, should not be taken to mean that amicable settlement is an inappropriate task for a judicial body.[91] Rather, expediency demands that the Court should concentrate on adjudicatory functions and leave the quasi-judicial functions to the Commission. Where the parties to a dispute agree to resolve it amicably, the Court may transfer the matter to the Commission for settlement. Accordingly, this would save the Court's time and also that of the parties.[92]

10.3   Procedures of the Court

---

88   Art 9 of the Court's Protocol provides that, 'the Court may try to reach an amicable settlement in a case pending before it in accordance with the provisions of the Charter.'

89   Van Der Mei (n 2 above) 121.

90   As above.

91   For the propriety or otherwise of having a judicial body performing both adjudicatory and conciliatory functions, see generally E Whinney *Judicial settlement of international disputes: Jurisdiction, justiciability and judicial law-making on the contemporary international court* (1991) 7; C Chinkin 'Alternative dispute resolution under international law' in M Evans (ed) *Remedies in international law: The institutional dilemma* (1998) 128-129.

92   Van Der Mei (n 2 above) 121.

Article 33 of the Protocol provides that the Court shall draw up its own rules and determine its own procedures in consultation with the Commission.[93] As at the moment, the Court's rules of procedure have not been drafted, therefore no detailed discussion on the Court's procedures may be meaningful. The Protocol, however, has scanty provisions that may serve as guidelines to some procedural aspects of the Court. These provisions touch on, for example, admissibility and consideration of cases, judgements and remedies.

10.3.1 ADMISSIBILITY AND CONSIDERATION OF CASES

Like its counterpart the African Commission, the starting point of consideration of cases by the Court is the admissibility stage. According to Article 6(2) of the Protocol, the Court 'shall rule on the admissibility of cases taking into account the provisions of Article 56 of the Charter.' Article 56 of the Charter lays down seven admissibility requirements that must be fulfilled before a communication is considered on merit. These requirements as well as the jurisprudence of the African Commission relating thereto were discussed at length in the previous chapter.

Noteworthy, the Court is permitted to request the opinion of the Commission before making a decision on the admissibility of a case instituted by relevant NGOs or individuals.[94] In such cases, the Commission is not mandated to give a 'ruling' but an 'opinion', meaning that the Court would then have to give a ruling on the admissibility of such a case.[95] Due to this, the Protocol is thought to be initiating an unnecessary movement of a case between the Court and the Commission.[96] This situation is aggravated by the fact that the Court may eventually decide to defer the determination of a case to the Commission.[97] Thereafter, assuming the case to be admissible,

---

93   Art 33 reads: 'the Court shall draw up its Rules and determine its own procedures.
       The Court shall consult the Commission as appropriate.'

94   Art 6(1) of the Court's Protocol.

95   Murray (n 47 above) 203.

96   O'Shea (n 49 above) 295.

97   Art 6(3) provides that 'The Court may consider cases or transfer them to the
       Commission.'

the Court may decide to refer the case back to the Commission for determination on merit.

The approach of the Inter-American system and its European counterpart (prior to the Protocol 11 amendment) differs from that of the African system in that the Commissions under both systems would make preliminary decisions on admissibility.[98] This limits the movement of a case between the Commission and the Court. The European Court at one time held that all admissibility questions had to be raised before the Commission first, and not come to the Court for the first time.[99] It would be expedient to have such an approach adopted under the African system.

In relation to post-admissibility consideration of cases, the Protocol does not indicate clearly the procedure to be followed or the conditions under which admissible cases may subsequently be referred to the Commission. The Protocol only provides that 'the Court may consider cases or transfer them to the Commission.'[100] Consequently, in exercising its discretion under Article 6(3), the Court is expected to act as a filter and channel some cases back to the Commission. This clearly demonstrates the inefficiency of a two-tier system where both organs may receive the same types of complaints.[101] The scanty provisions dealing with the relationship between the Commission and the Court give insufficient guidance on how the machinery will operate in practice.

In the course of its proceedings, the Court is expected to conduct public hearings, unless otherwise required by its Rules of Procedure.[102] Whereas the African Commission's complaints process has largely been conducted in private, it is encouraging to see the Protocol provide for public proceedings. As Murray argued, through public hearings, potential litigants will be acquainted with the procedures of the Court.[103] What remains is for the Court,

---

98   O'Shea A (n 49 above) 295.
99   *De Wilde, Ooms and Versyp v. Belgium* ECHR (18 June 1971) Ser A 12 para 48.
100   Art 6(3) of the Court's Protocol.
101   Dieng (n 5 above) 5.
102   Art 10(1) of the Court's Protocol.
103   Murray (n 47 above) 203.

preferably in its Rules of Procedure, to define the scope of 'public hearings'. Under the European system, for example, the concept of public hearing also requires the public disclosure of all documents.[104]

Litigants before the African Court have the right to legal representatives of their choice.[105] Where the interests of justice so require, free legal representation may be provided for an indigent litigant.[106] Given the abject poverty in many African states, it is believed that this is essential in trying to ensure that litigants, irrespective of their economic status, are heard by the Court. It is necessary for the Rules of Procedure to clarify the qualifications of the legal representatives that would appear before the Court. Additionally, the question of who should shoulder the expenses of the legal representative— whether it is the state party concerned or the Court— needs to be clarified.[107]

According to Article 26, the Court shall hear submissions by all parties and, if deemed necessary, hold an enquiry.[108] Such inquiries could be in the nature of on-site visits to establish allegations presented before it by the litigants. In this regard, the states concerned are obligated to assist in the process by providing relevant facilities for the efficient handling of the case.[109] This provision is important, especially because it safeguards the victim from the mischief of a recalcitrant state that may wish to destroy or withhold crucial evidence.

Pursuant to Article 26(2), the Court is empowered to receive written or oral evidence, including expert testimony. In tandem with this provision and given the vastness of the continent, the Court could receive foreign depositions instead of requiring the physical presence of witnesses for *de novo* trials. Video-taped recordings of witness testimony rendered on oath with all the guarantees of due

---

104   Rule 33(3) of the Rules of the European Court makes specific mention of documents being accessible to the public.

105   Art 10(2).

106   As above.

107   Murray (n 47 above) 203.

108   Art 26(1).

109   As above.

process could be used to facilitate this process.[110] These economical measures can go a long way towards accelerating the litigation of cases and mitigating related expenses. This will help to reduce the length of proceedings.

As part of its procedures, the Court is also empowered to adopt interim measures. Article 27(2) provides that 'in cases of extreme gravity and urgency, and when necessary to avoid irreparable harm to persons, the Court shall adopt such provisional measures as it deems necessary.' The importance of interim measures in preventing irreparable harm to victims of violations has been discussed at length in our discussion on the procedures of the African Commission. It is expected that the rules of procedure will address this issue comprehensively and, where need be, specify the consequences of breaching them. As already stated, states have not been taking seriously the interim measures pronounced by the African Commission. Hopefully, the Court will not be treated with equal contempt.

10.3.2 JUDGEMENTS OF THE COURT

The Court is entitled to make findings and order appropriate remedies when it establishes a violation of rights.[111] The judgements of the Court, decided by majority of the judges, would be final and not subject to appeal.[112] However, the Court can review its decisions in the light of new evidence.[113] In cases where the judgment of the Court is not unanimous, either in whole or in part, any judge would be entitled to deliver a separate or dissenting opinion.[114]

A novel feature of the Protocol that distinguishes the Commission from the Court is that it requires the Court to render its judgements 'within ninety days of having completed its deliberations.'[115] Perhaps, this is to ensure a speedier dispensation of justice. It is a prerequisite

---

110   Padilla (n 44 above) 192.
111   Art 27(1) of the Court's Protocol.
112   Art 28(2) of the Court's Protocol.
113   Art 28(3) of the Court's Protocol.
114   Art 28(7) of the Court's Protocol.
115   Art 28(1) of the Court's Protocol.

for the judgements to be reasoned, and must be read in open Court, due notice having been given to the parties.[116] The effect of this provision is to avert the possibility of the Court resorting to the initial practice of the Commission where judgements were neither reasoned nor detailed.

The above provisions notwithstanding, it should be stated categorically that the ability of the Court to impact the African human rights system will largely depend on how binding its judgements would be. Article 30 of the Protocol provides that states parties 'undertake to comply with the judgement in any case to which they are parties within the time stipulated by the African Court and to guarantee its execution.' This provision imputes on states the primary responsibility for the execution of the judgements of the Court. Apart from this Article, there does not seem to be any specific recourse provided in the Protocol against a state that deliberately refuses to comply with the Court's judgement.[117]

Arguably, Article 30 only emphasises the voluntary nature of the execution of judgements, and has nothing to do with imputing an obligation on states to ensure the same.[118] The phrase 'states undertake' does not seem to carry the requisite force to compel a recalcitrant state to comply with the Court's judgement. The Court does not therefore possess any express powers to ensure that its judgements are respected, and thus appears to be powerless to react when its decisions are ignored. Consequently, the effectiveness of the Court appears to hinge on the willingness of states to comply with its decisions.

On a more positive note, however, the Protocol provides for mechanisms which may be used to compel states to comply with the Court's judgements. For example, it requires judgements to be brought to the notice of the member states of the AU as well as the African Commission.[119] Additionally, the Court is required to submit, in each regular session of the AU Assembly, a report on its

---

116   Art 28(5) & (6) of the Court's Protocol.

117   Hopkins (n 87 above) 238.

118   As above.

119   Art 29(1) of the Court's Protocol.

work during the previous year.[120] The report would include cases in which a state has not complied with the Court's judgment.

Hopefully, the involvement of the Assembly in the activities of the Court will compel states to comply with its judgements.[121] This is because the Constitutive Act of the African Union provides for mechanisms to ensure compliance with supranational decisions. For example, it provides for sanctions against states that fail to comply with the Act.[122]

The AU is therefore expected to protect the integrity of the regional human rights system by adopting measures that are necessary to ensure compliance with the Court's judgement. Moreover, the involvement of the Executive Council of the AU in the monitoring of the Court's judgements should be seen as an added impetus to the effective operation of the Court.[123] The Council will perhaps be instrumental in ensuring that national courts play a crucial role in the enforcement of the judgements of the African Court. In the Inter-American system, the Inter-American Court's judgments on reparations are executed in national courts.[124] Unfortunately, there is no similar provision in either the African Charter or the Protocol on the African Court.

10.3.3 REMEDIES

Most international human rights instruments recognise the right of victims of human rights abuses to receive remedies. Remedies are diverse and their award depends on many different factors and circumstances.[125] Article 27(1) of the Protocol to the African Court deals with the issue of remedies in the following terms:

---

120 Art 31 of the Court's Protocol.

121 Hopkins (n 87 above) 238.

122 See the Constitutive Act of the African Union, art 23.

123 The Court's Protocol, art 29(2).

124 Art 26 of the American Convention.

125 A Waris 'The remedies, application and enforcement provisions of the African Court on Human and Peoples' rights' in Viljoen (n 7 above) 101.

If the Court finds that there has been a violation of a human or peoples' rights, it shall make appropriate orders to remedy the violation, including the payment of fair compensation or reparation....

Essentially, the Court is given a very wide discretion to order remedies whatever it deems 'appropriate'. This provision does not state the exact nature or type of orders or remedies the Court may grant, other than 'compensation' or 'reparation'. Thus, in exercising its wide discretion, the Court may choose to pronounce some remedial measures, such as injunctions and sanctions.[126] It is important that the Court avoids a restrictive interpretation of its remedial powers by ordering adequate reparation whenever the interests of justice demand.

When awarding remedies, the Court should also determine the issue of costs. The Protocol is silent on how this issue should be treated. While the Protocol provides for 'free legal representation', for example, there is no indication of who should bear the costs of such.[127] The rules of procedure should therefore clarify whether parties will be allowed to make prayers for costs and how the Court should determine such prayers.[128]

As a general analysis, the African Court has more potential to contribute to the effective enforcement of human rights in Africa than its counterpart, the African Commission. In order to ensure its place among the eminent judicial bodies[129], however, the Court, through its Rules of Procedure, must think strategically of how it will operate efficiently.[130] Among other ways, it should be innovative in the presentation and enforcement of its judgements.

126　As above.

127　Murray (n 47 above) 218.

128　As above.

129　Such as the Inter-American and European human rights Courts.

130　Murray (n 47 above) 218.

10.4   RELATIONSHIP BETWEEN THE COURT, THE COMMISSION, THE AU AND OTHER RELEVANT HUMAN RIGHTS BODIES

10.4.1   RELATIONSHIP BETWEEN THE COURT AND COMMISSION

The Court has not been established to replace but to complement and reinforce the Commission. This fact can be deduced from the preamble and other provisions of the Protocol. The last paragraph of the preamble to the Protocol emphasises that 'the attainment of the objectives of the African Charter on Human and Peoples' Rights requires the establishment of an African Court on Human and Peoples' Rights to complement and reinforce the functions of the African Commission on Human and Peoples' Rights.' In such circumstances, one would expect the Protocol to set out clearly the relationship between the Commission and the Court, yet it does not. Rather, as O'Shea correctly observed, the relationship between the two institutions is only dealt with in the most general terms, which give little if any hint as to how the machinery actually works.[131]

Article 2 provides that the Court shall 'complement the protective mandate' of the Commission. Article 8 requires that Rules of the Court should indicate when cases should be brought before it 'bearing in mind the complementarity between the Commission and the Court.'[132] This appears to suggest that the African Court will only consider cases which have gone through the Commission, thus following the initial approach of the European human rights system.[133]

Prior to the adoption of Protocol 11 to the European Convention, the European Commission looked at admissibility, tried to reach a friendly settlement, and reported if there was a breach.[134] It would send the case to the Committee of Ministers to be enforced, or it

---

131   O'Shea (n 49 above) 293.

132   Art 8 reads: 'The Rules of Procedure of the Court shall lay down the detailed conditions under which the Court shall consider cases brought before it, bearing in mind the complementarity between the Commission and the Court.'

133   O'Shea (n 49 above) 293.

134   Murray (n 47 above) 198.

could choose to submit the case to the Court, if the state concerned had accepted its jurisdiction. There was a presumption in this system that the European Commission, rather than the Court, would have primary responsibility for fact-finding.[135] This delegation of responsibility between a Commission, that deals with disputes of facts and a Court which looks at disputes of law, might be useful for the African system.[136]

Under the African system, the Commission is conferred with both a promotional and protective mandate. It may be deduced from the provisions of Article 2 of the Protocol that the complementarity between the Court and the Commission does not specifically affect the promotional, but rather the protective, mandate of the Commission. In relation to their common protective mandate, the Protocol does not, however, contain any significant details regarding how this will be shared between the Court and the Commission—especially in relation to the filing of complaints by individual 'victims' of human rights violations and NGOs.[137]

The Protocol also initiates a relationship between the Court and the Commission with regard to admissibility proceedings. Article 6(1) intimates that 'the Court, when deciding on the admissibility of a case instituted under Article 5(3) of this Protocol, may request the opinion of the Commission which shall give it as soon as possible.' Also, Article 6(2) provides that the Court shall take the provisions of Article 56 of the African Charter into account when considering the admissibility of all cases. While Article 56 of the Charter provides a catalogue of admissibility requirements, it has nothing to do with the Commission's relationship with the Court.

It is therefore necessary for the two institutions to harmonise their rules of procedure in order to enhance their relationship. Article 33 of the Protocol intimates that the Court 'shall consult as appropriate with the Commission' when it draws up its rules of

---

135   As above. See also J Merrills *The development of international law by the European Court of Human Rights* (1993) 10; L Clements 'Striking the right balance: The new Rules of Procedure for the European Court of Human Rights' (1999) 3 *European Human Rights Law Review* 267.

136   Murray (n 47 above) 198.

137   As above.

procedure. The Commission should also consider revising its rules to conform with those of the Court. The successes of the Court would depend on, among other things, its viable working relationship with the Commission.[138] A number of proposals on how to enhance the relationship between the two institutions have been mooted in the next part of this book.

10.4.2 RELATIONSHIP BETWEEN THE COURT AND AU AND ITS ORGANS

The AU and its organs relate with the Court in more than one way. For instance, the Assembly of the AU is paramount in the appointment of the judges of the Court.[139] Thus, it is instrumental in ensuring the competence or otherwise of the Court. Additionally, the Assembly may reverse a decision to suspend or remove a judge from office.[140] The Assembly also determines the seat of the Court and may change it after due consultation with the Court.[141] Further, the Court is required to submit to each regular session of the Assembly, a report on its work during the previous year.[142] The Union also determines the expenses of the Court, emoluments and allowances for judges and the budget of its registry.[143]

Another organ of the AU that has relationship with the Court is the Executive Council (formerly Council of Ministers). Article 29(2) of the Protocol indicates that the Council shall monitor the execution of judgements of the Court on behalf of the Assembly. Meanwhile, the African Commission does not have a direct relation with the Executive Council in as far as its reports are submitted directly to the Assembly.[144] It would therefore be important to involve the Council in the reports of the Commission to

---

138   I Badawi 'The future relationship between the African Court and the African Commission' (2002) *African Human Rights Law Journal* 253.

139   See arts 11-15 of the Court's Protocol.

140   Art 19(2) of the Court's Protocol.

141   Art 25(1) & (2) of the Court's Protocol.

142   Art 31 of the Court's Protocol.

143   Art 32 reads: 'Expenses of the Court, emoluments and allowances for judges and the budget of its registry, shall be determined and borne by the OAU, in accordance with criteria laid down by the OAU in consultation with the Court.'

144   Arts 52, 53, 54 & 58 of the African Charter.

ensure proper follow-up on the work of both the Court and the Commission, given the complementarity between them, especially in the protective mandate.[145]

The AU Court of Justice is also expected to have relationship with the African human rights Court, although both are encompassed in uncertainty on their future relationship. In the main, there is the ongoing debate on how to merge the two institutions.[146] The official explanation for such a merger was that it would be financially expedient to do so.[147] After the matter of the merged Court had been referred back and forth between the Permanent Representatives Council (PRC), Legal Experts and the Executive Council, a Meeting of Governmental Legal Experts was scheduled to be held in Algiers in order to consider a draft instrument prepared by the Algerian foreign minister and former president of the International Court of Justice, Dr Mohammed Bedjaoui.[148] However, due to the fact that only 22 member states turned up for this meeting and that the necessary quorum was therefore lacking, a working group was constituted instead to consider the matter.[149]

The meeting adopted a Draft Protocol on the Statute of the African Court of Justice and Human Rights, which introduced a number of fundamental changes to the Draft Protocol on the Integration of the African Court on Human and Peoples' Rights and the AU Court of Justice. The Draft Protocol attempted to change the content of the Protocol Establishing the Human Rights Court, in particular making individual petitions automatic.[150] This attempt, however, was resisted by a number of states in that, although

---

145   Amnesty International (n 14 above) 10.

146   See paras 4 & 5 of Assembly/AU/Dec 45(III). See also F Viljoen & E Baimu 'Courts for Africa: Considering the co-existence of the African Court on Human and Peoples' Rights and the African Court of Justice' (2004) 22/2 *Netherlands Quarterly of Human Rights* 241-267.

147   As above.

148   Bekker (n 1 above) 170.

149   As above. See also Report of the Meeting of Government Legal Experts on the Merger of the African Court on Human and Peoples' Rights and the Court of Justice of the African Union, EX.CL/211(VII).

150   Bekker (n 1 above) 170. See also art 32 of the Draft Protocol on the Statute of the African Court of Justice and Human Rights, UA/EXP/Fusion cours3(I).

a modified version of this draft was tabled at the AU Summit in Khartoum in January 2006, no decision was taken on it.[151]

Similarly, in a subsequent meeting held in May 2006, no agreement could be reached in relation to issues of jurisdiction, signature and ratification, and these matters were deferred for discussion at the AU Summit meeting in July 2006.[152] Again, no decision was reached, prompting the legal instruments to be referred to the Ministers of Justice and Attorneys-General from member states. The apparent lack of political will to conclude the issue of the merger of the two courts serves as a clear indication that the interests of states prevail over the dire need of a workable regional human rights system. States should be more committed to their obligation to ensure an effective regional human rights system.

10.4.3 RELATIONSHIP BETWEEN THE COURT AND OTHER HUMAN RIGHTS MECHANISMS IN THE REGION

While the question of the relationship between the Court and Commission has received some attention and suggestions, the same cannot be said of the relationship between the Court and other regional human rights enforcement institutions, such as the Committee of Experts on the Rights and Welfare of the Child.[153] As already argued above, the Court can apply human rights instruments adopted under the African system. Apart from the African Charter, other relevant human right instruments under the African system include the African Charter on the Rights and Welfare of the Child (ACRWC)[154] and the Protocol on the Rights of Women in Africa.[155]

Article 32 of ACRWC establishes an African Committee of Experts on the Rights and Welfare of the Child with a mandate 'to promote and protect the rights and welfare of the child.' Part of its protective mandate is to 'interpret the provisions of the Charter at the request of a state party, an institution of the Organisation of

---

151   As above.

152   As above.

153   Banderin (n 22 above) 147.

154   CAB/LEG/24.9/49 (1990); 9 IHRR 870 (2002).

155   See protocol to the African Charter on Human and Peoples' Rights on the Rights of Women in Africa.

African Unity or any other person or institution recognised by the Organisation of African Unity, or any state party.'[156] Article 44(1) of the ACRWC mandates the Committee to 'receive communication, from any person, group or Non-Governmental Organisation recognised by the Organisation of African Unity, by a member state, or the United Nations relating to any matter covered by this Charter.'

However, Article 5 of the Protocol of the African Court does not list the Committee on the Rights and Welfare of the Child as one of the institutions with direct access to the Court. Consequently, initiating a case alleging the violation of the ACRWC may depend on the goodwill of states parties to the Protocol or African intergovernmental organisations.[157] This is a complex situation given that most African states are unwilling to commence proceedings against each other. There is, therefore, the need to address this issue in the Court's Rules of Procedure in order to enhance the relationship between the Court and the Committee on the Rights and Welfare of the Child. Fortunately, the African Women's Protocol does not present this problem as its Article 27 confers its enforcement to the African Court.[158]

The relationship between the Court and other regional economic courts is also of concern. Possible conflicts may arise in relation to jurisdiction especially in the area of intersection between human rights and economic development.[159] Perhaps the African Court would do well to take such concerns on board, concentrating on ensuring that the African Charter is incorporated at both sub-regional and national levels. Viable lessons could be learned from the European experience where it has been stressed that there is the need for regional bodies to focus on ensuring rights are enforced at the national level.[160] One task of the African Court should therefore be to forge a relationship with the national judicial and human rights systems.

156   African Charter on the Rights and Welfare of the Child, art 42(c).
157   Banderin (n 22 above) 148.
158   As above.
159   As above.
160   L Hill 'Universality versus subsidiarity: A reply' (1998) 1 *European Human Rights Law Review* 75.

CHAPTER 11

AFRICAN COMMITTEE OF EXPERTS ON THE RIGHTS AND WELFARE OF THE CHILD

11.1 STRUCTURE AND COMPOSITION

The African Committee of Experts on the Rights and Welfare of the Child (hereafter 'the African Committee', 'Committee of Experts' or 'the Committee') is the main regional body exclusively mandated to promote and protect children's rights in Africa.[1] The Committee was established by the Assembly of Heads of State and Government (AHSG) of the former Organisation of African Unity (OAU) on 10 July 2001. It comprises 11 members of 'high moral standing, integrity, impartiality and competence in the matters of the rights and welfare of the child.'[2] The members, who are from different nationalities, serve in their personal capacity.[3] Normally, they are elected by the Assembly by secret ballot, from a list of persons nominated by the states parties to the African Charter on the Rights and Welfare of the Child (hereafter 'Children's Charter' or 'the Charter').[4]

Procedurally, each state party to the Children's Charter is allowed to nominate a maximum of two candidates, one of whom shall not be a national of that state.[5] Interested states are to nominate their candidates at least six months before the elections,[6] after which the list of nominees shall be communicated to Heads of State and

---

1   According to art 32 of the African Charter on the Rights and Welfare of the Child, 'An African Committee of Experts on the Rights and Welfare of the Child hereinafter called 'the Committee' shall be established within the Organisation of African Unity to promote and protect the rights and welfare of the child.'

2   Children's Charter, art 33(1).

3   Children's Charter, art 33(2) & (3).

4   Children's Charter, art 34.

5   Children's Charter, art 35.

6   Children's Charter, art 36(1).

Government at least two months prior to the elections.[7] Once elected, Committee members are liable to serve for a non-renewable term of five years.[8] However, the terms of four of the members elected at the first election expires after two years and the term of six others, after four years. In discharging their duties, members of the Committee enjoy the privileges and immunities provided for in the General Convention on the Privileges and Immunities adopted by the former OAU.[9]

A number of issues concerning the structure and composition of the Committee need to be underscored. First, it should be noted that, unlike the African Commission on Human and Peoples' Rights, the issue of independence and incompatibility of members of the Committee appears to have been taken more seriously.[10] The Committee has on a number of occasions sought to ensure that members' positions do not interfere with the functions of the Committee. For example, when one member, Mrs. Seynabou Diakhate was nominated as judge to the West African Monetary and Economic Union, and another one, Mrs. Dawlat Hassan, was appointed as Advisor to the MinIster of Agriculture and International Relations in her country, the Committee determined whether or not their new positions were incompatible with the functions of the Committee.[11] After deliberating on the issue in detail, the Committee concluded that the appointments were not incompatible with the functions of the Committee and therefore retained the two members.

Earlier, a Committee member from Togo, Mme Aho, tendered her resignation after being appointed the Minister of Health, Social Affairs, Promotion of Women and Protection of the Child,

---

7   Children's Charter, art 36(2) stipulates, 'the Secretary-General of the Organisation of African Unity shall draw up in alphabetical order, a list of persons nominated and communicate it to the Heads of State and Government at least two months before the elections.'

8   Children's Charter, art 37(1).

9   Children's Charter, art 41.

10   R Murray 'Children's rights in the OAU' in R Murray (ed) *Human rights in Africa* (2004) 168.

11   B Mezmur 'The 9th ordinary session of the African Committee of Experts on the Rights and Welfare of the Child: Looking back to look ahead' (2007) 7 *African Human Rights Law Journal* 547.

a position which threatened her independence and impartiality.[12] Similarly, former Committee members from Chad, Mme Motoyam, and Senegal, Mme Sow, resigned because they had secured new employment at UNICEF and the United Nations International Criminal Tribunal for Rwanda (ICTR), respectively.[13] Chad and Senegal therefore had to propose alternative candidates to serve the remainder of the members' terms, in accordance with Article 39 of the Children's Charter.[14]

Another issue concerning the Committee that needs to be underscored relates to its gender and geographical composition. The Children's Charter is silent on these two crucial issues. Although the gender balancing of the Committee has in the past been satisfactory (six female and five male),[15] geographical representation has been ignored. Initially the Committee had no member from North Africa, despite the fact that Algeria, Egypt and Libya are parties to the Charter. Notwithstanding the fact that this imbalance was addressed with the election of a Committee member from Egypt, Mrs. Dawlut Hassan, in 2006, states should always take heed of geographical representation in future appointments to the Committee.

Moreover, it is not understood why the drafters of the Charter preferred that members of the Committee should serve for a single non-renewable term. This is contrary to the other enforcement institutions under the African human rights system, such as the African Commission and Court on Human and Peoples' Rights. Commissioners of the African Commission, for example, are elected for a six-year term and are eligible for re-election.[16] Similarly, judges of the African Court are elected 'for a period of six years'

---

12   A Lloyd 'Report of the second ordinary session of the African Committee of experts on the rights and welfare of the child' (2003) 3 *African Human Rights Law Journal* 332.

13   As above.

14   Children's Charter, art 39 provides that 'If a member of the Committee vacates his office for any reason other than the normal expiration of a term, the state which nominated that member shall appoint another member from among its nationals to serve for the remainder of the term, subject to the approval of the Assembly.'

15   See J Sloth-Nielsen & B Mezmur 'Win some, lose some: The 10th ordinary session of the African Committee of Experts on the Rights and Welfare of the Child' (2008) 8 *African Human Rights Law Journal* 213.

16   See the African Charter on Human and Peoples' Rights, art 36.

and may be re-elected once.'[17] The motivation for restricting the appointment of members of the Committee of Experts to a non-renewable term of five years is therefore not clear.

Although the Executive Council of the African Union (AU) has requested the AU Commission to study measures to renew the terms of office of the Committee members for another term,[18] nothing seems to have been done in this regard. It would be expedient for the terms of office of the Committee members to be brought in line with those of the African Commission and the Court in order to encourage uniformity under the African human rights system.

Finally, it is apparent that the establishment of a Secretariat for the Committee has been taken for granted. Article 40 of the Children's Charter mandated the 'Secretary-General of the Organisation of the African Unity to appoint a Secretary for the Committee'. This provision remained a dead letter until as recently as 2007, when the Secretary was appointed.[19] Such a delay is rather unfortunate given that a Secretariat is very essential in the administration of Committees of this nature. Having formally acknowledged the importance of establishing a functional Secretariat, the AU should now assist in the recruitment of competent staff.

11.2   MANDATE OF THE COMMITTEE

The Committee's mandate is stipulated in Chapter 3 of the Children's Charter. Accordingly, Article 42 mandates it to perform four functions, namely[20]:

(a)   To promote and protect the rights enshrined in the Charter.

(b)   To monitor the implementation and ensure protection of the rights enshrined in the Charter.

(c)   To interpret the provisions of the Charter at the request of a state party, an institution of the AU or any other

---

17   See the Protocol to the African Charter on Human and Peoples' Rights Establishing the African Court on Human and Peoples' Rights, art 15 (1).

18   See Decision EX/CL/233(VII) of 2005 para 8.

19   Sloth-Nielsen & Mezmur (n 15 above) 210.

20   Children's Charter, art 42 (a)-(d).

person or institution recognised by the AU, or any state party.

(d)   To perform such other task as may be entrusted to it by the Assembly of the AU and any other organs of the AU or the United Nations (UN).

Noteworthy, like the African Commission, the Committee is entrusted with promotional, protective and interpretive functions. It is interesting to note that the Committee is equally mandated to take instructions from the UN. However, the Charter fails to clarify the nature and scope of the tasks the Committee can perform with instruction from the UN. Arguably, in the absence of clarity in this regard, this provision could be interpreted to mean that the Committee can only perform those tasks that are in line with its mandate and functions as stipulated in the Charter.

In addition to the above stated functions, the Committee possesses broad investigatory powers through which it may resort to any appropriate methods of investigating any matter falling within the ambit of the Charter, including measures a state party has taken to implement the Charter.[21] It may request from the state party any information that is relevant to the implementation of the Charter. By virtue of this mandate, the Committee is vested with considerable powers to hold states accountable if they fail to promote and protect the rights and welfare stipulated in the Charter. If this mandate is exercised properly, the Committee could become a formidable guardian of children's rights on the continent.[22]

11.2.1   THE COMMITTEE'S PROMOTIONAL MANDATE

11.2.1.1 GENERAL PROMOTIONAL ACTIVITIES

In the performance of its promotional functions, Article 42(a) mandates the Committee to, among other things, (i) collect and document information; (ii) commission inter-disciplinary assessment of situations on African problems in the fields of the rights and

---

21   Children's Charter, art 45(1).

22   G Naldi 'Future trends of human rights in Africa' in M Evans & R Murray (eds) *The African Charter on Human and Peoples' Rights: The system in practice: 1986-2000* (2002) 17.

welfare of the child; (iii) organise meetings, encourage national and local institutions concerned with the rights and welfare of the child; (iv)where necessary give its views and make recommendations to governments; and (v) cooperate with other African, international and regional institutions and organisations concerned with the promotion and protection of the rights and welfare of the child.[23]

The Committee has, since its inception, indulged in a number of activities that would ensure the promotion of the rights and welfare of the child throughout the continent. For example, it has initiated the Day of the African Child (DAC), Pan-African Forum for Children (PAFC) and lobbying and investigation missions. Moreover, in recent times it has allowed a number of national institutions and Non-Governmental Organisations (NGOs) to attend its sessions or participate in some of its activities. It has also drafted criteria for granting observer status to such organisations. During the 9th meeting, the Chairperson of the Committee called on interested organisations to submit their requests for observer status by the latest in May 2008.[24]

The DAC is a special day set a side by the former OAU Council of Ministers to be commemorated every year in every member state with a special programme.[25] This day has been recognised since 1991 and is celebrated every year on 16 June. It coincides with the 1976 Soweto uprising in South Africa, where thousands of black school children were massacred as they marched in the streets to protest the inferior quality of their education and to demand their right to be taught in their own languages.[26] The day serves as an advocacy and awareness tool through which the Children's Charter is popularised in states parties. Celebrations are carried out at all levels: the AU; governmental; NGO; and at grass-roots level-for example within schools, children's clubs and at village festivals.[27]

23   See Children's Charter, art 42(a)(i) & (iii).

24   See Sloth-Nielsen & Mezmur (n 15 above) 214.

25   Council of Ministers 52nd ordinary session, 3-8 July 1990; 'Resolution on African Decade for Child Survival, Protection and Development', CM/Res. 1290 (LII), http://www.africa-union.org (accessed 10 June 2010).

26   Sloth-Nielsen & Mezmur (n 15 above) 214.

27   Lloyd (n 12 above) 337.

The celebration of the DAC generally enlightens people on the activities and progress of the Committee of Experts, as well as draws attention to priority issues affecting children in Africa. However, to the disappointment of the Committee, states have been reluctant to celebrate this day. For example, although the theme for the 2007 DAC was communicated to all AU member states requesting them to submit reports on how this day is planned in their respective countries, no such reports were received.[28] This trend should be discouraged and states should show their commitment by taking the activities of the Committee more seriously.

The Committee has also initiated the PAFC which focuses on the future growth and development of the child. The first PAFC, convened in Cairo, Egypt, in 2001, culminated in a Declaration and Plan of Action for an Africa Fit for Children.[29] This Declaration and Plan of Action served as the basis for Africa's common position for the UN General Assembly Special Session on Children held in New York in 2002.[30] The Committee seized the opportunity to profile its activities during the second PAFC. The outcome of this forum was the 'Call for Accelerated Action on the Implementation of the Plan of Action towards Africa Fit for Children 2008-2012'.

Concerning lobbying missions and investigation, the Committee has attempted to visit those countries that have not ratified the Children's Charter in order to encourage them to do so. For instance, during its 8th meeting, it resolved to visit Gabon, Tunisia, Sao Tome and Principe, Democratic Republic of Congo (DRC), Liberia and Zimbabwe for lobbying.[31] Whereas Tunisia, Gabon and Zambia responded positively, it was reported that the DRC, Liberia and Sao Tome and Principe did not respond at all. In 2004, members of the Committee concluded lobbying missions in four countries, namely, Burundi, Madagascar, Namibia and Sudan. The missions were said to be successful in that the first three countries subsequently ratified the Charter.[32]

---

28   Sloth-Nielsen & Mezmur (n 15 above) 214.

29   As above, 217.

30   As above.

31   Mezmur (n 11 above) 549.

32   As above, 550.

The Committee had also recommended that a special mission be sent to Darfur to report on the situation of children in the area, in tandem with Article 45(1) of the Children's Charter. During the 9th meeting of the Committee, it was highlighted that the AU Department of Social Affairs was in consultation with the Department of Peace and Security to facilitate the visit to Darfur. Apart from Darfur, the Committee should also visit other war-torn parts of the continent so as to collect and collate information that would be vital to the promotion and protection of the rights of affected children. The AU should also cooperate with the Committee in terms of providing the necessary financial and material resources towards this end.

11.2.1.2 STATE REPORTING

Article 43(1) of the Children's Charter obligates states parties to submit to the Committee periodic reports on the measures they have adopted to give effect to the provisions of the Charter. Such reports are also to indicate the progress made by states parties in guaranteeing the enjoyment of the rights in the Charter.[33] Two types of state reports are provided for in the Charter: initial reports, to be submitted within two years of the entry into force of the Charter for the state party concerned;[34] and subsequent reports, to be submitted every three years after the initial report.[35]

It is essential that reports should contain sufficient information that would enlighten the Committee on how the Charter is being implemented in the concerned country.[36] Such information may include the factors and difficulties, if any, affecting the fulfilment of the obligations in the Charter.[37] In order to be creative and avoid unnecessary repetition, states ought to ensure that they do not resubmit basic information that has already been provided in their previous reports.[38] This would therefore mean that state reports must be as comprehensive as possible.

---

33   Children's Charter, art 43(1).
34   Children's Charter, art 43(1)(a).
35   Children's Charter, art 43(1)(b).
36   Children's Charter, art 43(2)(a).
37   Children's Charter, art 43(2)(b).
38   Children's Charter, art 43(3).

The process of preparing reports presents states the opportunity to conduct a comprehensive review of the various measures undertaken to harmonise their national law and policy with the Charter and to monitor progress made in the enjoyment of children's rights.[39] Hence, the process should be one that encourages and facilitates popular participation, national introspection and public scrutiny of government policies and programmes, private sector practices and generally the practices of all sectors of society towards the protection of children. Reporting also affirms the commitment of states parties to respect and ensure observance of the rights in the Charter and serves as the essential vehicle for a meaningful dialogue between them and the Committee.[40] Due to the importance of the process, the Committee resolved to formulate the 'Guidelines for Initial Reports of States Parties' (hereafter 'Initial Reporting Guidelines' or 'the Guidelines').[41]

According to the Guidelines, reports are to be accompanied by copies of the principal legislative and other texts as well as detailed statistical information and indicators.[42] The Guidelines are divided into eleven parts, namely: Introduction; General measures of implementation; Definition of the child; General principles; Civil rights and freedoms; Family environment and alternative care; Health and welfare; Education, leisure and cultural activities; Special protection measures; Responsibilities of the child; Specific provisions for the reporting process; and Amendments.

Under the 'General measures of implementation', states parties are requested to provide relevant information pursuant to Article 1 of the Charter.[43] Such information includes the[44]:

---

39   See 'Guidelines for Initial Reports of States Parties (prepared by the African Committee of Experts on the Rights and Welfare of the Child pursuant to the provision of Article 43 of the African Charter on the Rights and Welfare of the Child' (hereafter 'Initial Reporting Guidelines' or 'the Guidelines'), Cmttee/ACRWC/2 II. Rev 2 para, 3.

40   As above, para 4.

41   As above, para 5.

42   As above, para 6.

43   As above, para 8.

44   As above, para 8(a)–(d).

(a)   necessary steps taken, in accordance with their constitutional processes and with the provisions of the Charter, to adopt such legislative or other measures as may be necessary to give effect to the provisions of the Charter;

(b)   measures taken to realise the rights and welfare of the child in the law of the state party or in any other international convention or agreement in force in that state;

(c)   measures taken to promote positive cultural values and traditions and to discourage those that are inconsistent with the rights, duties and obligations contained in the Charter; and

(d)   existing or planned mechanisms at the national or local levels for coordinating policies relating to children and for monitoring the implementation of the Charter.

Additionally, states are requested 'to describe the measures that have been taken or are foreseen to make the principles and provisions of the Charter widely known to adults and children alike and to widely disseminate their reports to the public at large in their own countries.'[45]

The 'definition of a child' part of the Guidelines requires states parties to provide information, in conformity with Article 2 of the Charter, regarding the definition of a child under their laws and regulations.[46] Further, the part that deals with 'general principles' necessitates states to furnish 'relevant information, including the principal legislative, judicial, administrative or other measures in force or foreseen; factors and difficulties encountered and progress achieved in implementing the provisions of the Children's Charter' in respect of a number of provisions of the Charter.[47]

On 'civil rights and freedoms', it is incumbent on states to explain how they have implemented the children's rights to name, nationality, identity and registration at birth (Article 6); freedom of expression (Article 7); freedom of thought, conscience and religion

---

45   As above, para 9.

46   As above, para 10.

47   As above, para 11. The provisions in question relate to: non-discrimination (arts 3 & 26); best interests of the child (art 4); right to life, survival and development (art 5); respect for the views of the child (art 7); and provision of information to children and promotion of their participation (arts 4, 7 & 12).

(Article 9); freedom of association and of peaceful Assembly (Article 8); protection of privacy (Article 10); and protection against child abuse and torture (Article 16).[48]

When reporting on 'family environment and alternative care' states are expected to particularly underscore the measures taken to bring to realisation the 'best interests of the child' and 'respect for the views of the child' principles contained in the Charter.[49] In this regard, they are to highlight the factors and difficulties encountered and progress achieved in implementing the relevant provisions of the Charter in respect of parental guidance (Article 20); parental responsibilities (Article 20(1)); separation from parents, separation caused by state party, separation caused by internal displacement arising from armed conflicts, civil strife, or natural disasters (Articles 19(2) & (3) and 25); family reunification and children deprived of a family environment (Article 25(2)(b)); maintenance of the child (Article 18(3)); adoption and periodic review of placement (Article 24); abuse, neglect, exploitation including physical and psychological recovery and social integration (Articles 16 and 27).[50]

Additionally, the Guidelines require states to provide information on the numbers of children desegregated per year within the reporting period.[51] Such information should concern, among others, children who are homeless, abused, neglected or taken into protective custody. They are also to give an account of children placed in foster care, institutional care, domestic adoption and those entering and leaving the country through inter-country adoption procedures.[52]

On 'health and welfare', states are to report on the measures, particularly, programmes, projects and existing or future institutional infrastructure for implementing policies in this area.[53] The reports

---

48   As above, para 13.

49   As above, para 14.

50   As above.

51   As above, para 15.

52   As above.

53   As above, para 17. The provisions of the Charter under focus in this part are: survival and development (art 5); children with handicap (art 13); health and health services (art 14); social security and child-care services and facilities (art 20 (2)(a-c)); and care for orphans (art 26).

must also specify the nature and extent of cooperation between states and local, national, regional and international organisations, concerning the implementation of this area of the Charter.[54]

The part that deals with special protection measures mainly borders on the protection of children in situations of emergency (Articles 22, 23 & 25); children in conflict with the law (Article 17); children of imprisoned mothers (Article 30); children in situation of exploitation and abuse (Articles 15, 16, 28 & 29); children victims of harmful social and cultural practices affecting the welfare, dignity, normal growth and development of the child (Article 21); and children belonging to a minority group (Article 26).[55]

The Guidelines permit a state party that has already submitted a report to the UN Committee on the Rights of the Child (CRC) to use elements of that report in its report to the Committee of Experts.[56] However, such a report should reflect the provisions of the Children's Charter specified in the Reporting Guidelines. Further, such a report must specify the action taken by the state party in response to any recommendations made to it by the Committee and/or the CRC.[57] This approach is convenient because the Reporting Guidelines adopted by the Committee of Experts are almost identical to those of the UN Committee on the Rights of the Child. Their main difference relates to the additional provisions contained in the Children's Charter[58], thus, requiring from states parties information that is more particular to the issues affecting the African child.

The examination of state reports by the Committee of Experts has not begun in earnest, although reports are said to have been submitted by Egypt, Mauritius, Nigeria and Rwanda.[59] The Committee intends to appoint Rapporteurs from among its members, who would examine the reports. It was proposed that

54   As above, para 18.
55   As above, para 21.
56   See para 24, which relates to 'specific provisions for the reporting process.'
57   As above, para 25.
58   These provisions are: arts 1(3), 14(2)(g), (i) & (j), 20(1)(b) & (c), 23, 26, 31 & 44 of the Children's Charter.
59   See Sloth-Nielsen & Mezmur (n 15 above) 219; Mezmur (n 11 above) 551.

the examination session should comprise of not only the designated Rapporteurs but also of representatives of interested international and regional organisations and NGOs.[60] Perhaps, the Committee could also adopt a procedure similar to the one of the CRC, in order to expedite the examination of state reports.

Under the CRC procedure, reports are considered in three stages: the pre-session working group, the constructive dialogue and concluding observations.[61] The pre-session working group is a closed-door meeting of the Working Group, usually convened a week after a plenary session of the CRC. During the meeting, the main questions that would be discussed with the representatives of the reporting states are formulated.

The second stage, which involves constructive dialogue, permits the CRC and the representatives of the reporting state to discuss the issue which the CRC feels need to be addressed more comprehensively by the latter. At this stage, the CRC may make proposals on, for example, how the state may ensure the implementation of the rights in the Convention. In the concluding observations stage, the CRC presents its views on whether or not it is satisfied with the state's efforts to implement the Children's Convention.

The procedure contemplated under the Rules of Procedure of the African Committee of Experts is to the effect that the Committee shall make such suggestions and general recommendations on the implementation of the Charter by the reporting state, as it may consider appropriate.[62] Thereafter, the Committee shall transmit, through the Chairperson of the Commission, its suggestions and general recommendations to the concerned state party for its comments.[63] The Committee is authorised to include, in its Annual

---

60   Sloth-Nielsen & Mezmur (n 15 above) 219.

61   See 'Working methods of the CRC Committee' available at http://www.ohchr.org/
     english/bodies/crc/ workingmethods.htm#a1,(accessed 23 June 2010).

62   See Rule 71(1) of the 'Rules of Procedure of the African Committee of Experts on
     the Rights and Welfare of the Child', Cmttee/ACRWC/II.Rev 2 (hereafter 'The
     Rules of Procedure' or 'The Rules').

63   As above, rule 71(2).

Activity Reports, the suggestions and general recommendations together with comments, if any, received from states parties.[64]

Under the Rules, if, in the opinion of the Committee, a state's report does not contain sufficient information, the state may be requested to submit an additional report or information.[65] Additionally, the Committee may invite Regional Economic Commissions (RECs), the AU, Specialised Agencies, the United Nations organs, NGOs and CSOs, to submit to it reports on the implementation of the Charter and to provide it with expert advice in areas falling within the scope of their activities.[66]

In case of non-submission of reports, the Rules require the Committee to send a reminder to the concerned state party and to undertake any other measures in a spirit of dialogue.[67] If, despite these efforts, the state party fails to submit the required report or complementary information, the Committee shall consider the situation as it deems necessary and shall include a reference to this effect in its Annual Activity Reports.

To summarise this discussion, it is noteworthy that the Committee of Experts can benefit a lot from the experience of its counterpart, the CRC. However, the Committee seems to be failing in exercising its promotional mandate as it should. This is in spite of the overt fact that children's rights have continued to be violated with impunity throughout the continent. The Committee needs to be more aggressive in the execution of its functions.

11.2.2   THE COMMITTEE'S PROTECTIVE MANDATE

The Committee has jurisdiction to entertain communications from persons, groups, NGOs or the UN, relating to any matter in the Children's Charter.[68] This seems to allow it to consider complaints in the manner of the African Commission. However, neither the

---

64   As above, rule 71(3).

65   As above, rule 68.

66   As above, rule 69(1).

67   As above, rule 66(1).

68   Children's Charter, art 44(1).

Children's Charter nor its Rules of Procedure[69], have clear guidelines on how the Committee should deal with communications. Rule 74(1) of the Committee's Rules of Procedure casually provides that: 'the Committee shall develop guidelines relating to the admissibility and consideration of communications pursuant to the provisions of Article 44 of the Children's Charter.' The guidelines are yet to be developed.

In the absence of such guidelines, it is expected that the Committee will, to a large extent, follow a similar procedure to that of the African Commission. For example, before communications are considered on merit, they should meet certain admissibility requirements. Again, it is expedient for the guidelines to indicate whether the Committee would receive communications from states that are not parties to the Children's Charter. If Article 44(1) is anything to go by, one might conclude that the Charter allows all states to submit communications to the Committee, regardless of them not being party to the Charter. It is also necessary to ascertain the nature and scope of the communications to be submitted. The fact that communications could be brought on 'any matter covered by the Charter', is potentially contentious due to the vagueness of the phrase under Article 44(1).

While considering communications, the Committee shall draw inspiration from international law on human rights, 'particularly from the provisions of the African Charter on Human and Peoples' Rights, the Charter of the Organisation of African Unity, the Universal Declaration on Human Rights, the International Convention on the Rights of the Child, and other instruments adopted by the United Nations and by African countries in the field of human rights, and from African values and traditions.'[70] This is important because drawing inspiration, particularly from the African Commission, will enable the two regional human rights institutions to streamline their jurisprudence and avoid potential 'jurisprudential chaos.'

---

69 See generally the 'Rules of Procedure of the African Committee of Experts on the Rights and Welfare of the Child', (n 62 above).

70 Children's Charter, art 46.

Although the Committee is still at its infancy and nothing much can be said of its activities and mandate, it is necessary to state that there is the need to clarify the relationship between it and other regional institutions with human rights responsibility. The present institutional arrangement tends to encourage overlaps and duplicity in the functions of the Committee of Experts and the African Commission in as far as they are mandated to perform similar tasks, such as receiving state reports and communications relating to the violation of children's rights.

The Commission's mandate, which is broader, overlaps that of the Committee when it comes to handling issues relating to children's rights. Therefore, since the Commission has the mandate to receive communications, even those relating to the violation of the rights of the child, there is the potential danger of the two institutions evolving conflicting jurisprudence on this area of human rights law, if caution is not taken. The issue of overlaps and duplicity of human rights institutions under the African system has been addressed more comprehensively in Chapter 13.

Other than the potential overlaps and duplication that appear to threaten its intended innovativeness, the Committee has many challenges that it needs to tackle as it endeavours to advance the rights of children in Africa.[71] For example, like the African Commission, the Committee operates within a stifling budget, notwithstanding the fact that there are NGOs and UN agencies that continue to support its work. It is needless to emphasise that with the necessary financial and technical support, the Committee could emerge as a major tool for promoting and protecting children's rights in Africa.

The issue of limited resource allocation seems to affect the frequency of the Committee's meetings. For instance, some of the Committee's ordinary sessions have lasted for only three days.[72] This situation has been exacerbated by the fact that neither the Charter nor the Rules of Procedure of the Committee prescribe the minimum period that an ordinary session should last. Rule 2(1), which is most relevant in this regard, merely provides that 'the

---

71   Mezmur (n 11 above) 558.
72   Sloth-Nielsen & Mezmur (n 15 above) 210.

Committee shall normally hold two ordinary sessions annually not exceeding two weeks.'

The Committee has so far never utilised the two weeks at its disposal. It is inconceivable how the Committee, which works on a part-time basis, could achieve its maximum potential by confining its ordinary sessions to three days. It is no wonder therefore that the state reports that were submitted in 2006 have taken more than two years to be examined.[73] The Commission therefore needs to revisit, not only the frequency of its meetings in a given year, but also their length per ordinary session.

In order to avoid repetition of shortcomings, the Committee should draw viable lessons from its counterparts such as the African Commission. It is needless to have an institution that would only 'reinvent the wheel' or propagate unnecessary duplication and overlaps. The African human rights system did not require another institution that is plagued with inefficiency. By creating the Committee of Experts, it intended to evolve an institution that would challenge the 'straight-jacket' approach to the violation of the rights of children in Africa. The Committee therefore needs to resonate this gesture by exploring unique approaches to tackling the ever-rising violations of children's rights on the continent.

---

73   As above, 211.

PART IV

CHALLENGES AND REFORMS TO THE AFRICAN SYSTEM ON HUMAN AND PEOPLES' RIGHTS

CHAPTER 12

NORMATIVE CHALLENGES AND REFORMS TO AFRICA'S REGIONAL HUMAN RIGHTS SYSTEM

The African human rights system has largely been criticised as being ineffective, hence causing doubt on its potential to improve the continent's poor human rights record.[1] It is in this context that this chapter discusses the normative deficiencies of the system, as well as the possible reforms thereto. It should be appreciated that, although the African human rights system is plagued with numerous challenges and shortcomings, it has equally made some positive contribution to the international human rights law discourse.[2] As shown in the previous chapters, the system has not been static but has rather evolved over time to incorporate in its norms, institutions and practice, some aspects that were not given credence at its inception.

It is needless to emphasise that states have acted and continue to act in ways that are antithetical to their human rights obligations under the African human rights system. This has, by extension, rendered human rights illusory in the daily lives of the majority of people on the continent.[3] This perennial state of affairs aggravates the already precarious human rights situation in the region. As a result, some scholars have argued for the comprehensive reform

---

1   See generally E Bondzie-Simpson 'A critique of the African Charter on Human and Peoples' Rights' (1988) 31 *Howard Law Journal* 643-665; R Murray 'The African Charter on Human and Peoples' Rights 1987-2000: An overview of its progress and problems' (2001) 1 *African Human Rights Law Journal* 1-17; M Mutua 'The Banjul Charter and the African cultural fingerprint: An evaluation of the language of duties' (1995) 35 *Virginia Journal of International Law* 339-380; J Oloka-Onyango 'Beyond the rhetoric: Reinvigorating the struggle for social and economic rights in Africa' (1995) 26 *California Western International Law Journal* 1-73; P Amoah 'The African Charter on Human and Peoples' Rights: An effective weapon for human rights?' (1992) 4 *African Journal of International and Comparative Law* 226; C Welch 'The African Commission on Human and Peoples' Rights: A five-year report and assessment' (1992) 14 *Human Rights Quarterly* 43-61.

2   For a similar comment, see Murray (n 1 above) 1.

3   G Mugwanya *Human rights in Africa: Enhancing human rights through the African regional human rights system* (2003) XV.

and invigoration of the African system to enable it to, among other things, compel states to comply with their human rights obligations.[4]

Normative reform of the African human rights system may take different forms, including, for example, the amendment of certain aspects of the provisions of the African Charter[5], the Protocol Establishing the African Court on Human and Peoples' Rights[6], the Rules of Procedure of the African Commission[7], or any other instrument that is relevant to the system.[8] Since the African Charter is the main substantive instrument of this system, our debate on normative reforms shall be limited to the provisions of this instrument. As already stated, the Constitutive Act of the African Union (hereafter 'CAAU' or 'the Act'), some of whose provisions were highlighted elsewhere in this book, is not a source of substantive rights under the African system.

As for the African Charter on the Rights and Welfare of the Child and the Protocol to the African Charter on Human and Peoples' Rights on the Rights of Women in Africa, most of the rights contained therein resonate those in the African Charter. The only difference is that they have been 'contextualised' to guarantee the promotion and protection of rights of children and women. Otherwise, the scope and content of their provisions is more or less similar to that of the African Charter in many respects.

---

4   See generally H Steiner & P Alston *International human rights in context: Law, politics and morals* (1996) 689; Mutua (n 1 above) 339; Oloka-Onyango (n 1 above) 1; Amoah (n 1 above) 226; Welch (n 1 above) 43.

5   Art 68 of the African Charter provides for the amendment of the Charter by a majority of states parties.

6   Art 35 of the Protocol provides that: '1. The present Protocol may be amended if a state party to the Protocol makes a written request to that effect to the Secretary-General of the OAU. The Assembly may adopt, by simple majority, the draft amendment after all the state parties to the present Protocol have been duly informed of it and the Court has given its opinion on the amendment. 2. The Court shall also be entitled to propose such amendments to the present Protocol as it may deem necessary, through the Secretary-General of the OAU. 3. The amendment shall come into force for each state party which has accepted it thirty days after the Secretary-General of the OAU has received notice of the acceptance.'

7   Rule 121 & 122 provide that the Commission can change its own rules.

8   C Heyns 'The African regional human rights system: In need of reform?' (2001) 2 *African Human Rights Law Journal* 156.

When addressing the question of how to reform the African Charter, two approaches may be considered. The first would be to reform the 'flawed' or 'inadequate' provisions through interpretive and jurisprudential mechanisms. This approach contemplates a situation where the African Commission and the Court are given the opportunity to interpret the Charter and bring its provisions in line with international jurisprudence.[9] With regard to the Commission, this approach finds support from Articles 60 and 61 of the Charter. Article 60 provides:

> The Commission shall draw inspiration from international law on human and peoples' rights, particularly from the provisions of various African instruments on human and peoples' rights, the Charter of the United Nations, the Charter of the Organisation of African Unity, the Universal Declaration of Human Rights, other instruments adopted by the United Nations and by African countries in the field of human and peoples' rights as well as from the provisions of various instruments adopted within the Specialised Agencies of the United Nations of which the parties to the present Charter are members.

Article 61 adds:

> The Commission shall also take into consideration, as subsidiary measures to determine the principles of law, other general or special international conventions, laying down rules expressly recognised by member states of the Organisation of African Unity, African practices consistent with international norms on human and people's rights, customs generally accepted as law, general principles of law recognised by African states as well as legal precedents and doctrine.

A combined reading of the above provisions seems to suggest that the sources listed therein could be used by the Commission to define the substance and contents of the rights contained in the Charter to the best extent possible. Noteworthy, both Articles 60 and 61 use the 'shall' clause, meaning that the African Commission is under obligation to 'draw inspiration from', and 'take into consideration', other international human rights instruments. By extension, the Commission could give effect to the rights in the Charter in conformity with the standards of the universal and other regional human rights systems. Arguably, the Charter, as it stands, provides for

---

9   As above, 157.

its own development through the jurisprudence of the Commission and the Court.[10] This approach, however, will only be effective if the intention is to keep reforms to the barest minimum and under the control of the Commission and the Court.[11]

The second approach calls for the comprehensive reform of the normative framework of the Charter. This approach is premised on the argument that many events have transpired since the adoption of the Charter, justifying radical reforms to the content and substance of its provisions. From this viewpoint it has been contended that, while the Commission is entitled to develop the Charter through its jurisprudence, 'this is not a healthy practice in the long run, unless its interpretations are followed up by the reform of the Charter provisions.'[12] The jurisprudence evolved by the Commission and the Court may also not be regarded with the same degree of seriousness as the Charter provisions. It is much easier for one to understand the provisions of the Charter than to peruse through a lengthy judgement that purports to interpret the Charter.

Moreover, the African human rights system has been going through transformation, which may necessitate comprehensive reforms to the Charter in order to encourage normative and institutional homogeneity.[13] Good examples to be cited in this regard are the transformation of the OAU to AU and the establishment of the African Court to complement the African Commission. Since the emerging mechanisms of the system are more appealing and appear to be more superior than those that already exist, they provide a good indication that time is ripe to consider comprehensive reforms to the entire system in order to encourage uniformity.

---

10   See R Murray 'Report on the 1996 Sessions of the African Commission on Human and Peoples' Rights 19th and 20th Sessions' (1997) 18 *Human Rights Law Journal* 923.

11   Heyns (n 8 above) 157.

12   As above.

13   As above.

12.1 REFORMING THE CIVIL AND POLITICAL RIGHTS PROVISIONS OF THE AFRICAN CHARTER

As already stated, the African Charter is an innovative human rights instrument that incorporates into one document all the three generations of rights: civil and political rights; economic, social, and cultural rights; and group (peoples') rights. Sadly, however, the Charter's civil and political rights provisions have a number of shortcomings, although they constitute the bulk of its substantive provisions.

First, the Charter has conspicuously omitted several internationally recognised civil and political rights. For example, it does not guarantee the right to privacy which is an important right entrenched in all the regional human rights instruments, as well as in those of the Universal system.[14] The right to privacy protects individuals from unnecessary interference by the state or its agencies. It has various facets, including the right not to have: (a) their person or home searched; (b) their property searched; (c) their possessions seized; (d) information relating to their family or private affairs unnecessarily required or revealed; or (e) the privacy of their communications infringed.[15]

The rationale for the omission of this important right from the Charter cannot be understood, given the fact that it is always infringed in many domestic jurisdictions in Africa. The police, for example, have been the most notorious violators of this right, especially when arresting suspects and undertaking seizure and searches when enforcing criminal laws and procedures.[16]

The Charter also does not guarantee the right against forced labour. Article 5 of the Charter, where this right could possibly have fitted-in so well, protects a number of related rights, namely: (i) the right to the respect of the dignity inherent in a person; (ii) the right

---

14   Even the Constitutions of some states contain this right. See, for example, Section 76 of the Constitution of the Republic of Kenya, 1963, as amended in 2002.

15   See the Bomas Draft of the Constitution of Kenya, art 47, available at www.gov. ac.ke/bomasconstitution.2004 (accessed 12 June 2010).

16   See U Umozurike 'The significance of the African Charter on Human and Peoples' Rights' in A Kalu & Y Osinbajo *Perspectives on Human Rights* (1992) 45.

to the recognition of one's legal status; and (iii) the right against all forms of exploitation and degradation of man particularly slavery, slave trade, torture, cruel, inhuman or degrading punishment and treatment.[17] The right against forced labour is essential in Africa for a number of reasons. First, forced labour was a common practice during the slave trade and colonial periods. The possibility of this practice finding its way into the post-colonial societies cannot therefore be overlooked.

Secondly, forced labour is still evident in some African cultural and religious practices.[18] It is not uncommon to hear of people being forced to work in order to service their debts. Although it may be against their will, such people are threatened or even sent to prison to compel them to comply with their 'masters' demands.[19] Thirdly, the right against forced labour is essential in Africa because some governments have policies that require people to do certain jobs for the state against their will. Such jobs may include helping in the construction of roads and bridges, or similar community labour involvements that are largely meant to be the responsibility of the state to its people and not vice versa.

The Charter has also failed to explicitly give credence to the right to form trade unions and other civic organisations within states. Article 10 should have incorporated this right in clear and precise terms. The Article provides in part that '(1). Every individual shall have the right to free association provided that he abides by the law. (2)... no one may be compelled to join an association.' Although not explicitly stated, this Article intends to protect the rights and freedom of individuals who unite to form a collective entity that represents their common interests and objectives. These interests and objectives may be of a political, economic, religious, social, cultural, professional or labour union nature.[20]

---

17   Art 5 states:'Every individual shall have the right to the respect of the dignity inherent in a human being and to the recognition of his legal status. All forms of exploitation and degradation of man particularly slavery, slave trade, torture, cruel, inhuman or degrading punishment and treatment shall be prohibited.'

18   See M Mbondenyi 'Improving the substance and content of civil and political rights under the African human rights system' (2008) 17/2 *Lesotho Law Journal* 98.

19   As above.

20   O Nmehielle *The African human rights system: Its laws, practice and institutions* (2001) 110.

The Charter should therefore have clarified the scope of the right to freedom of association under Article 10, by specifically mentioning the right to form trade unions and other civic organisations. It is not enough just to mention freedom of association without defining its scope. It is common knowledge that many governments in Africa have attempted either to suppress or outlaw the formation of trade unions and civic organisations, particularly those suspected to be a potential 'threat to their smooth running'.[21] Many NGOs and trade unions have been banned or forced to desist from criticising the government of the day.[22]

The Charter should have gone ahead to require states to take legislative and other measures to promote and encourage trade unions and civil society participation in decision-making and in public affairs at all levels of government. It should also have provided for the guarantee of smooth running and operation of these organisations in order to curtail state interference. It is suggested that the Charter should have provided that any legislation purporting to regulate the registration or operation of civil society organisations or trade unions should ensure that: (a) registration is in the hands of a body that is independent of government or political control; (b) any fee chargeable is no more than is necessary to defray essential costs of the procedure; (c) there is a right to registration, unless there is good reason to the contrary; (d) any standards of conduct applied to organisations is formulated with input from the affected organisations; and (e) de-registration procedures provide for a fair hearing and for a right of appeal to an independent tribunal.[23]

Further, the provisions of the Charter guaranteeing the rights to liberty and security of the person and those of an arrested person do not reflect international standards and are inadequate.[24] Article 6, for example, provides that 'every individual shall have the right to

---

21   As above.

22   This was the order of the day in the single party days in Kenya. Many NGOs were either refused registration or deregistered when they commented on the inefficiency of the government of the day. See Mbondenyi (n 18 above) 99.

23   See the Bomas Draft of the Constitution of Kenya (n 15 above) art 44.

24   See arts 6 & 7 of the Charter which guarantee the right to liberty and security of person and the right to a fair trial, respectively. See also E Ankumah *The African Commission on Human and Peoples' Rights* (1996) 123-133.

liberty and to the security of his person. No one may be deprived of his freedom except for reasons and conditions previously laid down by law. In particular, no one may be arbitrarily arrested or detained.' First, the provision, through the use of a claw-back clause, entrusts to states the responsibility to define the parameters of this right. More likely than not, this responsibility will be abused.[25]

Secondly, the drafters of the Charter failed to acknowledge that this right goes beyond arbitrary arrest or detention to envisage important issues such as the right of every person: (a) not to be detained without trial, except in conditions that are clearly laid down under international law; (b) to be free from all forms of violence from either public or private sources; (c) not to be tortured in any manner, whether physically or psychologically; and (d) not to be subjected to corporal punishment or to be treated or punished in a cruel, inhuman or degrading manner.[26] The Charter provisions guaranteeing these rights need to be brought in line with these standards.

The same applies to the provisions on fair trial under Article 7 of the Charter, where some important rights of an accused or arrested person were either deliberately ignored or accidentally omitted. Before 'appealing to competent national organs' or even exercising the 'right to defence', an accused person is entitled to other forms of protection. For example, he or she has the right to be informed promptly, in a language that he or she understands, of the reason for the arrest.[27] The person also has the right to remain silent and in this regard must be informed of the consequences of not remaining silent.

Hence, an accused person should be protected from making forced confession or admission that could be used in evidence against him or her. Where the accused freely chooses to make a confession, it should be made before a competent authority mandated by law

---

25   As above.

26   See the scope of this right in, for example, the Bomas Draft of the Constitution of Kenya (n 15 above) art 45.

27   N Udombana 'The African Commission on Human and Peoples' Rights and the development of fair trial norms in Africa' (2006) 6 *African Human Rights Law Journal* 313.

to conduct such proceedings.[28] An accused person or a suspect should also be detained separately from persons serving a sentence because he or she is innocent until proved guilty. In most African states, due to the lack of adequate detention and prison facilities, it is not uncommon to find suspects and convicts sharing prison cells. Usually, the convicts either harass or mistreat the suspects, as a result of which one's right to be presumed innocent until proved guilty is rendered nugatory.

Further, although Article 7(1)(c) guarantees every person the right to be defended by Counsel of their choice, the Charter fails to make provision for state-provided legal assistance. By extension, it does not cater for indigent persons, who for lack of funds may fail to exercise the right to Counsel of their choice. The importance of legal representation, especially in criminal cases, cannot be overemphasised. It is the state's duty to legally assist indigent persons to secure fair trial. The omission in the Charter cannot easily be reconciled with the realities faced by African masses, who are generally poor and therefore lack the means to adequately hire legal services.[29] Some African countries have legal aid programmes, but these programmes are generally poorly funded and managed.[30] There ought to be some form of commitment by states and NGOs in this area, if the right to fair trial is to be enjoyed by the poor masses.

Additionally, the Charter has failed to provide that an accused person or a suspect must be brought before a court or tribunal as soon as is practically possible. Instead, Article 7(1)(d) guarantees the right to be tried 'within a reasonable time.' It is believed that the Charter makes reference to 'reasonable time' to ensure that proceedings are not unduly prolonged. The rationale of the provision is to ensure the speedy completion of proceedings, which has nothing to do with the presentation of an accused before a court or a tribunal to be charged. Thus, it does not cater for potential delays in the commencement of proceedings.[31] The Charter should have stated that an accused person must be brought before a court or tribunal,

---

28   Bomas Draft of the Constitution of Kenya (n 15 above) art 73.

29   Nmehielle (n 20 above) 98.

30   As above.

31   As above.

for example, not later than 48 hours after being arrested, or not later than the end of the first court day, if the period expires outside ordinary court hours.[32]

The Charter is also silent on the right to bail. The right of an accused person to be released on bond or bail pending trial or appeal should be mandatory, unless there are compelling reasons to the contrary. Other important rights of an accused person which have not been addressed in the Charter include: the right to judicial review of one's detention; the right to compensation for unlawful detention or release from such detention; the right to public hearing or the circumstances under which public hearing may be excluded; the right to adequate time and facilities to prepare a defence; the right of the defence to examine and cross-examine witnesses in court and the right to an interpreter; the right of those acquitted to compensation for miscarriage of justice and; the right not to be subjected to a new trial for the same cause.[33] The drafters of the Charter turned a rather blind eye to the importance of these rights.

Further, Article 13 of the Charter recognises the right to vote in a very superficial way. The Article guarantees every citizen the right to participate freely in the government of his or her country either directly or through freely chosen representatives. However, the inadequacy with which this right has been addressed in the Charter defeats logic. Africa has experienced series of undemocratic governments where democracy, constitutionalism, the rule of law and human rights have been ignored.[34] Military rule and undemocratic change of governments have also taken toll unabatedly.

Moreover, a large number of those in the political class almost literally 'purchase' the right to vote from their citizens and once voted, they use the power and state machinery for their personal benefits. At best, political power is used to reward cronies and sycophants, on the one hand, and on the other hand, to punish 'dissidents' and opponents. Under such circumstances, it cannot be understood how

---

32   Bomas Draft of the Constitution of Kenya (n 20 above) art 73.

33   See Mugwanya (n 3 above) 344.

34   For a detailed discussion on this, see generally, A Mangu 'The road to constitutionalism and democracy in Africa: The Case of the Democratic Republic of Congo' (2002) *LLD Thesis University of South Africa* Chapter 3.

the drafters of the Charter could have failed to entrench the right to vote and other related rights. This is a serious omission that needs to be addressed urgently.

The civil and political rights provisions of the Charter could therefore be enhanced by incorporating rights that were omitted or inadequately addressed but which are guaranteed under the universal and other regional human rights instruments. Variations may of course be permitted but not to the extent that the universal protection of such rights is compromised. One way to incorporate or reform those provisions could be through the adoption of Protocols to the Charter.[35] The other way may be through the constructive and progressive interpretation of the provisions in accordance with international standards and principles. Alternatively, states parties could exercise their mandate under Article 68 to amend the Charter as they deem appropriate.[36]

With regard to the approach that involves the constructive and progressive interpretation of the Charter's provisions, the Commission's elaboration on several substantive rights is commendable.[37] It has, for instance, found Article 5 of the Charter to protect, *inter alia,* the right to life.[38] The said Article guarantees the right against all forms of slavery, slave trade, torture and cruel, inhuman or degrading treatment. The Commission's findings were to the effect that deaths resulting from torture or from trials conducted in breach of the due process guaranteed in Article 7 of the Charter violated the right to life guaranteed in Article 4.[39] Additionally, it has

---

35   Heyns (n 8 above) 173.

36   Murray (n 10 above) 19.

37   See C Odinkalu 'The role of case and complaints procedure in the reform of the African regional human rights system' (2001) 2 *African Human Rights Law Journal* 239.

38   See communications 48/90, 50/91, 52/91 & 89/93, *Amnesty International, Comité Loosli Bachelard, Lawyers Committee for Human Rights and Association of Members of the Episcopal Conference of East Africa v. Sudan,* Thirteenth Annual Activity Report of the African Commission on Human and Peoples' Rights (Annex V) (hereafter 'the Sudan cases') and communications 54/91, 61/91, 98/93, 164/97 & 210/98, *Malawi African Association, Amnesty International, Ms Sarr Diop, Union Interafricaine des Droits de l. Homme and RADDHO, Collectif des Veuves et Ayant-droit and Association Mauritanienne des Droits de l. Homme v. Mauritania,* Thirteenth Annual Activity Report of the African Commission on Human and Peoples' Rights (Annex V) (hereafter 'the Mauritania cases').

39   See the *Sudan case* (n 38 above) para 48 and the *Mauritania case* (n 38 above) para 119.

interpreted Article 5 broadly to guarantee the enjoyment of certain economic, social and cultural rights. On this basis, it has condemned 'practices analogous to slavery' such as 'unremunerated work.'[40]

Further, the Commission has elaborated the contents of the right to a fair trial in both its casework and resolutions. To this effect, it has extended the right to fair trial to encompass such issues as legal aid and assistance and the protection of the independence of the judiciary.[41] In the *Sudan case* cited above, it linked Articles 7(1)(d)[42] and 26[43] of the Charter to achieve protection of the independence and integrity of the judiciary.[44] The Commission took the view that the purge of over 100 judicial officers by the Sudanese government deprived the courts of qualified personnel required to ensure their impartiality and thus violated these Articles. The Commission has also found the practice of setting up of special courts or tribunals, contrary to the standard judicial procedures, to be in violation of both Articles 7(1)(d) and 26 of the Charter.[45]

In the same spirit of constructive interpretation of the Charter, the Commission has held that Sharia is inapplicable to non-adherents of the Islamic faith unless they voluntarily submit to it. While finding a violation of the right to freedom of religion guaranteed under Article 8 of the Charter, it correctly observed that:

> . . . it is fundamentally unjust that religious laws should be applied against non-adherents of the religion. Tribunals that apply only Sharia

---

40   See *the Mauritania Case* (n 38 above) 137. See also the argument in C Odinkalu 'Analysis of Paralysis or paralysis by analysis? Implementing economic, social and cultural rights under the African Charter on Human and Peoples' Rights' (2001) 23 *Human Rights Quarterly* 358-365.

41   See 'Resolution on the Right to a Fair Trial and Legal Assistance in Africa, adopting the Dakar Declaration on the Right to a Fair Trial in Africa', DOC/OS(XXVI)INF 19.

42   Art 7(1)(d) guarantees every individual 'the right to be tried within a reasonable time by an impartial court or tribunal.'

43   Art 26 reads, in part: 'States parties to the present Charter shall have the duty to guarantee the independence of the courts. . .'

44   Odinkalu (n 37 above) 240.

45   Communication 151/96, *Civil Liberties Organisation v. Nigeria*, Thirteenth Annual Activity Report of the African Commission on Human and Peoples' Rights, para 71.

are thus not competent to judge non-Muslims, and everyone should have the right to be tried by a secular court if they wish.[46]

Significantly, the Commission recommended that trials must always accord with international fair trial standards.[47] Generally, the Commission should be applauded for its evolving practice of interpreting the Charter provisions progressively. In some cases, however, it remained passive and failed to develop its jurisprudence, even when an opportunity presented itself.[48]

In *Henry Kalenga v. Zambia*[49], for example, where the complainant had been detained without trial, the Commission concluded the case without developing its jurisprudence on Article 6. The complainant in this case had petitioned the Commission, demanding his release. Zambia's Ministry of Legal Affairs later informed the Commission of his release. The Commission proceeded to declare the matter amicably resolved without expounding on Article 6. This trend should not be encouraged, if the inadequate provisions of the Charter are to be reformed.

Apart from the inadequacy of some of its provisions, the Charter also deals with the limitation of civil and political rights in a very unsatisfactory manner. In the main, it has no derogation clause that would permit the suspension of certain rights and freedoms in strictly defined circumstances.[50] According to the African Commission, the absence of a derogation clause means that the Charter 'does not allow for states parties to derogate from their treaty obligations during emergency situations. Thus, even a civil war... cannot be used as an excuse by the state violating or permitting violations of rights in the African Charter.'[51] It further observed that the lack of a derogation clause 'can be seen as an expression of the principle that the restriction of human rights is not a solution to national

---

46   *The Sudan case* (n 38 above) para 73.

47   As above.

48   Nmehielle (n 20 above) 91-92.

49   Communication 11/88, *Henry Kalenga v. Zambia*, ACHPR/LR/A1 (1997).

50   Heyns (n 8 above) 160.

51   Communication 74/92, *Commission Nationale des Droits de l'Homme et des Liberties v. Chad* (1997) 4 *IHRR* 94, Para 21.

difficulties: the legitimate exercise of human rights does not pose dangers to a democratic state governed by the rule of law.'[52]

The Commission's observations on the absence of a derogation clause in the Charter may be rejected for two reasons. First, a derogation clause is essential because, in certain circumstances, rights must be limited in any society. This process, however, must be carefully managed, 'in order to ensure that such limitations are done in an acceptable way.'[53] Thus, derogation clauses serve the dual function of allowing infringements of rights and at the same time defining standards that must be met by such infringements.[54] The absence of a derogation clause in the Charter therefore means that states can infringe rights in cases of emergencies without being called to question.

Secondly, the Commission's approach should be rejected because, in reality, it can hardly be conducive to the protection of human rights. States under emergencies, for example, could easily ignore the Charter due to the impending danger. Under such circumstances the Charter would be discredited for failing to restrain states from violating or unduly restricting the rights of their citizens.[55] One would therefore concur with Heyns to the effect that, the Commission ought to reverse its interpretation of the Charter on this issue by acknowledging the right of states to derogate from certain Charter rights in certain defined circumstances.[56]

Besides the Charter's lack of a derogation clause, some of its provisions have claw-back clauses which subject the enjoyment of rights to national or domestic laws of states.[57] Claw-back clauses

---

52   Communications 48/90, 50/91/ 52/91 & 89/93, *Amnesty International and others v. Sudan*, Thirteenth Annual Activity Report of the African Commission on Human and Peoples' Rights (Annex V) para 79.

53   Heyns (n 8 above) 160.

54   As above. See also R Higgins 'Derogation under human rights treaties' (1976-77) 48 *The British Yearbook of International Law* 281.

55   As above. See also J Oraá *Human rights in states of emergency in international law* (1992) 210.

56   As above.

57   For example, art 8 guarantees the freedom of conscience and religion 'subject to law and order.' Art 9(2) states: 'Every individual shall have the right to express and disseminate his opinions within the law.' Additionally, art 10 guarantees the right to freedom of association to an individual 'provided that he abides by the law.' An

have rightly been criticised since they imply that international supervision of domestic law is limited in respect of certain rights, thus defying the very reason for the existence of a regional human rights system.[58]

The Commission has attempted to address this inadequacy by, for example, interpreting claw-back clauses to the benefit of the complainants.[59] Although the Commission's creativity in this regard is commendable, it is important that such efforts are succeeded by a modification of the Charter. Not only should claw-back clauses be scrapped, but also the Charter needs a general limitation clause.[60] The general clause should permit the limitation of rights only to the extent that the limitation is reasonable and justifiable.[61] Hence, limitation of rights under the African human rights system must be imposed only in strictly defined circumstances.

From the above analysis, one would agree with the observation that the Charter, as far as civil and political rights are concerned, has the capacity to be reformed. Unfortunately, 'its positive features are often under-estimated or overlooked, and its capacity for metamorphosis is yet to be fully explored.'[62] Noteworthy, a great impediment to the realisation of this category of rights in

---

individual's freedom of movement under art 12 is guaranteed 'provided he abides by the law.' Art 13(1) guarantees citizens the right to participate freely in their governments 'in accordance with the provisions of the law.' The same is evident in art 14 which permits the encroachment upon property 'in accordance with the provisions of appropriate law.'

58   See for example Ankumah (n 24 above) 176; R D'sa 'The African Charter on human and Peoples' Rights: Problems and prospects for regional action' (1981/83) 10 *Australian Yearbook of International Law* 110; R Gittleman 'The African Charter on Human and Peoples' Rights: A legal analysis' (1982) 22 *Virginia Journal of International law* 694; P Kunig 'The protection of human rights by international law in Africa' (1982) 25 *German Yearbook of International Law* 155; R Murray *The African Commission on Human and Peoples' Rights and International Law* (2000) 127.

59   Odinkalu (n 40 above) 358.

60   C Heyns 'Civil and political rights in the African Charter' in M Evans & R Murray *The African Charter on Human and Peoples' Rights: The system in practice: 1986-2000* (2002) 161.

61   Art 36 of the Constitution of the Republic of South Africa, 1996; art 33 of the Bomas Draft Constitution of Kenya (n 15 above).

62   C Odinkalu 'The individual complaints procedure of the African Commission on Human and Peoples' Rights: A preliminary assessment' (1998) 8 *Transnational Law and Contemporary Problems* 398.

Africa is constituted by, among other factors, illiteracy, ignorance and poverty.[63] For instance, whereas one may want to pursue his or her rights, the cost of litigation is prohibitive. It follows that, to many Africans, the rights entrenched in the Charter may be mere paperwork, irrelevant to their existence.[64] Former Tanzanian President, Julius Nyerere, captured this position when he argued:

> What freedom has our subsistence farmer? He scratches a bare living from the soil provided the rains do not fail; his children work at his side without schooling, medical care, or even good feeding. Certainly he has freedom to vote and to speak as he wishes. But these freedoms are much less real to him than his freedom to be exploited. Only as his poverty is reduced will his existing political freedom become properly meaningful and his right to human dignity become a fact of human dignity.[65]

Nyerere tried to highlight the apparent insubordination of civil and political rights to economic rights in Africa. However, his observation should not be interpreted as an excuse for ignoring or violating civil and political rights. What he meant was, civil and political rights could only be realised within favourable living standards that accord with human dignity. The relevance of all categories of rights cannot be overlooked, given that human rights are interrelated, interdependent and indivisible.

12.2   REFORMING THE ECONOMIC, SOCIAL AND CULTURAL RIGHTS AND OTHER SUBSTANTIVE PROVISIONS OF THE CHARTER

Like civil and political rights, the Charter does not comprehensively guarantee some economic, social and cultural rights in accordance with international standards. For example, under Article 15, it guarantees the right to equitable and satisfactory work conditions.[66] However, unlike Article 7 of both the International Covenant on

---

63   J Mubangizi 'Some reflections on recent and current trends in the promotion and protection of human rights in Africa: The pains and gains' (2006) 6 *African Human Rights Law Journal* 160.

64   As above.

65   Reproduced in (1969-1970) 2 *Africa Contemporary Record* 30-31.

66   Art 15 provides: 'Every individual shall have the right to work under equitable and satisfactory conditions, and shall receive equal pay for equal work.'

Civil and Political Rights (ICCPR) and the International Covenant on Economic, Social and Cultural Rights (ICESCR), it does not expressly guarantee the right to rest, leisure, limited working hours and paid holidays. This right also goes hand-in-hand with other rights, such as the right of workers to go on strike, which have not been included in the Charter.

Further, Article 16 guarantees the enjoyment of the best attainable state of physical and mental health. It then provides that 'states parties... shall take the necessary measures to protect the health of their people and to ensure that they receive medical attention when they are sick.' The provision, however, does not include at least some minimum requirements that states should fulfil in order to safeguard this right. The right to health demands more than receiving medical attention when one is sick. It includes the right to health care services and reproductive health care. The Charter fails to guarantee emergency medical treatment, which is usually denied in many African states.[67]

The Charter is also not elaborate in its provision that guarantees the protection of the right to education. It simply states that 'every individual shall have the right to education' without stipulating the parameters of this right. As stated earlier, this right embodies a number of essential components. For example, it consists of the right to primary education, secondary education, higher (tertiary) education, and the right to choice of schools, among others. One cannot understand whether the Charter also guarantees individuals the right to establish and maintain independent educational institutions that would further their religious, cultural or other pertinent interests.[68]

The Charter also does not contain certain economic, social and cultural rights, including the right to food, social security and adequate standards of living. These are basic rights which any state is expected to guarantee its citizens. Many African states have been violating these rights with impunity. State funds, which would have been used to safeguard these rights, have always been mismanaged

---

67   Umozurike (n 16 above) 48.

68   Nmehielle (n 20 above) 130.

or diverted to private accounts of the 'powers-that-be,' leaving many innocent citizens wallowing in abject poverty. It is therefore very unfortunate that these basic rights were not given any attention by the drafters of the Charter.

From the foregoing, it is inevitable to conclude that economic, social and cultural rights have not been fully addressed under the Charter and as such the relevant substantive provisions need to be reformed. Like with the civil and political rights provisions of the Charter, there is the need for both progressive interpretation and, in certain cases, the promulgation of protocols to address the shortcomings in this category of rights. Particularly, protocols should be adopted to protect the rights of vulnerable groups such as the aged, disabled and minority communities, thus expounding on Article 18(4) of the Charter. The inadequacies of the provisions relating to women and children's rights under Article 18(3) have been redressed through the adoption of the Protocol on Women in Africa and the African Charter on the Rights and Welfare of the Child, respectively.

It is recommended that economic, social and cultural rights should be taken as seriously as civil and political rights in both the agenda of the AU and the activities of the African human rights system. People should be educated on the existence of these rights and their enforcement procedures. It is sad to note that, while economic, social and cultural rights are very essential, they are generally not known to, or are ignored by, the lay person. This trend needs to be reversed.

Apart from the economic, social and cultural rights debate, the question of duties in the Charter also needs to be revisited. More should be done to clarify the status of the duties in the Charter because, as they are, they cannot easily be given meaning in a legal context.[69] For example, there is uncertainty on how the duty to preserve the harmonious development of the family under Article 29(1) could be enforced by a domestic court of law or the regional

---

69   See Mutua (n 1 above) 12.

enforcement mechanisms such as the African Commission and the Court.[70]

The scope and content of peoples' rights under the Charter also needs to be revisited. If peoples' rights are to be utilised to address some of the human rights challenges affecting the continent, it would be imperative for the Commission to put extra effort in their interpretation and application and in the promotion of their understanding. For purposes of legal certainty, it would also be crucial for the Commission to elaborate sufficiently clear criteria for determining the nature of the groups which qualify as 'people' within the meaning and context of the Charter.[71] A number of groups across the continent have been, and continue to be, subjected to gross human rights violations. In particular, some have been dispossessed of lands they consider their traditional homes.[72] Some of them have also been, and continue to be, subjected to discrimination and marginalisation as a result of their alleged inferior and outdated cultural practices.[73]

It is encouraging to note that the African Commission has begun to see the importance of protecting the rights of vulnerable communities. For example, it recently adopted a report that recognises certain groups as indigenous peoples.[74] The Commission should also be commended for some landmark pronouncements on certain aspects of peoples' rights. Particularly, in the *Social and Economic Rights Action Centre (SERAC) & another v. Nigeria*[75] ('*Ongoni case*' or '*SERAC case*') discussed earlier, it underscored the role of the

---

70   Heyns (n 8 above) 160.

71   S Dersso 'The jurisprudence of the African Commission on Human and Peoples' Rights with respect to peoples' rights' (2006) 6 *African Human Rights Law Journal* 380.

72   K Bojosi & G Wachira 'Protecting indigenous peoples in Africa: An analysis of the approach of the African Commission on Human and Peoples' Rights' (2006) 6 *African Human Rights Law Journal* 406.

73   As above.

74   See African Commission's 'Working Group on Indigenous Populations/Communities, Activity Report 2005' (April 2006); see also 'IWGIA Report, 39th ordinary session of the African Commission on Human and Peoples' Rights, Banjul, The Gambia, 11 to 25 May 2006'.

75   Communication 155/96, *Social and Economic Rights Action Centre (SERAC) & another v. Nigeria*, Fifteenth Annual Activity Report of the African Commission on Human and Peoples' Rights (Annex V).

state in providing socio-economic rights to peoples. It recognised the rights of 'peoples' and even recommended compensation for the victims. This has been hailed as a landmark precedent for international and domestic courts on socio-economic rights of a people.[76]

---

76   See C Odinkalu & C Christensen 'The African Commission on Human and Peoples' Rights: The development of its non-state communications procedures' (1998) 20 *Human Rights Quarterly* 278.

CHAPTER 13

INSTITUTIONAL CHALLENGES AND REFORMS UNDER THE AFRICAN HUMAN RIGHTS SYSTEM

The image of the African human rights system, particularly its enforcement mechanisms, is not very appealing. As Odinkalu noted, the system is generally perceived as a juridical misfit, with a treaty basis and institutional mechanisms that are dangerously inadequate.[1] Naldi and Magliveras observed that 'the [African] Commission does not give hope for optimism'[2] because, in their opinion, it adopts 'a generally pusillanimous approach too respectful of state sovereignty.'[3] The African Court, which is still at its infancy, has also already had a share of criticism. Some scholars are sceptical of its potential to improve the human rights situation in the region.[4] Those aspects of the Court that have contributed to this scepticism include its jurisdiction[5], access[6] and its relationship with the Commission, AU and other relevant human rights bodies in the region.[7]

---

1   C Odinkalu 'Analysis of paralysis or paralysis by analysis? Implementing economic, social, and cultural rights under the African Charter on Human and Peoples' Rights' (2001) 23 *Human Rights Quarterly* 328.

2   G Naldi & K Magliveras 'Reinforcing the African system of human rights: The protocol on the establishment of a regional court of human and peoples' rights' (1998) 16 *Netherlands Quarterly of Human Rights* 432.

3   As above.

4   See C Heyns 'The African regional human rights system: In need of reform?' (2001) 2 *African Human Rights Law Journal* 166-171; N Udombana 'Toward the African Court on Human and Peoples' Rights: Better late than never' (2000) 3 *Yale Human Rights and Development Law Journal* 90.

5   M Mutua 'The Banjul Charter and the African cultural fingerprint: An evaluation of the language of duties' (1995) 35 *Virginia Journal of International Law* 339.

6   See for example, W Kaguongo 'The questions of *locus standi* and admissibility before the African Court on Human and Peoples' Rights' in F Viljoen (ed) *The African Human Rights System: Towards the co-existence of the African Commission on Human and Peoples' Rights and the African Court on Human and Peoples' Rights* (2006) 81-85.

7   A O'Shea 'A Critical reflection on the proposed African Court on Human and Peoples' Rights' (2001) 2 *African Human Rights Law Journal* 293; I Badawi 'The future relationship between the African Court and the African Commission' (2002) *African Human Rights Law Journal* 253; F Viljoen & E Baimu 'Courts for Africa: Considering the co-existence of the African Court on Human and Peoples' Rights and the African Court of justice' (2004) 22/2 *Netherlands Quarterly of Human Rights* 241-267.

While the above observations are indisputably true, there are some prospects for an invigorated and efficient regional human rights system. As already pointed out, some developments of historical proportions have already taken place on the regional human rights landscape with the likelihood of impacting the future of Africans. This is a clear indication that the system has gradually been evolving as new institutions and norms are being initiated in order to facilitate its efficiency. In all fairness therefore, it will be more accurate to argue that in the journey towards an effective regional human rights system, both challenges and positive progress have been registered. In this respect, it is expedient to review the achievements, challenges and possible reforms to the key enforcement institutions of the system, namely, the African Commission and Court on Human and Peoples' Rights.

13.1   THE AFRICAN COMMISSION ON HUMAN AND PEOPLES' RIGHTS

The reform of the African Commission on Human and Peoples' Rights necessitates a multi-dimensional and incremental process, based on a careful and rigorous assessment of its actual performance and real potential. In tandem with this realisation, it is crucial to examine a number of aspects of the Commission which may be in need of reform. These aspects include, but are not limited to, its composition, organisation, mandates and functions.

To begin with, a number of concerns have been raised regarding the Commission's composition and organisation. These include the mode of election, independence and impartiality of its members; gender representation; and equitable geographic and legal cultural representation.[8] It has been noted, and correctly so, that the Commission is effectively under the control of the Assembly of the Heads of State and Government (AHSG), thus bringing to question its ability to function independently and impartially.[9] A number of provisions in the Charter attest to this fact. For example, it provides

---

8   See, for example, O Nmehielle *The African human rights system: Its laws, practice and institutions* (2001) 172; S Rembe *The system of protection of human rights under the African Charter on Human and Peoples' Rights: Problems and prospects* (1991) 25; E Ankumah *The African Commission on Human and Peoples' Rights* (1997) 18-19.

9   Nmehielle (n 8 above) 172.

for the establishment of the Commission 'within the OAU'[10]; its Commissioners are political appointees[11] and its power to make decisions, including the publication of measures taken lies with the AHSG.[12]

This situation is aggravated by the fact that the Commission cannot make binding decisions against state parties but only recommendations to the AHSG.[13] This is in stark contrast with, for instance, the European Convention on Human Rights and Fundamental Freedoms, which has provision for mechanisms with jurisdiction to make binding decisions against contracting states.[14] Moreover, the involvement of the AHSG in the election of the Commissioners has raised some doubt about the effectiveness of the Commission, as it appears to be subordinate to the AHSG.[15]

These fears are confirmed by the fact that since its establishment, the Commission has been served by Attorneys-General, Ambassadors, Ministers, Judges, Advocates and university lecturers, who are normally appointed as a result of their 'good standing' with their governments, and not necessarily on the basis of their

---

10   Art 30 of the Charter states as follows: 'An African Commission on Human and Peoples' Rights, hereinafter called 'the Commission', shall be established within the Organisation of African Unity to promote human and peoples' rights and ensure their protection in Africa.'

11   Art 33 of the Charter.

12   See the Rules of Procedure of the African Commission on Human and Peoples' Rights adopted on October 6, 1995.

13   Art 58 of the Charter provides: '1. When it appears after deliberations of the Commission that one or more communications apparently relate to special cases which reveal the existence of a series of serious or massive violations of human and peoples' rights, the Commission shall draw the attention of the Assembly of Heads of State and Government to these special cases. 2. The Assembly of Heads of State and Government may then request the Commission to undertake an in-depth study of these cases and make a factual report, accompanied by its findings and recommendations. 3. A case of emergency duly noticed by the Commission shall be submitted by the latter to the Chairman of the Assembly of Heads of State and Government who may request an in-depth study.'

14   See art 41 of the Convention for the Protection of Human Rights and Fundamental Freedoms.

15   Rembe (n 8 above) 25.

competence and human rights credentials.[16] Consequently, their election has seriously undermined the independence and credibility of the Commission. The independence of Commissioners is the cornerstone of the mechanism's credibility. The Charter emphasises that the Commissioners 'shall serve in their personal capacity.'[17] This means that they ought to serve independently without any iota of influence from their home governments, despite the fact that they were nominated by them.[18]

The appointment of Commissioners who are also Ministers or Ambassadors in their home governments has been condemned because they can hardly function independently or even effectively.[19] Their efficiency is largely impaired by the workload that comes with the performance of multiple tasks. Some of these political appointees also lack expertise, commitment and interest in human rights. Their attendance in the Commission's sessions is therefore largely due to formality and performance of duties. No wonder, it is not uncommon to find as many as between four and five Commissioners being absent as a result of engagements, not related to the Commission's work.[20] Consequently, the Commission's endeavours to improve the enforcement of human rights in the region has grossly been impaired.

In an apparent attempt to reverse this trend, the AU adopted guidelines on the election of Commissioners, particularly aimed at ensuring their independence and impartiality.[21] Among other things, the guidelines require states to only nominate and elect persons with requisite knowledge, expertise and commitment to human rights and whose regular assignments do not, or appear to,

---

16   See R Murray 'The African Charter on Human and Peoples' Rights 1987-2000: An overview of its progress and problems' (2001) 1 *African human Rights Law Journal* 7; G Wachira 'A critical examination of the African Charter on Human and Peoples' Rights: Towards strengthening the African human rights system to enable it effectively meet the needs of the African population' in Viljoen (n 6 above) 19.

17   African Charter, art 31(2).

18   Nmehielle (n 8 above) 173.

19   Ankumah (n 8 above) 18-19.

20   See Nmehielle (n 8 above) 173; Ankumah (n 8 above) 16.

21   See Assembly/AU/Dec.84 (V), on the election of members of the African Commission in Sirte, Libya (4-5 July 2005).

compromise their independence. It is interesting to note that in the recent nomination and election of Commissioners, these guidelines were adhered to and states only elected candidates whose positions and careers did not seem to conflict with their independence and impartiality.[22]

In line with the subordination argument, the AHSG has been accused of asserting its influence and position to interfere with the Commission's work. This is in light of, for example, the Assembly's decision to suspend the publication of the African Commission's 17th Activity Report and deletion of certain aspects of the 19th Activity Report before its publication.[23] At its sixth Summit in Khartoum, Sudan, in January 2006, the Assembly decided 'to adopt and authorise, in accordance with Article 59 of the Charter, the publication of the 19th Activity Report of the African Commission and its Annexes, except for those containing the Resolutions on Eritrea, Ethiopia, Sudan, Uganda and Zimbabwe.'[24]

The decision to suspend the publication of the Report was made after Zimbabwe protested that the report did not incorporate its response to the findings of the Commission on a fact finding mission. This is despite the fact that the Commission had solicited the said response to no avail.[25] The insubordination of the Commission has made it exceptionally difficult for human rights to be effectively enforced at the regional level simply because states have the last word in the Commission's work. It is therefore important for the Commission to clarify its status, and dialogue with the AHSG to ensure that interference with its work by both individual states and the Assembly is curtailed.

The geographical composition of the Commission has also remained unsatisfactory until recently. It is unfortunate that the Charter does not provide for geographical and gender balance in the Commission. Thus, over the years, most Commissioners have

---

22   Wachira (n 16 above) 21.

23   As above.

24   As above.

25   As above.

come from West Africa.[26] At its Twentieth Session, for instance, six Commissioners were from West Africa, two each from North and Central Africa, and one from East and Southern Africa. East and Southern Africa have particularly been under-represented. Equitable geographical representation at the Commission has often been made an issue, and rightly so. The reason for this is the connection between the geographical divides and legal cultures of Africa, and the need to have these legal cultures represented.[27]

Apart from geographic representation, the issue of gender balance in the Commission has also been of concern. From its inception, it appeared that the role of women in the Commission was taken for granted.[28] This trend has changed in the recent years and a more representative Commission is now in place. Its membership now reflects gender and regional balance. As at April 2007, the Commissioners were elected as follows: two from Eastern Africa[29]; three from Western Africa[30]; one from North Africa[31]; and four from Southern Africa.[32] Central Africa was the only region that was not represented.

It should be noted that the number of female Commissioners has also increased. As at April 2008, the Commission had five female Commissioners, which is almost half of the total number. The Chairperson was also a woman (Madame Salamata Sawadogo). This is a marked improvement that needs to be encouraged because the increasing participation of women in the Commission will encourage positive developments in promotional and protective activities in the areas of human rights that affect women.

---

26   In 1996, the Commission had seven members from West Africa and none from Southern or East Africa.

27   Nmehielle (n 8 above) 172.

28   As above, 173.

29   Mr. Yaser Sid Ahmad El-Hassan (Sudanese) and Mr. Bahame Tom Mukirya Nyanduga (Tanzanian).

30   Madame Salamata Sawadogo (Burkinabe), Madame Reine Alapini-Gansou (Benin) and Mr. Musa Ngary Bitaye (Gambian).

31   Ambassador Kamel Rezag-Bara (Algerian).

32   Dr. Angela Melo (Mozambican), Ms. Sanji Mmasenono Monageng (Botswana), Mr. Mumba Malila (Zambian) and Advocate (Ms) Faith Pansy Tlakula (South African).

Another area in which the Commission is in need of reform relates to its promotional mandate. Although initiative has been taken to promote human rights in the region, the same has not been satisfactory, partly because the Commission is hampered by a number of internal and external challenges. To begin with, it is inevitable to note, although publicity is essential to the realisation of the Commission's promotional mandate, the same has not been done effectively. Odinkalu noted that one of the reasons why the Commission has not had much impact is because many Africans are not even aware of its existence or, if they are, they do not appreciate its mandate and capacity.[33] There is the need to publicise the Commission and the Charter through, for example, publications, promotional missions, hosting more sessions in all states and through the mass media. Additionally, national human rights institutions, civil society and educational institutions have a great role to play in creating awareness and sensitising the general public of the regional human rights mechanisms.

Publicity, if taken seriously, would play an important role in enhancing the effective promotion of human rights. Individuals, NGOs and Inter-Governmental Organisations need reliable information to put pressure on governments.[34] The lack of publicity in the work of the Commission has contributed to the low esteem human rights have enjoyed on the continent. Moreover, it has led to the situation where national legislations, including Constitutions of states parties, are at variance with the provisions of the Charter, hence complicating its enforcement.[35]

Apart from the issue of publicity, the Commission has also somehow failed in its relationship with NGOs, though admittedly, they have greatly influenced its activities.[36] For example, it was through the efforts of NGOs that the Commission was able to appoint Special Rapporteurs on Prisons and Other Conditions of

---

33   C Odinkalu 'Implementing economic, social and cultural rights under the African Charter on Human and Peoples' Rights' in M Evans & R Murray *The African Charter on Human and Peoples' Rights: The system in practice: 1986-2000* (2002) 234.

34   M Killander 'Confidentiality versus publicity: Interpreting Article 59 of the African Charter on Human and Peoples' Rights' (2006) 6 *African Human Rights law Journal* 572.

35   Odinkalu (n 33 above) 234.

36   Murray (n 16 above) 13.

Detention[37], on Summary, Arbitrary and Extrajudicial Executions[38], on Refugees and Displaced Persons in Africa, on Human Rights Defenders and on Women's Rights.[39] As if to appreciate and acknowledge their involvement in its work, the Commission has so far granted observer status to more than 300 NGOs, to enable them to participate during its sessions.[40] Whereas the participation of NGOs should be encouraged, the Commission has seemingly developed the tendency of abandoning some of its responsibilities to these organisations.[41] For instance, one Commissioner, who merely was being assisted by an NGO, reportedly attributed his failure to deliver to the lack of funding from the NGO.[42]

The Commission ought to execute its mandate, within its available resources, without necessarily having to rely on NGOs. Sadly, even with support from NGOs, some of the Special Rapporteurs cannot boast of much success in their assigned areas. This has resulted to their usefulness being questioned. For example, upon her appointment, the first Special Rapporteur on Women's Rights failed to undertake any of the studies on the situation of women's rights in Africa that were initially planned.[43] The same

---

37   See generally, 'Report of the Special Rapporteur on Prisons and Conditions of Detention to the 21st Session of the African Commission on Human and Peoples' Rights'Tenth Annual Activity Report (Annex VII).

38   At the Commission's 14th session, held in Addis Ababa in 1993, Amnesty International proposed that the Commission appoints a Special Rapporteur on Extrajudicial Executions in Africa. See 'Statement of Amnesty International to the 15th session of the African Commission on Human and Peoples' Rights, April 1995'. See also 'Report on Extra-Judicial, Summary or Arbitrary Executions (by Hatem Ben Salem, Special Rapporteur)'Tenth Annual Activity Report (Annex VI).

39   See 'Draft programme of activities of the Special Rapporteur on women's rights in Africa for the period 1999-2001', DOC/OS/53(XXIV); 'Report of the Special Rapporteur on women's rights', DOC/OS/57(XXIV).

40   See the Twenty-Second Activity Report of the African Commission on Human and Peoples' Rights, June 2007, EX.CL/364(XI). See also 'Resolution on granting observer status to national human rights institutions in Africa', Twelfth Annual Activity Report of the African Commission on Human and Peoples' Rights (1998-1999) AHG/215 (XXXV) (Annex IV).

41   Murray (n 16 above) 13.

42   As above.

43   For the planned studies see, 'Draft programme of activities of the Special Rapporteur on women's rights in Africa for the period 1999-2001', DOC/OS/53(XXIV); 'Report of the Special Rapporteur on women's rights', DOC/OS/57(XXIV). See also Murray (n 16 above) 13.

is noted of the Special Rapporteur on Extrajudicial Executions. Harrington noted the following shortcomings about this particular Rapporteur:

> Firstly, the Special Rapporteur had no expertise in the subject, no concrete notion of how to proceed, and no written mandate to guide him... The second problem was that there were no material means— financial or administrative— made available to the Special Rapporteur, even for writing and sending faxes and making phone calls. The Secretariat of the African Commission proved manifestly incapable of playing the role of administrative arm for the Special Rapporteur's activities...Thirdly, the Special Rapporteur was professionally ill-placed to pursue investigations of, or negotiations with, African governments. At the time of his appointment he was a mayor. In 1997 he was appointed the Tunisian ambassador to Senegal.... Although superficially these positions might have seemed as presenting him with abundant opportunities to know and influence African governments, in practice the nature of his duty to represent his own state made it extremely difficult if not impossible for him to appear at other times in the guise of an independent Rapporteur.[44]

As evidenced by the above narration, it is not exclusively the inadequacy of the African Charter that hampers the African Commission's effectiveness, but also the lack of resources and, most critically, the lack of will and requisite expertise on the part of some Commissioners. The attempt by the Commission to designate Special Rapporteurs to minimise the constraints of the institution can only be successful where the individual appointed is competent and also devoted to the task.[45]

Additionally, the Commission's promotional activities have paid lip service to economic, social and cultural rights by being predominantly focused on civil and political rights.[46] Concerns have been raised by representatives of civil society organisations, in several of the Commission's sessions, that there is the need to focus

---

44   J Harrington 'Special Rapporteurs of the African Commission on Human and Peoples' Rights' in Evans & Murray (n 33 above) 256.

45   As above.

46   S Khoza 'Promoting economic, social and cultural rights in Africa: The African Commission holds a seminar in Pretoria' (2004) 4 *African Human Rights Law Journal* 334.

on socio-economic rights too.[47] As recently as 2004, the African Commission, in collaboration with the International Centre for Legal Protection of Human Rights (Interights), the Cairo Institute for Human Rights Studies and the Centre for Human Rights at the University of Pretoria, co-hosted a seminar on 'Economic, Social and Cultural Rights in Africa.'[48] The seminar highlighted the violation of economic, social and cultural rights on the continent, emphasising their neglect and relegation to a secondary status. More needs to be done by the Commission to give weight to the promotion of this category of rights on the continent.

At another level, it is evident that the Commission carries out its promotional activities only during the inter-session period. Even so, Commissioners have restricted themselves to visiting universities and other institutions of higher learning in countries assigned to them.[49] While so doing, the Commission is definitely seized with the knowledge that masses of Africans are ignorant of its existence. Hence, it needs to do more than just giving lectures in institutions of higher learning. It could, for example, organise public awareness campaigns in African towns and villages, targeting people from diverse backgrounds. This, however, requires the collaboration and cooperation of states. Additionally, sufficient resource allocation needs to be considered towards this end.

It is needless to emphasise that the size of the continent and the inadequacy of material and human resources present challenges to effective regional promotion of human rights. With one Commissioner working part time and responsible for promoting the Charter in three to five countries, chances of effective promotion are slim.[50] It is therefore necessary for the Commission to operate through a network of national, international and private organisations based in those areas. Because human rights promotion requires publicity in the mass media, which in many African countries are still

---

47   See, for example, the 'Report of the 17th session of the African Commission on Human and Peoples' Rights, Lomé, Togo, 13–22 March 1995', published by the African Society of International and Comparative Law 8.

48   Held in Pretoria from 13 to 17 September 2004. See generally Khoza (n 46 above) 334.

49   Nmehielle (n 8 above) 179.

50   As above.

controlled by governments, the Commission must seek the support of all stakeholders if its promotional mandate is to be a success.[51]

Another promotional activity of the Commission that warrants reform is the state reporting mechanism. The effectiveness of this mechanism is undermined by several factors, the first one being its inadequate legal framework.[52] As Kofi observed, the reporting obligation under Article 62 of the Charter is rather terse compared to that of other human rights instruments, such as the ICCPR.[53] Whereas the ICCPR requires states to report on 'the measures' they have adopted, the African Charter requires states parties to report on 'the legislative and other measures...'[54] This suggests that the African system places a greater emphasis on legislative measures.

Further, the African Commission lacks the explicit authority to make 'general comments.' On the other hand, the ICCPR gives the Human Rights Committee (now Human Rights Council) the authority to issue 'general comments'.[55] It was out of this realisation that the participants at the 1991 'Conference on the African Commission' recommended that the Commission should 'interpret Articles 45(1)(b) and 60 of the Charter as providing the Commission with the mandate to perform the functional equivalent of the Human Rights Committee's general comments.'[56]

The African Commission's initial guidelines on state reporting, which were unnecessarily complex, also contributed to the inefficiency of the reporting mechanism. In the formative years of state reporting, the Commission did not have clearly laid down procedures. Thereafter, at its 4th ordinary session in October 1991, it adopted the 'General Guidelines for National Periodic Reports.'[57]

---

51   As above.

52   See in this regard Q Kofi 'The African Charter on Human and Peoples' Rights: Towards a more effective reporting mechanism' (2002) 2 *African Human rights Law Journal* 273.

53   As above.

54   See ICCPR, art 40.

55   Kofi (n 52 above) 273. See also ICCPR, art 40(4).

56   As above.

57   See 'Guidelines on national periodic reports', Second Annual Activity Report of the African Commission on Human and Peoples' Rights (Annex XII).

These guidelines were too detailed, complex and difficult to follow.[58] They were later amended, only to find that states were already de-motivated and therefore unwilling to comply with their reporting obligations because no seriousness was attached to the process from the beginning.[59]

Other reasons for non-compliance by states with their reporting obligations include the general lack of political will and the lack of a co-ordinated effort between state departments.[60] The non-coercive nature of the reporting mechanism is also likely to have contributed to the lack of commitment to the reporting process. States that submit their reports do so as a mere formality or a public relations exercise.[61] Those that choose not to submit their reports are neither reproved nor punished. Simply put, many states do not seem to appreciate the importance of submitting their reports as required.[62] Partly because of the failure by states to submit reports as they should, the African Commission has not fully succeeded in enhancing the protection and promotion of human rights in the region.

The first report under the African Charter was submitted by Libya in January 1990.[63] As at 9th March 1992, only eight states parties had submitted their initial reports.[64] As at 30th March 2000, twenty-four states had never submitted a report and only twelve had no overdue reports.[65] As at June 2007, fifteen states had not submitted any report, fourteen states had submitted all their reports,

---

58   See Nmehielle (n 8 above) 189; Ankumah (n 8 above) 284; F Viljoen 'State reporting under the African Charter on Human and Peoples' Rights: A boost from the south' (1999) 44 *Journal of African Law* 112.

59   G Mugwanya 'Examination of state reports by the African Commission: A critical appraisal' (2001) 2 *African Human Rights Law Journal* 278.

60   As above.

61   As above.

62   See C Heyns & F Viljoen 'The impact of the United Nations human rights treaties on the domestic level' (2001) 23 *Human Rights Quarterly* 508.

63   Third Annual Activity Report of the African Commission on Human and Peoples' Rights, para 23.

64   Fifth Annual Activity Report of the African Commission on Human and Peoples' Rights, para 11.

65   Thirteenth Annual Activity Report of the African Commission on Human and Peoples' Rights, (Annex III).

while fourteen states had submitted one report but owed more.[66] Moreover, most reports lack serious self-evaluation.[67] Nigeria's initial report, for example, was very brief and uninformative.[68] Some initial reports, however, such as those of The Gambia, Mozambique and Algeria, were of a satisfactory standard.[69]

To overcome the problem of irregular submission and non-submission of reports, the Commission has, since November 1995, been willing to receive reports which combine several years.[70] However, this approach does not also seem to be working. Perhaps the approach of the UN Committee on Economic, Social and Cultural Rights and that of the Committee on the Elimination of all forms of Racial Discrimination could be adopted to salvage the situation. The two UN Committees have developed procedures that enable the examination of a country's human rights situation even when no report has been submitted.[71] Similarly, Heyns' recommendation, that an inter-departmental body responsible for state reporting should be formed in each country, ought to be considered.[72] Additionally, a reporting support unit should be formed under the African human rights system, to assist governments with all aspects of reporting.

Another inhibiting factor to effective state reporting is the lack of seriousness during the report examination proceedings. There is some indication that the report examination proceedings are taken lightly by both the Commission and reporting states.[73] For example, during the 18th session when the report of Tunisia was being examined, some shortcomings regarding the procedure were noted.[74]

---

66   See the Twenty-Second Annual Activity Report of the African Commission on Human and Peoples' Rights, 11.

67   Mugwanya (n 59 above) 278.

68   As above. It is said that the whole report was six pages long.

69   As above.

70   See *Note Verbale* ACHPR/PR/A046, 30 November 1995.

71   See UN Doc HRI/MC/1995/2 7; UN Doc HRI/MC/1996/2, 10-11. See also the arguments advanced in kofi (n 52 above) 275.

72   Heyns (n 4 above) 173.

73   See S Malstrom & G Oberleitner '18th ordinary and 2nd extra-ordinary session of the African Commission on Human and Peoples' Rights' (1996) 14 *Netherlands Quarterly of Human Rights* 93.

74   As above.

To start with, the Rapporteur and the Commissioners had not been provided with copies of the report and other relevant documents and background material. Further, no English translation of the report was provided, thus effectively locking out the English speaking Commissioners from participating in the proceedings. At the 21st ordinary session of the Commission, history repeated itself when the reports of Sudan and Zimbabwe were submitted only in English, as a result of which the non-English speaking Commissioners were excluded from the discussions.[75]

At the 28th ordinary session of the Commission held in Benin in 2000, the reports of Namibia and Ghana were not examined because their representatives did not show up.[76] Earlier, at its 25th ordinary session in 1999, the Commission was compelled to adopt a resolution concerning the Republic of Seychelles' refusal to present its initial report.[77] The resolution noted that the Commission had, since its 17th session, invited Seychelles to present its initial report. However, the government had refused to abide by the request, under the pretext of unavailability of resources to implement such an obligation.[78]

Considering this to be a breach of Article 62 of the African Charter, the Commission invited the AHSG 'to express their disapproval of such a persistent refusal that amounts to a deliberate violation of the Charter by the Republic of Seychelles.'[79] It further requested the Assembly 'to invite Seychelles to abide by the Charter and to consider the appropriate measures to be taken against the Republic of Seychelles.'[80] In spite of the Commission's efforts, Seychelles' report could still not be examined afterwards because there was no delegate to present it.[81]

---

75   See S Malstrom '21st ordinary session of the African Commission on Human and Peoples' Rights' (1997) 15 *Netherlands Quarterly of Human Rights* 382.

76   R Murray 'The African Commission on Human and Peoples' Rights' (2001) 19 *Netherlands Quarterly of Human Rights* 94.

77   As above.

78   Kofi (n 52 above) 277.

79   As above.

80   As above.

81   See 26th ordinary session of the African Commission on Human and Peoples' Rights, 1-15 November 1999, Kigali, Rwanda.

Even when delegates are sent to present reports, it sometimes happens that they are unable to provide the required information in response to questions from the Commission. A good example to be cited in this regard is that of Ghana's *Chargé d'Affaires* who presented the country's initial report in 1993.[82] The representative's incompetence warranted the Commission to urge the government of Ghana to submit in writing additional information and response to questions which could not be answered by the representative during the examination of the report.[83]

If the reporting mechanism is to be effective, it is necessary for both the Commission and reporting states to start taking the exercise more seriously.[84] The Commission should consider the approach of making concrete concluding observations.[85] This approach was once attempted in respect of reports submitted by Algeria, Congo, Ghana and Namibia, but was later discontinued for no apparent reasons.[86] Viljoen correctly noted that without concluding observations the reporting process 'has little meaning because no critical evaluation can be conducted without the Commission stating its position on the facts presented before it.'[87]

It has been said that the report examination process usually ends with profuse thanks to the representatives, without any advice to states on how to improve their human rights situations.[88] This defeats the logic and essence of having the process in the first place. It was equally noted that the Commission lacks sufficient time to examine reports in detail because it has too much to do within a fixed period in the course of its sessions.[89] The time allocated for

---

82   See Final Communiqué of the 14th ordinary session of the African Commission on Human and Peoples' Rights- ACHPR/FIN/COM (XIV).

83   As above.

84   See Malstrom (n 75 above) 382.

85   The approach of making concluding observations is provided for in Rules 85(3) & 86(1) of the Commission's Rules of Procedure.

86   See F Viljoen 'Examination of state reports at the 27th session of the African Commission on Human and Peoples' Rights: A critical analysis and proposals for reform' (2001) 16 *South African Journal on Human Rights* 576.

87   See Viljoen (n 58 above) 110.

88   Mugwanya (n 59 above) 278.

89   As above.

the examination proceedings should be extended since state reports inform the Commission on the extent to which the Charter's provisions have been given effect at the state level.

Some of the problems mentioned above, such as the lack of adequate time to consider reports and their non-submission in the approved languages, are linked to the Commission's budgetary constraints and the attendant lack of secretarial support.[90] These problems have given rise to other challenges such as limited periods of working sessions, inability to make documents available for circulation to those who need them, default in transcription and translation of reports; and the unavailability of easy access to modern communication technology such as e-mail and the Internet. The Commission's financial allocations from the AU have often declined rather than increased. This has partly been attributed to the difficulty of the Union to recover the pledged contributions from members states.[91]

Under Article 41 of the African Charter, the Commission of the AU is responsible for the costs of the African Commission's operations, including the provision of staff, financial and other resources, necessary for the effective discharge of its mandate.[92] During the 2006 financial year, the Commission was allocated US $ 1,142,436.[93] In the 2007 financial year, there was a five per cent increase to the budget, bringing it to about US $ 1,199,557.8.[94] Out of this amount, only US $ 47,000 was allocated for the Commission's programmes, including promotion and protection missions.

As per the Commission, this amount is enough to cover only four promotion missions in a year, whereas each Commissioner is expected to undertake at least two missions per year.[95] There is no allocation for research, training/capacity building, special mechanisms

---

90   See Wachira (n 16 above) 26; Nmehielle (n 8 above) 195.

91   Kofi (n 52 above) 263.

92   Art 41 states in part that '...the Organisation of African Unity shall bear the costs of the staff and services....'

93   See the Twenty-Second Activity Report of the African Commission on Human and Peoples' Rights, 17, para 100.

94   As above.

95   As above.

activities, projects, seminars and conferences, commemoration of human rights events, such as the Africa Human Rights Day, etc. This amount does not cover even a third of the costs of the promotion missions for Commissioners and special mechanisms earmarked for a year.[96]

This explains the magnitude of the financial strain the Commission is facing. Consequently, the Commission continues to resort to extra-budgetary sources to supplement its AU funding. It has therefore been relying on material and financial support from its partners, such as the Danish Human Rights Institute[97], Rights and Democracy[98], the Danish International Development Agency (DANIDA)[99], Open Society Initiative for West African (OSIWA)[100], and the Republic of South Africa[101], among others.

The lack of ample financial and material resources has also affected staffing at the Commission's Secretariat. By the end of 2007, the Commission had only 23 members of staff to undertake its enormous tasks.[102] It cannot be gainsaid that the effectiveness of the Secretariat is critical for the success of the African Commission. The Commission considers at least fifty communications at each ordinary session and a lot of research is needed to finalise a communication.[103]

---

96   As above, para 101.

97   As above, para 104. The Secretariat of the African Commission continues to be supported by the Danish Institute for Human Rights by financing the post of an Expert on Strategic Planning.

98   As above, para 105. The Canadian NGO, Rights and Democracy, has supported the Commission with personnel and has put at its disposal three Canadian *cooperants* since January 2006.

99   As above, para 106. DANIDA continues to support the activities of the Working Group on Indigenous Populations/Communities through the International Working Group on Indigenous Affairs (IWGIA). This support was expected to continue until June 2007. The European Union, through the International Labour Organization (ILO) is also supporting the activities of the WGIP.

100 As above, para 107. The Open Society for West Africa has provided the Commission with computers and printers and made available money to improve the website of the Commission.

101 As above, para 108. The Republic of South Africa has provided funding for activities of the Commission and also seconded one of its nationals to assist the Commission's Special Rapporteur on the Rights of Women in Africa.

102 Twenty-Second Activity Report of the African Commission on Human and Peoples' Rights, 19.

103 As above.

Given the workload of, for example, the Special Rapporteurs, each of them should have at least one full-time legal officer to coordinate their activities. At the moment, however, only two of them have been provided with legal officers on short term basis.[104] Legal officers should also be appointed to advise Commissioners on state reports. To promote human and peoples' rights and ensure their protection in Africa, a vast continent of 53 independent states, the current staff strength is clearly inadequate.

The above are the key factors inhibiting the effectiveness of the state reporting mechanism. There may be others that are either connected with or incidental to these. It should therefore suffice to state that the above discussed factors are only instructive but not exhaustive. It may not be possible to analyse in detail all the challenges to state reporting under the African human rights system.

Apart from the specific suggestions and recommendations discussed above, there are a number of other ways the state reporting mechanism can be invigorated and made more effective. One such way is to increase the role of NGOs and national human rights Institutions in state reporting. For example, the Commission can request these organisations to furnish 'shadow' or alternative reports to those of the states. The 'shadow' or alternative reports provide the requisite information that will enable the African Commission to engage in constructive dialogue with state representatives when the reports are considered.[105]

The practice of furnishing 'shadow' reports is also entrenched in the European system. Article 23 of the European Social Charter imposes on governments an obligation to send their periodic reports to national organisations of employers and trade unions. These organisations have the right to comment on the reports, and the governments have a duty to forward the comments to the monitoring bodies.[106] This approach could be given a thought under the African human rights system. The increased involvement of these organisations is essential because the Commission is logistically

---

104   As above.
105   Mugwanya (n 59 above) 280.
106   Kofi (n 52 above) 271.

limited to monitor every states' compliance with the Charter. Moreover, national human rights institutions and NGOs that have been granted observer status by the Commission may also be called upon to exert the necessary pressure on their governments to supply their reports.[107] If these institutions perform their functions as required, a more effective monitoring system could be guaranteed.

Another way to invigorate the state reporting mechanism is to involve AU organs. The success of the mechanism depends, to a significant extent, on the possibility of exposing and sanctioning non-compliant states. The exposure of non-compliant states may go a long way to improve state reporting because African governments are never comfortable with adverse publicity, especially with respect to their poor human rights records.[108] There is sufficient legal basis on which the African Commission can rely in order to bring on board some AU organs in its state reporting activities.

Article 45(1)(c) of the African Charter, for example, calls on the African Commission, when performing its functions, to 'co-operate with other African and international institutions concerned with the promotion and protection of human and peoples' rights.' This is a general provision that could be interpreted liberally to allow the Commission to work with any organ of the AU in its state reporting activities.[109] The Commission could, for instance, collaborate with relevant AU organs to induce some degree of political pressure on a recalcitrant state, as a way of strengthening the state reporting mechanism.

Other than its promotional mandate, the effectiveness of the protective mandate of the Commission, which is exercised mainly through the communications (complaints) procedure, has been and is still being, undermined by several factors. First, for a long time, there was uncertainty as to whether the Commission had the authority to consider individual complaints, and also about the exact mandate of the Commission when considering such complaints.[110]

---

107   As above.

108   As above, 282.

109   As above.

110   Heyns (n 4 above) 163.

Article 58 provides for a special procedure to be followed by the Commission in the case of 'a series of serious or massive' human rights violations. However, it was not entirely clear from the text whether individual communications could be considered by the Commission if these communications did not reveal such 'serious or massive violations.'[111] At its own volition, the Commission has resorted to considering individual communications, even when they do not reveal serious or massive violations.[112]

Moreover, the requirement under Article 58 that the Commission should draw the attention of the AHSG to *prima facie* situations of serious or massive violations, and then await further instructions from the Assembly, proved to be a dead letter, since the latter has apparently never responded to such requests.[113] This has, however, not deterred the Commission from finding 'a series of serious or massive violations' in a number of cases, without necessarily bringing such cases to the attention of the AHSG.[114] In some cases, the Commission has failed or ignored to deal with states against which several communications alleging serious and massive violations were pending. For example, in separate cases brought against Chad[115], Malawi[116], Zaire[117] and Rwanda[118], the Commission

---

111   As above.

112   As above. See also communications 147/95, 149/96, *Sir Dawda K Jawara v. The Gambia*, Thirteenth Annual Activity Report of the African Commission on Human and Peoples' Rights, para 42.

113   R Murray *The African Commission on Human and Peoples' Rights and international law* (2000) 20.

114   R Murray 'Serious or massive violations under the African Charter on Human and Peoples' Rights: A comparison with the Inter-American and European mechanisms' (1999) 17 *Netherlands Quarterly of Human Rights* 109.

115   Communication 74/92, *Commission Nationale des Droits de l'Homme et des Libertés v. Chad,* Ninth Annual Activity Report of the African Commission on Human and Peoples' Rights (Annex VIII).

116   Communications 64/92, 68/92 & 78/92, *Krishna Achuthan (on behalf of Aleke Banda), Amnesty International (on behalf of Orton and Vera Chirwa v. Malawi)*, Seventh Annual Activity Report of the African Commission on Human and Peoples' Rights (Annex IX); Eighth Annual Activity Report of the African Commission on Human and Peoples' Rights (Annex VI).

117   Communications 25/89, 47/90, 56/91 & 100/93, *Free Legal Assistance Group, Lawyers' Committee for Human Rights, Union Interafricaine des Droits de l'Homme, Les Témoins de Jehoveh v. Zaire,* Ninth Annual Activity Report of the African Commission on Human and Peoples' Rights (Annex VIII).

118   Communications 27/89, 46/91, 49/91, 99/93, *Organisation Mondiale Contre La Torture*

found that there were serious and massive violations, but it did not take any action.[119]

It is also evident that the Charter is not clear on what kind of findings the Commission is able to make after the consideration of individual communications and what the possible remedies are.[120] Nonetheless, the Commission has developed a practice of its own in this regard, which has already been discussed at length elsewhere. What needs to be done, however, is to entrench the Commission's procedure in the Charter or in the Commission's Rules of Procedure. It is advisable for the Charter to be revised to provide a clear legal basis for making of findings and recommendations by the Commission.[121]

On remedies, the Commission has displayed a general lack of uniformity and consistency.[122] For instance, while it ordered the annulment of offending decrees in *Civil Liberties Organisation v. Nigeria*[123], it failed to do the same in other cases with similar facts.[124] Additionally, some of the remedies it previously awarded were neither clear nor unambiguous. In many instances, it merely stated that the government was 'responsible for the reparation of these abuses.' This has brought to question its ability to chastise recalcitrant states.

---

and Association Internationale des juristes Democrates) Commission Internationale des Juristes (C.I.J) Union Interafricaine des Droits de l'Homme v. Rwanda, Tenth Annual Activity Report of the African Commission on Human and Peoples' Rights (Annex X).

119   R Murray 'Serious or massive violations under the African Charter on Human and Peoples' Rights: A comparison with the Inter-American and European mechanisms' (1999) 17 *Netherlands Quarterly of Human Rights* 109.

120   Heyns (n 4 above) 164.

121   As above, 163.

122   See G Mugwanya *Human rights in Africa: Enhancing human rights through the African regional human rights system* (2003) 373-374.

123   Communication 101/93, *Civil liberties Organisation in Respect of the Nigerian Bar Association v. Nigeria,* Eighth Annual Activity Report of the African Commission on Human and Peoples' Rights (Annex VI).

124   See, for example, Communication 102/93, *Constitutional Rights Project and Civil Liberties Organisation v. Nigeria,* Twelfth Annual Activity Report of the African Commission on Human and Peoples' Rights (Annex V); Communication 129/94, *Constitutional Rights Project (in respect of Lekwot and six others) v. Nigeria.*

The quality of the Commission's decisions is also quite unsatisfactory.[125] Generally, they are not detailed and seldom expound on the Charter's provisions.[126] It is therefore recommended that the Commission should make its decisions more elaborate. Other than expressly citing the relevant provisions of the Charter, the decisions should be supported with judicial precedents, as well as jurisprudence from national and other international mechanisms. Such elaborate and well formulated decisions are essential in deepening the normative understanding of the rights in the Charter.[127]

Another factor inhibiting the effectiveness of the Commission's protective mandate is the undue prolongation of its proceedings. The Commission is on record for taking between two to six years to render its decision on admissibility.[128] For example, *Diakité v. Gabon*[129] was filed with the Commission in April 1992. The Commission, however, declared this case inadmissible more than eight years later, a length of delay that is both unsatisfactory and worrisome. In *Association pour la defence des droits de l'homme et des libertés v. Djibouti*[130], where the Commission delayed the case for unduly long, the matter was later resolved amicably.[131]

The inadequate staffing and management of the Commission's Secretariat, particularly during the initial years of its existence, and the attendant failure of states to respond promptly to inquiries, are said to have contributed to these delays.[132] The Commission's recent approach of presuming the truth of allegations in communications and its proceeding to hear cases, notwithstanding a state's silence, is commendable for speeding up the dispensation of justice. Now,

---

125   Nmehielle (n 8 above) 249.

126   See the observations in M Mutua 'The African human rights court: A two-legged stool?' (1999) 21 *Human Rights Quarterly* 348.

127   Mugwanya (n 122 above) 368.

128   Nmehielle (n 8 above) 248.

129   Communication 73/92, *Mohamed L Diakité v. Gabon*, Seventh Annual Activity Report of the African Commission on Human and Peoples' Rights.

130   Communication 133/94, *Association pour la Défence des Droits de l.Homme et des Libertés v. Djibouti*, Thirteenth Annual Activity Report of the African Commission on Human and Peoples' Rights.

131   As above, paras 13–17.

132   Nmehielle (n 8 above) 248.

on average, the Commission is said to be rendering its admissibility decisions between six months and one and a half years after the filing of a communication.[133] There is still the need to increase the sessions of the Commission as well as the staffing of the Secretariat to avoid any further delays in the dispensation of justice.

Another factor that undermines the protective mandate of the Commission, which is also related to inordinate delay, is the lack of organisation at sessions.[134] Murray noted that although the Commission holds two sessions per year, lasting fifteen days each, the efficient use of time during the session is lacking.[135] It has further been noted that in some instances, the commitment of individual Commissioners to the discharge of their responsibilities has been pathetic and the Commission's internal checks on such conduct have not been sufficient.[136] Although the Commission has an obligation to police itself,[137] in most cases it has failed to do so.

Mugwanya observed that the Commission has always been reluctant to take action in cases where Commissioners' perpetual absence constituted negligence or the lack of commitment.[138] One example he cited in this regard is when the Commission failed to bring to the attention of the then OAU Secretary-General the fact that Commissioner Beye had not attended five consecutive ordinary sessions and two extraordinary sessions in 1989 and 1995.[139] It has further been noted that, in several instances, the Commission begins its session with the requisite quorum which later degenerates in the course of the session when some Commissioners leave prematurely.[140]

---

133   See Communication 106/93, *Amuh Joseph Vitine v. Cameroon*. See generally C Odinkalu & C Christensen 'The African Commission on Human and Peoples' Rights: The development of its non-state communications procedures' (1998) 20 *Human Rights Quarterly* 275-276.

134   Murray (n 16 above) 8.

135   As above.

136   Mugwanya (n 122 above) 377.

137   African Charter, art 39(2).

138   Mugwanya (n 122 above) 378.

139   As above.

140   See Ankumah (n 8 above) 48.

The Commission also lacks detailed written record of the debates and decisions taken at the sessions. Murray succinctly captured this position when she stated as follows:

> A final communiqué is produced at the end of sessions, but this is only a few pages long and often does not detail the discussions on specific points. As a result, there are many occasions where it is either not possible to remember what issues were raised, whether any decision was reached at a previous session or, if so, what it was. There is thus considerable repetition of previous discussions, which wastes valuable time. While submissions made by participants at the session are now collected, copied and disseminated to participants, sometimes by the end of that day, this has for long not been the case.[141]

She therefore suggested that the Commission could improve its own efficiency by requiring its Secretariat to make a detailed report of the session and disseminate it amongst the Commissioners, NGOs, states and other participants.[142]

Like its promotional activities, the protective activities of the Commission also lack ample publicity. The Commission has developed the practice of publishing its decisions on communications in detail in its Activity Reports. These reports, however, are not disseminated widely enough. Consequently not many international bodies and national judicial systems are aware of the Commission's decisions.[143] Indeed, it is not sufficient for the Commission to post its decisions on its website, more so as annexes in its Annual Activity Reports, without giving them ample publicity.

Another inhibiting factor to the effectiveness of the Commission's protective mandate is the lack of proper follow-up procedures.[144] Although the Commission recommends some forms of remedies, their enforcement is lacking. The African Charter is devoid of mechanisms that could compel states parties to abide by the recommendations; neither has the Commission laid down procedures to supervise their enforcement. This effectively confines

---

141   Murray (n 16 above) 8.

142   As above.

143   As above.

144   Mugwanya (n 122 above) 376.

the enforcement of the Commission's recommendations to the goodwill of the states concerned.[145] At present the Commission's follow up is made through diplomatic *note verbales,* during field missions and during its ordinary sessions when state delegates are present.[146] This approach, however, has failed to yield satisfactory results. It is recommended that a Special Rapporteur on follow-up should be appointed.

The Commission is also affected by the persistent lack of support and cooperation from states, especially when it comes to the enforcement of its recommendations. The eleven Commissioners cannot do much without states carrying out their obligations under the Charter. Political leaders are sometimes tempted to take a stand on human rights situation based on what they consider to be their own national interest. For example, there have been instances of democratic governments supporting dictatorial regimes in Africa. Beneath the ostensible reasons are profit motives and political or ideological advantages they wish to exploit.[147]

Some states have failed to comply with their obligations under the Charter by deliberately ignoring the recommendations made by the Commission. In 2004, for example, the Commission granted provisional measures to the Endorois community in Kenya.[148] It urged the state to take immediate steps to ensure that no further mining concessions were issued or land transferred prior to its decision on the substance of the matter. The provisional measures notwithstanding, mining went on in the region. Another example is the landmark *Ogoni* decision.[149] The recommendations made in the decision, including that environmental and social impact assessments

145   Wachira (n 16 above) 23.

146   As above.

147   See generally A Mangu 'The Road to Constitutionalism and Democracy in Post-Colonial Africa: The Case of the Democratic Republic of Congo' (2002), *LLD Thesis University of South Africa* ch. 3.

148   See *CEMIRIDE (On behalf of the Endorois Community) v. Kenya* available at http://www.minorityrights.org/news_detail.asp?ID=342 (accessed on 2 July 2010).

149   Communication 155/96, *Social and Economic Rights Action Centre (SERAC) & Another v. Nigeria,* Fifteenth Annual Activity Report of the African Commission on Human and Peoples' Rights (Annex V).

be conducted and the victims be adequately compensated, are yet to be implemented.

At its 24th Ordinary Session, the Commission adopted a resolution noting the lack of compliance by states parties with its recommendations. It called upon those states which had not implemented the recommendations to do so within 90 days from notification.[150] The resolution notwithstanding, most, if not all, concerned states are yet to implement the Commission's recommendations. It is hoped that the AU and its organs and programmes will provide a framework to ensure decisions reached by the African Commission and the African Court, when it commences its proceedings, are implemented.

It is also recommended that the AU, in accordance with its Constitutive Act, should exercise the right to intervene in a member state in respect of grave circumstances of human rights violations.[151] The recently established Peace and Security Council of the AU may also be useful in assisting the Commission to enforce some of its recommendations, especially where the continuing violations are serious or massive. Additionally, the Charter should be revised to enhance the Commission's powers to ensure that its decisions are complied with and its remedies are enforced. Where a state fails to do so, or where an amicable settlement is not forthcoming, the state should be punished accordingly.

It is needless to stress that the Commission also faces the challenge of inadequate financial support to enable it to conduct its protective activities as it should. The magnitude of the financial ineptitude of the Commission has been discussed under the challenges facing the state reporting mechanism. Sadly, this situation has forced the Commission to engage the services of legal officers, volunteers and interns funded by organisations from outside Africa, in order to overcome the shortcomings at the Secretariat. Some of these personnel are non-Africans, and students without much experience.[152] This could lead to fundamental problems,

---

150   Wachira (n 16 above) 24.

151   Constitutive Act of the African Union, art 4(h).

152   Nmehielle (n 8 above) 185.

which would undermine the legitimacy and credibility of the Commission.[153] Africans should have direct involvement in the work of the Commission because of the need to develop African human rights jurisprudence.[154]

The effectiveness of the African Commission can also be enhanced through strengthening its Secretariat. This would entail a number of things, for instance, increasing the number of its professional staff.[155] In particular, legal experts and competent press personnel are needed to expedite and publicise the work of the Commission. Moreover, the quality of personnel should be emphasised. Recruitment of the staff should include, among others, African legal experts and scholars. The Commission could also initiate programmes that would attract people from across the continent to visit it and contribute to its work. This may include a fully-funded legal researchers' programme for post-graduate students from African universities, pursuing degrees that are relevant to the Commission's work.

African universities and institutions of higher learning should also be encouraged to send researchers, students and distinguished scholars to the Commission on a regular basis. In addition, they should develop comprehensive courses on the African human rights system where students would spend a couple of years studying and researching on the system.[156] For example, certificate, diploma or degree courses could be structured on this subject. The more people get to understand the system, the better. This is because an insight into the system will reveal the potential areas of reforms thereto.

---

153   Ankumah (n 8 above) 33.

154   As above, 34.

155   See the Twenty-Second Activity Report of the Commission on Human and Peoples' Rights 20-21. As at June 2007, the Commission had 23 personnel whereas the required number was 36. See also the Executive Council Decision EX.CL/322 (X) on the Twenty-First Activity Report of the African Commission on Human and Peoples' Rights adopted at its Tenth Ordinary Session held from 25–26 January 2007 in Addis Ababa, Ethiopia. The decision 'CALL[s] ON the Commission of the African Union in collaboration with the ACHPR to propose a new Structure for the latter to the next Ordinary Session of the Executive Council taking into consideration the broad mandate of the ACHPR.'

156   See a similar recommendation in Heyns (n 4 above) 172.

The efficiency of the Commission could also be enhanced if sub-commissions, entrusted with promotional activities are established. The sub-commissions, based on the main geographical divides of the continent, will represent the Western, Eastern, Northern, Central and Southern regions of the continent. Apart from conducting promotional activities, the sub-commissions could receive communications, from their regions, on behalf of the Commission and process them in accordance with the requirements of the Charter and the Rules of Procedure.[157] The admissible communications would then be forwarded to the Commission's headquarters to be determined in accordance with the laid down procedures.

As far as accessing the Court is concerned, the sub-commissions would assist in the admissibility process, in accordance with the Court's Protocol and the Rules of Procedure. They could also examine the reports from states within their sub-regions. The rationale for the creation of sub-commissions is to bring the activities of the African human rights system closer to the people. As argued earlier, the African continent is vast, consisting of states with ideological, social, economic and political differences. Thus, sub-commissions will create a sense of identity and cohesiveness amongst the few states within a sub-region.

Given the diversity of the continent, it is possible for sub-regional arrangements to be more readily accepted than global, or even regional, arrangements. Again, it is obviously more convenient for a case to be heard within the sub-region than elsewhere. This is largely because, complainants will not have to travel long distances and more witnesses could be summoned than it may be the case with a regional arrangement.[158] Commissioners are also more likely to take interest in human rights violations in their sub-regions than on the continental level.

Definitely, the pragmatism of establishing sub-commissions may be contested on grounds of their financial implication. It

---

157   W Eno 'The African Commission on Human and Peoples' Rights as an instrument for the protection of human rights in Africa' (1998) *LLM Thesis, University of South Africa* 156.

158   As above.

may be argued that since the Commission is faced with financial constraints, it is not conducive at this time to implement the idea of sub-commissions, especially if their budgets would strain the meagre resources of the human rights system. To overcome the financial implications of establishing sub-commissions, it is proposed that each sub-region should take care of the expenses of its sub-commission. The Commissioners who come from the sub-region will then be in-charge of the activities thereof and report to the Commission. Thus, their emoluments will continue to be drawn from the AU coffers.[159]

The creation of sub-commissions would encourage division of labour and efficiency of the Commission. It would also ensure that the Commissioners are put to more productive use that it is currently the case. The involvement and participation of NGOs from within a sub-region would also be enhanced. Further, the Commission will also be more accessible to people who will not have to travel to The Gambia to have their rights vindicated, unless it becomes very necessary for them to do so. Finally, the Commission's interaction with sub-regional mechanisms such as ECOWAS, COMESA and SADC, and the tribunals established under them, will be invigorated through the proposed sub-commissions.[160] This will have a positive impact on the jurisprudence of the African human rights system.

13.2   THE AFRICAN COURT ON HUMAN AND PEOPLES' RIGHTS

At the moment, the African Court is not yet fully operational in the sense that it has not commenced its judicial proceedings, its Rules of Procedure are still being drafted, its Registry has not been set up and it is not known when it will consider its first case. In 2006, the Court submitted its first Activity Report to the AU Summit, noting that it had held three meetings since the appointment of the first bench.[161] The Report cited a number of challenges already encountered by

---

159   As above.

160   As above, 157.

161   Activity Report of the Court for 2006, Assembly/AU/8(VIII). The meetings dealt with drafting the Court's Rules of Procedure, discussing its budget and the seat of the Court.

the Court in its initial months of operation. These include heavy dependence on the AU Commission, lack of awareness among those in the AU Commission of the importance and status of the Court and lack of headquarters. After deliberating on the Activity Report, the Assembly, among other things, instructed the AU Commission to liaise with Tanzania in order to facilitate the establishment of the headquarters of the Court in Arusha.[162]

Generally, the process of establishing the Court has been very slow. This is evidenced by the fact that, it took longer than five years to secure the fifteen ratifications required for the entry into force of the Court's Protocol. This is not very encouraging, given the fact that the establishment of the Court took more than thirty years from the time it was first mooted.[163] With the atrocities in Darfur (Sudan), Somalia, Democratic Republic of Congo, Chad, Zimbabwe, and other violations taking place across the continent, it is obvious that the Court is essential and its delayed operationalisation cannot be countenanced. The AU could not continue to fold its hands, while many Africans continue to be victims of human rights violations.

The prolonged operationalisation of the Court is a culmination of the apparent resistance to the establishment of a powerful regional judicial mechanism. It has been argued in some quarters that there are adequate mechanisms for the protection of human rights at the national level.[164] A regional human rights court, according to this argument, will therefore encourage unnecessary duplication of the mandates of these courts.[165] This proposition should, however, be rejected given the ineptitude of national courts of most African states. Not every African state can boast of a robust legal system that is capable of protecting human rights.

Another challenge to the potential effectiveness of the Court may be linked to resource allocation. African states are ravaged by poverty and are in most cases left with no option but to prioritise

---

162   As above.

163   The quest for a regional human rights Court began in the 1961 Lagos Conference that was organised by the International Commission of Jurists.

164   O'Shea (n 7 above) 287.

165   As above.

their resource allocation. Already, there are a number of new pan-continental institutions that require support from states in terms of resources. Additionally, a majority of the states rely on donor aid to manage their huge economic burdens. Given such circumstances, supporting a regional court that would more likely than not create further adverse economic implications, is not an idea most states are prepared to embrace.

Further, certain provisions on the jurisdiction of the Court also present some challenges which may possibly have negative implications to its effectiveness. Article 3(1) provides that: 'the jurisdiction of the Court shall extend to all cases and disputes submitted to it concerning the interpretation and application of the Charter, this Protocol and any other relevant human rights instrument ratified by the states concerned.' Article 7 further states: 'the Court shall apply the provisions of the Charter and any other relevant human rights instruments ratified by the states concerned.' These provisions could create a whole range of uncertainties. It has been argued, they give the Court a very wide adjudicatory jurisdiction.[166]

The provisions, it has been suggested, could be interpreted to mean that the Court has jurisdiction to consider cases brought before it under any human rights instrument ratified by the states concerned, including UN and other African human rights treaties.[167] Consequently, Article 3(1) should be amended to restrict the Court's jurisdiction to cases involving the violation of the African Charter and other relevant human rights instruments promulgated under the OAU/AU.[168] In the event an amendment is not preferred, the African Court should make it clear at the earliest opportunity that it

---

166   Naldi & Magliveras (n 2 above) 435.

167   See generally the arguments in E Quasigah 'The African Court of Human Rights: Prospects in Comparison with the European Court of Human Rights and the Inter-American Court of Human Rights' in African Society of International and Comparative Law *Proceedings of the Tenth Annual Conference, held in Addis Ababa 3–5 August 1998* (1998) 61–62.

168   See a similar argument in Heyns (n 4 above) 168, where the author argued that art 3(1) should be amended to provide that the Court exercises jurisdiction over 'the African Charter and all Protocols to the Charter.'

does not exercise jurisdiction over the entire corpus of human rights treaties ratified by African states.

Another area of equal importance to the Court's efficiency is its power to issue binding judgements. The ability of the system to bring about change depends on how binding the judgements of the African Court will be.[169] Article 30 of the Protocol provides that states parties 'undertake to comply with the judgement in any case to which they are parties within the time stipulated by the African Court and to guarantee its execution.' Apart from this provision, the Protocol does not seem to provide for any sanction against a state that deliberately refuses to comply with the Court's judgements. Consequently, the effectiveness of the Court seems to be largely at the mercy and willingness of states to comply with its decisions.[170]

States parties therefore ought to be compelled to comply with, and enforce the judgements of the Court. At least one of two approaches could be used to achieve this intention. First, Article 30 of the Protocol could be amended with an express provision spelling out the consequences of a state's failure to comply with, or enforce the Court's judgements. Alternatively, the Court's Rules of Procedure could provide for the enforcement of the Court's judgements at the national level because supra-national enforcement of decisions is normally practically difficult.[171] This difficulty is mainly caused by the reluctance of states to enforce decisions against each another. Perhaps, this is instigated by the general fear that if a state chastises another, the same would be done to it sooner or later.[172]

Suffice it to state that the success, or otherwise, of the African Court will to a large extent depend on the willingness of states to embrace the core values of the African human rights system. As Mutua noted, this is a two-dimensional obligation: first, it necessitates that states incorporate the provisions of the African Charter into their own municipal laws and ensure compliance with it. Secondly,

---

169   K Hopkins 'The effect of the African Court on the domestic legal orders of African states' (2002) 2 *African Human Rights Law Journal* 238.

170   As above.

171   N Sibongile 'Implications of the establishment of the African Court on Human and Peoples' Rights on domestic legal systems in Africa' in Viljoen (n 6 above) 44.

172   As above.

it necessitates that states accept and obey the judgements of the Court notwithstanding ideological conflicts that may exist between their own jurisprudence and that of the Court.[173]

The Court will only be useful if it will manage to correct the shortcomings of the African system and provide victims of human rights violations with an effective and accessible forum to vindicate their rights.[174] It is needless to state that the Court will not meet the expectations of Africans if it is not provided with material and other forms of support that it may require for its effective performance.[175]

---

173   As above.

174   Mutua (n 126 above) 357.

175   As above.

CHAPTER 14

MAINSTREAMING AND RATIONALISING THE AFRICAN HUMAN RIGHTS SYSTEM

The developments registered over the last few decades are a clear indication and a positive sign that the African human rights system is gradually moving towards success. The complete success of the system, however, calls for a close relationship between all its institutions. As Baimu suggested, these institutions should complement rather than compete with one another; the relationship between them should be one of collaboration, as distinguished from that of control.[1] In the meantime, ways and means will have to be explored on how all the regional institutions with human rights responsibility in Africa can jointly pursue the common goal of a peaceful, stable and developed Africa, in tandem with human rights protection and promotion.[2]

While it is encouraging to note that the African human rights system is registering positive developments, there is an emerging trend of institutional proliferation which needs to be checked. This is because, the existing and emerging institutions tend to overlap and duplicate each other's functions in a way that is rather disturbing. Currently, there are a number of institutions and initiatives on the continent with the mandate to promote and protect human rights. Proliferation of institutions is likely to present certain problems, especially with regard to resources and personnel allocation and their attendant obligations on states.

The foregoing therefore stresses the need to mainstream and rationalise the existing regional human rights institutions in a way that they can complement but not duplicate each other. In this context, 'mainstreaming' should be understood to mean the process that would involve the consolidation of the existing human rights

---

1   See E Baimu 'Human rights in NEPAD and its implications for the African human rights system' (2002) 2 *African Human Rights Law Journal* 318.

2   K Kithure 'Overlaps in the African human rights system' in F Viljoen (ed.) *The African human rights system: Towards the co-existence of the African Commission on Human and Peoples' Rights and the African Court on Human and Peoples' Rights* 141.

mechanisms within the AU framework in order to enhance their relationship with each other.[3] The AU, as the 'parent' institution of the African human rights system would therefore hold the central place in ensuring the co-ordination and synergy of the existing human rights mechanisms in the region.

Rationalisation, on the other hand, would involve defining the relationships and synergies between these institutions in order to minimise or overcome overlaps and duplication within the African human rights system. Hence, while mainstreaming would be initiated to improve the 'vertical relationship' (between the AU and the regional institutions with human rights responsibility), rationalisation should be seen as a way to improve the 'horizontal relationship' (between the human rights institutions). What follows, therefore, are proposals of some ways in which rationalisation could be achieved. Our discussion shall, however, be confined to certain institutions whose relationship is at the moment quite problematic, yet they are pertinent to the success of the regional human rights system. These are the African Court on Human and Peoples' Rights, African Commission and AU Court of Justice.

14.1   INSTITUTIONAL OVERLAPS AND DUPLICATION IN THE AFRICAN HUMAN RIGHTS SYSTEM

It has been observed that the failure to mainstream the African human rights system within the former OAU may have contributed to the dismal performance of the regional human rights system.[4] Similarly, failure to anchor the system in the newly created AU is more likely to reproduce the marginalisation experienced under the OAU. As already stated earlier, the African human rights system has not remained static since its inception. Rather, it has been advancing both normatively and institutionally. For instance, while the African Commission used to be its sole enforcement mechanism, the African Court has lately been established to complement it and there is also the possibility of the AU Court of Justice being instrumental in human

---

3   See also this position in S Gutto 'The reform and renewal of the African regional human and peoples' rights system' (2001) 2 *African Human Rights Law Journal* 181-184.

4   As above, 176.

rights protection in the region. Additionally, the AU has undertaken a number of initiatives geared towards human rights promotion and protection in the region. These include the creation of the New Partnership for Africa's Development (NEPAD) and African Peer Review Mechanism (APRM), as well as other organs created under the Constitutive Act of the AU (hereafter 'CAAU' or 'the Act'). As a result of these developments, the regional human rights system suffers from normative and institutional overlaps, tending towards duplication and proliferation.[5] A number of examples could be cited to vindicate this argument.

Most notable is the duplication of certain functions between the African Commission and the Committee of Experts on the Rights and Welfare of the Child (hereafter 'the Committee'). The Committee, established under Article 32 of the African Charter on the Rights and Welfare of the Child (hereafter 'Children's Charter'), has promotional and protective mandates that are more or less similar to those of the African Commission. For example, the protective mandate includes examining periodic reports by states[6] and receiving and determining complaints by individuals and groups, as well as intestate complaints.[7] This is regardless of the fact that the rights and freedoms of children, although elaborated and expanded in the Children's Charter, can easily be interpreted and enforced through the African Commission, as well as the African Court.[8]

At another level, duplication is apparent between the AU Court of Justice (hereafter 'Court of Justice') and the African human rights Court (hereafter 'African Court'). As stated earlier, the jurisdiction of the African Court 'shall extend to all cases and disputes submitted to it concerning the interpretation and application of the Charter, this Protocol and any other relevant human rights instrument ratified by the states concerned.'[9] Undoubtedly, therefore, the enforcement of human rights is its core business. The Court of Justice, on the other hand, has a broader jurisdiction extending to all AU treaties

---

5   Kithure (n 2 above) 125.

6   African Charter on the Rights and Welfare of the Child (ACRWC), art 43.

7   As above, art 44.

8   Gutto (n 3 above) 178.

9   Protocol Establishing the African Court on Human and Peoples' Rights, art 3.

and conventions and other issues concerning international law, including bilateral issues between AU members states.[10] Moreover, the Assembly of the Union may confer jurisdiction on the Court of Justice over any other dispute.[11]

Hence, there is a broad symmetry in both Courts in relation to their composition and jurisdiction.[12] Like the African Court, the Court of Justice has the competence to interpret and apply the CAAU.[13] Thus, their jurisdictions overlap in the sense that, while the Court of Justice could adjudicate on human rights matters that fall within the competence of the African Court, the latter could be requested to give advisory opinions or hear cases based on the human rights provisions of the CAAU. There is therefore the possibility of the two Courts rendering conflicting judgements on human rights issues if allowed to operate independently from each other.[14]

There is also potential duplication and jurisdictional conflicts likely to be experienced by the African Court and Commission. Both the Commission[15] and the Court[16] are mandated to interpret the Charter and receive communications. However, there is no clarity as to when it would be appropriate to submit a complaint to the Court rather than to the Commission, or vice versa. It is equally important to note that the AU is not precluded from establishing more institutions than those currently in place. The CAAU mandates the AU Assembly to establish more institutions if this would be desirable for the achievement of the Union's objectives.[17]

One would therefore concur with Magliveras and Naldi that 'the number of organs of the Union appears to be very large and in

---

10   See the Protocol Establishing the Court of Justice.

11   As above, art 9.

12   Both Courts consist of eleven Judges, no more than one from each of the states parties and with the president serving full-time. See E Baimu & F Viljoen 'Courts for Africa: Considering the co-existence of the African Court on Human an Peoples' Rights and the African Court of Justice' (2004) 22/2 *Netherlands Quarterly of Human Rights* 250.

13   Protocol Establishing the Court of Justice, art 19(1)(a) & (d).

14   Baimu & Viljoen (n 12 above) 250.

15   African Charter on Human and Peoples' Rights, art 45(3).

16   Protocol Establishing the African Court on Human and Peoples' Rights, art 3.

17   CAAU, arts 5(2) & 9(2).

the long run it could not only result in the cumbersome operation of the Union but also present a financial burden.'[18] The proliferation of institutions should be a source of concern, since understaffing and under-funding already plague the existing human rights institutions and mechanisms on the continent.[19] As stated earlier, the African Commission is currently under severe shortage of human and financial resources, which restricts its effective functioning.

14.2   RATIONALISING THE AFRICAN COURT AND COMMISSION

It should be emphasised that the mere establishment of a regional Court cannot be construed as the end to the many challenges encompassing the enforcement of human rights under the African system. Much still needs to be done, especially with regard to its relationship with its counterparts, such as the African Commission, to ensure its efficiency. Further, it should be reiterated that the Court was not established to replace, but rather to complement and reinforce the Commission. On this premise, one would expect the Court's Protocol to define, in no uncertain terms, the relationship between the Commission and the Court, yet it does not. Instead, as O'Shea correctly noted, the relationship between the two institutions is dealt with very superficially.[20]

Two approaches are therefore mooted to rationalise these institutions. The first approach contemplates a situation where the Court and the Commission are vested with protective and promotional functions, respectively.[21] The second one prefers that both institutions are vested with clearly defined protective functions. Additionally, the Commission would continue with its promotional functions.[22] This would then mean that the Court will only

---

18   G Naldi & K Magliveras 'The African Union: A new dawn for Africa?' (2002) 51 *International and Comparative Law Quarterly* 419.

19   Baimu (n 1 above) 313.

20   A O'Shea 'A critical reflection on the proposed African Court on Human and Peoples' Rights' (2001) 2 *African Human Rights Law Journal* 293.

21   See M Mutua 'The African human rights court: A two-legged stool?' (1999) 21 *Human Rights Quarterly* 360.

22   W Kaguongo 'The questions of *locus standi* and admissibility before the African Court on Human and Peoples' Rights' in Viljoen (n 2 above) 84.

concentrate on protective functions since it is intended to serve as a judicial institution and nothing more.

The first approach is motivated by a number of factors. First, it is important to have a clear division of labour between the Commission and the Court. This arrangement will therefore enable them to be more effective in their areas of specialisation and will also enhance cooperation and mutual reinforcement between the two institutions.[23] Secondly, it is both time and cost effective. It is questionable whether the allocation of resources to have two separate organs with a judicial mandate is rational, given that the Commission is already severely hampered by inadequate resources.[24] Instead of the institutions duplicating each others' functions, it is expedient that each be vested with distinct roles.

Thirdly, if both the Commission and the Court are involved in the interpretation of the Charter, but do so separately, then it is possible that the African human rights system may have two separate voices saying two different things.[25] In such circumstances, it would be appropriate to allow only the Court to conduct judicial functions. Other than that, the Court comprises of judges who, unlike Commissioners, may exude competence in their work. Further, all measures should be taken to ensure that the Court operates independent of the Commission which has been accused of suffering from severe image problems.[26]

While the first approach makes sense given the reasons fronted to justify it, it has been argued, and rightly so, that the Protocol establishing the Court contemplates a sharing of the protective mandate between the Commission and the Court.[27] Indeed, Article

---

23   See Amnesty International *Credibility in question: Proposals for improving the efficiency and effectiveness of the African Commission on Human and Peoples' Rights* AI Index: IOR 63/02/1998.

24   W Benedek 'The judiciary and human rights in Africa: The Banjul seminar and the training Workshop for a Core of Human Rights Advocates of November 1989' (1990) 11 *Human Rights Law Journal* 250.

25   Kaguongo (n 22 above) 84.

26   See generally, Mutua (n 21 above) 361.

27   J Harrington 'The African Court on Human and Peoples' Rights' in M Evans & R Murray *The African Charter on Human and Peoples' Rights: The system in practice: 1986-2000* (2002) 332.

2 confirms this position when it states, 'the Court shall, bearing in mind the provisions of this Protocol, *complement the protective mandate of the African Commission on Human and Peoples' Rights...*' (emphasis mine). It is on this premise that the second approach, which prefers that the Commission performs both protective and promotional functions, is recommended. This is essentially because stripping the Commission of its protective mandate and reducing it to a 'human rights promotion body' would not be in line with Article 2 of the Protocol.[28]

The Commission and Court may complement each other in a number of ways. For instance, as Harrington suggested, the two institutions could divide the consideration of communications, with the Commission deciding the admissibility as the Court determines the merits.[29] After all, Article 6(1) of the Protocol gives the Court the right to ask for the opinion of the Commission on questions of admissibility. Henceforth, the Commission could desist from holding hearings and instead work as a screening body which determines the admissibility of cases for the Court.[30] Since the Court does not have promotional mandate, the Commission could continue with these activities.

Alternatively, the Court could leave collection and collation of facts to the Commission and restrict itself to the determination of cases chiefly on the basis of the Commission's written records. Hearings before the Court could be restricted to oral arguments by Counsel, rather than the examination of witnesses. On the other hand, hearings before the Commission could be restricted to the examination of witnesses and evidentiary documents.[31] However, a fundamental prerequisite for the adoption of this practice would be for the Commission to be divided into sub-commissions as proposed in the previous chapter. This will then resolve the issue of whether the Commission and the Court should be located in the same place.

---

28   As above.
29   As above.
30   As above.
31   As above.

In the long run, this approach will guarantee the evolution of consistent African human rights jurisprudence. It will also mark a departure from the way communications have traditionally been dealt with by the Commission. Suffice it to state that there could be more ways of perfecting the relationship between the Commission and the Court. However, the most important factor to be considered when selecting the most suitable approach is whether duplication and overlaps are avoided. The preferred approach should also be cost effective, convenient and time saving.

14.3   RATIONALISING THE AFRICAN COURT AND AU COURT OF JUSTICE

When considering the possible ways of rationalising the African Court and Court of Justice, it is appropriate to enquire whether in the first place the continent needs more than one regional court. This is because, it is possible that the agitation for two regional courts in Africa is motivated more by the ongoing events in Europe than by the need to improve on supra-national adjudication. As Udombana observed, a critical evaluation reveals that institutions such as the AU are patterned along the lines of their counterparts in Europe.[32] Similarly, Europe has two regional courts–a human rights court and a court of justice, which arrangement might have impressed those fronting for the same in Africa.

While such an institutional arrangement could possibly succeed in Europe, it is certainly clear, at the moment, Africa is not prepared to host more than one regional court. The continent is not prepared to tackle the challenges that come with maintaining two regional courts which, apart from a few aspects, have more or less the same mandate. We have already elaborated how there is the danger of conflicting interpretation of treaties by the two institutions. Moreover, vast resources will definitely be required to effectively operate the two institutions. Udombana succinctly captured this phenomenon when he stated as follows:

---

32   N Udombana 'An African human rights court and an African Union Court: A needful duality or a needless duplication?' (2003)23/3 *Brook Journal of International law* 852.

To start with, each of the... courts will require a building to house the court rooms, judges' chambers, and the offices for secretariats, including the Registrars. These offices must be equipped with furniture and other necessary supplies. Accommodation for the judges and their support staff will also have to be provided....Another major resource the courts will require is a library and documentation centre. The library must be stocked with rich legal materials dealing with both African and comparative law. It must also maintain a comprehensive collection of the laws of member states. In addition, there should be facilities for users, such as legal research and photocopy services and separate similar facilities for the judges of the courts. Furthermore, like any modern library, they must be equipped with computers and internet access. Competent librarians will need to be employed. They will also have to be trained in each of the principal legal systems and the courts' languages and regularly exposed to modern information systems.[33]

The above analysis identifies just some, not all, of what the two courts will require to function properly. It is not surprising that the AU, perhaps compelled by the fear of operating two regional courts, resolved to integrate them.[34] However, the failure to reach a consensus on the modalities of the integration made the AU Assembly to permit the operationalisation of the African Court.

The idea of an integrated regional court is very noble and can only be ignored to the continent's peril. First, it would avoid the splitting of resources towards maintaining two courts. Secondly, an integrated court will result in simplicity and is an antidote to the ongoing proliferation of regional institutions.[35] Thirdly, it would help to concentrate efforts, energy and focus on one institution rather than two. Finally, an integrated regional court will offer the opportunity to develop unified and cohesive jurisprudence for Africa.[36]

---

33   As above, 860.

34   See 'Decisions of the AU Assembly of Heads of State and Government', Third Summit held in Addis Ababa, Ethiopia, 6-8 July 2004; document Assembly/AU/ Dec.45 (III) available at www.africa-union.org (accessed on 16 June 2010).

35   On the likely impact of proliferation of human rights and other institutions in Africa see generally, E Baimu 'Human rights mechanisms and structures under NEPAD and the African Union: Emerging trends towards proliferation and duplication' *Occasional Paper no. 15* 2002 Centre for Human Rights; Naldi & Magliveras (n 18 above) 421.

36   N Udombana 'Toward the African Court on Human and Peoples' Rights: Better late than never', (2000) 3 *Yale Human Rights and Development Law Journal* 102.

Noteworthy, however, integration of the two courts, now that the African Court is operational, will be much more difficult because they are at different stages of development. According to Kithure:

> The question to be grappled with remains: Should the integration of the courts be realised, what will happen to the judges of the African Human Rights Court who may not secure slots in the integrated court? Under such circumstances it is likely that vested interests might make submerging of the African Human Rights Court into the Court of Justice very difficult even though it could be the most pragmatic thing to do. There are bound to be deep-seated vested interests (of judges and others) that may lead to a vehement opposition against any kind of interference with an already functioning human rights Court.[37]

Apart from the different stages of development being an obstacle to the integration process, the required qualifications and expertise of the judges of the two courts are also different and may present a problem.[38] To be a judge of the African Court one is required to be competent in human and peoples' rights,[39] while competence in international law is the pre-requisite for appointment to the Court of Justice bench.[40]

The issues relating to the differences in jurisdiction and expertise of the judges of the two courts, however, could be resolved. To start with, the Court of Justice, given the nature of its jurisdiction, can resolve human rights disputes. Its core business is the 'interpretation and application' of the CAAU.[41] It is needless to reemphasise that pursuant to this Act, the objectives[42] and the fundamental principles[43] of the AU are concerned with various aspects of human rights promotion and protection. Further, it should be noted that since human rights have a nexus with international law, experts in the

---

37   Kithure (n 2 above) 135.

38   As above.

39   Protocol Establishing the African Court on Human and Peoples' Rights, art 11(1).

40   Protocol to the Court of Justice, art 4.

41   CAAU, art 19.

42   As above, art 3(g) & (h).

43   As above, art 4(h), (m), (n) & (o).

latter will ordinarily have some knowledge in the former.[44] This will then resolve the issue of competence and experience of the judges with regard to resolving human rights cases. Alternatively, in the election of the judges of the integrated court, members states could be advised to nominate some candidates with expertise on human rights who, if elected, would deal with cases on this subject.[45]

When integrating the courts, the AU may settle for one of two approaches. The first would be to replace the existing protocols of the two courts with a new protocol establishing an integrated court. The new protocol could draw inspiration from the provisions of the two court's protocols. This approach will then lead to the creation of one court, but with different 'Divisions' or 'Chambers'. One Division or Chamber could specifically deal with regional enforcement of human and peoples' rights, while the other, with international law matters.[46] With the prevalence of genocide, war crimes and crimes against humanity on the continent, it would be appropriate to create a special division that would prosecute such crimes. We prefer this approach based on our earlier argument that Africa is, at the moment, not prepared to host two regional courts.

In pursuit of an approach similar to the one proposed above, a group of seven experts produced a 'Draft Protocol' prior to the AU Assembly summit of 2005.[47] The document proposed an integrated court, with the African Court as a 'specialised human and peoples' rights division.'[48] The new court would be composed of fifteen Judges of which at least seven would be competent in human and peoples' rights.[49] However, the AU Permanent Representatives' Committee was not impressed with some aspects of the Draft and proposed the operationalisation of the African Court.

The second integration approach, which is mooted as an afterthought, would be to maintain the jurisdiction of the two

---

44   Kithure (n 2 above) 137.

45   As above, 138.

46   Udombana (n 32 above) 865.

47   Draft Protocol on the Integration of the African Court on Human and Peoples'
      Rights and the Court of Justice of the African Union. EX.CL/162 (VI) Annex I.

48   Art 2(3) of the Draft Protocol.

49   As above, art 4.

courts but amend their protocols to enhance their relationship.[50] In this regard, the integration of the two institutions would be based more on 'essence' rather than 'form'. In other words, it is the interaction of the institutions that would be integrated and nothing else. Matters could be referred from one court to another whenever the need arises, in order to utilise the competence of both courts to the fullest extent. While so doing, the African Commission could still execute its promotional and protective mandate uninterrupted, and also serve as a 'screening body' for the African Court. From this arrangement, it would be prudent for the Commission to defer its protective mandate to the African Court so as to avoid duplicity and overlaps.

It is only after the two regional courts and the Commission have been streamlined that it will be possible to properly mainstream them within the AU framework. The current situation is pathetic because the relationships between these institutions are not clearly defined. For the African human rights system to be effective, the criteria to be followed when setting up new structures or mechanisms need to be defined. In this regard, some inquiry should be conducted to ascertain important issues such as: the added value of a proposed structure or mechanism; its legal, financial and administrative implications; and how the proposed structure would interface with the existing structures and mechanisms. As a matter of fact, no institution should be established prior to such an inquiry.[51]

It is also important to conduct an 'impact assessment' before mechanisms are established. The efficiency of the African human rights system is not on the number of institutions established, but rather on their relevance and impact. In line with the proposed 'impact assessment' is the need to conduct an 'audit' on the existing mechanisms. Whereas an 'impact assessment' should be conducted prior to the establishment of new mechanisms, an 'audit' should be done on the already existing ones to gauge their efficacy. It is proposed that the AU should create a special unit that would be involved in both institutional impact assessment and auditing.

---

50   Kithure (n 2 above) 141.

51   Baimu (n 1 above) 318.

While it is appreciated that annual activity reports may be useful in gauging the performance of the existing institutions, it is also important to have an independent body to do so. External evaluation is usually more critical and thorough than an internal one. Thus, a unit vested with monitoring and evaluation functions should be formed, specifically to monitor and evaluate the existing regional human rights mechanisms. The unit would then be in a position to advise on issues such as, the need, or otherwise, to create a new human rights institution, financial matters, mainstreaming and rationalisation of the human rights mechanisms, ways to improve the efficiency of the system, etc.

CONCLUSION

A number of issues have been discussed in this book, including the historical antecedents, normative, institutional and other aspects of the African system on human and peoples' rights. In the main, it has been shown that Africa is in dire need of effective regional human rights mechanisms. Having passed through the eras of slave trade and colonialism and now struggling with post-colonial uncertainties, the continent needs to direct its attention, resources and efforts to the attainment of reasonable standards of human rights, particularly at the regional level. While it is true that the African human rights system has made remarkable progress since its inception, much still remains to be done.

The journey towards an effective regional human rights system is far from being completed; the road leading thereto is rather narrow and long, yet the prospects and promises of attaining this goal are quite high. In other words, amidst the conflicts, uncertainties and confusion associated with the system, there is hope for a brighter and a better future for effective human rights enforcement in Africa. The alarming scepticism on the future of the regional human rights system may therefore be dismissed as unmeritorious, farce and sham.

As indicated in our earlier discussions, the system has registered unending academic debates, both negative and positive, on its past, present and future. The merits of some of these debates were discussed comprehensively. The study has therefore served as an added voice to the ongoing discussions on the various aspects of the African human rights system. It is not a conclusion in itself, but both an addition to, and a summation of, whatever has already been discussed on this subject that is crucial to the future success of the continent. In tandem with this concern, the study has illuminated the promises, pitfalls as well as the prospects for effective regional enforcement of international human rights law in Africa.

While our focus has largely been on normative and institutional challenges, it should be recalled that there are other factors that pose a threat to the effective enforcement of human rights under the African system. For example, due to the close nexus between regional and national protection of human rights, events at the national level could in one way or the over inhibit the effective functioning of the regional human rights system. Some of the inhibiting factors include, but are not limited to: historical factors, poverty, internal and international conflicts, civil disobedience, foreign interference, poor governance and cultural and ideological differences.

Historical factors have played a fundamental role in shaping the human rights discourse of the continent. For example, foreign invasion subjected African societies to political, economic and social domination. Besides tampering with the socio-economic and political fabrics of the then societies, it was characterised by gross violations of human rights. One would therefore agree with Odinkalu that the effective protection of human rights in post-colonial Africa necessitated a re-orientation of states away from the institutional infrastructure and attitudinal orientation inherited from the colonial period.[1] Unfortunately, this process was never undertaken let alone achieved. In fact, most of the laws, institutions and attitudes that underwrote the violations of human rights during colonialism did not just survive independence, they prospered thereafter.[2] Oloka-Onyango noted that:

> Nearly half a century after most countries on the continent attained independence, so many of them continue to utilise colonial laws governing political association, public health, education and free expression. The consequence is that their very claim to have made a difference in the human rights reality of the people they govern is effectively negated.[3]

Civil wars and conflicts also have a hand in impeding the effective enforcement of human rights in the region. Peace and stability are a prerequisite for effective human rights enforcement, be it nationally or internationally. Sadly, a wave of atrocities continues to rock the continent unabatedly. These conflicts not only violate

---

[1]   C Odinkalu 'Back to the future: The imperative of prioritising for the protection of human rights in Africa' (2003) *Journal of African Law* 2.

[2]   As above.

[3]   J Oloka-onyango 'Human rights and sustainable development in contemporary Africa: A new dawn or retreating horizons?' (2000) *Human Development Report 2000 Background Paper* 4, available at http://www.undp.org/hdro/Oloka-Onyango2000. html, (accessed 12 June 2010).

the rights entrenched in the African Charter, but also consume a large percentage of countries' national budgets.[4] For instance, it is reported that Uganda spends two per cent of its Gross Domestic Product (GDP) on defence[5] and less than one per cent on education.

As a result of civil wars and conflicts, resources which would otherwise be spent on strengthening the regional human rights system are mostly diverted to national defence and related concerns. Hence, human rights promotion and protection in the region has more or less become a secondary issue. In the words of Kofi Annan, the former UN Secretary-General, 'conflict in Africa poses a major challenge to United Nations' efforts designed to ensure global peace, prosperity and human rights for all.'[6]

Adverse socio-economic conditions have also affected regional enforcement of human rights in Africa in many ways. Some of the adverse socio-economic conditions affecting the continent are: poor economies, inadequate infrastructure, poor telecommunication facilities, poverty and diseases, lack of quality education, famine and attendant food shortage and the persistent lack of adequate socio-economic policies, among others.[7]

Poverty in most African countries has also translated to the lack of funds and resources to support the efforts to promote and protect human rights at the regional level. As already stated elsewhere above, both the promotional and protection activities of the human rights system have been hampered by the lack of adequate financial resources. The problem is evident from the fact that African states have routinely defaulted in meeting their financial obligations to the pan-continental bodies.

---

4   J Mubangizi 'Some reflections on recent and current trends in the promotion and protection of human rights in Africa: The pains and the gains' (2006) 6 *African Human Rights Law Journal* 166.

5   As above. See also A Mutumba-Lule 'Uganda defence budget "too little!"' available at   http://www.nationaudio.com/News/EastAfrican/08072002/Regional/ Regional140.html, (accessed 30 June 2010).

6   See 'Report of the Secretary-General on the Causes of Conflict and the Promotion of Durable Peace and Sustainable Development in Africa' available at http://www. un.org/ecosocdev/geninfo/afrec/sgreport/ report.htm, (accessed 1 March 2010).

7   See J Mubangizi 'Know your rights: Exploring the connections between human rights and poverty reduction with specific reference to South Africa' (2005) 21 *South African Journal on Human Rights* 32.

With regard to culture as an inhibiting factor, it should be pointed out that the concept of human rights has been construed differently due to the cultural differences between traditional African and Western societies. Because of these disparities, human rights have ignorantly been dismissed as a foreign ideology that is irrelevant to Africa. It was on this basis that the establishment of robust enforcement mechanisms under the African human rights system was resisted. For instance, the establishment of the African human rights Court was challenged on cultural grounds. According to this argument, a regional human rights court was not appropriate for Africa because African traditions dictated that disputes be resolved amicably.[8] The same was said to justify the African Commission's weak enforcement capacity.[9]

From the foregoing, it is inevitable to note that, generally, the African human rights system has been struggling through difficult and uncertain phases, having to contend with both internal (meaning normative and institutional) and external de-stabilising forces. The system has nonetheless registered some positive progress during its period of subsistence. The future of human rights in Africa is, after all, not as bleak as it may have been purported to be. What is currently needed is the concerted effort of all the role players, with the African states and peoples being in the lead, towards an effective regional human rights system.

---

8   U Umozurike 'The African Charter on Human and Peoples' Rights' (1983) 77 American Journal of International Law 909.

9   As above.

SELECTED BIBLIOGRAPHY

TEXT BOOKS

Ake, C (1996) *Democracy and development in Africa* Washington, D.C: Brookings Institution

Alston, P (ed) (1996) *Human rights law* Oxford: Clarendon Press

— (1992) *The United Nations and human rights: A critical appraisal* Oxford: Clarendon Press

Ambrose, B (1995) *Democratisation and the protection of human rights in Africa: Problems and prospects* Westport Connecticut: Praeger

Amin, S (1973) *Neo-colonialism in West Africa* New York: Monthly Review Press

Ankumah, E (1997) *The African Commission on Human and Peoples' Rights* The Hague/London/Boston: Martinus Nijhoff Publishers

Arambulo, K (1999) *Strengthening the supervision of the International Covenant on Economic, Social and Cultural Rights: theoretical and procedural aspects* Oxford: Hart

Austin, J (1985) *The province of jurisprudence determined,* Cambridge: Cambridge University Press

Ayittey, G (1992) *Africa betrayed* New York: Transnational Publishers Inc

Baah, R (2000) *Human rights in Africa: The conflict of implementation* Lanham: University Press of America

Benet, T (1995) *Human rights and African customary law under the South African Constitution* Kenwyn: Juta

Burgenthal, T (ed) (1995) *International human rights in a nutshell* Minnesota: West Publishing Company

Busia, K (1967) *Africa in search of democracy* (1967) London: Routledge and Kegan Paul Publishers

— (1951) *The position of the chief in the modern political system of Ashanti: A study of the influence of contemporary social changes on Ashanti political institutions* Oxford: Oxford University Press

Cassese, A (1990) *Human rights in a changing world* Cambridge: Polity

— (1986) *International law in a divided world* Oxford: Clarendon Press

Clapham, C (1996) *Africa and the international system: The politics of state survival,* Cambridge: Cambridge University Press

Clarke, P (1982) *West Africa and Islam: a study of religious development from the 8th to the 20th century* London: E. Arnold

Clements, C *et al* (1996) *European human rights: Taking a case under the Convention* London: Sweet & Maxwell

Cranston, M (1973) *What are human rights* London: Bodley Head

Curtin, P (1965) *The Atlantic slave trade: A census* Madison London: University of Wisconsin Press

Dahl, A (1992) *Democracy and its critics* New Haven: Yale University Press

Davidson, S (1992) *The Inter-American human rights system* Brookfield: Dartmouth Publishers

Dike, K (1956) *Trade and politics in the Niger delta, 1830-1885: An introduction to the economic and political history of Nigeria* Oxford: Clarendon Press

Donnelley, J (1989) *Universal human rights in theory and practice,* Ithaca: Cornell University Press

— (1985) *The concept of Human Rights* London: Croom Helm

Dowrick, F (ed) (1979) *Human rights problems, perspectives, and texts: a series of lectures and seminar papers delivered in the University of Durham in 1978, with supporting texts* West mead, England: Saxon House

Elias, T (1988) *Africa and development of international law* London: Martinus Nijhoff

— (1962) *British colonial law: A comparative study of the interaction between English and local laws in British dependencies* London: Stevens

— (1962) *The nature of African customary law* Manchester: Manchester University Press

Evans, M & Murray, R (eds) (2002) *The African Charter on Human and Peoples' Rights: The system in practice, 1986-2000* Cambridge: Cambridge University Press

Eze, O (1984) *Human rights in Africa: Some selected problems* Lagos: Macmillan Nigeria Publishers Limited

Fawcett, J (1987) *The Application of the European Convention on Human Rights* New York: Oxford University Press

Ghai, Y & McAuslan, B (1970) *Public law and political change in Kenya: A study of the legal framework of government from colonial times to the present* Nairobi: Oxford University Press

Gluckman, M (1967) *The judicial process among the Barotse of Northern Rhodesia* Manchester: Manchester University Press

Hannum, H (ed) (1999) *Guide to international human rights practice* New York: Transnational Publishers

Harris, D & Livingstone, S (eds) (1998) *The Inter-American system of human rights* Oxford: Clarendon Press

Harris, D *et al* (1995) *Law of the European Convention on Human Rights* London: Butterworths

Henkin, L (1990) *The Age of rights* New York: Columbia University Press

Heyns, C (ed) (1999) *Human rights law in Africa: 1997* The Hague: Kluwer Law International

Hooker, B (1975) *Legal pluralism: An introduction to colonial and neo-colonial laws* Oxford: Clarendon Press

Institute for Human Rights and Development (2004) *African human rights law reports* Lansdowne: Juta Law

Finnis, J (1980) *Natural law and natural rights* New York: Oxford University Press

Lindholt, L (1997) *Questioning the universality of human rights: The African Charter on Human and Peoples Rights in Botswana, Malawi and Mozambique* Aldershot: Ashgate/Dartmouth

Llewellyn, K (1962) *Jurisprudence: Realism in theory and practice* Chicago: University of Chicago Press

Macdonald, J *et al* (1993) *European system for the promotion of human rights* Dordrecht: Martinus Nijhoff Publishers

Maina, C (1990) *Human rights in Africa: A comparative study of the African Human & Peoples' Rights Charter & the new Tanzanian bill of rights* New York: Greenwood Press

Mamdani, M (1996) *Citizen and subject,* Princeton: Princeton University Press

— (1988) *et al* (eds) (1988) *Social movements, social transformation and the struggle for democracy in Africa,* Dakar: Council for the Development of Social Research in Africa (CODESRIA)

Marx, K (1964) *The economic and philosophic manuscript of 1844* New York: International Publishers

Mbiti, J (1994) *The African religions and philosophy* New York: Anchor Books

McCarthy-Arnolds E *et al* (1994) *Africa, human rights and the global system,* Westport Connecticut: Greenwood Press

Meek, C (1931) *A Sudanese kingdom* London: Oxford University Press

Merrils, G (1993) *The development of international law by the European Court of Human Rights* Manchester: Manchester University Press

Mouton, J (2001) *How to succeed in your Master's and Doctoral studies* Pretoria: Van Schaik

Mowbray, A (2001) *Cases and materials on the European Convention on Human Rights* London: Butterworths

Mudimbe, Y (1988) *Invention of Africa: gnosis, philosophy, and the order of knowledge,* Bloomington: Indiana University Press

Mugwanya, G (2003) *Human rights in Africa: Enhancing human rights through the African regional human rights system,* New York: Transnational Publishers

Murray, R (2004) *Human rights in Africa: From the OAU to the Africa Union* Cambridge: Cambridge University Press

— (2000) *African Commission on Human and Peoples' Rights & International Law* Oxford: Hart

Murray, R & Evans, M (eds) (2001) *Documents of the African Commission on Human and Peoples' Rights* Oxford: Hart

Nickel, J (1987) *Making sense of human rights: philosophical reflections on the Universal Declaration of Human Rights* Berkeley: University of California Press

Nmehielle, O (2001) *The African human rights system: Its laws, practice and institutions* The Hague/London/New York: Martinus Nijhoff Publishers

Nowak, M (2003) *Introduction to the international human rights regime,* Leiden: Martinus Nijhoff

Nzongola-Ntalaja, G & Lee, M (eds) (1997) *The state and democracy in Africa* Harare: AAPS Books

Nzongola-Ntalaja, G (1998) *From Zaire to the Democratic Republic of Congo* Uppsala: Nordiska Afrikainstitutet

Piotrowicz, R & Kaye, S (2000) *Human rights in international and Australian law* New South Wales: Butterworths Australia

Pollis, A & Schwab, P (eds) (1979) *Human rights cultural and ideological perspectives* New York: Praeger

Rattray, R (1969) *Ashanti law and constitution* Oxford: Clarendon Press

Rembe, S (1991) *The system of protection of human rights under the African Charter on Human and Peoples' Rights: Problems and prospects* Lesotho: Institute of African Studies, National University of Lesotho

Robertson, H & Merrills, J (1993) *Human rights in Europe: A study of the European Convention on Human Rights* Manchester: Manchester University Press

Rommen, H (1998) *The natural law: A study in legal and social history and philosophy* Indianapolis: Liberty Fund

Sands, P & Klein, P (2001) *Bowett's law of international institutions,* London: Sweet & Maxwell

Seighart, P (1982) *The international law of human rights,* London: Oxford University Press

Shepherd, G Jr & Mark, A (eds) (1990) *Emerging human rights: The African political economy context* New York: Greenwood Press

Shivji, I (ed) (1991) *State and constitutionalism: An African debate on democracy* Harare: Southern African Political Economy Series Trust

Sohn, L & Buergenthal, T (1973) *Basic documents on international protection of human rights* Indianapolis: Bobbs-Merrill

Steiner, H & Alston, P (1996) *International human rights in context: Law, politics and morals* Oxford: Clarendon Press

Symonides, J (ed) (2003) *Human rights: International protection, monitoring and enforcement* Burlington: Ashgate

Umozurike, U (1997) *The African Charter on Human and Peoples' Rights* The Hague: Martinus Nijhoff Publishers

— (1979) *International law and colonialism in Africa* Lagos: Nwamaife

United Nations (1996) *The United Nations & Human rights 1945-1995* New York: United Nations

Van Dyke, P & Van Hoof, G (1990) *Theory and practice of the European Convention on Human Rights* Deventer: Kluwer

Viljoen, F (ed) (2006) *The African human rights system: Towards the co-existence of the African Commission on Human and Peoples' Rights and the African Court on Human and Peoples' Rights,* Nairobi: International Commission of Jurists, Kenya Section

Welch, C (1995) *Protecting human rights in Africa: Roles and strategies of Non-Governmental Organisations* Philadelphia: University of Pennsylvania Press

Wilks, I (1975) *Ashanti in the nineteenth century: The structure and evolution of political order* Cambridge: Cambridge University Press

Wiseman, J (1989) *Democracy in black Africa* New York: Paragon House Publishers

Zartman, W (1989) *Ripe for resolution: Conflict and intervention in Africa* New York: Oxford University Press

CHAPTERS IN BOOKS

Adedeji, A 'From the Lagos Plan of Action to the New Partnership for African Development and from the Final Act of Lagos to the Constitutive Act: Wither Africa?' in Nyong'o, P, Ghirmazion, A & Lamba, D (eds) (2002) *New Partnership for Africa's Development (NEPAD): A New Path?* Washington D.C: Heinrich Boll Foundation

Alemika, E 'Protection and realisation of human rights in Africa' in Kalu, A & Osinbajo, Y (1992) *Perspectives on human rights* Lagos: Federal Ministry of Justice

Azinge, E 'Milestone decisions on human rights' in Kalu, A & Osinbajo, Y (1992) *Perspectives on human rights,* Lagos: Federal Ministry of Justice

Badawi, E 'The African Commission on Human and Peoples' Rights: A call for justice' in Koufa K (ed) (1997) *International Justice* Burlington: Ashgate

Benedek, W 'Peoples' rights and individuals' duties as special features of the African Charter on Human and Peoples' Rights' in Kunig, P, Benedek, W & Mahalu, C (eds) (1985) *Regional protection of human rights by international law: The emerging African system* Baden-Baden: Nomos Verlagsgesellschaft

Bernhardt, R 'General Report' in Bernhardt, R & Jolowicz, C (eds) (1987) *International enforcement of human rights* Berlin New York: Springer-Verlag

Busia, K 'The status of human rights in pre-colonial Africa: Implications for contemporary practices' in McCarthy-Arnolds, E, *et al* (1994) *Africa, human rights, and the global system: The political economy of human rights in a changing world* Westport Connecticut: Greenwood Press

Cranston, M 'Human rights: Real or supposed' in Raphael, D (ed) (1967) *Political theory and the rights of man* Melbourne: Macmillan.

Dankwa, V 'The Promotional role of the African Commission on Human & Peoples' Rights' in Evans, M & Murray, R (eds) (2002) *The African Charter on Human & Peoples' Rights: The system in practice, 1986-2000* Cambridge: Cambridge University Press

Donnelly, J 'Human rights and Western liberalism' in An-na 'im, A & Deng, F (eds) (1990) *Human rights in Africa: Cross-cultural perspectives* Washington D.C: Brookings Institution

Eide, A 'Economic, social and cultural rights as human rights' in Eide, A, Krause, C & Rosas, A (eds) (2001) *Economic social and cultural rights: A text book,* London: Martinus Nijhoff Publishers

Elmadmad, K 'The rights of women under the African Charter on Human and Peoples' Rights' in Benedek, W & Heinz, W (eds) (1992) *Regional systems of human rights in Africa, America and Europe: Proceedings of the conference* The Hague: Martinus Nijhoff Publishers

Enemo, I 'Self-determination as the fundamental basis for the concept of legitimate governance under the African Charter on Human and Peoples' Rights' in Edward, K *et al* (eds) (1999) *Legitimate governance in Africa: International and domestic legal implications* The Hague: Kluwer Law International

Eze, O 'Human rights, legal rights or social rights: The socio-economic order and problems of human rights' in Inadu, L & Ivowi, O (eds) (1982) *Human rights in Nigeria* Lagos: Macmillan Publishers

Fernyhough, T 'Human rights and pre-colonial Africa' in Cohen, R (1993) *Human rights and governance in Africa* Gainesville: University Press of Florida

Flinterman, C & Ankumah, E 'The African Charter on Human and Peoples' Rights' in Hannum, H (ed) (1999) *Guide to international human rights practice* New York: Transnational

Gitonga, A 'The meaning and foundations of democracy' in Oyugi, W *et al* (eds) (1998) *Democratic theory and practice in Africa* New York: Cambridge University Press

Gittleman, R 'The Banjul Charter on Human and Peoples' Rights: A legal analysis' in Welch, C Jr & Meltzer, R (eds) (1984) *Human rights and development in Africa* Albany: State University of New York Press

Gutto, S 'The Compliance to regional and international agreements and standards by African governments with particular reference to the rule of law and human and peoples' rights' in Nyong'o, P, Ghirmazion, A & Lamba, D (eds) (2002) *New Partnership for Africa's Development (NEPAD): A New Path?* Washington D.C: Heinrich Boll Foundation

Harrington, J 'The African Court on Human and Peoples' Rights' in Evans, M & Murray, R (2002) *The African Charter on Human and Peoples' Rights: The system in practice 1986-2000* Cambridge: Cambridge University Press

Henkin, L 'Human rights' in Bernhardt, R (ed) (1985) *Encyclopaedia of international law* New York: North-Holland Publishing Company

Heyns, C 'Civil and political rights in the African Charter' in Evans, M & Murray, R (2002) *The African Charter on Human and Peoples' Rights: The system in practice, 1986-2000* Cambridge: Cambridge University Press

Higgins, R 'The European Convention of Human Rights' in Meron, T (ed) (1984) *Human rights in international law: Legacy and policy issues* Oxford: Clarendon Press

Hountondji, P 'The master's voice: The problem of human rights in Africa' in Ricoeur, P (ed) (1986) *Philosophical foundations of human rights,* Paris: Unesco

Howard, R 'Dignity, community and human rights' in An-Na'im, A (ed) (1992) *Human rights in cross-cultural perspectives: A quest for consensus* Philadelphia: University of Pennsylvania Press

Joiner, J 'Beyond commitments, towards practical action' in Sall, E & Wohlgemuth, L (eds) (2006) *Human rights, regionalism and the dilemmas of democracy in Africa* Dakar: CODESRIA

Kenyon, J 'Constitutionalism in revolutionary America' in Pennock, J & Chapman, J (eds) (1979) *Constitutionalism* New York: New York University Press

Kithure, K 'Overlaps in the African human rights system' in Viljoen, F (ed) (2006) *The African human rights system: Towards the co-existence of the African Commission on Human and Peoples' Rights and the African Court on Human and Peoples' Rights,* Nairobi: International Commission of Jurists Kenya Section

Kohler, C 'The Court of Justice of the European Communities and the European Court of Human rights' in Igor, I (1992) *Supranational and constitutional courts in Europe: Functions and sources* New York: W.S. Hein

Kroeze, I 'Legal positivism' in Roederer, C & Moellendorf, D (eds) (2006) *Jurisprudence* Lansdowne: Juta & Company

Lalive, A 'The protection of human rights within the framework of existing regional organisations' in Robertson, A (ed) (1968) *Human rights in national and international law: The proceedings of the Second International Conference on the European Convention on Human Rights held in Vienna under the auspices of the Council of Europe and the University of Vienna, 18-20 October 1965,* Manchester: Manchester University Press

Lavoyer, J 'Implementation of international humanitarian law and the role of the International Committee of the Red Cross' in Carey, J *et al* (eds) (2004) *International Humanitarian Law: Challenges* New York: Transnational Publishers Inc

Legesse, A 'Human rights in African political culture' in Thompson, K (ed) (1980) *The moral imperatives of human rights: A world survey* Washington, D.C: University Press of America

Lewis, S 'Treaty-based procedures for making human rights complaints within the UN system' in Hannun, H (ed) (1999) *Guide to international human rights practice* New York: Transnational Publishers

M'Baye, K 'Human rights in Africa' in Vasak, K & Alston, P (eds) (1982) *The international dimensions of human rights* Westport Connecticut: Greenwood Press Paris France: Unesco

Marasighe, L 'Traditional conceptions of human rights in Africa' in Welch, C & Alston, P (eds) (1984) *Human rights and development in Africa* Albany: State University of New York Press

Markovic, I 'Implementation of human rights and domestic jurisdiction of states' in Eide, A & Shou, L (eds) (1968) *International protection of human rights* Indianapolis : Bobbs-Merrill

Naldi, G 'Future trends in human rights in Africa: The increased role of the OAU?' in Evans, M & Murray, R (eds) (2002) *The African Charter on Human & Peoples' Rights: The system in practice, 1986-2000* Cambridge: Cambridge University Press

Odinkalu, C 'Implementing economic, social and cultural rights under the African Charter on Human and Peoples' Rights' in Evans, M & Murray, R (2002) *The African Charter on Human and Peoples' Rights: The system in practice, 1986-2000* Cambridge: Cambridge University Press

Oloka-Onyango, J 'The concept of human rights in the international order' in Kalu, A & Osinbajo, Y (1992) *Perspectives on human rights,* Lagos: Federal Ministry of Justice

Panikkar, R 'Is the notion of human rights a Western concept?' in Alston, P (ed) (1995) *Human rights law* New York: New York University Press

Pollis, A 'Liberal, socialist and Third World perspectives on human rights' in Pollis, A & Schwab, P (eds) (1982) *Towards a human rights framework* New York: Praeger

Rodley, N 'United Nations non-treaty procedures for dealing with human rights violations' in (1999) *Guide to international human rights practice* New York: Transnational Publishers

Scheinin, M 'Economic and social rights as legal rights' in Eide, A, Krause, C & Rosas, A (eds) (2001) *Economic social and cultural rights: A text book* London: Martinus Nijhoff Publishers

Shestack, J 'The philosophic foundations of human rights' in R McCorquodale (2003) *Human rights* Aldershot: Ashgate

Sibongile, N 'Implications of the establishment of the African Court on Human and Peoples' Rights on domestic legal systems in Africa' in Viljoen, F (ed) (2006) *The African human rights system: Towards the co-existence of the African Commission on Human and Peoples' Rights and the African Court on Human and Peoples' Rights* Nairobi: International Commission of Jurists, Kenya Section

Sieghart, P 'International human rights law: Some current problems' in Robert, B & Taylor, J (eds) (1991) *Human rights for the 1990's: Legal, political and ethical issues,* London: Mansell

Teson, F 'International human rights and cultural relativism' in Alston, P (ed) (1996) *Human rights law* Oxford: Clarendon Press

Umozurike, U 'African concept of human rights' in Kalu, A & Osinbajo, Y (eds) (1992) *Perspectives on human rights* Lagos: Federal Ministry of Justice

— 'The significance of the African Charter on Human and Peoples' Rights' in Kalu, A & Osinbajo, Y (eds) (1992) *Perspectives on human rights* Lagos: Federal Ministry of Justice

Viljoen, F 'Admissibility under the African Charter' in Evans, M & Murray, R (eds) (2002) *The African Charter on Human and Peoples' Rights: The system in practice 1986-2000* Cambridge: Cambridge University Press

— 'Overview of the African regional human rights system' in Heyns, C (ed) (2001) *Human rights law in Africa 1998* The Hague: Kluwer Law International

— 'Review of the African Commission on Human and Peoples' Rights: 21 October 1986 to 1 January 1997' in Heyns, C (eds) (1999) *Human rights law in Africa 1997* The Hague: Kluwer Law International

Wachira, G 'A critical examination of the African Charter on Human and Peoples' Rights: Towards strengthening the African human rights system to enable it effectively meet the needs of the African population' in Viljoen, F (ed) (2006) *The African human rights system: Towards the co-existence of the African Commission on Human and Peoples' Rights and the African Court on Human and Peoples' Rights*, Nairobi: International Commission of Jurists, Kenya Section

Wai, D 'Human rights in sub-saharan Africa' in Pollis, A & Schwab, P (eds) (1979) *Human rights: Cultural and ideological perspectives*, New York: Praeger

Waris, A 'The remedies, Application and enforcement provisions of the African Court on Human and Peoples' rights' in Viljoen, F (ed) (2006) *The African human rights system: Towards the co-existence of the African Commission on Human and Peoples' Rights and the African Court on Human and Peoples' Rights* Nairobi: International Commission of Jurists, Kenya Section

Welch, C 'Human rights as a problem in contemporary Africa' in Welch, C & Meltzer, R (eds) (1984) *Human rights and development in Africa* Albany: State University of New York Press

Wiredu, K 'Democracy and consensus in African traditional politics: A plea for a non-party polity' in Eze, O (1997) *Postcolonial African philosophy: A critical reader* Cambridge: Blackwell

JOURNAL ARTICLES

Abass, A & Baderin, M 'Towards effective collective security and human rights protection in Africa: An assessment of the Constitutive Act of the new African Union' (2002) 49 *Netherlands International Law Review*

Acheampong, K 'Reforming the substance of the African Charter on Human and Peoples' Rights: Civil and political rights and socio-economic rights' (2001) 2 *African Human Rights Law Journal*

Addo, M 'Implementation by African states of the plan of action for the United Nations Decade for Human Rights' (2000) 44 *Journal of African Law*

Agbakwa, S 'A path least taken: Economic and social rights and the perspective of conflict prevention and peace building in Africa' (2003) 47/1 *Journal of African Law*

—— 'Reclaiming humanity: Economic, social and cultural rights as the cornerstone of African human rights' (2002) 5 *Yale Human Rights and Development Law Journal*

Aidoo, K 'Africa: Democracy without human rights?' (1993) 15 *Human Rights Quarterly*

Aka, C 'Military, globalisation and human rights in Africa' (2002) *New York Law School Journal of Human Rights*

Akinyemi, A 'The Organisation of African Unity and the concept of non-interference in internal affairs of member-states' (1972-3) 46 *British Year Book of International Law*

Akokpari, J 'Policing and preventing human rights abuses in Africa: The OAU, the AU & the NEPAD Peer Review' (2004) 32/2 *International Journal of Legal Information*

Alston, P 'UNESCO's procedure for dealing with human rights violations' (1980) 20 *Santa Clara Law Review*

Amoah, P 'The African Charter on Human and Peoples' Rights: An effective weapon for human rights?' (1992) 4 *African Journal of International and Comparative Law*

Ankumah, E 'Universality of human rights and the African Charter on Human and Peoples' Rights' (1992) *Universaliteit van Mensenrechten*

Anthony, E 'Beyond the paper Tiger: The challenges of a human rights court in Africa' (1997) 32 *Texas International Law Journal*

Appiagyei-Atua, K 'A rights-centred critique of African philosophy in the context of development' (2005) 5 *African Human Rights Law Journal*

Arts, J 'The international protection of children's rights in Africa: The 1990 OAU Charter on the Rights and Welfare of the Child' (1993) 5 *RADIC*

Askin, K 'Sexual violence in decisions and indictments of the Yugoslav and Rwandan Tribunals: Current status (1999) 93 *American Journal of International Law*

Badawi, I 'The future relationship between the African Court and the African Commission' (2002) *African Human Rights Law Journal*

Baimu, E 'Commission and the Court' (2001) 3 *Conflict Trends*

— 'Human rights in NEPAD and its implications for the African human rights system' (2002) 2 *African Human Rights Law Journal*

— 'The African Union: Hope for a better protection of human rights in Africa?' (2001) 2 *African Human Rights Law Journal*

— 'Human rights mechanisms and structures under NEPAD and the African Union: Emerging trends towards proliferation and duplication' (2002) 15 *Occasional paper*

Baimu, E & Viljoen, F 'Courts for Africa: Considering the co-existence of the African Court on Human an Peoples' Rights and the African Court of Justice' (2004) 22/2 *Netherlands Quarterly of Human Rights*

Banda, F 'Building on a global movement: Violence against women in the African context' (2008) 8 *African Human Rights Law Journal*

Banderin, M 'Recent developments in the African regional human rights system' (2005) 5/1 *Human Rights Law Review*

Baxi, U 'Voices of suffering and the future of human rights' (1998) 8/2 *Transnational Law and Contemporary Problems*

Bekker, G 'The African Court on Human and Peoples' Rights: Safeguarding the Interests of African states' (2007) 51/1 *Journal of African Law*

Bello, E 'Human rights: The rule of law in Africa' (1981) 30 *International & Comparative Law Quarterly*

Benedek, W 'The judiciary and human rights in Africa: The Banjul Seminar and the Training Workshop for a Core of Human Rights Advocates of November 1989' (1990) 11 *Human Rights Law Journal*

— 'The African Charter and Commission on Human and Peoples' Rights: How to make it more effective', (1993) *1 Netherlands Quarterly of Human Rights*

Benedek, W & Ginther, K 'New perspectives and conceptions of international law: An Afro-European dialogue' *Australian Journal of Public and International law* (1983)

Blay, K 'Changing African perspectives on the right to self-determination in the wake of the Banjul Charter on Human and Peoples' Rights' (1985) 29 *Journal of African Law*

Bojosi, K & Wachira, G 'Protecting indigenous peoples in Africa: An analysis of the approach of the African Commission on Human and Peoples' Rights' (2006) 6 *African Human Rights Law Journal*

Bondzie-Simpson, E 'A critique of the African Charter on Human and Peoples' Rights' (1988) 31 *Howard Law Journal*

Boukongou, J 'The appeal of the African system for protecting human rights' (2006) 6 *African Human Rights Law Journal*

Boven, T 'The relations between peoples' rights and human rights in the African Charter' (1986) 2/4 *Human Rights Law Journal*

Buergenthal, T 'The advisory practice of the Inter-American Human Rights Court' (1985) 79 *American Journal of International Law*

Busia, K 'The status of human rights in pre-colonial Africa: Implications for contemporary practices' (1996) 2 *Afrika Zamani*

Busia, K & Mbaye, K 'Towards a framework for the filing of Communications on economic, social and cultural rights under the African Charter, Phase I' (1994) *East African Journal of Peace and Human Rights*

Chanda, A 'The Organisation of African Unity: An appraisal' (1989-92) 21-4 *Zambia Law Journal*

Charlesworth, H *et al* 'Feminist approaches to international law' (1991) 85 *American Journal of International law*

Charney, J 'Is international law threatened by multiple international tribunals?' (1998) 271 *Recueil des cours*

Cherif, B 'Universal jurisdiction for international crimes: Historical perspectives and contemporary practice' (2001) 42/1 *Virginia Journal of International Law*

Cobbah, J 'African values and the human rights debate: An African perspective' (1987) 9 *Human Rights Quarterly*

Cornwell, R 'Madagascar: First test for the African Union' (2003) 12 *African Security Review*

Cullen, A 'Defining torture in international law: A critique of the concept employed by the European Court of Human Rights' (2003) 34 *California Western International Law Journal*

Curran, E & Bonthuys, E 'Customary law and domestic violence in rural South African societies' (2005) 21 *South African Journal of Human Rights*

D'sa, R 'The African Charter on Human and Peoples' Rights: Problems and prospects for regional Action' (1981/83) 10 *Australian Yearbook of International Law*

— 'Human and Peoples' Rights: Distinctive features of the African Charter' (1985) *Journal of African Law*

Dersso, S 'The jurisprudence of the African Commission on Human and Peoples' Rights with respect to peoples' rights' (2006) 6 *African Human Rights Law Journal*

Dieng, A 'Introduction to the African Court on Human and Peoples' Rights' (2005) 15 *INTERIGHTS Bulletin*

Diganke, O 'Protection of human rights in Africa' (2000) 10 *Transnational law & Contemporary Problems*

Dlamini, C 'The OAU and the protection of human rights in Africa' (1991) *Obiter*

— 'Towards a regional protection of human rights in Africa: The African Charter on Human and Peoples' Rights' (1991) *XXIV CILSA*

Donnelly, J 'Human rights and human dignity: An analytical critique of non-Western conceptions of human rights (1982) 76 *American Political Science Review*

El-Obaid, A & Appiagyei-Atua, K 'Human rights in Africa: A new perspective of linking the past to the present' (1996) 41 *Mc Gill Law Journal*

Emerson, R 'Faith of human rights in the Third World' (1975) Vol. XXVII No. 2 *World Politics*

— 'Pan-Africanism' (1962) 16/2 *International Organisation*

Enonchong, N 'The African Charter on Human and Peoples' Rights: Effective remedies in domestic law?' (2002) 46 *Journal of African Law*

Gaer, F 'First fruits: Reporting by states under the African Charter on Human and Peoples' Rights' (1992) 10 *Netherlands Quarterly of Human Rights*

— 'Human rights: What role in U.S Foreign Policy?' (1998) *Great decisions, special issue*

Gardham, J & Charlesworth, H 'Protection of women in armed conflict' (2000) 22 *Human Rights Quarterly*

Gittleman, R 'The African Charter on Human and Peoples' Rights: A legal analysis' (1982) 22 *Virginia Journal of International law*

Gross, E 'Legal aspects of tackling terrorism: The balance of the right of a democracy to defend itself and the protection of human rights' (2001) 6 *Journal of International Law and Foreign Affairs*

Gumedze, S 'Bringing communications before the African Commission on Human and Peoples' Rights' (2003) 3 *African Human Rights Law Journal*

Gutto, S 'The reform and renewal of the African regional human and peoples' rights system' (2001) 2 *African Human Rights Law Journal*

Hatchard, J 'Reporting under international human rights instruments by African Countries' (1994) 38 *Journal of African Law*

Heyns, C 'A human rights Court for Africa' (2004) 22/3 *Netherlands Quarterly of human rights*

— 'The African regional human rights system: In need of reform?' (2001) 2 *African Human Rights Law Journal*

— 'The African regional human rights system: The African Charter' (2004) 108/3 *Pennsylvania State Law Review*

Heyns, C, Padilla, D & Wolfgang, S 'A schematic comparison of regional human rights systems' (2003) 3 *African Human Rights Law Journal*

Heyns, C & Viljoen, F 'An overview of international protection of human rights in Africa' (1999) 15 *South African Journal of Human Rights*

— 'The impact of the United Nations human rights treaties on the domestic level' (2001) 23 *Human Rights Quarterly*

Hopkins, K 'The effect of the African Court on the domestic legal orders of African states' (2002) 2 *African Human Rights Law Journal*

Howard, R 'Cultural absolutism and the nostalgia for community' (1993) 15 *Human Rights Quarterly*

— 'Evaluating human rights in Africa: Some problems of implicit comparisons' (1984) 6 *Human Rights Quarterly*

— 'The full-belly thesis: Should economic rights take priority over civil and political rights?, Evidence from sub-Saharan Africa' (1983) 5 *Human Rights Quarterly*

Howard, R & Donnelly, J 'Human dignity, human rights and political regimes' (1986) 80 *American Political Science Review*

Jaycox, E 'Ghana' (1993) 1/2 *Human Rights Quarterly*

Kaime, T 'The Convention on the Rights of the Child and the cultural legitimacy of children's rights in Africa: Some reflections' (2005) 5 *African Human Rights Law Journal*

Khoza, S 'Promoting economic, social and cultural rights in Africa: The African Commission holds a seminar in Pretoria' (2004) 4 *African Human Rights Law Journal*

Kibwana, K 'Human rights and/or economic development: Which way Africa?' (1993) *Third World Legal Studies*

Killander, M 'Confidentiality versus publicity: Interpreting Article 59 of the African Charter on Human and Peoples' Rights' (2006) 6 *African Human Rights Law Journal*

Kirby, M 'The role of the judge in advancing human rights by reference to international human rights norms', (1988) *62 Australian Law Journal*

Kithure, K 'The normative and institutional framework of the African Union relating to the protection of human rights and the maintenance of international peace and security: A critical appraisal' (2003) 3 *African Human Rights Law Journal*

Kiwanuka, R 'The Meaning of "People" in the African Charter on Human and Peoples' Rights' (1988) *82 American Journal of International Law*

Kofi, Q 'The African Charter on Human and Peoples' Rights: Towards a more effective reporting mechanism' (2002) 2 *African Human rights Law Journal*

Kois, L 'Article 18 of the African Charter on Human and Peoples' Rights: A progressive approach to the women's human rights' (1997) 3 *East African Journal of Peace and Human rights*

Kunig, P 'The protection of human rights by international law in Africa' (1982) 25 *German Yearbook of International Law*

Kwakwa, E 'Internal conflicts in Africa: Is there a right of humanitarian action? *African Journal of International Law*

Lloyd, A 'Report of the second ordinary session of the African Committee of experts on the rights and welfare of the child' (2003) 3 *African Human Rights Law Journal*

Magliveras, K & Naldi, G 'The African Union: A new dawn for Africa?' (2002) 51 *International and Comparative Law Quarterly*

Magnarella, P 'Some milestones and achievements at the International Criminal Tribunal for Rwanda: The 1998 Kambanda, Akayesu cases' (1998) 11 *Florida Journal of International Law*

Mahmud, S 'The state and human rights in Africa in the 1990s: Perspectives and prospects' (1993) 15/3 *Human Rights Quarterly*

Mahoney, P 'Speculating on the future of the reformed European Court of Human Rights' (1999) 20 *Human Rights Law Journal*

Maina, C 'The proposed African Court of Justice: Jurisprudential, procedural, enforcement problems and beyond' (1993)1 *East African Journal of Peace and Human Rights*

Malstrom, S '21st ordinary session of the African Commission on Human and Peoples' Rights' (1997) 15 *Netherlands Quarterly of Human Rights*

Malstrom, S & Oberleitner, G '18th ordinary and 2nd extra-ordinary session of the African Commission on Human and Peoples' Rights' (1996) 14 *Netherlands Quarterly of Human Rights*

Maluwa, T 'International law making in the Organisation of African Unity: An overview' (2000) 12 *African Journal of International and Comparative Law*

Mangu, A 'Assessing the effectiveness of the APRM and its impact on the promotion of democracy and good political governance' (2007) 7 *African Human Rights Law Journal*

— 'The Changing human rights landscape in Africa: Organisation of African Unity, African union, New Partnership for Africa's Development and the African Court' (2005) 23/3 *Netherlands Quarterly of Human Rights*

Marks, A 'Emerging human rights: A new generation for the 1980s?' (1981) *Rutgers Law review*

Matthews, S & Solomon, H 'Prospects for African development in light of the New Partnership for Africa's Development (NEPAD)' (2002) 3 *African Institute Briefing Paper*

Mbazira, C 'A path to realising economic, social and cultural rights in Africa? A critique of the New Partnership for Africa's Development' (2004) 4 *African Human Rights law Journal*

— 'Enforcing the economic, social and cultural rights in the African Charter on Human and Peoples Rights: Twenty years of redundancy, progression and significant strides' (2006) 6 *African Human Rights Law Journal*

Mbondenyi, M 'The right to participate in the government of one's country: An analysis of Article 13(1) of the African Charter on Human and Peoples' Rights in the light of Kenya's 2007 elections crisis' (2009) *African Human Rights Law Journal*

Meron, T 'Rape as a crime under international humanitarian law' (1993) 87 *American Journal of International Law*

Mezmur, B 'The 9th ordinary session of the African Committee of Experts on the Rights and Welfare of the Child: Looking back to look ahead' (2007) 7 *African Human Rights Law Journal*

Mistry, P 'Africa's record of regional co-operation and integration' (2000) 99 *African Affairs*

Motola, Z 'Human rights in Africa: A cultural, ideological and legal examination' (1989) *Hastings International & Comparative law review*

Mubangizi, J 'Know your rights: Exploring the connections between human rights and poverty reduction with specific reference to South Africa' (2005) 21 *South African Journal on Human Rights*

— 'Some reflections on recent and current trends in the promotion and protection of human rights in Africa: The pains and the gains' (2006) 6 *African Human Rights Law Journal*

Mugwanya, G 'Examination of state reports by the African Commission: A critical appraisal' (2001) 2 *African Human Rights Law Journal*

Mujuzi, J 'An analysis of the approach to the right to freedom from torture adopted by the African Commission on Human and Peoples' Rights' (2006) 6 *African Human Rights Law Journal*

Murray, R 'A feminist perspective on reform of the African human rights system' (2001) *African Human Rights Law Journal*

— 'Report on the 1997 sessions of the African Commission on Human and Peoples' Rights-21st and 22nd sessions: 15-25 April and 2-11 November 1997' (1998) 19 *Human Rights Law Journal*

— 'A comparison between the African and European courts of human rights' (2002) 2 *African Human Rights Law Journal*

— 'A feminist perspective on reform of the African human rights system' (2001) 2 *African Human Rights Law Journal*

— 'Decisions by the African Commission on individual communications under the African Charter on Human and Peoples' rights' (1997) 46 *International and Comparative Law Quarterly*

— 'Developments in the African human rights system 2003-04' (2006) 6/1 *Human Rights Law Review*

— 'Report of the 1996 Sessions of the African Commission on Human and Peoples' Rights' (1997) 18 *Human Rights Law Journal*

— 'Serious or massive violations under the African Charter on Human and Peoples' Rights: A comparison with the Inter-American and European mechanisms' (1999) 17 *Netherlands Quarterly of Human Rights*

— 'The African Charter on Human and Peoples' Rights 1987-2000: An overview of its progress and problems' (2001) 1 *African Human Rights Law Journal*

— 'The African Commission on Human and Peoples' Rights' (2001) 19 *Netherlands Quarterly of Human Rights*

Murray, R & Wheatley, S 'Groups and the African Charter on Human and Peoples' Rights' (2003) 25 *Human Rights Quarterly*

Mutua, M 'The African human rights system in a comparative perspective' (1993) 3 *Review of the African Commission on Human and People' Rights*

— 'The Banjul Charter and the African cultural fingerprint: An evaluation of the language of duties' (1995) 35 *Virginia Journal of International Law*

— 'The African human rights court: A two-legged stool?' (1999) 21 *Human Rights Quarterly*

Naldi, G 'Limitation of rights under the African Charter on Human and Peoples' Rights: The contribution of the African Commission on Human and Peoples' Rights' (2001) 17 *South African Journal of Human Rights*

Naldi, G & Magliveras, K 'Reinforcing the African system of human rights: The protocol on the establishment of a regional court of human and peoples' rights' (1998) 16 *Netherlands Quarterly of Human Rights*

— 'The African Union: A new dawn for Africa?' (2002) 51 *International and Comparative Law Quarterly*

Neff, S 'Human rights in Africa: Thoughts on the African Charter on Human and Peoples' Rights in the light of the case law from Botswana, Lesotho and Swaziland' (1984) 33 *International and Comparative Law Quarterly*

Nguema, I 'Human rights perspectives in Africa' (1990) *Human Rights Law Journal*

Nmehielle, O 'Towards an African court of human rights: Structuring and the Court' (2000) 6/1 *Annual Survey of international and Comparative Law*

Nsibirwa, M 'A brief analysis of the Draft Protocol to the African Charter on Human and Peoples' Rights on the Rights of Women' (2001) 1 *African Human Rights Law Journal*

Nwankwo, C 'The OAU and human rights', (1993) *Journal of Democracy*

O'Shea, A 'A critical reflection on the proposed African Court on Human and Peoples' Rights' (2001) 2 *African Human Rights Law Journal*

Odinkalu, C & Christensen, C 'The African Commission on Human and Peoples' Rights: The development of its non-state communications procedures' (1998) 20 *Human Rights Quarterly*

Odinkalu, C 'Back to the future: The imperative of prioritising for the protection of human rights in Africa' (2003) *Journal of African Law*

— 'Proposals for review of the Rules of Procedure of the African Commission on Human & Peoples' Rights' (1992) 21/2 *Human Rights Quarterly*

— 'The role of case and complaints procedures in the reform of African regional human rights system' (2001) 2 *African Human Rights Law Journal*

Ohiorhenuan, J 'NEPAD and dialectics of African underdevelopment' (2002) 7 *New Agenda*

Okeke, C 'A note on the right of secession as a human right' (1996) III *Annual Survey of International and Comparative Law*

Okere, B 'The protection of human rights in Africa and the African Charter on Human and Peoples' Rights: A comparative analysis with the European and American systems' (1984) 6 *Human Rights Quarterly*

— 'Human rights and the African Charter' (1984) 6 *Human Rights Quarterly*

Okongwu, O 'The OAU Charter and the principle of domestic jurisdiction in Inter-African affairs' (1973) 13 *Indiana Journal of International Law*

Oloka-Onyango, J 'Beyond the rhetoric: Reinvigorating the struggle and cultural rights in Africa' (1995) 26/1 *California Western International Journal*

Olowu, D 'Protecting Children's Rights in Africa: A Critique of the African Charter on the Rights and Welfare of the Child' (2002) 10 *International Journal of Children's Rights*

Österdahl, I 'Implementing human rights in Africa: The African Commission on Human and Peoples' Rights and individual communications' (2002) *Swedish Institute of International Law Studies in International Law*

— 'The Jurisdiction *Rationae Materiae* of the African Court of Human and Peoples' Rights: A Comparative Critique' (1998) 7 *Revue Africaine des Droits de l'Homme*

Othman, H 'Africa and the protection of rights' (1995) 6/1 *African Law Review*

Padilla, D 'An African human rights court: Reflections from the perspective of the Inter-American system' (2002) 2 *African Human Rights Law Journal*

Parker, C & Rukare, D 'The New African Union and its Constitutive Act' (2002) 96 *American Journal of International Law*

Pasqualucci, J 'Advisory practice of the Inter-American Court of Human Rights: Contributing to the evolution of international human rights' (2002) 38/2 *Stanford Journal of International Law*

Quashigah, K 'The African Charter on Human & Peoples' Rights: Towards a more effective reporting mechanism' (2002) 2 *African Human Rights Law Journal*

— 'The philosophic basis of human rights and its relations to Africa: A critique' (1992) 2 *Journal of Human Rights Law and Practice*

Reisman, W 'Through or despite governments: Differentiating responsibilities in human rights programs' (1987) 72 *Iowa Law Review*

Ress, G 'The effect of decisions and judgments of the European Court of Human Rights in the domestic legal order' (2005) 140 *Texas International Law Journal*

Reyntjens, F 'Authoritarianism in Francophone Africa from colonial to the post-colonial state' (198) *Third World Legal Studies*

Rosa, S & Dutschke, M 'Children rights at the core: The use of international law on South African Cases on Children's Socio-economic rights' (2006) 22 *South African Journal of Human Rights*

Sermet, L 'The absence of a derogation clause from the African Charter on Human and Peoples' Rights: A critical discussion' (2007) 7 *African Human Rights Law Journal*

Shelton, D 'Improving human rights protection: Recommendations for enhancing the effectiveness of the Inter-American Commission on human Rights' (1988) 3 Fall *American University Journal of International Law and Policy*

— 'The jurisprudence of the Inter-American Court of Human Rights' (1994) 10 *American University Journal of International Law and Policy*

Shestack, J 'The philosophic foundations of human rights' (1998) 20 *Human rights Quarterly*

Singh, D 'When a child is not a child: The scourge of child soldiering in Africa' (2007) 7 *African Human Rights Law Journal*

Sloth-Nielsen, J & Mezmur, B 'Surveying the research landscape to promote children's legal rights in an African context' (2007) 7 *African Human Rights Law Journal*

— 'Win some, lose some: The 10th ordinary session of the African Committee of Experts on the Rights and Welfare of the Child' (2008) 8 *African Human Rights Law Journal*

Sohn, L 'The new international law: Protection of the individual rather than states' (1982) 32 *American University Law Review*

Swanson, J 'The emergence of new rights in the African Charter' (1991) 12 *New York Law School Journal of International and Comparative law*

Takirambudde, P 'Six years of the African Charter on Human and Peoples' Rights: An assessment' (1991) 7/2 *Lesotho Law Journal*

Tucker, C 'Regional human rights models in Europe and Africa: A comparison' (1983) 10 *Syracuse Journal of International and Comparative Law*

Udombana, N 'An African human rights court and an African Union Court: A needful duality or a needless duplication?' (2003) 23/3 *Brook Journal of International Law*

— 'Can the leopard change its spots? The African Union treaty and human rights' (2002) 17 *American University International Law Review*

— 'How should we then live? Globalisation and the New Partnership for Africa's Development' (2003) 20 *Boston University International Law Journal*

— 'The African Commission on Human and Peoples' Rights and the development of fair trial norms in Africa' (2006) 6 *African Human Rights Law Journal*

— 'The institutional structure of the African Union: A legal Analysis' (2002) 33 *California West International Law Journal*

— 'Toward the African Court on Human and Peoples' Rights: Better late than never' (2000) 3 *Yale Human Rights and Development Law Journal*

Umozurike, U 'The African Charter on Human and Peoples' Rights' (1983) 77 *American Journal of International Law*

— 'The domestic jurisdiction clause in the OAU Charter' (1979) 311 *African Affairs*

Van Der Mei, A 'The new African Court on Human and Peoples' Rights: Towards an effective human rights protection mechanism for Africa?' (2005) 18 *Leiden Journal of International Law*

Venter, D 'Black Africa and the Apartheid issue: A South African response?' (1981) *Journal of Contemporary African studies*

Viljoen, F 'Africa's contribution to the development of international human rights and humanitarian law' (2001) 1 *African Human Rights Law Journal*

— 'A human rights court for Africa and Africans' (2004) 1/30 *Brooklyn Journal of International Law*

— 'Examination of state reports at the 27th session of the African Commission on Human and Peoples' Rights: A critical analysis and proposals for reform' (2001) 16 *South African Journal on Human Rights*

— 'State reporting under the African Charter on Human and Peoples' Rights: A boost from the South' (2000) 44 *Journal of African Law*

— 'The Application of the African Charter on Human and Peoples' Rights by domestic courts in Africa' (1999) *Journal of African Law*

— 'The realisation of human rights in Africa through sub-regional institutions' (2001) *African Yearbook of International Law*

Viljoen, F & Baimu, E 'Courts for Africa: Considering the co-existence of the African Court on Human and Peoples' Rights and the African Court of justice' (2004) 22/2 *Netherlands Quarterly of Human Rights*

Viljoen, F & Louw, L 'The status of the findings of the African Commission: From moral persuasion to legal obligation' (2004) 48/1 *Journal of African Law*

Welch, C 'The African Commission on Human and Peoples' Rights: A five-year report and assessment' (1992) 14 *Human Rights Quarterly*

Yeshanew, S 'Utilising the promotional mandate of the African Commission on Human and Peoples' Rights to promote human rights education in Africa' (2007) 7 *African Human Rights Law Journal*

THESES AND DISSERTATIONS

Abdul-Razag, M 'The OAU and the protection of human rights in Africa (1988) *Ph.D Thesis, University of Hull*

Ayinla, A 'The African Union (AU) human rights agenda: the panacea to the problem of non-compliance with human rights norms in Africa?' (2003) *LLM Thesis Makerere University*

Eno, W 'The African Commission on Human and Peoples' Rights as an instrument for the protection of human rights in Africa' (1998) *LLM Thesis University of South Africa*

Kithure, K 'Humanitarian Intervention in Africa: The Role of Inter-Governmental Organisations' (2002) *LLD Thesis, University of Pretoria*

Mangu, A 'The Road to Constitutionalism and Democracy in Post-Colonial Africa: The Case of the Democratic Republic of Congo' (2002) *LLD Thesis University of South Africa*

Mbondenyi, M 'The potential of Taita Customary law in the promotion and protection of human rights in Kenya: A critical survey' (2003) *LLB Dissertation, Moi University*

REPORTS

African Commission Report on the Mission of Good Offices to Senegal of the African Commission on Human and Peoples' Rights, Tenth Annual Activity Report (1996-1997) Annex VIII

Human Rights Watch '*Prohibited persons': Abuse of Undocumented Migrants, Asylum Seekers and Refugees in South Africa* (1998)

— *World Report 2007* (2007)

Report of the African Commission Working Group of Experts on Indigenous Population/Communities (Banjul and Copenhagen: ACHPR and IWGIA, 2005)

Report of the Secretary-General on the Implementation of the Sirte Decision on the African Union, OAU Council of Ministers, EAHG/DEC. 1(V), CM/2210 (LXXIV)

Report of the Special Rapporteur on Prisons and Conditions of Detention to the 21st Session of the African Commission on Human and Peoples' Rights, Tenth Annual Activity Report, Annex VII

Report of the United Nations High Commissioner for Human Rights on the mid-term global evaluation of the progress made towards the achievement of the objectives of the United Nations Decade for Human Rights Education (1995-2004), Adopted at the 55th session of General Assembly, UN Doc A/55/360 (2000)

Twenty-Second Activity Report of the African Commission on Human and Peoples' Rights, June 2007, EX.CL/364(XI)

DECLARATIONS AND RESOLUTIONS

'Algiers Declaration on Unconstitutional Changes of Government', OAU Doc.AHG/Dec.1 (XXXV) (July 1999)

'Decision on the Interim Period', 1st Ordinary Session of the AU Assembly of Heads of State and Government, 9-10 July 2002, Durban, South Africa, AU Doc ASS/AU /Dec 1(1)

'Decision on the Pan African Forum on the Future of Children', AHG/Dec.11 (XXXVII)

'Declaration on Democracy, Political, Economic and Corporate Governance', AHG/235(XXXVIII), Annex 1, adopted by the HSIC at its Third Meeting in June 2002

'Declaration on Political and Socio-Economic Situation in Africa and the Fundamental Changes taking Place in the World', 11 July, 1990, 26th session of AHSG

'Declaration on the Elimination of Violence against Women', GA Res 48/104 of 20 December 1993

'Declaration on the Inter-Sudanese Peace Talks in Darfur', Assembly/AU/Decl. 3(V)

'Declaration on the Resolution of the Land Question in Zimbabwe', AHG/Decl.2 (XXXVII)

'Declaration on the Review of the Millennium Declaration and the Millennium Development Goals (MDGs)', Assembly/AU/Decl. 1 (V)

'Declaration on the Rights and Welfare of the African Child', AHG/ST.4 Rev.l, adopted by the Assembly of Heads of State and Government of the Organization of African Unity, at its Sixteenth Ordinary Session in Monrovia, Liberia, from 17 to 20 July 1979

'Declarations and decisions adopted by the Thirty-Sixth Ordinary Session of the Assembly of Heads of States and Government', AHG/Decl.1-6 (XXXVI) AHG/Dec. 143-159 (XXXVI) AHG/OAU/AEC/Dec.1 (IV)

'Grand Bay Mauritius Declaration and Plan of Action', adopted by the Ministerial Conference on Human Rights in April 1999, CONF/HRA/DECL (I)

'Resolution on Granting Observer Status to National Human Rights Institutions in Africa', Twelfth Annual Activity Report of the African Commission on Human and Peoples' Rights (1998.1999), AHG/215 (XXXV), Annex IV

'Resolution on Guidelines and Measures for the Prohibition and Prevention of Torture, Cruel, Inhuman or Degrading Treatment or Punishment in Africa in Recommendations and Resolutions of the Commission'

'Resolution on the African Commission on Human and Peoples' Rights', Sixth Annual Activity Report (1992-1993) ACHPR/RPT/6th

'Resolution on the Celebration of African Day of Human Rights', Second Annual Activity Report (1988-1989) ACHPR/RPT/2nd, Annex VII

'Resolution on the Ministerial Conference on Human Rights in Africa', CM/Res.1673 (LXIV)

'Resolution on the Right to Freedom of Association', adopted by the African Commission on Human and Peoples' Rights, at its 11 Ordinary Session (Documents of the African Commission)

'Resolution on the Right to Recourse Procedure and Fair Trial', Fifth Annual Activity Report of the African Commission on Human and Peoples' Rights, 1991-1992, ACHPR/RPT/5th, Annex VI (Documents of the African Commission)

'Resolution on the Robben Island Guidelines', adopted by the African Commission at its 32nd ordinary session, 17-23 October 2002, Banjul, The Gambia

'Resolution on the United Nations Reform: Security Council', Assembly/AU/Resolution.1 (V)

'Sirte Declaration on the Reform of the United Nations', Assembly/AU/Decl. 2 (V)

'Solemn Declaration on Gender Equality in Africa', Assembly/AU/Decl 12 & 13 (III), Assembly of Heads of State and Government 3rd ordinary session 6-8 July 2004, Addis Ababa

'United Nations Commission on Human Rights Resolution 1994/45 on the question of integrating the rights of women into human rights mechanisms of the UN and the elimination of violence against women', adopted on 4 March 1994

'UN Declaration on the Rights of Disabled Persons', UNGA Resolution 3447 (XXX) of 9 December 1975

'Universal Declaration of Human Rights' of 1948

Lightning Source UK Ltd.
Milton Keynes UK
UKOW01f1628260615

254186UK00009B/221/P